ROSARY

MYSTERIES, MEDITATIONS,
AND THE
TELLING OF THE BEADS

KEVIN ORLIN JOHNSON, PH.D.

PANGÆVS.

PANGÆUS PRESS

DALLAS, TEXAS

MCM XC VII

Nihil Obstat
Msgr. Glenn D. Gardner, Vicar General, Diocese of Dallas,
Censor Librorum

Imprimatur
✠ Most Reverend Charles Grahmann, D.D.
Bishop of Dallas

The *Nihil Obstat* and *Imprimatur* are official declarations
that a book or pamphlet is free of doctrinal error.

No implication is contained therein
that those who have granted the *Nihil Obstat* and *Imprimatur*
agree with the contents, opinions, or statements expressed.

Quotations from the Bible usually follow the
New American Catholic Edition of the Holy Bible,
Confraternity version, Benziger Brothers, New York, 1961;
some follow the *Biblia Sacra
iuxta Vulgatam Clementinam, nova editio*,
ed. Alberto Colungo, O.P., and Laurentio Turrado, Madrid, 1977.

Quotations from *The Collected Works of St. John of the Cross*,
translated by Kieran Kavanaugh and Otilio Rodriguez
copyright © 1979, 1991, by Washington Province of Discalced Carmelites,
and from *The Collected Works of St. Teresa of Avila*, Volumes One and Two,
translated by Kieran Kavanaugh and Otilio Rodriguez copyright © 1976, 1980,
by Washington Province of Discalced Carmelites,
ICS Publications, 2131 Lincoln Road, N.E., Washington, D.C. 20002 U.S.A.,
are used by permission.

Library of Congress Catalog Card Number
97-91838

ISBN 0-9653660-1-4

First Edition April 7, 1997

Design by David Lloyd Beck, Dallas
Cover: Orazio Gentileschi, Annunciation, 1624.
Galleria Sabaudia, Turin.
Photo © Scala/Art Resource. Used by permission.

Manufactured in the United States of America

TO JESUS
THROUGH
MARY

WITH THANKS TO

M.E.S.
AND
J.D.W.

בתחבלות תעשה־לך מלחמה ותשועה ברב יועץ

משלי כ"ד

THANKS

to Tad Roberts, whose questions inspired this book,
and to all who helped in its production, especially
Mr. and Mrs. Orlin C. Johnson, Staunton, Illinois,
Mark Schwartz, Esq., Houston, Texas, and
Jonathon Warner, Esq., New York,
who made it possible;
and to
Mr. Eldon Clem, Hebrew Union College, Cincinnati;
Rev. Thomas Cloherty, University of Dallas;
Rev. Robert M. Coerver, Director for the Spiritual Development of
Sacramental Life, Catholic Conference and Formation Center, Dallas;
Rabbi Barry Diamond, Temple Emmanu-El, Dallas;
Rev. Paul Hinnebusch, O.P., University of Dallas;
Mr. and Mrs. James D. Lancaster, Dallas, Texas;
Ms. Bonnie Langhaar, Urbana, Illinois;
Dr. and Mrs. Mark Lowery, Dallas, Texas;
Mr. Warren K. Miller, Silver Spring, Maryland;
Mr. Michael Nikonchuk, Cottage City, Maryland;
D. Harry Prestwood, Our Lady's Rosary Makers, Louisville, Kentucky;
Mr. E. William Sockey III, National Executive Director, World Apostolate
of Fatima, Washington, New Jersey;
Ms. Alison Thomas, Allen, Texas;
Ms. Margaret Jean Weidler, Staunton, Illinois;
and Prof. Ladislav Zgusta,
Director Emeritus, Institute for Advanced Study,
University of Illinois, Urbana-Champaign.

E V A ❀ A V E

SPECIAL NOTE FOR YOUNGER READERS

THE ROSARY IS A WAY TO MEDITATE FRUITFULLY ON THE IMPORTANT episodes in the lives of Jesus and Mary, the basic events that established Christianity on Earth, and it's a very, very old way to pray. Its roots are found deep in the practices of the first Christians in the first century, and it has grown and unfolded as the Church herself has grown; but its purpose and the truths that it teaches have always stayed exactly the same. Today, when you pray the whole Rosary well, you learn more and more about all of the things that Jesus Christ did during his stay here on Earth; you hold the whole Gospel, and the whole Faith, in your hand. You share in a devotion that has been dear to the hearts of kings and queens, popes, priests, and the greatest saints from every age and from every country. Yet it's so simple that everybody in your family can pray it together, even the littlest ones.

It's best to have somebody teach you what the Rosary is, what it means, and how to pray it. It helps to have books on the subject, too. This book is designed to answer the questions that most people have about the Rosary, questions about how the devotion got started and how it connects to the rest of Christianity. But it's also designed to get you to ask questions about the Rosary, yourself.

So be sure to have a look at the Biblical passages that are cited, chapter and verse, throughout this book; but remember that they're cited as examples. The Rosary is intimately connected with everything in Scripture, so you'll need to consult a Bible as you read this book. Remember that not all books sold under the title *Holy Bible* are complete and not all are accurate; look for the *imprimatur* at the beginning, and check to see that your copy contains the Book of Wisdom and the other books that are excluded from Protestant editions. Remember, too, that there are different systems for numbering the psalms and, sometimes, the verses in other books of the Bible. If a reference here doesn't make sense, try the psalm before or after.

And when you find something that you hadn't heard before—the name of a saint or a battle, for instance—look it up, first in the index here and then in a good encyclopædia. In the same way, you might not have heard some of the words that are used here, but you can find them in a good dictionary, which is how you learn new words no matter what you read. Try not to pass by anything that you don't know: look it up. That's one of the best ways to learn more about your Faith, and about what Christianity teaches.

Look carefully, too, at the Hebrew, Greek, and Latin words and phrases that are given here, even if you don't know much about those languages. Latin, in particular; it's still the official language of the Church, and you ought to know your way around that language. The equivalents of the Hebrew letters are given here, according to a widely used system of transliteration (š means the "sh" sound, and h is sometimes just a breath), but any good dictionary will list the Hebrew and the Greek alphabets for you so that you can sound out the root words, and you'll probably find that you already know more about those languages than you think you do. As you get older, you may start to study all of these languages so that you can understand the Bible better, and so that you can open up all of the other great treasures of the mind and heart written in those languages for so many thousands of years. You may study history, too, or archæology. The sections of this book that give some extra details of those studies are set off from the rest of the page the way that this paragraph is set off from the rest.

As you expand your studies, you might want to read the other books referred to in this one, and you might want to contact some of the organizations listed here. They'll give you a lot of information, and a lot of insight, into the skills of prayer in general and into the Rosary in particular.

CONTENTS

ROSARY

MYSTERIES, MEDITATIONS, AND THE TELLING OF THE BEADS

MOST PEOPLE IN THIS WORLD WOULD probably recognize a set of rosary beads, that familiar circlet of beads punctuated with larger beads or with holy medals in a sort of a necklace arrangement, usually with a shorter string of beads attached to it, ending in a cross or crucifix. Nobody has ever been required to have one, but for at least a dozen centuries most people in the Church have owned a rosary in one form or another, just as so many do today. But they don't have them just for ornament, nor do they treasure them because they believe that those beads have any power in and of themselves.

Rosary beads are only a way of counting repetitions of vocal prayers, so you have to do something with them before you get any good out of them. In fact, the repetitions—perfectly good prayers in their own right—aren't really the point of the devotion, either. The vocal prayers are intended as an aid to meditative prayer, to raising your mind and heart to God by meditating on the episodes in the life of Jesus and Mary in which Christ came, suffered, and triumphed over sin and death. These meditations constitute the Rosary itself, properly so called.

Without these meditations, Paul VI Montini reminded us, "the Rosary is a body without a soul, and its recitation is in danger of becoming a mechanical repetition of formulas" (*Marialis cultus*, 1974). So the only reason for having the beads is that they structure the practice of meditation. In fact

1

the Rosary is the easiest and most certain way for anybody to acquire the skill of meditative prayer. Regular meditation on the Mysteries of the Rosary keeps Christ and his work always before your eyes, and always in your heart; and the habit of meditative prayer draws you ever closer to him, which opens the way to greater and greater graces.

The immense spiritual, emotional, and even intellectual benefits of meditative prayer are the reason that so many millions of people pray the Rosary regularly—daily, in many cases. The Rosary works; the graces drawn down by this form of meditative prayer answer all petitions and supply all necessities, even final salvation. That's why a mystic as gifted as St. Teresa of Avila could say that this string of beads is a chain that pulls down Heaven to Earth, and it's why Michelangelo painted into his Last Judgement a clutch of repentant souls being pulled up into Heaven on just such a chain.

But of course all of this promise doesn't reside in the beads themselves, even if they're blessed, as they should be. The promise resides in the Covenant of Christ; the Rosary simply draws out the power that resides within you, the power to embrace that Covenant, and strengthens it. Constant practice of the Rosary works because it deepens your faith. It asks effectively for the graces that you need, a request that's never denied; and it enriches your participation in the sacraments. That's how it helps you make yourself into the person that you'd like to be. And, more to the point, those graces help you make yourself into the kind of person that God would like you to be.

THE FERTILE GROUND

THE LIVING PRAYER KNOWN METAPHORICAL-ly as the Rosary weaves together many separate branches of devotional practice, all of them ancient beyond telling, and most of them unique to Christianity. It consists of meditative prayer of a kind that doesn't occur in other religions. Those meditations are linked to repeated vocal prayers that are also distinctively Christian, and those prayers are counted on beads.

Like almost all of the other great Christian devotional practices that have developed since the time of the Apostles—the litanies, the Angelus, and a good many of the other devotions counted on chaplets of beads—the Rosary was instituted not by the hierarchy and not by any particular great saint, but by the laity.

Yet the Rosary belongs to the whole Church. As the laity shaped it, slowly, deliberately, over many centuries into a devotion that fits their own way of life, they always patterned their prayers on the ways in which the great orders of monks and nuns prayed, and they constantly sought the approval of the hierarchy. The orders and the hierarchy, for their part, listened, and they watched the way the laity prayed, often taking up ideas and practices to improve their own skills of prayer and those of Christians everywhere.

That's why the histories of all of the Church's other devotions are threaded together by the history of the Rosary. Even the orders themselves grew as the Rosary grew; even many of the vocal prayers that the Church uses in her public devotions and her liturgies—except those that come straight from Scripture—were developed, at least in part, to be used in the Rosary or in those devotions from which it sprouted. So the Rosary's roots are intertwined with those of every other Christian devotion, and they reach all the way back through the Book of Acts straight to the Gospels—

all the way to Genesis, in fact, by way of the prophets and the Book of Psalms. That's why the Rosary really can't be understood out of its Biblical context, any more than it can be understood apart from its historical context. And, like any other devotional practice, it has to be understood within the whole framework of Christian prayer.

Prayer is the purposeful act of communicating with God; prayer is the essential activity of a person alive to the existence of God and the reality of religion. Outward observance alone is not prayer; the study of divine things alone is not prayer: but lively attention to these things is part of prayer, and it can even be a cause of prayer. People pray because their religion is alive in them. People pray because their hearts are stirred to talk with God, and because they want God to answer.

The primal seed of that pattern of Christian prayer called the Rosary must have been that sudden awareness of the relationship between God and Man that came so forcefully to so many when they first heard the words of Jesus himself. That seed still drops today, and in fertile ground it grows into the gift of conversion. Conversion is a turning of the heart toward God, which means that the heart has to turn away from the quick and transient satisfactions of this world in favor of its birthright, which is everlasting reunion with God (Gn 25:29-34). To turn to God, the heart has to turn from sin, from selfishness, and—perhaps most difficult of all—even from indifference. Sometimes it happens as it must have happened to those who heard Christ on the Mount of Beatitudes, or to St. Paul on the road to Damascus, all at once. Often it happens drop by drop; sometimes it happens against the person's will.

But sooner or later there comes a pivotal point in conversion, after which nothing can possibly be the same any more. This, too, can come in a single stunning instant, but everybody who enters upon the lifelong process of conversion ends up somewhat astonished sooner or later. And anybody who sees at last the goodness of God, anybody who comes to know the inexpressible joy of that supreme goodness, wants more and more to turn his gaze to God in praise, in thanksgiving, and in simple adoration—that is, to pray. And a good many of these people who must look again at this world can do nothing other than offer the continual "sacrifice of the lips", praying constantly in atonement for sin, and begging God's mercy without ceasing.

In the second century after Christ, and probably even in the first, some Christians converted so decisively that they walked away from the world and retreated to the desert to give their lives over to that sacrifice. They were the first monks, but they didn't necessarily live in monasteries. Often, they would sit alone in the wilderness, concentrating on their heartbeat and silently repeating "Jesus Christ, Son of God," as they breathed in, and "have mercy on us," as they breathed out.

Of course, there are any number of forms of this "Jesus Prayer", as St. John Climacus later called it. This particular formula comes from the anonymous sixth-century Egyptian *Life of Abba Philemon*, which was written at about the same time St. John Climacus wrote his own *Ladder of Divine Ascent*, but there were many others used. St. John himself didn't prescribe a form for the prayer, and other eastern teachers of prayer at the time, like St. Barsanuphius of Gaza, suggest formulas like "Lord Jesus Christ, have mercy on us," "Lord Jesus Christ, save us," "Master Jesus, protect us," or simply "Jesus, help me." But no matter what the exact words were, the intention is identically the same. By repeating this or some similar prayer over and over again, they could relax their own wills, absorb themselves in this act of merciful prayer for all Mankind, and become immersed in an awareness of the presence of God.

This is the goal of Christian meditative prayer, generally: not to achieve a mental or spiritual emptiness like that sought by oriental meditatives, but to purposefully open the mind and heart to God's grace. Regular practice of Christian meditation, as Evagrius Ponticus explained in the fourth century, lets the soul see itself in the light of God, which is the gift of knowledge. It may even open the way to the extraordinary grace in which "the naked soul", he said, "becomes that which sees the Trinity" (*Problemata* 3:15). But certainly the regular and proper practice of meditative prayer lets the soul see itself, and God, more clearly.

This particular practice of meditative prayer is really the kernel of the Rosary, and of lots of other devotions, too. But in its simple form it didn't spread very far, nor did it last very long, in either the eastern or the western side of the Church. This technique required isolation, unlimited time, and a level of detachment that is simply not possible for the overwhelming majority of Christians. Still, pious Christians in all walks of life took it as the basis for various other techniques of raising their minds and hearts to God, not only because they wanted so urgently to turn away from sin, but because they could not bear to be separated from him. To do this they developed methods of meditative prayer that would let them spend some time each day thinking about God and his goodness; but they took care to design methods that would not require them to abandon their own perfectly legitimate vocations, which tied them to responsibilities of families, students, or parishioners.

Only a few Christian monks and nuns, in fact, could devote their full time and attention to practices like the Jesus Prayer. They all gave prayer the first place in their schedules, but they too had responsibilities—to the poor, to their own bodily sustenance, and to the well-being of the community. These had to be scheduled around that first priority of prayer. So they promised to say a certain number of vocal prayers like the Jesus Prayer at certain times every day, a thousand, perhaps, or five hundred or three hundred.

For that, they needed some method of counting the prayers, and the oldest and most universal way that people count things is with pebbles. They're easily available, they're convenient in size, and they have no particular value of their own, so you can use as many as you need and throw them away afterwards. Pebbles have been used everywhere since earliest times for every kind of reckoning, from counting prayers to calculating business transactions—in fact, our word "calculate" is from the Latin *calculus*, which means "little stone".

That's how other religions developed practices like piling up heaps of stones, each stone a record of a prayer uttered. There are occasional hints of this practice among Christians as early as the writings of St. John (Rv 2:17), but the earliest surviving explicit record of it comes from the writings of the fifth-century Greek historian Salaminius Hermias Sozomen. He tells about a monk named Paul the Hermit, who had died about a hundred years before Sozomen wrote. Paul would pick up three hundred pebbles every morning and put them in his pocket (whatever Paul wore, it evidently had pockets) and throw one away each time he had repeated his prayer. As the centuries rolled on, monks and nuns continued to pray in this way even when they lived in large communities, which, being usually in the wilderness, had plenty of pebbles available.

Counting their prayers helped the monks and nuns make sure that they didn't say fewer prayers than their vow required, but that was really the least of their reasons for keeping a tally. The point of repeating vocal prayers, then as now, wasn't just to tally up a great number of prayers, as it is in some eastern religions. In Tibetan Buddhism, for example, the number of prayers repeated is the whole point, so that ticking off beads, or even mechanically spinning a wheel with a prayer painted on it, completes the devotion in and of itself, without any real requirement of thought on the part of the person himself. In general, the repeated prayers of the eastern religions are not designed to ask anything from anyone who would have the power to grant it. Because the eastern religions that encourage some form of this practice don't believe in a unique personal God, their meditational practice consists of a skill that can be developed so that a natural state somewhat like a trance can be achieved, but it's a suspension of the mind that doesn't involve the soul. But when Christians pray they're communicating, directing their attention to a living and personal God, one who would hear and respond.

So the minds and hearts of the early monks had to remain engaged in God as they said their prayers. In fact, that's the main reason that Catholic

Christianity keeps track of vocal prayers: not just because of the inherent value of repeating vocal prayers, but because they're used as a framework for meditative prayer. This, too, is exactly the opposite of the meditative techniques practiced by the great eastern religions, even those that use prayer beads of their own. Oriental meditation is thinking about nothing, simply emptying the mind of all conscious thought. Christian meditative prayer is thinking about something, about God or something related to God.

Because Christian meditative prayer involves both the mind and the soul, Christianity would never instruct a person to suspend the workings of his mind. Far be it from Christians to try to keep faith without thinking, St. Augustine wrote to his disciple Consentius in about 410, "because if we weren't endowed with reason, we couldn't believe at all." So, unlike their oriental counterparts who try to empty their minds, Christian monks and nuns fill their minds with thoughts of God's goodness and his mercy, or some other aspect of his divinity, as they repeat their vocal prayers. And unless you can walk away from all human ties and live out your days alone in the desert, this kind of prayer requires that you keep count of the vocal prayers that lead you into this deep meditative state, for purely practical reasons.

When you use repetitive vocal prayer as a way of drawing yourself into meditative prayer, you soon forget the passage of time. "The hours glide past like minutes," St. John Vianney used to say; "it is a foretaste of Heaven." You can suddenly come to yourself and find that it's the middle of the night, if you started meditating during morning prayers, or that it's the middle of the morning, if you had planned to meditate before bedtime. At a certain initial level, this is like becoming absorbed in some occupation: you're alert and focussed on the object of your meditations, but you aren't aware of anything else going on around you. But most people who develop the skills of meditative prayer pass this initial stage fairly quickly, and the deep recollection that characterizes this kind of prayer is a different state altogether.

Recollection may even look like indolence, to the casual observer, but it's not. Certain separated groups, like the fourth-century Messalians and other Quietist sects, took the refusal to work as a sign of holiness—and the more violently their members refused, the holier they were supposed to be. But the Church doesn't see things that way; so even if some slackers might try to dismiss a call to duty by saying, "I'm praying," the chances are that they couldn't get away with it. Their superiors can perfectly well tell the difference between prayer and idleness.

People usually need quiet and physical relaxation for recollection. That's why the early monks took to the desert, and it's why people today find it difficult to pray meditatively while jostling along in a car or a train. Normally people at prayer simply remain quiet, focussed and detached, but they're obviously not sleeping or even resting. They don't usually close their eyes, and in the deepest levels of recollection they might not even blink. Their breathing remains regular, but shallow, not like the deep rhythmic breathing of sleep. In the lowest degree of ecstasy—if God draws them to ecstasy—some have neither breath nor pulse.

People praying meditatively often kneel, and some few in the past have knelt with chains around their knees, if their spiritual directors permitted them that kind of penance. Others stand, and some stand or kneel with their arms outstretched, reflecting the image of the Cross. They may stay in one of these rigorous postures for hours. Of course, a person who meditates may sit, or even lie down, as people sometimes do when they meditate while hospitalized, but no particular posture is necessary for genuine meditative prayer. The point is simply that even in the most ordinary kind of recollection the body of a person praying meditatively is clearly not the body of a person in idleness, because the mind is occupied with living thoughts of God, and the soul isn't idle at all—it's doing exactly what it was created to do, standing in rapt adoration of God himself. And the body probably isn't idle, anyway, because many, probably most, people who pray meditatively repeat vocal prayers while they do so.

In fact, vocal prayer is necessary, St. Augustine noted (*On the Sermon on the Mount* 3:14), "precisely because the attention to prayer clears and cleanses our hearts". Through vocal prayer, he said, "the heart is turned toward Him who is always ready to give ... there's a change of heart ... a cleansing of that inner eye through the exclusion of ... temporal things. And the gaze of the undivided heart is able to bear the undivided light divinely shining, without any motion ... and also to abide in that light ... with inexpressible joy."

Vocal prayer is an avenue to higher forms of prayerlike meditation and contemplation, or even to opening oneself to those mystical states in which God, in his own time and in his own way, reaches back to touch the soul that approaches him in prayer. Properly performed, vocal prayer is so effective in this way that great saints like St. Philip Neri or St. Ignatius of Loyola would fall into deep recollection after only the first few words— many saints had to be excused from the vocal prayers required by their vows because they simply could not recite even one without rising immediately into meditation, or even being drawn up by God in ecstasy.

St. Teresa of Avila recalled (*Way of Perfection* 30) an elderly nun who came to her, troubled that she could only pray vocally, "and if she didn't recite vocal prayers her mind wandered so much that she couldn't bear it... She spent several hours reciting a certain number of Our Fathers, in memory of the times Our Lord shed his blood, as well as a few other vocal prayers... I saw that though she was tied to the Our Father she experienced pure contemplation and that the Lord was raising her up and joining her with himself in union." This high mystical gift, the "prayer of union", came upon the old nun so quickly and so smoothly that she herself was not aware of it; she evidently thought that all of this was simply the normal result of good vocal prayer. "So," St. Teresa said, "I praised the Lord and envied her for her vocal prayer."

But even lesser lights can become deeply recollected by means of vocal prayer and lose track of time entirely. So even the earliest monks and nuns needed a way to bring themselves out of meditation when duties called. Some would force themselves to stand, or to walk; others would make themselves focus on some thing or some activity around them. But these things take tremendous effort, because the soul, transfixed in its meditation on God's goodness, never wants to turn its gaze away from him and back into this world.

Some people, like St. John Berchmans, S.J., have to be roused forcefully by their brethren when duties call them from prayer; they cannot do it alone. Some communities appointed a monk to walk around at certain times, striking a wooden clapper or simply calling loudly to bring the others to attention. In fact, bells were invented in the West in about the fourth century for exactly that purpose; the word itself is from the Anglo-Saxon *bellan*, to bellow, and the bellow of the bells has regulated the communal prayers of the Christian world ever since.

The quietest and most effective way to regulate your meditative prayer, though, is simply to count the vocal prayers that lead you into meditation. That puts an automatic limit on the amount of time spent in meditation, and it gives you a gentle signal that the allotted time is up. The early monks and nuns found that while their hands moved automatically through the given number of pebbles, their attention stayed focussed on the words of the prayers that they were addressing to Heaven, to the exclusion of the world around them, while their minds stayed free to meditate on God's goodness. And when they ran out of pebbles, it was time to get back to a different kind of prayer, the prayer of work.

Some of these monks and nuns continued to say the Jesus Prayer as they ran through their daily quota of pebbles, and in fact it's still said today, in some form, and in some devotions based on the modern Rosary. After about the third or fourth century, though, the form most often used to implore God's mercy was the Greek prayer, the Κύριε ἐλέησον—in Latin letters, the *Kyrie Eleison* (KEE-ree-ay ay-LAY-ee-son; Lk 18:9-14). Like the Jesus Prayer in all of its other forms, the *Kyrie* evidently got its start in the East very early, being used by the second century in litanies.

The *Kyrie* still stands at the beginning or at the end of every litany today. A litany is a form of public prayer in which a priest, deacon, or other prayer leader intones a series of petitions or invocations and the congregation responds with a formula of prayer in answer. Outside the Mass, litanies can be addressed to Christ, to Mary—hers is called the Litany of Loreto, from the city in Italy that popularized it—to another specific saint, or to a series of saints. Within the Mass itself, the Prayer of the Faithful is a litany, and so is the *Kyrie*; the Lamb of God (*Agnus Dei*) is a litany, too. Sometimes, particularly in the Greek East, the litanies were prayed not antiphonally but in unison, priest and people chanting the petitions and the plea together.

The *Kyrie* was quickly integrated into all kinds of devotional practices all across Christendom. No matter where it went, into the Coptic Rite, the Ethiopian, or the Syrian, it stayed in Greek, but it was the Latin Rite that built the prayer into its definitive form, the simple Κύριε ἐλέησον alternating with Χριστὲ ἐλέησον, "Christ, have mercy". In the Mass, this alternation is repeated three times, as it has been since at least the fourth century:

Κύριε ἐλέησον	*Kyrie, eleison*	Lord, have mercy
Χριστὲ ἐλέησον	*Christe, eleison*	Christ, have mercy
Κύριε ἐλέησον	*Kyrie, eleison*	Lord, have mercy
Χριστὲ ἐλέησον	*Christe, eleison*	Christ, have mercy
Κύριε ἐλέησον	*Kyrie, eleison*	Lord, have mercy
Χριστὲ ἐλέησον	*Christe, eleison*	Christ, have mercy

But the monks and nuns of the West chanted the *Kyrie* three hundred, five hundred, or a thousand times a day, begging God to forgive their own sins and the sins of others (Lk 18:1-5). When they prayed together for the repose of the souls of their departed brethren and benefactors, they combined the *Kyrie* with other prayers, mostly with readings from the Book of Psalms. In fact, they sang psalms for many different reasons—begging mercy is only one purpose of prayer, and the Book of Psalms encapsulates the most eloquent patterns of prayer for praise, thanksgiving, and simple adoration as well.

So from earliest times monks and nuns often sang psalms. Sometimes they sang all hundred and fifty psalms, and sometimes they chose certain ones appropriate to the intention of their prayers; but either way they all used psalms as a basis for meditative prayer—"I will pray with the spirit, but I will pray with the understanding also; I will sing with the spirit, but I will sing with understanding also", as St. Paul advised (1Cr 14:15-16). And they all added standard prayers like the *Kyrie* after each, no matter what arrangement of psalms they sang.

Historians like Eusebius, John Cassian, and, long before them, St. Paul himself (Eph 5:19; Cl 3:16) testify that the laity, too, established the Psalter as the basis of their private devotions very early in the Church's history. Day and night, the people flocked to the oratories of the monasteries and convents to participate in those devotions, and they were certainly welcome; the communal prayers of monastic communities are above all the prayers of the whole Church for the whole Church, and for the salvation of the whole world.

> In fact, the monks didn't just admit people who happened by; they invited the laity to join in. By the turn of the fifth century St. Porphyrius of Gaza had already added an *invitatorium* to the psalmodic prayers of the monks in his diocese; he put Psalm 94—Come, let us sing joyfully to the Lord—at the beginning of the devotions, and there it has stayed ever since, across Christendom. The Mozarabic Rite still calls this psalm the *sonus*, because it's sung while the bells are being rung to summon people to prayer, and since at least the time of Charlemagne the rubrics in Europe have specified that it should be sung slowly, to give people enough time to get there.

Now, from St. Paul's day and really up to the time of St. Porphyrius, Christianity was an urban phenomenon, by and large. The Apostles went to cities and towns, where the most people congregated (Mt 10:11-15). That made sense, because the area had been settled for so long, and comparatively few people lived out in the countryside; even farmers spent their nights within the safety of the city walls. So a church in Antioch or Pergamum could serve thousands of Christians; the cities gave rise to the churches, in those regions.

It was just the opposite in northern Europe—the churches gave rise to the cities. In Apostolic days, the whole region that today includes Ireland, England, France, Germany, Scandinavia, all of eastern Europe and much of Spain was still covered with virgin forest, punctuated by bog and moor, pierced only occasionally by a few shreds of Roman road that led to the scattered urban outposts there, the Roman military colonies. By the fourth century or so, these fortified towns were falling into ruin, and so were the roads that had once connected them to the civilized world. Not even the Roman Empire had made inroads through the native pagan religions, but as the darkness of the fall of Rome spread across the known world, monks and nuns from southern Europe moved into the north and built the great monasteries, lanterns in the darkness from which the lamps of civilization could be lighted.

Eventually, these outposts developed into cities like Rouen and Munich, whose very name *München* means simply "monks". But for centuries the monasteries of northern Europe were the only permanent buildings in the region, and liturgies in monastic oratories were the only church services available. The laity gathered in the monastery oratories for Mass on Sundays, and those who lived close enough responded to the *Invitatorium* and gathered there every day to take part in the psalmodic devotions as best they could. They evidently took the monastic patterns of prayer home with them, too. After all, when the laity there looked for examples of Christian life, they had only the monks and nuns before them, so they did as the clerics did.

With both religious and laity shaping their devotions on psalms and on the *Kyrie*, a good many penitential and meditative practices had grown up on the framework of these prayers by the middle of the fifth century. Some monks and nuns would add Gospel readings after the conclusion of each psalm, recalling not just the Passion but another episode in the life and redemptive work of Christ that was foretold in the psalm. Most would echo the Angelic Salutation to Mary—Lk 1:28— after each psalm, and then follow that with the Gospel passage prefigured by that particular psalm.

> The Angelic Salutation, "Hail, Mary, full of grace; the Lord is with thee," consists of the first words spoken when the Old Covenant was at last to be fulfilled and the New Covenant instituted. This instant in time is pivotal to the whole course of history: it's the Incarnation of Christ, the moment at which the Word took flesh and dwelt amongst us. All of Christ's work, the work of redemption that made salvation possible, started at that moment. Naturally, Christians have always taken the Annunciation as the epoch that ended the Age of the Law and began the Age of Grace. And, just as naturally, Christians have always repeated the angel's greeting to Mary in pious exercises based on the correspondences among prophetic passages, which predict that certain events in the Messiah's life on Earth will happen, and Gospel passages, which affirm that those events did happen. All of these correspondences, all of the correspondences among Scriptural passages Old and New, hinge on that verse, "Hail, Mary, full of grace;" and all of the fulfillment of prophecy since Genesis hinges on the events that immediately followed it.

To aid the memory and to draw the deepest significance out of these psalmodic devotions, many monastic communities patterned the Gospel episodes in sets of five, ten, fifteen, or even twenty passages that tell of the joys, sorrows, and triumphs of Mary and Jesus, just as the psalms themselves tell of the joys, sorrows, and triumphs of the Faithful and indeed of the Messiah who was to come.

But there were problems with all of these psalmodic devotions that were not to be solved for hundreds of years. It's often thought that the problem was illiteracy, but that's not really true. Europe in the Middle Ages was not so much illiterate as pre-literate; life generally ran along without the written word. It really just wasn't worthwhile for most people to learn how to read, in those days. Still, plenty of people could read, in the Middle Ages. In fact, the Book of Psalms was the basic textbook that the Church used to teach people to read. And the practice is as old as Scripture itself—it's why Psalms 110, 111, and 118 are arranged as little alphabet-books for Hebrew children.

The real problem was that before the invention of printing nobody could figure out how to make enough copies of the liturgical books so that everybody who could read could use one. We sometimes forget that mediæval Europe didn't even have paper; a single sheet of parchment or vellum costs the life of a farm animal, not to mention weeks of preparation. Even today good ink is costly, brewed by hand. Manuscripts took years to copy, and they were unbelievably expensive. A Psalter was worth a farm and a Bible a whole village.

Instead, people in those days used memory, and a surprising number of people knew the Psalter by heart, straight through. As early as the fourth century St. Jerome wrote to a monk named Rusticus—whose name implies that he didn't have much education to start with—and told him to "gather the various fruits of Scripture and enjoy the pleasures that it offers you; learn the Psalter by heart; pray it unceasingly." St. Jerome's friend St. Paula and her daughter St. Eustochium Julia not only learned the Psalter but learned Hebrew so that they could chant it in that language, as it was originally chanted, with no trace of an accent. So did their friend Marcella. Two hundred years later St. Benedict laid it down as a rule that the monks who weren't priests should work on memorizing the Psalter in whatever time they had left after Matins in the middle of the night.

The interesting thing is that so many of the laity knew the Psalter, too. St. Basil says that his congregation was familiar with it, generally, and so do many other Fathers of the Church. Even up to the time of the First World War, any psalm could be recalled to people's minds by a snippet of quotation on a coin or in a popular song, or in any other circumstances (cf. Mt 27:46; Ps 21; Lk 23:46; Ps 30:6). Literate, illiterate, or pre-literate, people knew their psalms.

That meant that even monks and laymen who couldn't read could join in the singing, but without access to written texts it might take them years of hearing psalms to learn the whole book. Besides, to perform these devotions from memory, they'd have to know not just Psalms but the whole Bible, and beyond all of that they'd have to know the particular patterns of texts appropriate to each day. And the effort required to keep up with the devotions by memory would divert too much attention from the process of prayer itself.

So, despite everybody's best efforts, most Christians were excluded from participating fully in the great psalmodic devotions performed by the orders that were teaching Europe to pray. That's why the monks started carefully editing their psalmodic devotions into simpler and more manageable forms for the lay brethren and the laity at large. By about the year 800, monks in Ireland had already divided the hundred and fifty psalms of their long devotions into three parts—*na tri coicat*, "the three fifties", they called the practice.

That made it easier for the rank and file to perform a psalmodic devotion within the framework of their workday, because they could say one or two "fifties" during the night when no manual tasks could be done anyway, and then complete the third "fifty" during the day, leaving time for necessary work during the hours of light. Within a few years, the arrangement had spread to the great abbeys of Kemble and Canterbury, and by the ninth century it had been introduced to the great German centers like the abbeys of St. Gall and Fulda, to Reichenau on its island in Lake Constance, and to many other monasteries and convents throughout northern Italy.

But the practice of the "three fifties" still didn't do much for people who couldn't read, or who could read but couldn't afford a manuscript book; it was impossible for those who couldn't learn the psalms, or who hadn't learned them yet. So the lay brethren and the laity outside the monastic enclosures simply continued the process of editing and condensing the monastic devotions. They said the "three fifties" using prayers that they already knew in place of the Book of Psalms and all of the other texts that they fairly could not know. That is, by about the year 1000, they were praying the "Poor Man's Psalter", repeating the Our Father fifty or a hundred and fifty times instead.

This was already an old custom in the monastic life of the Church. In fact, the Our Father was the prayer that Paul the Hermit had repeated seven hundred years earlier while tossing away his pebbles, and countless monks since his time had done the same thing. Substituting the Our Father for extracts from the Book of Psalms was an old and universal practice, too, because the two texts are so closely interrelated. "If we pray rightly and in a becoming manner," St. Augustine said, "no matter what words we use, we're offering no petition that isn't found in this prayer of Our Lord's."

And, looking at it the other way around, any number of people since St. Augustine have noticed that these psalmodic devotions are only the Our Father carried into detail, expanded, and commented upon. The Our Father, after all, is a kind of psalm, and a psalm written by Christ himself; and it was customarily said at the end of each section of the psalmodic devotions that the monks prayed—"Definitely," St. Benedict wrote in his *Rule*, these devotions should not finish "without the Our Father being recited at the end by the superior, while all listen." It's exactly what Christ himself told us to say when we pray (Mt 6:9-13).

Those in authority speedily approved the use of the Our Father—the *Pater noster*, in Latin—as the basis for meditative devotions, not only in view of its divine authorship and these venerable devotional practices but for practical reasons too. They knew that everybody can memorize the Our Father; it's not very long, it's the first prayer a Christian learns, and it's kept fresh in the memory by being repeated at every Mass. They knew that the whole point wasn't to labor at prodigious feats of memory but to pray well; and most of all they knew that you can meditate while saying any vocal prayer, not just the whole Book of Psalms.

The Poor Man's Psalter meant that people in any walk of life could assign some of their time every day to meditation on the life and work of Christ while saying "three fifties" of the Our Father, often adding the Angelic Salutation after each, as the monks and nuns added it after each psalm. You sometimes hear objections to this form of prayer because people think that Mt 6:7 says that we shouldn't repeat prayers. But the Bible says that we should repeat prayers; and this objection really stems from reading the Bible too narrowly.

It's based specifically in the mistake of focussing on a word in the King James Version that's a little too old to be understood clearly now. In fact, the King James Version, published in 1611, changes Mt 6:7 even more, rendering the important phrase as "use not vain repetitions", but there's absolutely no way to get that meaning out of the texts that James's royal Biblical commission started with. They changed it purposefully, as they changed so many other verses, to suppress the ancient Christian customs of England—in this case, to suppress the custom of meditative prayer.

James I's predecessor, his cousin Queen Elizabeth I, had continued the policies of her father, Henry VIII, to stamp out all of the Church's practices and devotions in England. She had passed an act (13 Eliz. ii) that prohibited the manufacture and use of "Crosses, Pictures, Beads, and such like superstitious Things", but evidently it didn't work—people still used imported rosaries. James himself had to reinforce Elizabeth's prohibition with an act (3 Jas 1) specifying that "no person shall bring from beyond Seas … any Popish Primers, Ladies Psalters, Manuels, Rosaries."

The fact that the government had to specifically outlaw the practice again and again shows how devoted the English had always been to this ancient form of prayer. They were the most devoted nation in Europe, in fact—they all go to Mass every day, the surprised Venetian ambassador had written home in 1496, "and they pray many *paternosters* in public, all of the women carrying long strings of beads". The English were not about to give up the custom of praying while fingering a string of beads. Law or no, they could point to the Bible, which supports the practice, principally with that passage in Matthew but also with lots of other verses—to say nothing of the Church's uniform experience and practice since before Matthew was written.

To understand Mt 6:7 clearly, you have to go back to the Church's Bible, which was the only Bible in existence when the King James commission started working on their own version. The original Greek is προσευ-χόμενοι δὲ μὴ βατταλογήσητε ὥσπερ οἱ ἐθνικοί, etc. In its classical sense, the word βατταλογέω means "to stammer", and it's also used to mean to chatter any empty, meaningless sound. Eustathius, the twelfth-century bishop of Thessalonika—who certainly knew his Gospel—used it in his commentary on Homer to refer to the twittering of birds. Either way, the word doesn't mean saying the same thing over and over; it means hemming and hawing, babbling meaninglessly instead of saying what you want to say, or just not getting to the point.

In the Latin Bible, the Vulgate or the Latin of St. Jerome, Mt 6:7 says *Orantes autem, nolite multum loqui, sicut ethnici, putant enim quod in multiloquo suo exaudiantur*. You can't get the verb "multiply" out of the *multum* in that verse; it isn't even a verb. *Nolite loqui* is the verb, and it simply means "don't talk". And *multum*, there, means "much" or "a lot". So *nolite multum loqui* just means, "don't talk a lot; don't run off at the mouth; don't rattle on like the pagans do: get to the point"—exactly what the Greek means. Today, we'd understand that verse as saying something like "But when you pray, don't talk a lot as the Gentiles do, thinking that they'll be heard simply because they talk so much." The idea is that you should simply say what you want: "for your Father knows what you need before you ask him" (Mt 6:8).

So Mt 6:7 is a warning against confusing quantity with quality; "first of all," St. Augustine said, "Our Lord excluded loquaciousness" (*Sermon* 56:4). Christ advised against twittering and talking too elaborately, which is a different thing entirely from repeating the same prayers over and over. In fact—like pious people in the Old Testament (1Kn 12)—he himself spent whole nights in prayer; he himself repeated what he said time and again (Mt 26:44), and he himself said that repeated prayers work even beyond the claims of justice (Lk 11:5-8, 18:1-8; *cf.* Jm 5:16-17; 3Kn 17-18). Besides, he followed this advice immediately with the Our Father as a pattern, and then he repeated it himself—the full version in Matthew is part of the Sermon on the Mount, but the abbreviated reminder of it in Luke happened on another occasion altogether.

Christ set the pattern to be repeated, and he told us to say it when we pray. Pray this way, he said, and pray without ceasing—commandments that the Church has never forgotten (Lk 18:1, 21:36; 1Th 5:17). So the repetition of vocal prayers is certainly in harmony with all of his instructions in the matter of prayer, and it follows his own example.

But King James set up his Biblical commission to write its own version of the Bible, removing or changing whatever parts of Scripture supported teachings and practices that they wanted to get rid of. Civil laws against those practices hadn't worked, so the commission took out the central part of Mt 6:7, the advice against running off at the mouth when you pray, and substituted "use not vain repetitions", a phrase directly aimed at suppressing the Rosary but entirely different from what the Bible says.

The simple answer to the objection, then, is that proper repetitions of vocal prayers aren't vain, in either sense of the word. The words of vocal prayer are not meaningless—it's a fault to babble them out without paying any attention to them (Mr 7:6), but words have meaning and, because the human mind operates in terms of language, words have power, the power to change the way you think. If you repeat the words automatically, you've wasted this power, and you've missed the point of vocal prayer, which is after all communication that asks for an answer. Certainly, there can't be any objection to repeating a communication, least of all a prayer, and least of all prayers drawn straight from the Bible; and if you say those prayers well each time, it can't matter whether that repetition follows immediately, an hour later, or a day later—God stands outside of Time, and a thousand years in his sight are as yesterday (Ps 89:4). If you're saying it right, you can't say it often enough; and if you're saying it wrong, it doesn't matter how often you say it.

But beyond that an objection to the repetition of vocal prayer in devotions like the Rosary misses the point, precisely because these vocal prayers are repeated as a way to achieve a state of clear meditation, a lively regard of God or of some aspect of God: he who only follows words has nothing, but he who possesses his own mind cares for his soul (Pr 19:7-8). Repetitions aimed at that goal can appear vain only to those who have not been taught the skill of meditative prayer.

Naturally, people who adopted the practice of meditative prayer while repeating the Our Father fifty or a hundred and fifty times wanted to be sure that they hadn't stopped at forty-nine or a hundred and forty-nine, and they, too, had to keep from spending all day and all night rapt in meditation. For that matter, it probably wasn't easy for them to develop the skill of meditation at all. These simple folk were not used to detaching themselves from this world and standing still in the presence of their God; their lives, like ours, left them extremely wary of anything even remotely resembling idleness.

But they knew that the repetitive manual tasks around the house and farm—shelling beans, churning butter, plowing fields—let them fall into a reverie and be alone with their thoughts. If we're working with our hands on earthly things, Richard Rolle asked in the fourteenth century, "what is to keep us from working with our hearts on heavenly things?" What, indeed—in those days Bl. Bonavita of Lugo worked at his smithy so deeply recollected that he failed to notice that the whole town was on fire; but when his neighbors finally got his attention turned to the emergency, he extinguished the flames by making the Sign of the Cross toward them, and then he went back to work and to prayer.

Even if few reached that degree of recollection, the laity across Europe had the habit of praying as they worked, too. Many, perhaps most, set aside a quiet time each day, alone or with the family gathered together, specifically to pray; and they structured their meditations on another repetitive task, taking up the ancient practice that you find all over the world and in all cultures that pray. They counted their prayers by means of little stones, or they knitted those prayers together with a length of string, a circlet of cord knotted or strung with beads.

In fact, our English word "bead" really means "prayer". It's related to the modern German *beten*, which means to pray, and to *Bitte*, which is used as we use "please", in polite requests. "Bead" itself comes from the Old English word *biddan*, which is also the root of our word "bid", as when you bid a favor of somebody, bid someone do something, or even bid people good morning—that is, when you ask something of somebody or when you express a desire. That's why the old term for saying the Rosary is "telling your beads", which means really "saying your prayers". It's also why the venerable St. Bede, the eighth-century English writer, was named that; his name means prayer. For the word to enter our language as it did, the Angles must have used beads almost exclusively for counting prayers, and the Saxons must have worn their strings of prayer beads around the waist—the Saxon word for prayer is *belt*. A canon of the English synod of Cealcythe held in 816, for instance, ordered seven belts of Our Fathers, *septem beltidum Paternoster*, to be prayed for deceased bishops.

The Angles, the Saxons, and their joint progeny were particularly fond of bead-counted devotions, but all through Christendom this practice stood as the basis of prayer-lives of the poor. It was particularly dear to the hearts of the country folk who lived in the lands around monasteries. They were the ones whose example taught meditative prayer to the rich and powerful; and when the great ones of the Earth started practicing meditative prayer by repeating fifty Our Fathers, the beads that they used started to get fancier, as suitable to the earthly rank of the people who used them. Lady Godiva, who died in about 1075, had precious stones threaded on a cord so that "by fingering them she could count her prayers exactly," the English historian William of Malmesbury said. St. Rosalia of Palermo kept her simpler beads with her always—they were found with her bones in 1624 in her hermit's grotto in which she had died in 1160—but she undoubtedly had finer ones in her earlier life as a princess of the family of Charlemagne.

After the twelfth century, the business of making the beads—which were then called *filæ de paternoster, numeralia de paternoster,* or simply "paternosters"—grew to keep pace with this increasingly popular devotion. By 1268 there were already four separate guilds of professional *patenôtriers* registered in Paris, and the street in London where their English counterparts had their shops is still called Paternoster Row.

The craftsmen who made these strings of beads, these "chaplets", had plenty of work to do, because circlets of beads were used for any number of devotional practices counting many different prayers, not just the *Pater noster* from which they took their generic name. These prayer cycles all consisted of meditations regulated by vocal prayers—usually the Our Father alternated with a short prayer of petition to St. Michael, St. Peter, St. Paul, or another specific angel or saint—and they were all counted on beads strung together in some specific number and arrangement.

Many of these devotions have faded over the centuries, but many of them took root and, in time, were approved by the Universal Church. You can still find the chaplets for many of them in religious-goods stores today. But from about the twelfth century to the fourteenth, one of these bead-measured devotions started to outgrow all of the others, and its increasing popularity came to be reflected in language, too. In fact, the German name Rosenkranz, which means "rose wreath", tells you that at some point in the past this family distinguished itself as makers of the circlets of beads used for this particular devotion—as makers of rosaries.

That name, like the modern Rosary itself, lay far in the future in the year 800. But by then all of the elements were there: the Faithful throughout Christendom, lay and clerical alike, were regularly practicing meditative prayer; they were structuring their meditations on the repetitions of vocal prayers anchored to the Lord's own prayer, the Our Father; they added the Angelic Salutation after each *Pater noster,* and they counted these vocal prayers on beads, after the pattern of the psalms, grouping them in fifties for a total of a hundred and fifty. These elements continued to develop and grow, step by step, with the psalmodic devotions of the great Orders; both the chaplet-based prayers of the laity and the monastic devotions grew and flourished together, all of them reaching their definitive forms at about the same time.

THE HOURS OF PRAYER

THE MONASTIC DEVOTION FROM WHICH THE ROSARY SPROUTED—AND THE most important devotion based on Psalms—is the "Prayer of the Hours". All clerics in the major orders are required to pray the Hours every day, which is why this devotion is also called the Office, from the Latin *officium*, which means "service" or "duty". Sometimes it's called the Divine Office, and sometimes the Great Office, to distinguish it from all of the other, lesser, duties of prayer embraced by clerics and laity.

Like most of the Church's devotional practices, the devotion of the Hours has its direct roots in the practice of the Apostles, who gathered to say certain prayers at certain hours of the day or night (Ac 3:1; 10:9, 30; 16:25). This is really just a continuation of Jewish practice, as you can see in passages like 1Kn 10:5 or Ps 118:164, or in the prescriptions for the services of the Temple in Exodus and Deuteronomy. There is no time in the memory of Christianity when Christians did not do this, and although the devotions took various forms and patterns they all had certain key features in common. Chiefly, they were all based on psalms, which were selected as appropriate to the day and hour; and they all combined these psalms with Gospel readings and the prophecies they fulfilled, excerpts from explanatory homilies by the Fathers of the Church, and penitential prayers like the *Kyrie*.

Normally, certain sections of the Office are to be said at each of the canonical hours, which are different from horological hours; the canonical hours didn't occur at the same time every day during the year, not until the invention of reliable mechanical clocks. Timekeeping in early Christian and mediæval days followed the ancient Roman practice of dividing the daylight, no matter how long or short it was, into twelve hours.

There were six hours between dawn and solar noon, and six between solar noon and sunset; nobody fussed about minutes and seconds, in those days. So the monastery bells pealed out at first light, at high noon, and at sunset, and when the Sun was at the halfway mark between dawn and noon, or between noon and sunset. Those five peals marked the major divisions of the twelve daylight hours, and five of the canonical hours were set on that frame of reference; but there are two canonical hours during the night, for a total of seven—seven times a day I praise thee (Ps 118:164).

THE HOURS OF PRAYER

The cycle of the canonical hours really started long before sunrise, with Lauds at about midnight; "at midnight I rose to give thanks unto thee," as the Psalmist said (118:62). Sometimes this midnight observance was called "Matins", from the Latin word for morning, but as its name "Lauds" implies, its prayers are devoted to praise, so they include psalms of praise like Ps 148, 149, and 150.

After Lauds, Prime came at dawn; as its name says, it was the first of the hours in the daytime. Terce came at the end of the third hour of the day, halfway between Prime and Sext; Sext is at the end of the sixth hour of the day, always at solar noon. Nones at the end of the ninth hour fell halfway between Sext and sunset; sunset itself was the hour of Vespers, from the Latin *Vesper* and the Greek ἕσπερος, the name of the evening star.

Vespers was, and is, the most solemn of the hours, the one at which candles were lighted, really more for ceremonial purposes than for illumination—the Hour used to be called *Lucernarium*, lamplighting time, too—and incense was offered, as at the evening sacrifice at the Temple (2Pr 13:11). Compline, so named from the Latin *completorium*, complement or completion, finished the cycle at about nine at night, after which the monks and nuns got a few hours of sleep before rising again at Lauds. So, with the reading of the Hours, the Church has always fulfilled Christ's command to pray always (Lk 21:36) as well as the prophetic ideal in Psalms, that from the setting to the rising of the Sun all nations should praise the Name of the Lord (Ps 112:3).

The devotion of the Hours has never been required of the laity, but during the first few centuries of the Church's life almost every Christian attended the services anyway, as the Book of Acts indicates. Those who couldn't, like people living outside the main cities or far from any monastic outpost, were still in the habit of pausing to pray at least at dawn, noon, and sunset. But the culture of the Middle Ages and the Renaissance practically required the Divine Office of princes and the nobility.

Like the monks, they had a good many duties to attend to in the course of the day, and their retainers had to have some idea of where they'd be and what they'd be doing at any given time; and the monastery bells that announced the daylight Hours were as close to standard timekeeping as the Middle Ages had. For these practical reasons, and because the lords of the Earth ought to be devoted to the Lord of the Heavens, the nobility structured their daily schedules around prayers at the times announced by the monastery bells pealing forth the Hours. By the eighth or ninth century, the practice was virtually universal among the movers and shakers of Christendom.

The devotional practices of the rich and powerful naturally set the fashion in devotions for the poor and obscure, just as the devotions of the monks and nuns set the patterns for the laity's prayers, and just as the prayers of the poor taught the gentry to tell their beads. But although the Hours were better organized and more logical in sequence than the free-wheeling psalmodic devotions of earlier centuries, they were even broader in the range of readings that they included, and even more complicated. The skills that the Hours demanded and the hours of time that they took still meant that most Christians couldn't perform them at all.

No two days' Hours are exactly alike, and with seven canonical hours for each of three hundred and sixty-five days, there are more than twenty-five hundred different patterns of prayer in the entire devotion. At first, all of these prayers of the Great Office had to be read out of a whole library of books, not just the Psalter but the other books of the Bible, as well as the Lectionary that indicated the Bible readings for Masses on particular feast days—that helped group the passages thematically—the Antiphonary, the Responsorial, and the Hymnal, and of course certain writings of the Fathers of the Church. The Passionary, which records the histories of the martyrs, and the Legendary, which contains *legenda* ("readings", from the Latin *legere*, to read) on the lives of the saints in general, also had to be at hand to supply additional texts, and a calendar was indispensable.

Obviously, it was extremely difficult to keep everybody singing from the same page. As early as the fourth century, St. Jerome put together the first Lectionary, a collection of psalms for the different hours, at the request of Pope St. Damasus I, and eventually people developed indexed versions of the lectionaries. These indices took on independent lives of their own, under the title *breviarium*, meaning abridgement or, more literally, abbreviation; the earliest of these breviaries were simply lists of instructions as to which readings were to be said on which days. By about the sixth century most orders and a good many Christian communities copied out all of the passages indicated by their breviaries into books known as "plenaries", or in Latin *plenarium*, from *plena*, full—the full complement of texts indicated in the breviaries.

By about the time of Charlemagne (742-814), breviaries in the original form had become unnecessary, since the only thing that people needed to perform the devotion of the Hours was a plenary. As the old-fashioned breviaries fell into disuse, people naturally transferred the title to the books that started life as plenaries—so, after that time, the plenaries were called breviaries. It made sense to call them that, because they were collections of all of the texts required for the Office of the Hours, taken out of the Bible and their various other sources and compiled into a single volume. So they really were abridgements of all of those books: each was a *breviarium* in its own right. That's why you never hear of a plenary any more, but a book that contains the prayers of the Divine Office is still called a breviary. Nowadays the Church's standard version is the *Breviarium Romanum*, the Roman Breviary or simply the Breviary, with a capital B.

Pope St. Gregory VII shortened the liturgy of the Hours again in the eleventh century, which reinforced the name *breviarium* for the collection of its texts, and Innocent III dei Conti di Segni did the same thing again in the twelfth, further abbreviating the Breviary. It still filled volumes—even today a printed copy of the Roman Breviary fills at least four thick tomes, one for each season of the year; in manuscript it looks like an encyclopæ-dia. But at least the texts in those volumes were in order, and at least there was only one place to look for them.

Still, writing the devotions down didn't solve the problem, because books were so few and so expensive. There were other practical problems that kept the majority of Christians from practicing the devotion of the Hours, too. Family duties and the hard labor of ordinary life made it vir-tually impossible for the laity to rise every few hours during the night to pray. For that matter, rising so often in the night wasn't really possible for all monks and nuns, either, particularly for those who had strenuous phys-ical labor to accomplish during the day. These religious have always been allowed to "anticipate", to group the prayers of the Hours together so that they can get the rest they need to maintain strength and health.

In some cases, they were allowed to limit their observance to Terce, Sext, and Nones, which fall in broad daylight. These "Little" Hours have a long history as a separate devotion, too; the practice is mentioned in Ps 54:18 and Dn 6:11, and evidently the community at Wadi Qumran—where the Dead Sea Scrolls were found—followed it. But the Little Hours have never been observed with the liturgical solemnity that accompanies Lauds and Vespers; their texts all follow the same simple pattern of a hymn, an antiphon, three psalms, a short lesson from the Bible, a few psalm verses with responses (the "versicles"), and a final prayer, virtually always the Our Father.

A few monks and nuns were simply dispensed from the specific obliga-tion, but they still sang as many psalms as they knew by heart while they worked, usually in combination with other prayers. Even those under the obligation did this, for that matter, and they all had a certain freedom in it; "We emphasize that if anyone is dissatisfied with this arrangement of psalms," St. Benedict specified in the *Rule*, "that he is to organize them oth-erwise, as he finds best." So monks and nuns were all required to pray the psalms, but the Scriptural passages that they might add, like the arrange-ments that they made in the order of the prayers, the time at which they said them, and even the tunes to which they sang them, were left to their judgement so that these devotions could fit their particular preferences as well as their other obligations.

This freedom was another reason that a myriad of different patterns of devotion based on the Book of Psalms developed, everywhere from Ireland to Russia. But, more importantly, after the Hours stabilized in the breviaries, it meant that the devotions always got simpler rather than more complicated as they had in previous centuries. From time to time, abbots and bishops took stock of developments; they called for the gathering and editing of these "extras" and "accretions" that had grown up spontaneously among the lay brethren and among the laity at large, whose culture was so tightly interwoven with that of the great Orders, and they evaluated them.

In these popular practices there were naturally some abuses that had to be corrected, but real contributions far outnumbered these innocent enthusiasms. The laity regularized the patterns and improved the formulations of psalm-based prayers, and they invented countless hymns and little canticles—pious folk-songs, really—that were often insightful and always simple enough for anybody to learn. And by further condensing the monastic devotions and sharpening their focus, these popular devotions were making it easier and easier for people in any walk of life to raise their hearts to God through meditative prayer.

As these psalmodic devotions grew from the Great Office, or as they were condensed out of it, the Church as a whole came to distinguish and approve several different devotions based on the Hours—the Hours of the Cross, the Hours of the Holy Spirit, and the Offices of the Passion, of the Dead, and so on. Across the face of Christendom, there have been any number of "psalters" that grouped the psalms and their attendant versicles and hymns in focus on a certain facet of Christ's redemptive work. There was the "Jesus Psalter", which was once immensely popular in England but disappeared entirely; there were "Lady Psalters" or "Angelic Psalters" that proved far more durable.

They range from the *Weddâsê Mâryâm*, the *Praises of Mary*, of the Ethiopian Rite to the *Psalter Mariæ* written by Stephen Langton, the great thirteenth-century archbishop of Canterbury, which separated all hundred and fifty psalms into individual verses and followed each and every one of them with a single line of petition to God through Mary, in an elaborate kind of litany. Langton's successor St. Edmund Rich wrote a Lady Psalter of his own, and so did many another luminary of the Middle Ages. Even St. Bonaventure had one attributed to him, the *Psalter Immus Beatæ Mariæ Virginis*.

By far the most important of these variants of the Divine Office is the Hours of the Virgin, often called the "Little" Office, to distinguish it from the massive volumes of the Great Office itself. This was the devotion that the nobility took up, in particular, and its development marked the next stage in the condensation of the popular devotions that eventually crystallized into the modern Rosary. But it evidently didn't start out specifically as a devotion to Mary. It's really a condensation of a condensation, a breviary drawn from the Breviary to give further system and clarity to psalmodic devotions and to make them more readily accessible to a greater number of Christians.

The Little Office consists largely of those parts of the Divine Office that are sung on the great feast days of the year, the days that commemorate the Incarnation of Christ, his death on the Cross, and the other events from the Annunciation to the Assumption that surround and complete the work of these great events, including the Nativity, Pentecost, and the others. Now, if you draw out those parts of the Roman Breviary that commemorate these great events, Mary features importantly in all of them, either taking a pivotal role or standing at her son's side in intimate co-operation with him.

In fact, Mary's role in Christ's work of redemption has had specific commemorations during the canonical Hours since patristic times. These were gathered together into special books, in only slightly variant forms, just as the breviaries themselves were being compiled, and it all happened at almost exactly the same moment throughout the Church. St. Ildelphonsus wrote an Office of the Blessed Virgin for the West in about 660, and St. John Damascene wrote one for the East only a little later, in about 730.

So the condensed Little Office came naturally to focus on Mary. Because its texts came out of the Divine Office itself, the Little Office has always been based on the Book of Psalms, and like all of the other psalmodic devotions it sets patterns of prayer to be sung on appropriate dates. Exactly as in the Great Office itself, these devotions consist of applicable Gospel verses, prophecies, hymns, antiphons, and commemorations of the saints—principally Mary. The commemorations of Mary include her own great canticle, the *Magnificat*; more recent hymns that monks and laymen had written in her honor, like *Vergine Madre* (contributed by Dante), *O Gloriosa Virginum*, and *Ave, Maris Stella*; and of course the Angelic Salutation, which features in all of the old variants of the Little Office.

In the Little Office, each Hour's devotions are followed by the Our Father and an antiphon of Our Lady. The antiphon was often composed especially for the Little Office, but some are drawn from the Marian commemorations of the particular liturgical season like Lent or Advent, or from the offices written especially to accompany the votive Masses customarily celebrated on Saturdays, a day that's always been devoted particularly to Mary. By 750 Pope St. Zachary ordered such a Little Office observed strictly at Monte Cassino, in addition to the Great Office. By the turn of the tenth century its texts had been collected into a volume called a Primer, after the canonical Hour of Prime, and by 950 it was celebrated in addition to the Great Office at monasteries and convents throughout the Holy Roman Empire.

The custom of praying the Little Office came along at exactly the right moment. As it happened, the tenth century was a particularly sad one for the Church, in terms of discipline, and it was a chaotic time politically, too. The disorder was so bad that people thought that it must be the tribulations leading to the Millennium, and the approach of the year 1000 did nothing to make them think differently. But looking back on it now the decay of morals and the disorder of public life only serve as a dark background against which the astonishing effects of the Little Office shine more clearly by contrast. In those countries where significant numbers of the laity adopted it, the Little Office was the key to restoring structure and order to religious observance, to morals, and to daily life itself.

England, for example, just before the Millennium, was convulsed by endless civil wars of unification. As King Æthelstan fought to make himself recognized as the first *rex totius Britanniæ*, King of All Britain, monasteries were laid waste, or fell into ruin; priests fled their duties, or drifted from them; and ancient paganism sprang up again in the absence of regular Christian ministry—it reportedly reached the point of human sacrifice, again.

But Æthelstan's successor Eadmund appointed Dunstan, Abbot of Glastonbury, to restore the Faith in Britain. Dunstan busied himself with reforming the clergy and the laity alike, not just as a royal official and bishop but by personal example. He attended Mass regularly, and he spent long hours in prayer, while most British clergy frankly did neither. Most important, he celebrated the Little Office publicly, with splendid liturgy, taking care to teach the participants about all of the prayers that it involved. The devotion was never required, of course, but even so the laity voluntarily crowded into the churches every day, many times a day, and even in the middle of the night.

St. Dunstan's onetime deacon, St. Æthelwold, helped him in establishing public devotion to the Little Office. Virtually everywhere these two great reformers went in Britain, the laity took the Little Office to their hearts, and in very short order it became basic to the prayer life of the realm. It became basic to education, too—the Primer was used to teach children how to read, just as the Psalter had always been used to teach priests and religious to read. After all, its texts were comparatively simple, and every monastery and convent had to have at least one copy so that the devotion could be celebrated there; and all of the schools were in those selfsame monasteries and convents.

For a thousand years after St. Dunstan, anybody who could read in England had been taught to read from the Primer. It was the basic British textbook four hundred years later when Chaucer wrote about the "litel clergeon seven years of age" who "sate in the scole at his prymer", and not even the Reformation could stamp it out. John Dryden translated the hymns for a primer published in 1706, and as late as 1773 Samuel Johnson defined a primer simply as "a small prayer-book in which children are taught to read." But however great the educational effects of the Little Office were, they take second place to the devotion's spiritual effects, which were nothing short of tremendous.

B y urging people to attend the celebration of the Little Office, by encouraging them to pray along with it as best they could, and by teaching them to do so, St. Dunstan and St. Æthelwold established peace and order in England, Scotland, and Wales such as nobody could remember. By the time they died the whole realm was filled with new and orderly monasteries and convents, with schools using their primers to teach morals as well as reading, and with churches restored and filled with people singing praises to Jesus and his Mother.

That might sound like a lot to credit to a devotional practice, but it stands to reason. After all, civil order can be achieved and maintained in a society in one of two ways: the government can force people to behave by means of an external power, or the people can behave themselves, in response to an internal power. When the internal power of virtue fails, Pius XI Ratti wrote (*Ingravescentibus malis*, 1937), when "the supreme and eternal authority of God, who commands and forbids, is despised and completely repudiated by Mankind, the result is that the consciousness of Christian duty is weakened, and that faith becomes tepid in souls or entirely lost; and this afterward affects and ruins the very basis of human society." There remains, of course, the expedient of using force, Benedict XV della Chiesa noted (*Ad beatissimi Apostolorum*, 1914), "but what is the result? Force can hold back the body, but it cannot govern the souls of Men."

The soul of Man can only be governed by itself; and people who are praying—particularly those who are praying meditatively—are thinking deeply about God's will and about his love every day, many times a day. They're sharpening their awareness of his justice; and in turning their hearts toward God they're turning more and more decisively away from sin. That is, they're turning toward virtue; and it is virtually impossible that people who have the habit of meditative prayer should be unjust in their dealings with others, or that they should think to commit crimes— "meditation and sin cannot exist together," as St. Alphonsus of Liguori used to say, categorically. A nation that establishes the habit of meditative prayer among its citizens is certainly going to come closer to achieving the Christian ideal of peace than a nation that doesn't.

Devotion to Mary has proved to be a particularly effective way of achieving this ideal. "Anyone who studies with diligence the records of the Catholic

Church will easily recognize," Pius XI continued, "that the victory won through her brought the return of tranquillity… Among the various supplications with which we successfully appeal to the Virgin Mother of God, the Rosary [which some call the *Psalter of the Virgin* or the *Breviary of the Gospel and of Christian Life*] without doubt occupies a special and distinct place."

Of course, in the year 1000 the Rosary as we know it had not yet developed. So when St. Peter Damiano saw civil disorders tear Italy to shreds a generation or so after St. Dunstan and St. Æthelwold had rebuilt England, and when he saw that the Church there was too weak to contest them— parish offices openly bought and sold, priests publicly "marrying" the women they lived with, riots in the very cathedrals, schism, heresy, and indifference on all sides–he took the Little Office of the English saints as one of his principal weapons. Like his English counterparts, he brought clarity and order to life by example and by insisting on the firmest discipline for those clerics under his governance. Like them he constantly encouraged the laity to embrace the devotion of the Little Office, and he let nothing interfere with clerical observance of both Offices, Great and Little.

In fact, while he was lying ill in February of 1072 at the monastery of Santa Maria degl' Angeli in Faenza, he got up to sing the Lauds appropriate to that day, and as soon as they were over he died. But by the end of his earthly career he could report that many of the Faithful, and virtually all of the secular clergy, prayed the Little Office daily throughout Italy and even throughout France, and that both of those lands had returned to regular observance of their religion.

They had returned also to something like civil order, and in fact to a kind of early Renaissance of art and learning. Times were still complicated, of course, as they always are to some degree or another; but most scholars still recognize that the turn of the eleventh century marks the first dawn that broke the Dark Ages. For his contributions to this reawakening, St. Peter Damiano was named a Doctor of the Church; but he himself attributed the change to the laity's return to prayer, specifically to their devotion to the Little Office of the Blessed Virgin Mary.

When the monastic orders saw its effect on faith and morals, many of them took up the Little Office in preference to the various other devotions that they had used, praying it in addition to the Divine Office itself. So did those who couldn't pray the Great Office—the illiterate, the laity, and the tertiaries, lay people who join the "third order" after the orders for men and for women, taking no solemn vows and living outside the order's religious community but participating in its devotions and other good works. They all continued to clarify and condense the many forms of the Little Office that had developed in different times and places, and they continued to count those prayers, or whatever prayers they substituted for the psalms and readings, on their beads as they had always done. Eventually, the Little Office was standardized in the reformed Roman Breviary promulgated by St. Pius V Ghislieri in 1568, and, most recently, it was edited again by John XXIII Roncalli, and then by the Second Vatican Council.

To this day, the Little Office is prayed instead of the Great Office by Dominican, Carmelite, Augustinian, and Franciscan tertiaries, and by the members of most of the congregations of women engaged in active work like nursing or teaching. It's also prayed by many lay people who, like their early Christian forebears, want to take part in the liturgical prayers of the Church. The Little Office of the Blessed Virgin is ideal for people who can't manage the Divine Office, because it complements the Little Hours; it's prayed at Matins, Lauds, Vespers, and Compline, the four Hours during which the Little Hours aren't prayed.

So anybody observing both the Little Hours and the Little Office would be rising to pray seven times a day, even if he anticipated and grouped the devotions along the lines of his work schedule. And he would be praying devotions that, compared to the voluminous complexities of the Divine Office, are simplicity itself. In fact, the Little Office of the Blessed Virgin is simple enough to be set down in a single volume, a Book of Hours. It's the devotion that fills so many beautiful manuscripts from the Middle Ages and the Renaissance—but then, you still needed to have a book, and you still had to know how to read Latin, before you could really perform this devotion.

That's why people still speak of "reading" the Hours, in contrast to "hearing" Mass; but that age-old need for books still made most of western Christendom feel left out. Anybody could attend the celebration of the Little Office, and by the year 1000 millions did; but the scarcity of written texts and the ability to read them still excluded most Christians from participating fully, in those long centuries before printing.

But the mediæval day itself was punctuated by the ringing of the bells of the canonical Hours. Evidently just after bells were invented, the laity had started using the monastic signal of the daytime Hours to pause in their work and meditate for a few minutes on the Incarnation, the Passion, or the Resurrection of Jesus. At that same moment, at least at Prime and Compline, the monks and nuns themselves would be singing psalms and praying the Hours, in whatever form the Hours stood at that time and place.

The Hours included a feature called simply the "Prayers", the *orationes* or *preces*. These are verses from Psalms, each split into an invocation and a response, in a kind of litany of antiphons. One common set of *preces* for Lauds, for instance, included these verses (in written versions of these devotions, "V." indicates the verse recited by the leader, and "R." indicates the response):

V. Let thy mercy, O Lord, be upon us
R. in such measure as we have hoped in thee (Ps 32:22)

V. Save your people, and bless your inheritance
R. and govern them, and exalt them forever (Ps 27:9)

V. Remember your flock
R. that you built up of old (Ps 73:2).

The sequence ended with a call from the leader, something like "Let us pray for the Faithful Departed" or "Let us pray for our absent brethren", to which the response was "O Lord, grant them eternal rest," or "Save thy servants who trust in thee," as appropriate.

Most *preces* included about a dozen of the split verses, but St. Æthelwold had edited them down to three. When the effects of his renovation of the English Church became known, this particular custom of the *tres preces* or *tres oraciones* spread, with the rest of his ideas, into Germany and from there to Italy. Soon, the peasantry all across Europe began their daytime prayers with some form of Three Prayers; most of them evidently added a triple repetition of the little verse that the monks and nuns used at the beginning of those Hours: *Angelus Domini nuntiavit Mariæ*, the Angel of the Lord declared unto Mary. In the space of a generation or so this practice itself came to be called the Angelus; and while it too started out at many places at once and took many various forms, the Angelus has always been brief enough to fit anybody's workday and simple enough to fit anybody's memory.

As in the *preces* and the other collective devotions, normally at least two people prayed this way, antiphonally—that is, one person said the first verse, the other (or the rest) answered with the second, and then they alternated the other verses. Everybody recites the Angelic Salutation together, and the leader intones the final prayer of petition. The Angelus took a long time to develop, and it varied in form from place to place, but basically it is as follows:

V. The Angel of the Lord declared unto Mary

R. and she conceived of the Holy Spirit (*cf.* Lk 1:28, 35).

   Hail, Mary, full of grace; the Lord is with thee.

V. Behold the handmaiden of the Lord;

R. let it be done unto me according to thy word (Lk 1:38).

   Hail, Mary, full of grace; the Lord is with thee.

V.   And the Word was made flesh, and dwelt amongst us (Jn 1:14).

Hail, Mary, full of grace; the Lord is with thee.

V.   Pray for us, O holy Mother of God

R.   that we may be made worthy of the promises of Christ.

V.   Let us pray. Pour forth, we beseech you, O Lord, your grace into our hearts, that we, to whom the Incarnation of Christ your Son was made known by the message of an angel may, by his Passion and Cross, be brought to the glory of his Resurrection. Through the same Christ, our Lord.

R.   Amen.

Notice that this follows the pattern of the *tres preces* exactly, with a sequence of three split verses, this time drawn from the Gospel, followed by calls to prayer from the leader. The Angelic Salutation occurs three times here, to make a parallel to the *tres orationes*. People who couldn't recite the whole Angelus—little children, for instance, or invalids, or people in remote areas who couldn't read it and hadn't been taught it—would simply pause and repeat that Bible verse three times, raising their minds and hearts to God in meditation on the Incarnation as they did. As the centuries rolled by, this verse was linked with the greeting of Elizabeth at the Visitation. By about the year 1300 both verses came to be followed by the ancient petition of the Council of Ephesus for Mary's intercession—Holy Mary, Mother of God, pray for us sinners—a combination that's the basis of the Hail Mary as we know it today. So people naturally integrated that prayer into the Angelus itself.

Those who didn't know the whole sequence of verses in the Angelus would simply repeat the Hail Mary three times as the bells pealed, and pause to think about the life and work of Christ on Earth. By about the thirteenth century, a general pattern had condensed out of all of the varied practices of the laity: people generally meditated on the glory of the Resurrection in the morning (suitable for the time of rising from the "little death" of sleep), the sorrow of the Passion at noon, and the joy of the Annunciation in the evening, taking the promise of the Savior with them as they slept.

Whatever form it took, though, the Angelus was so popular in its simplicity that it became virtually universal in Christendom by the end of the tenth century. Just as the Hours governed the schedules of monks and princes, just as the Little Hours punctuated the daily lives of those who could gather at monastic oratories or parish churches, the Angelus came to structure civil life for everybody else, even in the fields. The bells of Prime signalled the first exercise of the prayer as well as the time to rise and start work; at Sext work paused for lunch and for meditation again; at Vespers or, more usually, at Compline the bells summoned people to their homes for prayers, and by the eleventh century at the latest this was understood as curfew, after which nobody was to be out in the streets.

The Angelus is still rung on the campuses of some of the Church's universities—the institutional children of the monasteries—and it was so basic to mediæval life that it became the main reason that parish churches came to be built with bell towers. The bells themselves, some of which still peal today, were often inscribed with the Angelic Salutation or with related verses like "Behold! this bell of faithful Gabriel sounds", "Gabriel the Messenger bears glad tidings to Mary", and "I bear the name of Gabriel, sent from Heaven". In the Middle Ages, repetition of the Angelic Salutation was literally in the air.

T he Angelus dissolved a good many of the barriers that had kept the laity and the clerics apart in their devotions. It linked all Christians in prayer at certain given hours of the day, it was briefer than the Breviary, and it was simpler than even the Little Office. It reminded people to raise their minds and hearts to Christ through Mary during the day, and its spiritual and emotional benefits were noticeable.

But the Angelus alone is not enough. It's the ultimate condensation of the Hours, but its very brevity limits the depths of meditation that can be achieved. And, although its occurrence at regular intervals helps sanctify the whole day, the fact that it occurs during the work day means that it usually can't be extended. So pious people everywhere continued to supplement the Angelus by cultivating other meditative practices along the same lines, as they had always done.

By the turn of the twelfth century most of the Church's laity, east and west, rich and poor, supplemented the meditations of the Angelus by reserving some time during the day to tell their beads as they always had, meditating while counting off a hundred and fifty Our Fathers. Most still followed each with an Angelic Salutation—praying the Psalter of the Virgin, or, as they began to call it, the Breviary of the Gospel or the Breviary of Christian Life. The great lady Blanche of Castile (1188-1252), was particularly devoted to telling her beads in this way, and it ran in her family, unlikely as that must have seemed to those who knew her father, Alfonso VIII of Castile (1158-1214).

Alfonso was not pious by nature or by upbringing. He had inherited the throne at the age of eighteen months, and his childhood was an endless nightmare of narrow escapes from the great nobles who wanted to kill him and take his kingdom. Naturally, the boy had no religious training to speak of, and his adolescence is most charitably described as disorderly. He grew up leading his ragged armies in a hopeless campaign of reconquest of his own kingdom, not only from the Moors but from his own vassals. At last, his foes beat him back to a city held by one of his few loyal vassals, and it so happened that St. Dominic de Guzmán was there, too, preaching the practice of bead-counted prayers.

In one of his sermons, St. Dominic mentioned in passing Mary's promise that whoever shall pray the beads devoutly, applying himself to the consideration of the sacred mysteries, shall never be conquered by misfortune. The king sent for the preacher afterwards and asked him if that were really true; nothing could possibly be more true, St. Dominic said. Alfonso vowed on the spot to pray that way every day, and he kept his promise for a whole year. He never went to battle without first telling his beads devoutly, on his knees; he encouraged his court, his officers, and all of his servants to practice the devotion, too. Through this devotion, he obtained not only the return of his rightful kingdom but other special graces, too, like the cure of his wife's blindness. He even managed to arrange the marriage of his daughter Blanche to Louis VIII, King of France.

The marriage was a brilliant political alliance, and Louis and Blanche were personally happy in it, too, which is rare in the arranged marriages of princes. But for the first twelve years of their marriage they had no children. When St. Dominic saw her again while he was preaching in France, he reminded her of her father's great devotion and of the wonderful graces that it had brought him. So she, too, took up the beads, and about a year later, in 1213, she gave birth to her first son, Philippe. He died in infancy, as so many children did in those days, but she kept to her devotions and encouraged the whole French nation to join her. She had twelve children in all, six of whom lived to adulthood. One of them reigned after her husband as Louis IX, Louis the Saint.

Louis the Saint regularly heard Mass twice a day and participated in both of the Offices, the Great one and the Little; every day of his life he rose at midnight to dress for Lauds at midnight, in somber silks in summer and in gray woolens in winter. When his duties as King and crusader took him on long journeys, he rode surrounded by priests mounted on horseback who chanted the Hours so that he would never have to neglect those devotions. And in private—it would not be known to us if his servants hadn't seen him—he took up a devotion similar to his mother's that had been popularized by St. Aybert fifty or sixty years before. The king of France repeated the Angelic Salutation itself, the verse that stood at the head of so many of the hourly devotions of both clerical and lay life, a hundred and fifty times every day while meditating on some aspect of Christ and his work. At each repetition, he would genuflect or bow, as a penance and as a courtesy to the Lady with whom he shared his prayers.

THE FERTILE GROUND

This courteous attention to Mary is not at all surprising, because this was the great age of courteous attention to ideal ladies. In fact, the courtly culture of the Age of Chivalry grew up interwoven on the framework of the Hours, the Little Office, and the Angelus; and in return the ideals of chivalry, however imperfectly that knightly code achieved them, prompted the laity to ask for clearer and clearer definitions of Mary's role in the economy of salvation. Both impulses, the religious and the courtly, worked together toward the same goals, and in the process they shaped western civilization from at least the time of Charlemagne in the ninth century until the time of Cervantes in the sixteenth. And really the benefits of this quest extended until the complete collapse of the knightly code in the eighteenth, at the French Revolution.

The Age of Chivalry didn't get off to a very promising start, though. After the collapse of the central government of Rome, the legions withdrew, or they were absorbed into the local populations. With the legions gone, those local strong men who could maintain a gang of henchmen fought among themselves to extract goods and services from the peasantry and to establish their title to land by force, land being the source of all wealth in those days. Gradually, the strongest of these gangsters established leadership over any number of other tribal leaders less strong, and eventually, by about the sixth century, a system of oaths, extortion, and alliances grew into a tangled network of force that covered most of the continent.

This early feudal system was by no means stable, and it wasn't much concerned about actually governing anything. The men who fought their way to the top of the heap may have taken Roman titles like *comes*, count, *dux*, leader or "duke", or *rex*, king—some even modernized *Cæsar* into *Kaiser*—but they took almost nothing of Roman civilization along with them. Living on their loot, they could afford weapons and horses to carry them, while the peasantry, living on the land, could not; and so the mighty of the Earth ran roughshod over the meek, with nobody to stop them. Nobody, that is, except the monks and nuns. They had their work laid out for them on all sides: on the one hand, the masses of peasants had to be helped toward a more settled and prosperous life, and on the other hand the bands of bullies had to be kept from unsettling those people and stealing the fruits of their labors.

Because the Church could not take up arms against the leaders, she converted as many as would listen; and because she could not force any of them to put down their arms, she developed a policy of sanctifying those arms. That is, the Church used every means of persuasion at her disposal to make early feudal leaders understand that there are higher considerations in life than knocking people down or slicing them up; she pointed to goodness and mercy, and above all to justice, as the proper aims of worldly might.

So, as the feudal system stabilized and clarified itself, the Church constantly exhorted its leaders to concern themselves with the defense of the people living on those lands they claimed (which after all was in the leaders' best interests anyway, as securing their wealth and defusing rebellion). She planted the seeds of a strict code of morals and of honor. This was the code of *chivalry*, from the French *chevallerie*, horsemanship, the code of the mounted warriors, and it was imposed on them by the Church—certainly the men who eventually adopted it hadn't thought of imposing it on themselves. As time went on, public order and moral order grew together, and the Church cultivated certain forms and ceremonies of civil and military life, consecrating weapons to the work of justice and blessing knightly vows to use those arms only in defense of virtue.

Eventually this devotion of might to right led to massive international campaigns like the Crusades, but more to the point it had a great and growing effect on the general tenor of life in Europe. Rather than contending for land or riches alone, Christian knights contended to see who could endure the longest fast, complete the longest pilgrimage, or achieve the highest standard of virtue—contention itself runs against virtue, of course, and Christian knights blew a great many trumpets for themselves, but at least they were aiming their efforts at something beneficial to themselves and harmless to others, and setting an example for the lower orders.

By about the eleventh century, again at the urging of the Church and with her blessing, the flower of knighthood organized itself into great orders, avowed and devoted to the justice of civilization as the orders of the monks were dedicated to the Justice of Heaven. They still wasted a lot of blood and even more energy, and the lower classes were still living in conditions that would appall the average American. But gradually bands of knights bent on loot and plunder gave way to knights banding together in international networks of mercy, building hospitals, ransoming captives, taking in orphans, and seeing to the care of widows and the disabled. To a surprising extent, these chivalric orders—the Order of St. Stephen, of St. George, of St. Andrew, and many, many others—maintained a standard of honor and honesty among society's powerful that had been utterly unknown before and has been all too rare since.

In the long run, though, the most lasting achievement of chivalry was a recognition in the West of the value of the feminine side of life. When the warrior caste of Europe started to practice what the Church had always preached to them, it occurred to them that the noble things of life, the things worth fighting for, all centered around the women. They had learned of clemency from the Church, but when they sought models of selflessness and compassion, they found them in their women; when they needed examples of gentleness, they found them in the nurturing and the sweetness that seems to accompany maternity as perfume comes with flowers. Kindness—something that would never have occurred to a classical Roman—suddenly became the mark of real nobility.

It was during this time that Christians were first able to investigate the more agreeable aspects of the fact that the greatest of virtues is love. It was true when St. Paul first said it, of course, but there had been all of those ages of persecution and martyrdom in between. Now love motivated everything that the knights did, or were supposed to do; and the love of the feminine blossomed along with the love of the delicate, the fragile, and the fragrant—the grace of love, you might say. People studied love, the earthly kind and its heavenly model; they developed the theology of love to a study of great depth and clarity, and they put their studies into practice through courtesy. Men made themselves into gentlemen, and women became ladies.

If this great awakening to the civilizing power of the feminine was not yet the rebirth of culture that was the Renaissance, at least it was no longer the Dark Ages—the times were a kind of Middle Age between the two, which is why they're called that. People still had to live in fortified houses, but they gave them cheerful names like Plaisance and Beauté instead of horrifying ones like Malvoisin, and they called them Montjoie rather than Montfort. They took the effort to make them lovely as well as defensible, painting them bright colors and hanging them with pennants. They left space inside the curtain-walls for flower gardens; they built fairy-webs of weightless stone a hundred or a hundred and fifty feet tall and walled them with colored glass, vaulted cathedrals of an impossible delicacy from which the whole court of Heaven smiled in rainbow light. And they dedicated most of these confections to the perfect lady, the ideal lady, the lady most beautiful, most elegant, and most graceful, in both senses of the word. They dedicated them to Mary.

It was during this time that Mary herself came to be called *Madonna*, my Lady, or *Notre Dame*, Our Lady; you can hardly tell, reading some mediæval love lyrics, if the ideal gentlewoman eulogized is Mary or a more corporeal lady. The Age of Chivalry was a time in which people read the *Romance of the Rose* along with their Bibles, and troubadours like St. Francis of Assisi and Bl. Ramon Lull wrote songs of both kinds, at different stages in their careers. Devotion to Mary impelled western Christendom to a higher standard of civilized behavior, and in return the idealization of the pure love of a knight for his Lady encouraged people to think more deeply about Mary and her position in Christian theology. That position never changed, of course, but by the time of Saint Louis understanding of it had certainly clarified immensely, compared to what it had been only a few hundred years before. And the implications of that position were clarified during those centuries, too, as devotions to Mary brought down a rain of graces more constant and more copious than resulted from any other kind of pious practice.

Like St. Louis's repetitions of the Angelic Salutation, the most popular devotional practices were, basically, the very same ones adopted by the earliest hermit monks; and they were all expressions of the same basic technique of meditative prayer that the laity had never really abandoned. The devotions based on this technique required no reading, no books, no prodigious feats of memory; they centered the attention on repeated vocal prayers; and they left the mind free to meditate on the key episodes in Christ's work of redemption.

This is how it came about that, by the early thirteenth century, the monks and nuns were still singing psalms, as they do even today in the Office of the Hours; lay brethren and the laity at large focussed more closely on the key episodes in the lives of Mary and Jesus in the Little Office that had condensed out of the Great one. Those who could not attend these liturgies, or who could not attend to them by reason of youth, age, occupation, or lack of education, still focussed on those episodes in the work of salvation at least three times a day, at the Angelus.

And apart from these intervals of meditative prayer during the day, everybody in Christendom—prince, priest, peasant, monk, and nun—was taking the time to meditate while saying the Poor Man's Psalter, a hundred and fifty Our Fathers, or while meditatively repeating Our Lady's Psalter, "three fifties" of the Angelic Salutation punctuated with the prayer that Jesus himself had taught them; and all of them counted their vocal prayers on chaplets of beads. That is, by the thirteenth century Christians were praying the Rosary in all but name.

אמת

PRAYER-BEADS AND CROWNS OF ROSES

THE FIRST PERSON TO WRITE ABOUT THE MEDITATIVE DEVOTION OF THE beads using the name "Rosary" was Thomas of Chantimpré, who was born at the turn of the thirteenth century. Thomas, often called *Brabantinus*, the little man from the Brabant in the Netherlands, was a Dominican who studied under St. Albert the Great, the Universal Doctor, the Expert Doctor, of the Church. Like his teacher, Thomas set encyclopædic goals for his own writings. He decided to collect everything that anybody had ever known about nature, with special attention to the properties and characteristics of creatures.

For fourteen or fifteen years he ransacked every known text about the physical world, from Aristotle to his own day. He put anything interesting that he found into a huge work called *De Natura rerum*, "On the Nature of Things", which is a suitably broad title for an encyclopædia that includes treatises on everything from the marrow in lion's bones to the making of compasses. The *De Natura rerum* was the standard reference text at all of the great universities for a long time thereafter. Philippe IV le Bel had to set an equitable official price for it at the University of Paris at the turn of the fourteenth century, because in those days before printing the bidding for manuscript copies of it kept getting out of hand.

Thomas was up to date or ahead of his time—*De Natura rerum* includes the first technical essay on how to install regular lead-soldered plumbing like we have today. But his main purpose in this great work was moral rather than scientific; he wanted to use all of this information to illustrate moral points, thereby making it easier for preachers to convey those points in terms that anybody would understand.

No matter what in the world he investigated, Thomas of Chantimpré looked past its literal, natural meaning and found a higher and holier significance for it. His *Book of the Bees* (*Liber de apibus*), for instance, isn't really a work of natural history at all but an allegorical account of the early days of the Dominican Order of Preachers. So it's perhaps entirely in the nature of things that he should speak metaphorically of the meditative prayers that the laity, through no requirement but that of love, offered to Heaven every day.

As a good Latin scholar—and as one of history's greatest anthologists— he was perfectly familiar with the use of the word *rosarium* to mean a compilation, a bouquet of little blossoms of information or literary delight. And to him these cycles of prayer, counted on little circlets of beads, seemed like little crowns of spiritual roses presented to the Blessed Virgin. So Thomas of Chantimpré, in the thirteenth chapter of the second part of his *Book of the Bees*, became the first to compare a circlet of beads to a chaplet of roses, and to refer to this devotional practice as praying the Rosary.

S trictly speaking, the word "rosary" really means a garden in which roses are grown, just as an orangery is a place where orange trees are grown, and even as a fishery is a place where fish are grown. And the word "chaplet", as the circle of beads is called, means a little crown of flowers or leaves, or a circlet of gold or precious stones, to be worn around the head. To understand why people started calling this particular devotion a "wreath of roses" or even a "garden of roses", and to understand why any devotion of this kind is called a "chaplet", it's important to remember what a wreath is for, and what roses symbolize.

Ever since the Old Stone Age, people almost everywhere have strung up garlands of flowers at times of rejoicing, woven wreaths for mourning, and crowned victorious heroes with flowers, even if sometimes these crowns were made of gold flowers instead of real ones. The Romans used one and the same word for all of these things: *corona* means garland, wreath, and kingly crown, all at once. Like the Greeks and most other ancient peoples, the Romans would deck the streets with *longæ coronæ*, long garlands, on joyous occasions like the advent of a ruler into his city—that's why the Israelites cut branches on the spur of the moment in Mt 21:8.

Sometimes they'd weave flowers into crowns of rejoicing, too, as the people in Ws 2:8 did, and in the ages before Christ priests generally wore them while they were offering sacrifices. Greeks, Romans, and other ancient peoples put up wreaths like those that we still offer at funerals, too, and they laid them on tombs in tribute to the remembered dead, as we still lay them today. When a Roman general liberated a city, his soldiers caught up whatever grasses and wildflowers grew in the fields around it, twisted them into a *corona obsidionalis*, the crown of the siege, and presented it to him as a sign of triumph. In fact, when a Roman general was paraded in triumph thorough the city of Rome itself, a man was appointed to stand behind him in his chariot, holding over his head a crown of laurel, of olive branches, or of flowers—a *corona triumphalis*.

Most of these floral tributes were woven together spontaneously, but they were all understood as primary signs of happiness, sadness, or honor; all of them were offerings of a kind, tributes that signified the state of the heart. They were used on so many different occasions that distinct words were invented to distinguish different kinds of *coronæ*. By about the year 1000 the word "crown", the English form of the Latin *corona*, began to be restricted to mean that little head-wreath of gold and jewels worn by kings and nobles; a twist of grass and flowers came to be called a "wreath" in English, which is related to our word "writhe", meaning to twist or wind around.

By the fourteenth century the wreaths of flowers to be worn on the head had come to be called "chaplets", which, like our word "cap", is from the same root as the French word *chapeau*, meaning hat or headgear—all of which come from the Latin *caput*, head. A chaplet, then, is simply a wreath, like the old Roman laurels, to be worn on the head as a sign of the feelings in the heart at occasions of joy, mourning, or triumph. Until recent years, everybody understood what it meant to offer a chaplet to somebody—in 1648, when Robert Herrick's lady love sent him a chaplet of willow, the plant symbolic of sadness, he knew instantly that it "did but only this portend, I was forsooke by thee" (*The Willow Garland*).

I f Herrick's lady had sent a chaplet of roses, the story would have had a different ending entirely. No flower conveys the idea of love more perfectly than the rose, and no floral symbol is understood more universally. Ben Jonson's lady understood perfectly well that the gift of a chaplet of roses is intended as a pledge of undying love, so, to reject that love, she simply sent it back to him (*Song to Celia*, 1616).

Roses are practically universal—no matter where you look in the northern hemisphere, roses were either introduced there by our prehistoric ancestors or were waiting to greet them when they got there. The word "rose" itself is basically the same in all western languages, and in all of its forms it's so ancient that nobody knows for sure where it came from, either. The Greek ῥοδέα is a possible root, but then again that word itself seems to have come from a word in an earlier mother-language that people used to refer to this flower long before Greece was even settled.

And just as everybody knows roses, everybody loves them. They have an inborn tendency to sport double and even triple flowers in every color from spotless white to deep red, almost black, by way of yellow, pink, and orange, and in every combination and pattern. Even in their wildest state they have a superlative and penetrating fragrance, and cultivated varieties yield the richest and sweetest perfumes known to Man.

The earliest pictures of roses seem to date from about twelve thousand years before Christ, and there may well be earlier ones that haven't been found yet; but at any rate the rose been a symbol of perfection, of love, and of superiority, even divinity, ever since Mankind can remember. It's the royal flower *par excellence*—it was the symbol of the god-kings of Persia long before Sappho named it the Queen of Flowers in the ode of praise that she wrote to it. And of course no other flower features more often in the heraldry of the Middle Ages. The houses of York, Lancaster, and Tudor are only some of the most prominent of the princely houses that adopted roses as their emblems. The most prominent person whose emblem is the rose, though, is Mary, the Mother of God.

The association between Mary and the rose is even stronger than the symbolism of the lily that shows up in almost every Annunciation ever painted—but often in close proximity to the rose, as in the Song of Songs (Cn 2:1). The rose's delicacy, sweetness, fragility, and above all its fragrance seem to recall the virginal majesty of Mary more than those of any other flower.

And Mary herself seems to have chosen the rose as her special favorite. Early Christian accounts say that when the Apostles opened her sealed tomb three days after her burial, they found the sarcophagus empty after her bodily Assumption into Heaven, but garlanded with fresh, sweet-smelling roses. Mary herself sent fragrant mystic roses, caught up in the *tilma* of Juan Diego, as her special signal to Bishop Zumárraga when she appeared at Guadalupe in Mexico in 1531. At La Salette in 1846 the Lady of the apparition stood crowned with roses, and she had roses on her shawl and slippers; at Lourdes she appeared standing on a little eglantine, a wild rose, that grew on the floor of the grotto there.

And the insistent smell of roses above earthly flowers, coming from a branch of the holm-oak at Fátima cut in 1917, convinced Maria Rosa dos Santos that her daughter Lucia was telling the truth about the Lady whom she claimed to have seen standing above that tree. In fact, the Odor of Sanctity, that penetrating and amazingly persistent fragrance of heavenly roses that emanates from the possessions, the apparitions, and even the incorruptible bodies of so many of the great saints associated with Mary, is most often described as that of superlative roses.

So Christian artists have always depicted the Mother of God in a rose garden, the enclosed garden of the Song of Songs, the New Eve in the New Paradise of Salvation; or standing under a bower of roses, crowned with roses, or handing a rose to the infant Christ. Mary herself is called the Rose E'er Blooming in the Christmas carol and the Mystic Rose, *Rosa Mystica*, in the Litany of Loreto that honors her, and many of her most devoted clients have been called that, too. The close association of Mary and roses is why St. Rosalia of Palermo was called that, even though in the twelfth century she was too early in history to use the same name for her prayer beads.

The Marian symbolism of roses is why the convent in which St. Rose of Viterbo was buried was called St. Mary of the Roses, back in the thirteenth century; it's why, in sixteenth-century Peru, little Isabel de Flores del Oliva started calling herself Rosa de Santa María, and why she's known today as St. Rose of Lima. It may even have had something to do with why the housemaid in Acts 12:13 was named Rhoda, a name that stems directly from the rose's ancient Greek root. Certainly, the connection between Mary and roses is the reason that so many little girls in the past two or three centuries have been named Mary Rose, or Rosemary.

The Rosary is indeed "an admirable garland, woven from the Angelic Salutation, together with the Lord's Prayer, joined to meditation," Leo XIII Pecci said (*Diuturni temporis*, 1898). And, in fact, during the centuries after Thomas of Chantimpré's *Book of the Bees*, the name *Rosary*—rose garden, rose-crown—was reinforced time and again through devotional tracts, sermons, and even visions that turned on the symbolism of the rose. In his *Secret of the Most Holy Rosary*, St. Louis-Marie Grignion de Montfort reports that the Jesuit Alfonso Rodríguez, who was deeply devoted to the Rosary, often saw mystic roses dropping from his own lips when he prayed it—a red one falling at each Our Father, and a white one at each Hail Mary.

But the Rosary didn't flourish because everybody likes roses; it grew to surpass all of the other chaplet devotions because it's associated with Mary.

E VA ❧ AV E

MARY

PAUL VI MONTINI NOTED "THAT THE ROSARY IS, AS IT WERE, A BRANCH sprung from that ancient trunk of Christian liturgy, the Psalter of the Blessed Virgin, by which the humble were associated in the Church's hymn of praise and universal intercession… In fact, like the liturgy … it draws its inspiration from Sacred Scripture and is oriented toward the mystery of Christ." The Rosary, he reminded us, draws from the Gospel the presentation of the Mysteries, as well as its main formulas of vocal prayer. It is an important part of Christian devotion to Mary, the devotion that fits "into the only worship that is rightly called 'Christian' because it takes its origin and effectiveness from Christ, finds its complete expression in Christ, and leads through Christ in the Spirit to the Father" (*Marialis cultus*, 1974; see also *Lumen gentium*, especially chapter 8).

Mary is so closely united with her son, so integral to Christianity, that no matter where you begin to study theology you encounter her almost immediately. No single book, no single library full of books, can adequately explore Mary's role in her son's continuing work of redemption. But to understand the Rosary only two facets of her participation in the economy of salvation really need to be understood: her unparalleled powers of intercession and the great devotion that Christians have always had for her.

Christian devotion to Mary is stronger and higher than the devotion given to any other saint, but it's not substantially different from that devotion, and it's entirely different from the worship given to God alone. The worship given to God is *latria*, a Latin word that comes from the ancient Greek λατρεία, which means strictly the adoration that humans owe to the divine. The honor given to any saint is called *dulia*—δουλεία, in Greek—which means rather "duty" or "courtesy". Specifically, dulia is the respect paid to a superior by an inferior; anyone who has some excellence is entitled to this kind of respect.

In the natural order of things, respect is owed to parents, teachers, and government officials, because these have some quality conferred upon them as part of that position that makes them excel the child, the student, and the person who lives under their governance (Ex 20:12; 3Kn 1:16, 23; Pr 5:13, 24:21; Mt 22:21). So the respect paid to them obviously isn't anything like worship; it's a kind of dulia. Natural respect is also due to anybody who has a personal excellence, too—we'd naturally respect somebody kinder, stronger, or holier than we are, and the exact character of that respect would vary according to the exact quality by which that person excels us.

THE FERTILE GROUND

In the supernatural order, dulia is due to the saints because their heroic virtues excel ours, as the Church has recognized. This duty to the saints only honors God; the thousands of tiny stars only make us see how much greater the Sun is, you might say. We look up to the saints for their heroic virtues, but, as they themselves know, those virtues come from God; his is the power that's revealed to the world through these saints' exercise of those virtues—which really only serve to draw other people to him by example. So the saints are treated with respect; they are loved, and they are honored.

The honor given to Mary, greatest of saints, is called *hyperdulia*, a word made from the same *dulia* with the added prefix *hyper-*, meaning above. The hyperdulia accorded to Mary is a uniquely elevated form of the same honor given to any saint, but it's still that same dulia, and it's nothing like worship—let Mary be honored, St. Epiphanius cautioned some enthusiastic parishioners in the fourth century: "let the Father, Son, and Holy Spirit be adored, but let no one adore Mary."

The Church has always held to that position, but Mary rightly receives a higher form of honor than any other saint because she plays a unique and essential role in the cycle of redemption and in the economy of salvation: she is the mother of Jesus. That is the basic fact on which Mary's position in Christianity stands; "Mother of Jesus" is the title most often applied to her by the Gospels, which use the term eight times. Theologically, her fullness of grace, her sinlessness, and her immaculate conception are all attendant and necessary conditions of her motherhood of Jesus; her motherhood is the fact that brought her these extraordinary graces.

Devotionally, all of the honors that the Church extends to her, all of the expressions of the affection warm in the hearts of Christians around the world and in all ages, come to Mary by reason of her divine maternity—no matter how full the graces and glory that she received, the special honor of hyperdulia would not be due to her unless she had also been made the Mother of Jesus. Liturgically, virtually all of the titles by which the Church calls her are derived from the principal title *Sancta Dei Genetrix*, Holy Mother of God; all of the others speak of some aspect or characteristic of her divine motherhood, as for example Mother of Christ, Mother of Divine Grace, Mother Most Pure, Mother Most Chaste, Mother Inviolate, Mother of Our Savior, Seat of Wisdom—Christ being the Divine Wisdom, of course. Titles like Virgin Most Prudent and Virgin Most Faithful are assigned to Mary because she had the faith and prudence to accede to the will of God and accept her vocation to be the mother of Jesus.

Those extraordinary graces that Mary received—Mary alone since Adam and Eve—give her unparalleled powers of intercession. Intercession is simply the process of praying for someone else, whether they ask you to or not; but it usually involves praying for someone who has requested your help, or, on the other hand, asking someone else to pray for you and with you (Mt 18:20; Gn 20:7; Jb 42:8; Rm 15:30-31; Cl 4:3; 1Th 5:25; 2Th 3:1; Hb 13:18; Jm 5:16).

Christ himself always answered prayers submitted to him on behalf of others, those who could not pray themselves, for whatever kind of physical or spiritual disability (Mt 8:5-13, 9:2-7; 9:18-19, 10:32; 15:21-22; etc.). And he framed a special parable to show us that intercession for other people works (Lk 13:6-9). In fact, it would almost seem that Christ would rather hear prayers that are supported by the community (Mt 18:19; Mr 6:4-6). He certainly spoke of his followers as a body unified and whole, and he certainly didn't like for people to be alone, cut off from that body (Jn 15:5). And Scripture is quite definite on the fact that it's more effective to ask those who have found favor with God to pray for you (Nm 21:7; Jb 5:1, 42:8; Ps 80:5; 2Mc 15:14; Jm 5:15-18). In fact, as St. Louis-Marie Grignion de Montfort pointed out, it's a real failure of humility to bypass these mediators, whom God has given us because of our weakness; it would be presuming that you don't need any help, or that your virtues are as great as theirs.

The principal ones favored by God, of course, would be the angels who stayed with him in obedience and those humans who have run an heroic race and now stand forever in the joy of his presence—the saints. Angels and saints do hear prayers addressed to them; they present these petitions to God (Rv 5:8, 8:3), and God lets them help in granting the requests. Raphael carried the prayers of Tobit to God, and he was allowed to intervene extraordinarily to help the man when he faced extraordinary difficulty (Tb 12:12). So were Onias and Jeremia, holy men who had died centuries before Judas Machabeus needed their prayers for Israel's victory over Nicanor (2Mc 15:1-17). Christ himself told how the rich man communicated with Lazarus, who had died and gone to be with Abraham (Lk 16:19-31), although in that case the request had to be denied.

Still, even though the answer occasionally has to be "No," Christians, like the Israelites before Christ, have never failed to ask the Faithful Departed to intercede. People speak to St. Anthony of Padua, to St. Thérèse of Lisieux, or to many another favorite saint as familiarly as they'd speak to a faraway friend by telephone, and the saints answer just as clearly, if not exactly by vocal communication. It's as if you had a distant relative or a former teacher who now lives so far away that you can't meet face to face, but who keeps in touch and is always ready to help you when you need sympathy, understanding, and the benefits of superior resources. In fact, the connection is so intimate between the Pilgrim Church on Earth and the Triumphant Church in Heaven that time, space, and even death itself are no barrier between the two.

This intimate union is called the "communion of saints", from the Latin *cum-*, together, and *unitas*, oneness—unity. It's the same root that gives us the word "community", and in fact the communion of saints forms a single great community embracing the Church here and the Church hereafter. The phrase "communion of saints" is, and always has been, part of the Apostles' Creed, because in a fundamental sense, the communion of saints is the Church—to repudiate the communion of saints is to deny the Church, and to repudiate the Church you must deny the communion of saints. And that isn't easy; after all, Christianity is a salvational religion, and salvation means that physical death doesn't make any difference. Christianity teaches that the soul is immortal, and that—given acceptance and observance of the Covenant—it will be re-joined to the physical body in a better and everlasting life of inexpressible happiness in the presence of God. If this is not true, then our faith is in vain, as St. Paul pointed out (1Cr 15:12-19).

Those saints who have gone before us marked with the sign of faith are still alive, still distinct personalities, and still united with us in the Church whose head is Christ. The only difference is that they are now standing immediately before God, while we stand encumbered by this mortal clay; they can see God in his full glory, while we can see God only, as it were, through a glass, darkly. That difference means that they are in an immeasurably better position to pray, so it makes sense to ask them to pray for us. The formal process of canonization, in fact, is really only a matter of using human investigation and the confirmation of extraordinary miracles to establish that the person in question does, indeed, stand with God, and that he may therefore assuredly be asked to present your petitions.

So you can ask the Faithful Departed to pray for you in Heaven, just as you ask your friends here on Earth to pray for you. On the other hand, whenever you pray for anybody, you're interceding for that person. That's all that intercession means. Of course, here or there, anybody who prays for you depends absolutely on God for favors and graces no less than for existence. The angels and saints can do nothing more than present your petitions to God, the way you do for your friends here on Earth and they do for you, the way whole orders of clergy pray for all of us, the way the secular clergy does at every Mass—the way all Christians pray for all others, living or dead. After all, when you love somebody you want more good for him than you can possibly give him yourself, so you pray for him. Intercession is driven by love; praying for others, and begging others to pray for them, is nothing other than an act of love.

Mary's intercession, like that of any other saint, has to do with the distribution of graces, because she is not the source of those graces—Christ is. Still, the Church has always known that Mary's influence with Christ is unparalleled, and in fact the way in which she intercedes is unique. In the Gospels, she is the one in his inner circle who asks favors on behalf of others—the Apostles don't, as a rule. They alone received the power to forgive sin, and they alone constituted the priesthood of Christ's Church (Mt 16:19, 18:18; Jn 20:22-23; Is 22:22; etc.), but Mary was the normal channel for exceptional graces and favors. And she never asked them for herself: only for others.

Mary's petitions on behalf of others were never refused; she is the only person in Christ's inner circle that he obeyed, even when her request changed the timing of what he had in mind to do. "You can approach," St. Peter Damiano called out to Mary, "not simply to ask, but to command; no longer a handmaiden, but Queen" (*On the Nativity of the Blessed Virgin*). Christ performed his very first miracle, at the marriage feast at Cana (Jn 2:1-11), because Mary presented the host's needs to him, although as he said he hadn't planned to reveal himself at that time and place. For that matter, he had been ready to go forth and engage the leaders of the Old Covenant as soon as he reached the age of manhood, but Mary interceded, and he obeyed her (Lk 2:41-51).

So Scripture and Sacred Tradition affirm that whenever Mary asks anything of Christ for someone else he grants it; whenever she holds him he allows himself to be restrained. That is, he allows her to mediate on behalf of others; she stands as *mediatrix*, which is the feminine form of the Latin word *mediator*. Naturally, a mediator's effectiveness comes from the influence that he has with both parties to the mediation; the perfect mediator would be someone who was essentially one with both parties. Jesus Christ is the only person who is identical with God and identical with Man; so, being both God and Man, Jesus is the one and only perfect mediator between the two. That's what St. Paul was talking about in 1Tm 2:3-6, and it's what the Church has always taught.

Mary's mediation is different. Christ's mediation is primary; hers is secondary, depending utterly on Christ in the very nature of things. Christ's mediation is self-sufficient; hers, again, depends absolutely on his will— although her will has always been understood as being in perfect accord with his. Christ's mediation is absolutely necessary for human salvation; Mary's is not, strictly speaking. That is not to say that her mediation can be ignored or rejected, because in the particular way that God unfolded the plan of salvation it can't be; Mary is the mother of Jesus; she is the one who brought that perfect mediator forward to stand between the two parties to the mediation. And therefore she can't be extracted from Christianity as God implemented it on Earth.

That is, Mary's mediation is indispensable because it's a necessary part of the particular way in which God implemented Christianity; she is integral to God's specific plan for the salvation of humankind. God could have made another plan that did not include her, and, hypothetically, Mary could have refused to become the mother of the Redeemer: but then Christianity would be entirely different. Not that Man would not have been redeemed if Mary had refused, but that redemption certainly would not have happened in the way that it did. Not that the Redeemer would not have come, necessarily, had God made another plan; but while the God-Man might have been precisely the same God, he would have been a different man. The Redeemer is Jesus of Nazareth, and Jesus of Nazareth is the son of Mary; "the flesh of Jesus is the flesh of Mary," St. Augustine pointed out, "and however much it was exalted in the glory of his resurrection, nevertheless the nature of his flesh, derived from Mary, remained and still remains the same" (*On the Assumption*).

That's how Mary stands in an absolutely unique relationship to God. On the other hand, she stands in a unique relationship to Mankind, too, because her mediation is significantly different from the intercession of any other creature, whether saint or angel. Their intercession is effective only in certain particular cases, and for specific graces; hers is understood to be constant and universal, because through her came Christ, the source of all graces. The intercession of other creatures—other saints, the angels, and other human beings on Earth—has to do with the application of graces, but Mary's also has to do with the acquisition of graces, with meriting graces, as well as with their application.

"In bringing about the work of human redemption," Pius XII Pacelli explained, "the Most Blessed Virgin Mary was, by the will of God, so indissolubly associated with Christ that our salvation proceeded from the love and sufferings of Jesus Christ intimately joined with the love and sorrows of his mother" (*Haurietis aquas*, 1956). She was not simply the passive receptacle of grace. She contributed, through specific and voluntary acts, to the reconciliation of God and Man that was brought about by her son.

That is, everything that any of the other saints have done, even the Apostles themselves—which is also indispensable to the way in which God worked out salvation among us—has to do with the ways in which the "fruits", the benefits, of Christ's acts may be applied to individual souls. But Mary, unlike any other creature, co-operated directly in Christ's redemptive acts, not just in the application of their fruits to individual souls. Again, it was through her, and by her will, that Jesus was born. That fact is the pivot of her existence, and of all of the honor that Christians have always bestowed upon her. It's the reason for all of the centuries of prayer to her, in all of the forms that those prayers took, since the first moments of the fulfillment of the Old Covenant.

ST. DOMINIC

ALL OF THOSE PATTERNS OF PRAYER THAT HAD DEVELOPED SO STEADILY since the earliest moments of the Church had come together definitively as the Rosary by the end of the fifteenth century. Still, the Rosary didn't really attain its definitive form until the early seventeenth century, when the Dominicans published the works of Bl. Alan de Rupe, whose name is sometimes given as Alan de la Roche. Oddly enough, Alan de Rupe had died about two hundred years before anybody knew what he had done for the Rosary.

Alan de Rupe was one of those outstanding intellects who come forward from obscurity to distinguish themselves in the service of the Church, so very little is known about his early life. He seems to have been born in Brittany, in about 1428; he certainly entered the Order of Preachers at an early age at Dinan. There's little evidence that he preached very much himself, but if he wasn't much of a preacher he was a great teacher. He taught at Lille, Douai, and Ghent, ending up in the home town of Thomas à Kempis, Zwolle in Holland, where he died in 1475.

The details of his earthly life don't matter, of course, because his writings weren't discovered until after it had ended. When he died, his superiors ordered that all of his manuscripts be gathered together and prepared for publication, and it's safe to say that they were surprised at the quantity of writings that he had left, no less than by their quality. The editing took a long time, and it was not easily done, because Alan didn't always compile his notes into finished form. But his works appeared in print, finally, in 1619, under the title *Beatus Alanus de Rupe Redivivus—Blessed Alan de Rupe Revived*, it would be in English.

Even this edition was incomplete, and frankly it hadn't been edited so well as might be hoped. To this day scholars debate over exactly what Alan de Rupe said and how he meant it. But his words are exceptionally clear when he wrote on the Rosary. After all, he was a Dominican, and the Dominican house at Dinan had the oldest known chapel dedicated to Mary under the title Our Lady of the Rosary.

As his fellow Dominicans had done so often in the past, Alan de Rupe had carefully studied all of the various bead-counted Rosaries that had been prayed for so long all over Europe, but unlike his predecessors he hadn't just condensed these devotions: he had crystallized them. He had reduced the devotion to those elements that were common to them all, establishing the standard arrangement of vocal prayers: fifteen decades, each of ten Hail Marys, separated by an Our Father said before each decade, and divided into three groups of five decades each, dedicated to the mysteries of the birth, passion, and glory of Christ.

Oddly, too, Alan isn't remembered for shaping this most popular devotion into its definitive form. His connection with the Rosary is better known because he wrote that the Blessed Virgin appeared to St. Dominic de Guzmán, showed him a Rosary in this form, told him how to pray with it, and promised certain specific graces. Alan said that his account of this vision was based on the accounts of earlier writers, but no earlier account has survived, evidently. At least, none has been found. The thirteenth-century *Golden Legend* of Jacobus da Voragine, which compiles the main significant data about the saints of the liturgical year, for instance, doesn't mention St. Dominic's interest in the Rosary at all.

Later papal documents that mention the apparition cite its source as the tradition of the Dominican Order, but none asserts that the story of the vision is true. The popes are perfectly well familiar with the long development of the Rosary and its roots in the most ancient forms of meditative prayer, so they make only passing reference to the popular belief that the Rosary in its definitive form came to be popularized by St. Dominic. And they preface the reference with a qualifying phrase like "as it is said". The Order of Preachers itself acknowledges that St. Dominic was instructed in the Rosary by the Blessed Mother, but, it seems, nobody asserts that the devotion was given to him literally out of the blue.

It is certainly true that St. Dominic chose the Blessed Mother as the special patroness of the great order that he founded, and that he encouraged people to pray the Angelic Psalter, as the Rosary was usually called in his day; and it's true that his order has done more than any other to extend the devotion. It was through the Dominicans that the Rosary proved that its effectiveness surpasses even that of the Little Office, because the Rosary, in the developing form it had at the turn of the thirteenth century, was St. Dominic's primary weapon when he turned back the tide of heresy in the south of France.

The whole region at the turn of the thirteenth century was plagued by the Albigensian heresy and its related heterodoxies, the Waldensian and the Catharist heresies. Naturally, these offered nothing positive, heresy being the process of taking out those of Christ's teachings that you find bothersome, and they offered nothing new—Albigensianism is nothing more than the same old Manichænism that St. Augustine had extinguished nearly a thousand years before, and fragments of it and its related heresies still come up today. These schemes are always attractive because they offer an easier morality than Christianity does; they virtually always claim that you can be assured of your salvation if you join, and that nothing that you do or fail to do really makes any difference. That's why so many separated sects are founded even today on the basis of these same heresies, new ones arising literally every week.

In fact, the heresy that took its name from the city of Albi got started in Toulouse, the capital of the district. When the first Albigensian heretics began teaching this sort of thing there in about 1020, though, the laity refused to hear it. They arrested the Albigensian preachers, tried them for heresy, convicted them of civil sedition and treason, and burned them. Even so, the heresy persisted underground for about a hundred years. Then in about 1119 William IX, Duke of Aquitaine, heard an Albigensian preacher, and it occurred to him that if he adopted this heresy he'd be free from the moderating hand of the Church. The idea appealed to his neighboring noblemen, too, particularly to the powerful Count of Toulouse. They could openly keep mistresses or even have more than one wife—heresies always begin by trying to demolish the sacraments—and they would not be bound by any real moral considerations in dealing with the rights of their subjects. With the support and protection of these and a few other powerful nobles, the Albigensians soon displaced the Church in the region, often by burning the churches and murdering the clergy.

Naturally, the lords got more than they bargained for. They were free to carry on as they pleased, raping and burning without let or hindrance, but the heresy also taught the laity itself that they wouldn't have to bother observing any kind of law at all, moral or civil, either. The heresy tore the whole principle of law out of life, and the richest provinces in France were plunged into chaos. Whenever the mood struck them, the populace would burst out in raping and burning, without let or hindrance, too, but violent civil disorders weren't the worst part of the chaos. In fact, most of the Albigensians still went to church most of the time. But they had overturned the altars and murdered or exiled the priests; so they sang hymns and heard sermons, but they never attended Mass, and they certainly never heard any moral principles there.

They heard instead a muddle of teachings centered around the idea that the creator Lord of this World is Satan, in constant struggle with the pure spirit of the Lord of Heaven. Satan created the body, the Albigensians said, and God created the spirit; so all souls end up with God sooner or later, while anything having to do with a material body is gross and evil. The Albigensians taught that this world is in the thrall of an evil demi-urge, that people are depraved and evil by their very nature; so we may as well do as we please, free from any moral prohibitions or religious duties—provided that we're one of the elect, not created damned like the common herd, and provided that we prove it by undergoing a "baptism of the Spirit". People who attended Albigensian churches every Sunday heard that because spirit is pure and good it's not affected by anything that the body does—so nothing that a person does can work toward salvation of the soul or even be good. They heard that no act has any consequence worth worrying about; their faith, or their predestination, would save them. The one and only sin, for which the heretics would burn people at the stake, was to adhere to the Catholic Church.

As a result, crime was entirely out of hand, even when there were no riots. The police and even the armies were too little to enforce order on the population at large. The courts didn't punish anybody for anything—when you teach that humans are by nature depraved, people naturally draw the conclusion that nobody's responsible for his acts, and people can't be punished for something they're not responsible for. Nobody was safe on the streets or even at home; cities fell into ruin as governments found themselves powerless to maintain order in them. Families were ruined, too; with the sacrament of Matrimony despised, people just coupled at pleasure and then coupled again with other partners, doing all that they could to avoid conception and leaving any children of their unions virtually to fend for themselves.

The nobles who had encouraged the heresy fought desperately to impose some kind of order with steel. At last, Raymond VI, Count of Toulouse, saw that he could not even defend his own rank and position against the chaos, and he offered to renounce the heresy and return his subjects to the fold of the Church; but by then it was far beyond his power to decide the religion of his subjects. The Albigensian Wars raged on for more than a century and a half, a foreshadowing of the Wars of Religion that erupted again in the time of Luther and Calvin. The fighting was so fierce for so long that today virtually no buildings from before the middle of the thirteenth century stand in the south of France. During this sad time the cathedral of Albi itself was rebuilt, taking the form almost of a fortress, which in fact it was.

St. Dominic de Guzmán, the man who finally defeated the Albigensian heresy, wasn't a native Frenchman. He was a Spaniard, born in Castile to rich and noble parents, but he was a serious young man, austere, even; his only extravagance was his alms. Once while he was a student at Palencia he sold his books to feed the starving poor, and more than once he tried to sell himself into slavery to replace people unjustly held in servitude. He was always quiet about all of this, but he was such a good man, and such a good student, that while he was still enrolled at Palencia the Bishop of Osma appointed him to the cathedral chapter to help reform it. Dominic did it so well that he was soon promoted to serve as the chapter's prior.

ST. DOMINIC

During the time he served at the cathedral, Dominic hardly ever set foot outside the chapter house. He spent most of his time running the cathedral, of course, but in his free time he liked nothing better than to pray. Apart from that, nothing is known about his life for those nine years. Then in 1203 he was called out of the chapter house—not on his bishop's business, but on his king's. Alfonso IX el Baboso, King of León, appointed the Bishop of Osma to travel to Denmark as his ambassador, asking the Danish king for the hand of his daughter in marriage to Alfonso's son. The bishop took Dominic along as his companion, crossed the frontier into France, and headed north toward the city of Toulouse.

Dominic and the bishop had heard all about Albigensianism, but they were astonished to see what had happened to the southern French countryside since the outbreak of the heresy. Clearly, no human beings were supposed to live in that kind of devastation, chaos, and moral disorder, and there was nowhere they could turn for help. Without Mass celebrated publicly and regularly, even those who would like to remain faithful could not hear the Word of God in its fullness or receive the sacraments; the heretics wouldn't hear Mass even if it were offered. This was an extraordinary situation, and, to Dominic, it appeared to require an extraordinary solution. He saw at once that these people needed, urgently, somebody to teach Christianity to them, as the Apostles had taught Christianity to the pagans. He decided on an order of preachers.

Preaching isn't required of priests, outside of the homily at Mass. But it isn't forbidden, either, as long as abuses are avoided; people are generally required to have the permission of the Bishop before they can preach, to ensure that they won't be preaching false doctrine or false morals. Preaching is a powerful means of reaching people outside the Church, to teach them, and people inside the Church, to minister to their spiritual and pastoral needs. Christ himself preached both kinds of sermon—the Sermon on the Mount as a *magisterial* address (from the Latin *magister*, teacher), and the discourse after the Last Supper as a *ministerial* one (from the Latin *minister*, servant; Jn 14-16), for instance.

From earliest times the Church has recognized that the ability to preach is a gift, which is why St. Paul sent Timothy and Titus out to do it. She has also recognized that even a gifted preacher has to be adequately trained, and Fathers of the Church like St. Cyprian and St. Gregory Nanzianus applied all of the skills of classical rhetoric to homiletics. St. Augustine was a professor of rhetoric before his conversion, and he used all that he knew about it for his sermons after. By the early Middle Ages, books of homiletics virtually replaced books of rhetoric in advanced education, and right through the Renaissance preaching was immensely popular all over Europe and the Levant.

Sermons served the same purpose in festivals that orations used to in Roman times, or really as they did in this country's celebrations of Independence Day until the First World War—they reminded people of the aims and ideals of their community, and they helped them think about the issues of the day. Good orators were always in demand; many famous travelling preachers used to leave towns quietly at night, so that people wouldn't detain them. University students sharpened their skills by posting propositions on church doors, giving the time and place of their sermons, and they'd schedule debates on theological questions among themselves, always attracting an audience. Eminent professors easily drew thousands. If anything, religious controversy attracted more preachers than ever before to the region—it heightened interest.

So the problem during the Albigensian heresies wasn't that there were no preachers, nor was it that people wouldn't listen to preachers. The problem was that the preaching that people were hearing was wrong. Not only was the regular institution of the Church in ruins, but heretics actively pushed a religion with no requirements except simply saying that you recognize Christ as your Lord, after which you were free to do as you pleased. Somebody had to move into Albigensian territory and offer accurate Christian teaching by the same means. That's why St. Dominic himself established the Order of Preachers.

St. Dominic adopted the Rule of St. Augustine for his preachers, along with other rules, the *Institutions* that he wrote himself. Innocent III dei Conti di Segni approved the Order by pontifical letters in 1205, and it was strict. The Dominicans were to take vows of poverty, chastity, and obedience; they were to use only wool for clothing—too many other preachers had worn silk—and only of black and white. They were to sleep in a common dormitory, on hard beds. They perpetually abstained from meat, and they fasted on all Fridays as well as from September until Easter. Silence reigned throughout their houses, except when they rose to chant the Hours or the Office of the Blessed Virgin.

Dominic set up his first house at Prouille, in the heart of the diocese of Toulouse. It was like a military base, and there Dominic trained his troops for the reconquest of the south of France. From that outpost, the first Dominicans walked through France, and through Spain and Italy as well, targeting on the major cities. By the time Dominic died, they had sixty houses in eight provinces. They set up good schools wherever they went— St. Albert the Great and St. Thomas Aquinas were both students and later professors in Dominican schools. They wrote an unending stream of good books on the Faith. They did a lot to reform the discipline of the Church, serving as ambassadors, inquisitors, legates, bishops, cardinals, and popes. But most of all, they preached.

The Dominicans patterned their sermons on the sequence of three of the great mysteries of the Faith—the Incarnation, the Redemption, and Eternal Life—and they simply told the truth, reporting Christian doctrine plainly, without any kind of compromise, and in no uncertain terms, as people have the right to hear it. And people saw that Christianity makes sense, while the heresies were really based on inaccuracies and indeed on downright falsehood, and that they didn't stand to reason. The Dominicans received heavenly help, too, in the form of miraculous cures, multiplications of food, and other mystic phenomena that the heretics could not match.

Then as now, these miracles exerted a powerful influence on those who would demand signs of the truth of their religion (Mt 16:4; Mr 8:1-12; Jn 20:29). More to the point, though, St. Dominic endlessly asked the people to pray. If only they would pray, they must eventually start to live as Christians are supposed to live, loving the Lord, their God, with their whole heart, and whole mind, and whole soul, and loving their neighbors as themselves. And only if they would do so would life in the region start to improve; only then would everybody be living together in harmony, being of one mind and one heart (Ac 4:32; Ps 132:1).

Like St. Dunstan, St. Æthelwold, and St. Peter Damiano before him, St. Dominic understood that the chief preachers, the basic preachers, the indispensable preachers in the Church are the laity. Parents, in teaching their children the elements of the Faith, are preaching to them magisterially; friends, by discussing the Faith with friends or studying together, are preaching ministerially, and those who answer questions knowledgeably, fully, and frankly are doing both. The highest and most effective form of lay preaching, of course, is by example (Jn 13:35). So St. Dominic knew that the conversion of the south of France would be accomplished by the conversion of each person there, individually; and he knew that the key to converting each of those who had been led astray by the heretics was to affirm very clearly the doctrines by which Albigensianism differed most radically from Christianity: the divine maternity of Mary, and her virginity before, during, and after the Incarnation. All of the facts about Christ and his nature that the heretics denied pivoted precisely on those two particular points. With those facts firmly established, Albigensianism would fall of its own weight.

That's why St. Dominic, "defending to the limits of his strength the holiness of these doctrines, invoked the help of the Virgin Mother herself... she used his ministry to teach the most holy Rosary to the Church, the Spouse of her Son: the prayer that, being both vocal prayer and meditation ... on the Mysteries of religion, is best adapted to fostering piety and every virtue," Benedict XV della Chiesa recalled (*Fausto appetente die*, 1921). "Rightly, then, did Dominic order his followers to inculcate this manner of prayer—the utility of which he had experienced—frequently in their preaching."

The pattern of meditation of that devotion—which was already coming to be called the Rosary—the sequence of meditations on the Incarnation, Passion, and Resurrection and on the events around them, focussed people's attention on those same great mysteries that shaped his sermons. As it had always done in the past, and as it was to do so often in the future, the conversion of the populace to meditative prayer worked wonders in the region. The Dominican fathers were almost overwhelmed by tens of thousands of penitents asking for the sacrament of Reconciliation; they were hard pressed to restrain the crowds from the most extravagant kinds of self-imposed penances. "Thus," Benedict XV della Chiesa concluded, "by the valor of Dominic Europe was freed from the danger of the Albigensian heresy." Things settled down politically as well as religiously; people who set aside a special time every day to pray the Rosary almost certainly don't have to be monitored by the police.

The difference was astonishing. Naturally, folk tales grew up around St. Dominic's miraculous re-conversion of the whole region, and his advocacy of the "Angelic Psalter", the Rosary, features importantly in many of these. However the story started, Alan de Rupe set it down for all time in a treatise usually called the *Apologia*, which means *Explanation*.

The story, according to Alan, is that St. Dominic at one point became down-hearted by the enormity of the heresies. He went into the forest near Toulouse and spent three days and nights in austerities and prayer. The Blessed Virgin appeared to him, accompanied by three queens and fifty maidens. She explained to St. Dominic that intellectual preaching would not be enough to convert the heretics; they needed the higher illuminating grace that comes immediately from the Holy Spirit. Then she asked him, "Do you know which weapon the Holy Trinity wants to use to reform the world?"

St. Dominic answered, properly, that the Mother of God would know that better than he would, because she was so much closer to Jesus than he could be. "I want you to know," the Lady continued, "that the battering ram in this kind of warfare has always been the Angelic Psalter, which is the foundation stone of the New Testament. Therefore, if you want to reach these hardened hearts and win them over to God, preach my Psalter."

In fact, the title under which Alan's book about the Rosary was originally published is *De Dignitate Psalterii, On the Dignity of the Psalter*. The reference to the foundation stone of the New Testament is allegorical; Christ is the foundation stone, as he himself said (Mt 21:42), but the term is applied metaphorically to the Our Father. "It is a summary of the New Testament," Tertullian said, a thousand years before the Albigensian problem arose. "It contains all of the duties that we owe to God, all of the acts of all of the virtues, and the petitions for all of our spiritual and corporal needs," St. Louis-Marie Grignion de Montfort added five hundred years after St. Dominic's day. The Hail Mary is an integral part of the Angelic Psalter, too, because it's based on the Angelic Salutation to Mary, which, for several hundred years, was the only verse repeated between the Our Fathers of the early Rosary.

Of course, St. Dominic's campaign to defeat the forces of heresy wasn't the first spiritual war fought by the Church Militant here on Earth; Jesus himself foretold these struggles to his Apostles (Mt 10:34-35), and the Church must enter upon a daily war, Leo XIII wrote (*Octobri mense*, 1891), so that she might teach Men the truth, and lead them to eternal salvation. Throughout the course of ages, he added, she has fought even to martyrdom; and, certainly since St. Dominic's day, the Rosary has always been there to help her fight those battles.

E VA ❀ AV E

BATTLE

SOMETIMES THE WARFARE OF THE ROSARY WORKS NOT ONLY SPIRITUALLY but also literally, and in those cases it usually does so against such extreme odds, in such hopeless campaigns, as to leave little room for doubting the power of its graces. The increasing power of devotions like those adopted by St. Dunstan, St. Æthelwold, and St. Peter Damiano showed that the development was moving ahead in a way ever more pleasing to Heaven. But the pivotal case showing the power of the Rosary against civil disorders came during the chaos of Albigensianism, through St. Dominic himself, at the Battle of Muret.

Philippe II Auguste, King of France, had been fighting to restore order in the Languedoc since the beginning of his reign in 1180. Naturally, as long as the people didn't restrain themselves voluntarily with any particular moral system, it was hopeless; the heretics who murdered priests didn't hesitate to kill royal commissioners, certainly. At last Pope Innocent III, looking back over the failures of a hundred years of missionaries, councils, and other peaceful means, asked Philippe to send his armies in.

That was a lot to ask, in those days. The King of France was only nominally ruler of the lands that we think of as France today, and the name itself was only applied to the little province around Paris—a province entirely surrounded by larger and more powerful states, so that it was called the "Island" France, the *Ile de France*. Philippe had few troops to send and a region to subdue, the whole southern half of the lands he called his kingdom. It was impossible from the outset, and it got worse.

For six long years the royal armies did the best they could, but by 1213 they were utterly exhausted. Philippe himself had no more money and no way to raise any. His forces in the south had dwindled to a mere thousand horsemen or so, ill equipped, far from home, and commanded by a minor nobleman. Fortunately, this obscure knight turned out to be the Gedeon of his day: Simon IV, Count of Montfort l'Amauri, the "strong mountain" of Montfort being just a little hill with a fortified manor house on top of it.

> This Simon IV, Count of Montfort l'Amauri (*c.* 1160-1218), is the father of Simon de Montfort, Earl of Leicester (*c.* 1208-1265), who is better known to history than his father is. Simon the son inherited the English title through his father's mother, who was the heiress of the Beaumont family that had been earls of Leicester before. He married the sister of Henry III of England (1207-1272), raised a rebellion against the king, and ruled England as a kind of military dictator—but ruled

it so well that the commoners of England wanted him canonized.

Simon IV de Montfort l'Amauri had been a crusader, twice, and on the whole he was a good general. But on the morning of September 13, 1213, before the city of Muret just south of Toulouse, Simon IV de Montfort and his thousand ragged knights faced an Albigensian army numbering something over a hundred thousand. Simon's knights, booted, spurred, and mounted in their saddles, lined up their horses that morning before the open doors of the little church of St. Jacques and heard Mass celebrated by St. Dominic himself. Then they charged down on the Albigensian forces, and in that one charge they defeated them utterly.

The victory at Muret was like the multiplications of loaves and fishes— it was not expected, and for that matter it wasn't possible; nobody was sure how it was happening as it happened, but the scraps left over proved that it really had happened. It isn't mentioned in many English-language history books any more, but the Battle of Muret was every bit as pivotal in the history of western civilization as the week-long Battle of Tours had been five hundred years before, when Charles Martel turned the Moors out of France in October of 732. If Simon de Montfort had lost the Battle of Muret, the monarchy of France would have been crippled and probably extinguished; Christendom would certainly have sunk into chaos, and the existence of the Church herself would have been threatened.

Some historians like to say that the victory of Muret isn't all that remarkable because the Albigensian forces consisted almost entirely of footsoldiers—no, of peasants who picked up whatever weapons they could find, a mob more than an army. But the numbers of such a mob would be overwhelming in themselves, with more than a hundred foot against each of Simon's thousand horsemen; and the Albigensian forces were not such a mob. They were not even made up primarily of untrained locals—there weren't that many locals left alive in the region, much less that many organized into a group.

Those natives in the force were principally experienced marauders, commanded by such local horsemen as had survived until then, but the vast bulk of the host was made up by the formidable armies of the brother-in-law of Raymond of Toulouse, King Pedro II of Aragon, who had hurried across the Pyrenees to tear off whatever territories he could for himself. Pedro's army outnumbered Simon's by at least a hundred to one, all by itself. Nothing short of the most extraordinary graces could have saved the orthodox forces; nothing short of a miracle could have brought them victory.

Certainly Simon de Montfort himself considered Muret a miracle. He publicly attributed the victory to the prayers of St. Dominic and to those of the faithful laity, through the Rosary; and as a monument he built a chapel in the little church of St.-Jacques dedicated to Our Lady of the Rosary, apparently the first in Christendom to bear that title.

After the Battle of Muret it was entirely natural that the Church as a whole turned to the Rosary as a way to pray, united, for the special graces necessary whenever Christendom was threatened by overwhelming forces. Time and again, regions and territories that embraced the habit of the Rosary rose up against immense odds to restore themselves to order and decency, and many great preachers—none more fervent than the Dominicans—kept the devotion alive through their exhortations and their examples.

No Dominican was a better example than Michele Ghislieri (1504-1572), born at the turn of the sixteenth century to a poor but noble family in Lombardy. Michele had entered the Order of Preachers after having been educated in their schools in Voghera, near Pavia. He was intelligent enough to be permitted Holy Orders after only two years in school, but his piety was even more remarkable, although few people noticed it at the time, which is exactly how piety is supposed to operate. As a priest, he undertook exceptional fasts and penance without ever speaking of them, and he passed long hours of the night alone in the meditative prayer of the Rosary. He was happy in that life, austere and obscure as it was, but because of his tranquil cheerfulness through it all, his immense charity, and his acute mind, he was elected master of novices and then prior of whatever house of his order he was living in.

He took these positions of authority in obedience, against his own will, always urging his superiors to find somebody better; but having taken the offices under obedience he never let their power go to his head, any more than he let the duties keep him from his own Rosary. And he performed those duties so exceptionally well that he soon came to the attention of the Master General of the Order, and then to the notice of the Pope.

Paul IV Carafa (1476-1559) gave Father Michele one assignment after another, always bigger and more important for the whole Church. Father Michele accepted all of these offices under obedience, too, sometimes through tears, because he only wanted to go back to the friary and live as an ordinary Dominican. But he made the best of it; he used each of his offices to keep both the clergy and the laity on the right track, urging them to avoid the heresies that were so prevalent in those days, reminding them constantly of accurate doctrine, and begging them to remember the Rosary.

At last he asked to be allowed to retire again to his friary. Paul IV's answer was to make him Bishop of Sutri, another promotion that he accepted under obedience, and another that he used as a broader field for his efforts to keep the Faith strong. But in addition to seeing to the needs of his diocese, Bishop

Michele was often called to Rome to advise the Holy Father. He had sharp-ened his inborn gifts with great experience, by then, and he was remarkably able to find fair, workable answers to the most difficult problems. Most of all, he was never afraid to oppose the pope when he thought that he was ill-advised in some matter of policy or discipline.

In spite of that, or really because of that, Paul IV made Michele Ghislieri a cardinal in 1557, again over his emotional objections. Now he had no choice but to wear the scarlet robes of the cardinalate, but he never changed his austere personal habits. As before, he saw his new office only as a broader stage for his exhortations to convert the laity.

Then in 1559 Paul IV died. He was succeeded by Pius IV, born Giovanni Angelo de' Medici—a member of the Milanese Medici, a much humbler family than the Florentines of the same name. Except for his wholehearted insistence on the reforms of the Council of Trent, Pius IV was entirely the opposite of Paul IV. He might have put Cardinal Ghislieri to good use in implementing the reforms of Trent, except that Ghislieri firmly blocked his efforts to appoint his thirteen-year-old nephew, Ferdinand de' Medici, to the College of Cardinals. Pius IV retaliated by appointing Cardinal Ghislieri Bishop of Mondovì, high in the mountains of Piedmont northeast of Nice—as far from Rome as could be, in Italy. So the cardinal obediently went there to live quietly, away from the papal court and all of the great changes that Pius IV was working in the discipline of the Church.

Michele Ghislieri probably liked it. Being out of favor with the Pope was almost like being in the friary again, except that he had a cardinal's income to work with. He distributed almost all of his office's income as alms instead of maintaining his palace as people thought he should, and he spent most of his time visiting the sick, embracing beggars, and washing and feeding both; and at least twice a day he knelt before the Blessed Sacrament to pray meditatively, at least once through the Rosary.

But his retirement ended abruptly when Pius IV died in 1565. Con-claves in those times were always webs of politicking among the cardinals of the great and powerful families, the Florentine Medici, the Roman Farnese, the Milanese Borromeo, and the rest. In this one, nobody gave much thought to the obscure and modest Cardinal Ghislieri during all of the deal-making, but at one point the whole Sacred College suddenly found themselves flocking together toward his cell. He guessed why they were there, and he hinted broadly that if he were elected he'd refuse, so they all went away to more politicking. But then the College came together before him again and almost picked him up bodily to take him to the Pauline Chapel in the papal apartments.

He resisted again, so the cardinals voted orally, one by one. They all said the same thing: I elect Michele Cardinal Ghislieri as my Pope. Cardinal Ghislieri began to weep, and in tears he begged the cardinals to think of some candidate more able and more worthy. But one after another they voted for him, not for any of the cardinal princes. When the vote was over, he sat in stunned silence. When the Cardinal Dean asked him if he accepted, he didn't answer, so the Dean prodded him and asked again. *Mi contento sù*, he said: I am content; I accept it.

People thought that he would take the name Paul, after Paul IV, who had liked him so much and had raised him so high in the hierarchy. He surprised everybody by taking the regnal name Pius, after his fearsome predecessor. But that was only the first surprise; he never did anything the way anybody expected him to. Not even the papal dignity changed the man's piety any more than it affected his austere style of life. He kept to his devotional practices, reviving the old custom of long (and exhausting) papal pilgrimages and processions, and praying the Rosary at least once a day no matter how much work he had to do.

In fact, few popes ever had more work to do than Pius V. Christendom at that moment was pressed on both sides by forces bent on its destruction. In the North, the Germanies were sunk in chaos worse than the agonies inflicted by the old Albigensians. In the East and in the South, the Turks had swept forth with an invincible host of armies and navies that had conquered every Christian kingdom between Constantinople and the gates of Vienna—people often forget that the Turks had overrun Hungary like a flood in 1526, and that after 1547 the central part of the kingdom was part of the Turkish Empire. By the time Pius IV died in 1565 Selim II Mest was boasting that he'd make good on the Turks' age-old threat to put a crescent atop the dome of St. Peter's and wrap the pope's head in a turban, whether it was connected to his body or not. Not everybody was sure that a quiet, pious little friar like Michele Ghislieri would have what it would take to throw off both arms of these pincers, or even to keep the Church alive. "With God's help," he said when he saw the reaction to his election, "I will try to govern so that the public's grief at my death will be even greater than their grief at my election."

Pius V worked tirelessly for the renewal of faith and the renovation of morals in western Europe, and he never stopped urging people to take up the Rosary as the best defense against error and heresy. At the same time, he struggled to get the Christian monarchs of Europe to form a Holy League, an alliance that would marshal enough forces to oppose the enemy in the East.

The monarchs squabbled as the situation became desperate. By 1571 the Turks were besieging Cyprus, the last Christian outpost in the eastern Mediterranean. They slaughtered many of the population, and, as they usually did in these cases, they flayed the Christian commander alive, stuffed his skin, and dragged it through the streets so that the survivors could see what happened to those who opposed them. Then they gathered their fleet at the ancient port of Naupactos, called Lepanto in Italian, which is in Epirus in Greece. And they armed themselves for the invasion of Italy itself.

The pope had expected this for some years, already. He had redoubled his advocacy of the Rosary, and now he exhorted all the Faithful of Europe, including those Christians held in territories already conquered by the Turks, to pray the Rosary daily to beg Mary's intercession to save the Church and to liberate the captives. The Rosary Confraternities of Rome itself held special processions every Sunday, after which they prayed the Rosary publicly together with the crowds who followed them, and Confraternities in all the cities and towns of faithful Europe did the same. There can be few occasions in the history of the world in which so many people were united in prayer in the same way for the same intention; and few prayers can have been more fervent. Like the early Christian martyrs, like Christ himself in Gethsemane, the laity of Europe was praying for help against those who would kill them happily, and kill them horribly, in hatred of the Faith.

On a more mundane level, the pope acquired three galleys to patrol the eastern coast, and he hurried to rebuild the crumbling fortifications at Ancona and Civitavecchia, and at Ostia, the port city of Rome. This was the most that he could do alone, and it seemed pitifully little against the Turks' two hundred and eighty-two warships and fifty thousand men at arms. But the monarchs of Europe, at long last, were alarmed enough to settle their differences and join forces. Through the Pope's diplomacy, they formed the Holy League and got ready to meet the Turks head on. The Christian fleet, two hundred and thirty-six warships and some thirty-three thousand men, sailed into the bay of Lepanto on the morning of Sunday, October 7, 1571.

The wind was in favor of the enemy that morning, and the Christian fleet was almost immediately surrounded by the Turks. But the Holy League's admiral Don Juan of Austria and the Christian commander-in-chief Marcantonio Colonna fought desperately all day. At last, they managed to make one sure, swift stroke: they sailed straight for the flagship of the Turkish "Capitan Pasha", Muesinsade Ali. The sea was already red with blood and so choked with wreckage that the galleys could hardly row, but Don Juan and Colonna pushed their ships ahead. They grappled their galleys to Ali's huge flagship so tightly that the fighting seemed like a battle on land. Between them the two Christian commanders took Ali's ship by about four in the afternoon, and the Capitan Pasha himself was killed in the struggle.

The Turks, seeing the Christians winning against superior forces on every side, broke ranks and fled when they saw their flagship lost. At that moment the wind changed, and a violent storm blew up, wrecking many of the Turkish galleys before they could reach the harbor. The Battle of Lepanto was won. The Christians found that they had sunk fifty Turkish ships and captured a hundred and seventeen, while losing only twelve of their own. It had not been easy; but it was like a dream to us all, Marcantonio Colonna later wrote to Felipe II of Spain, and we saw in it the direct intervention of God.

At that same moment, about four o'clock in the afternoon of October 7, 1571, Pius V Ghislieri was sitting in his office at the Vatican, reviewing accounts with his Treasurer-General, Bartolomeo Busotti. The pope suddenly rose and walked to the open window. He stood there, looking out to the east in deep recollection, for a long time; and then he said, "A truce to our business. Now it is our task to give thanks to God for the victory that he has given the Christian armies."

The question arises instantly: how did he know? News travelled slowly in those days, and the papal court didn't even receive the information that the Turkish fleet was gathering at Lepanto until October 13, a week after Pius V announced the victory. That same dispatch was also the first news that anybody in Rome had that the Christian fleet had sailed out on September 30. It wasn't until the night of October 21-22 that a courier rode into the Vatican carrying a letter to the Pope from the papal nuncio in Venice, telling him of the great victory at the Battle of Lepanto.

Somehow, though, St. Pius V had known instantly. This wasn't the first insight that he'd had on the matter, and evidently not the first he'd had on many another important matter, either. The Roman agent of the Holy Roman Empire, Galeazzo Cusano, had written to the Emperor in May of 1570—a year and a half before Lepanto—to say that Pius had said privately that he'd already seen that the Christian fleet would triumph over the Turks. "He said that this often happened when he prayed God with all his heart about some most important matter," Cusano wrote.

However it came to him, none of his advance knowledge dulled Pius's joy when the Cardinal Secretary of State woke him up in the middle of that October night. The pope rose from his bed and spoke the Canticle of Simeon: Lord, let now thy servant depart in peace (Lk 2:29-32). At dawn he went to St. Peter's to celebrate a special Mass of thanksgiving, but by that afternoon he was so exhausted from the excitement that he had to ask one of the cardinals to preside at the requiem for those who had fallen in the battle—the first time in his life he had ever missed a liturgy. He also missed the sermon that, coincidentally, was preached by an eminent French scholar whose family name was the same as the name of his home town: Marc-Antoine Muret.

All over Europe, churches resounded with the *Te Deum*, the Church's great hymn of thanksgiving. Miguel de Cervantes, a veteran of the battle, wrote of it in his *Don Quixote* as "that most happy day, that most happy day in which so many won freedom, which was the Battle of Lepanto." Orations, poems, festivals, fireworks, statues, and paintings everywhere celebrated the victory. The Venetian Senate commissioned a picture of the Battle of Lepanto for the Doge's palace, specifying in the resolution that under it should be written the legend, "Not our power and arms, not our leaders, but the Madonna of the Rosary helped us to victory."

The Confraternity of the Rosary in Venice built a commemorative chapel at SS. Giovanni e Paolo, which included a picture of the battle by Tintoretto and a statue of St. Dominic. Other organizations, princes, and merchants followed suit, commissioning memorials from Titian, Veronese, and every other major painter in Christian Europe; churches and oratories dedicated to Our Lady of Victory began to spring up immediately. Some cities, like Genoa, put images of the Madonna of the Rosary over their gates, while others adopted the image of Mary standing on the crescent moon—which happened to also be the symbol of the Turkish empire—as their coats of arms.

In the great wave of rejoicing after Lepanto, Pius V decreed that a feast day should be kept on that day, the first Sunday in October, every year in perpetuity as the commemoration of Our Lady of Victory. But he himself didn't live long enough to see even the first celebration of that commemoration. His repetition of the Canticle of Simeon had been as much a prophecy as a hymn of thanksgiving, and he died a few months after the battle, on the first day of May, 1572—and the grief at his passing echoed across Europe, utterly drowning out any memory of the misgivings that had arisen at his election.

Pius V's successor, Gregory XIII Buoncompagni, was elected a few days later, on May 13. He was the pope who reformed the whole calendar, which is why it's called the Gregorian Calendar today. In doing this, he had to reconsider each feast day on the calendar and to adjust its commemoration suitably. The Feast of Our Lady of Victory, only two years old in 1573, was the only one commemorating a specific modern military victory; and, with the power of the Turkish empire broken, Gregory had to look forward to the spiritual victory over the heresies of the North. And anyway the point of Lepanto wasn't so much Lepanto itself as the fact that it was through the Rosary that the destruction of Christendom had been averted. So he restructured the feast on October 7, giving it the name by which it's still known today, the Feast of Our Lady of the Most Holy Rosary.

The Battle of Lepanto was epochal in many ways. It was the last in which rowed galleys, the standard warship since Hellenistic times, were used. It was the last Crusade, really, too, the last time that the forces of Christendom united at the urging of the Pope to avert the destruction of Christianity. But it wasn't the last victory attributed to the intercession of Mary in response to the Rosary, any more than it had been the first. "Ancient and modern history and the more sacred annals of the Church," Leo XIII wrote (*Supremi Apostolatus Officio*, 1883), "bear witness to the public and private supplications addressed to the Mother of God, to the help that she has granted in return, and to the peace and tranquillity that she has obtained from God. Hence her illustrious titles of helper, consoler, mighty in war, victorious, and giver of peace. And amongst these specially is to be commemorated that familiar title derived from the Rosary, by which the signal benefits that she has gained for the whole of Christendom have been solemnly perpetuated."

The whole of Christendom, though, no longer prayed the Rosary as it had before; English and German laws since Luther's day had stamped it out in those countries that fell away from the Church. Yet the great public miracles continued in those countries that kept the Faith, particularly in France. When Louis XIII took the Calvinist port city of La Rochelle—a siege as crucial to the survival of the French monarchy as the Battle of Muret had been so long before—he attributed the victory to the Rosaries prayed publicly at the Dominican church in the Faubourg St.-Honoré, at the suggestion of his mother, Marie de Médicis.

Even as late as the First World War, the Maréchal Ferdinand Foch—who incidentally was born at Tarbes, in the heart of the old Albigensian territory—said that he never omitted to pray the Rosary for a single day, even during the most terrible times of battle and when he had to go without sleep for days and nights on end. It sustained him, and, he said, he often saw Mary's obvious intercession in the decisions that he took and the strategies that he chose. "Take the advice of an old soldier," he said: "Do not neglect praying the Rosary for any reason."

אמת

THE HABIT OF HERESY

CHRISTENDOM IS NOT LIKELY TO FACE A CONCERTED MILITARY ATTACK LIKE that of Lepanto in our days, but the other half of that pincer that so pressed St. Pius V is still upon us: heresy. Heresy isn't just a difference of opinion about a lot of old teachings that don't matter any more. Heresy is the process of deleting those parts of Christ's teachings that you find bothersome—the word comes from the Greek αἵρεσις, meaning "to pick and choose". Heresy takes many forms, and it has many degrees of intensity: some few people indignantly shred the Bible and everything else, and some vehemently reject religion altogether, but heresy really tears most savagely while it tears most quietly, by misleading and misrepresenting.

All people have the right to hear Christ's teachings fully and accurately, and the Church is open to all people of all nations. The Church's view, therefore, is that all humans are members of the Church, potentially at least or actually to some degree or other; but it's the phrase "to some degree" that's important. It's crucial to be fully a member of the Church. Christianity, as a revealed religion, is really a take-it-or-leave-it proposition; if Christ is God, then no human can presume to improve upon his teachings. To pick and choose among them to suit yourself is to assert that some of his teachings are not important, or that Christ mandated something wrong—it's to disagree with Christ. So the Covenant is accepted as a unit, or it's not.

Turning away from that Covenant to some degree or another is heresy, which is, in that sense, the opposite of conversion. It's a progressive rejection of Christ's teachings rather than a progressive embracing of them. And it does always progress, from the loss of one teaching to the loss of others. As Dean Swift recognized in his *Argument to Prove that the Abolishing of Christianity in England May, as Things Now Show, Be Attended with Some Inconveniencies* (1708), Christianity is "a Sort of Edifice, wherein all the Parts have such a mutual Dependance on each other, that if you happen to pull out one single Nail, the whole Fabrick must fall to the Ground."

Heresy today seems to take two main forms. There are still those who rise up on purpose to start another sect calling itself Christian; they rewrite or reinterpret the Bible, and they take it upon themselves to dictate which of Christ's teachings their followers have to observe and which they don't. But these are only in the minority. Many more people seem to simply fall into the habit of heresy, ignoring some precepts or thinking that the rules don't matter—thinking that they know better than Christ what Christianity is, and what it requires. This is undoubtedly the most widespread form of heresy in this country. Even within the Church it shows up among those who still receive the sacraments while ignoring the Church's moral teachings, or even among people who lead regular lives but are shy about professing their Faith fully and accurately.

In fact, that shyness—a form of cowardice, really—is so widespread in this country that it's been called the "American" heresy. "In order to bring over more easily to the Catholic Faith those who dissent from it," Leo XIII Pecci explained (*Testem benevolentiæ*, 1899), some Americans, clergy and laity, think that "the Church ought to adapt herself somewhat to our advanced civilization and, relaxing her ancient rigor … pass over certain sections of doctrine, as if of lesser importance, or soften them so that they may not have the same meaning that the Church has invariably held."

That is, there's a tendency in some times and places to hold back information, to evade clear answers, or even to say that differences in doctrine don't matter. But that's more than misrepresentation; it's materially deleting doctrine, which is heresy. "We cannot approve the opinions that some embrace under the title of 'Americanism'," Leo XIII continued. That word is best reserved, he said, to refer to those characteristic qualities that reflect honor on the people of America, the condition of our commonwealths and the laws and customs that prevail in them; it should not be dishonored by application to a heresy. In that case, "the bishops of America should be the first to repudiate it, as being especially unjust to them and to the entire nation as well. For it raises the suspicion that there are some among you who conceive of and desire a church in America that is different from that which is in the rest of the world."

Then he quoted the First Vatican Council: "The doctrine of faith that God has revealed is not proposed as if it were a theory of philosophy that is to be elaborated by human understanding, but as a divine deposit delivered to the Spouse of Christ to be faithfully guarded and infallibly declared… That sense of the sacred dogmas is to be faithfully kept … and is not to be departed from". It may be difficult, socially, to embrace those doctrines in their fullness when your friends and family won't; it may be difficult to state the differences between the Church's doctrine and the teachings of separated sects when asked; but that's what fortitude is about, the fortitude that took the martyrs to their deaths.

THE HABIT OF HERESY

Answering questions about the Faith truthfully is an obligation on all the Faithful (*Catechism of the Catholic Church* §§ 900-906), and it requires not only fortitude but also enough knowledge of what the Church teaches, too, which means that each of the Faithful is required to learn all he can. But no one can properly withhold information or ignore doctrine to avoid stating the Church's teachings. And certainly inducing people to join any organization by giving them incomplete or misleading teachings is fraud, whether it happens through people inside the Church who take conciliation far enough to impair doctrine, or through those outside the Church who propagate the incomplete or incorrect doctrine of separated sects.

In any event, there's little doubt that most people cheated by heresy are good people, people sincerely wanting to know Christ and abide by his teachings, to make those teachings real in their lives and on Earth. In good faith, they enter or stay with a denomination whose founders fell into the more active kind of heresy, maybe three hundred years ago, maybe last week; they may enter the Church herself on an insufficient reason; or they may think that one denomination is as good as another, as long as it calls itself Christian. Any of these events pushes the person to some degree of separation from the Church.

But nobody would reject these good people as Christians, because they have made every possible effort to know what Christ teaches and to live by it, and because they have not willfully rejected Christ. "Those who seek the truth with care and prudence, who are ready to accept it when they discover it, are not to be counted among the heretics," as St. Augustine said (*Letters* 43:1). Those who received an heretical creed from their parents, he added, "are by no means to be counted among the heretics", because they didn't do the picking and choosing themselves. The Second Vatican Council pointed out that the same goes for those who at present are born into these communities and in them were brought up believing in Christ; their baptisms are valid, usually, and "the catholic Church accepts them with respect and affection as brethren".

Yet not quite brethren in full communion with the Church. Anybody who looks carefully at what any two Christian sects teach will see that they're saying things that aren't the same. Christ came, and he stood before us, and he taught; either he said something or he didn't. His commandment to the Church that he founded was explicit: teach all nations to observe what he commanded her, all things whatsoever (Mt 28:19-20). Separated sects, though, distinguish themselves by citing those parts of his teachings that they have rejected, or that they have replaced with different teachings.

So heresy is alive and flourishing today. It's wrong, in the sense of being inaccurate; and it does keep good people from full communion with Christ. If people are to find a full understanding of Christ and embrace his Covenant fully, they need to have full access to his teachings, and they need to know clearly the differences between those teachings and teachings that claim to be Christian while they are not. No separated sect, no vague or evasive answers, can offer Christ's teachings in their fullness; and, because the Church is a living entity who responds anew to any situation that arises, no sect cut off from her can offer a consistent view of how those teachings shape the lives of those humans who embrace them (Jn 15:4). The similarities between the Church's teachings and the teachings of heretical sects are a sound basis of common belief, but the differences really do make a difference.

C hrist intended that his Church should stand until the end of Time (Mt 16:18, 28:18-20). He intended also that it should be one Church, which is why he founded one Church, not more, and for that matter he said explicitly that his followers were to remain unified (Jn 17:1-26). That, too, means that each and every Christian has to know enough about Christ's teachings to stand firmly with them and to live in accordance with them, just as each needs to know enough to tell the difference between accurate presentations of those teachings and incorrect ones. Each Christian needs to keep in touch daily with the central mysteries of Christianity, and each needs to pray always (1Th 5:17), connecting life on Earth with life in Heaven by means of prayer, so that God himself will answer and complete the connection with grace. Prayer is the life's blood of Christianity; prayer is the way the earthly body of the Church keeps in living connection with its head, which is Christ himself. This living blood flows through the Church's collective prayers—the Mass above all—as through the heart, but it must also flow through all of the members of that body, as the constant individual prayers of each person each day.

Without prayer, people are severed from that body, and prayer alone can bring them back. It may seem inconceivable today that Christendom could be healed again after such a long and bloody separation, but then the Albigensian heresy stretched across centuries, too. It built churches, schools, and even convents, some of which were in operation for more than two hundred years. It imposed its own free-for-all morals on the laws of the region as well as on its customs. It broke families, violated property rights, and tied the hands of courts and police, generation after sad generation. On a larger scale, the Albigensian heresy loosed the same horrors as those we've seen across Europe and the world since the Reformation—mob rule, legitimate rulers decapitated, death camps, and all the chaos that always erupts when people turn their backs on God to one degree or another.

The difference today is precisely that for so many people it's unthinkable that the situation can be redeemed by prayer; in Albigensian days it was assumed that prayer was the only way that it could be. Yet heresy is the same today as it ever was, and the Rosary, as the proven preventive and remedy for it, stands next to the sacraments themselves as a favorite target of those who would edit or ignore Christ's teachings. "What have not the modern heretics ... said to throw discredit on the use of the beads?" St. Alphonsus of Liguori exclaimed. "But everybody knows the immense good that this noble devotion has done. How many, by means of the Rosary, have been delivered from sin! How many led to a holy life!" (*Glories of Mary*).

The Rosary works to heal heresy in two ways, of course: internally and externally. Internally, it draws people away from false or incomplete doctrine, because people who meditate about the mysteries of the Faith are more intimately familiar with those truths. Consequently, they're far less likely to be led astray by incomplete or nonsensical presentations of them. Externally, the Rosary has always been advocated as an effective way to beg God to heal heresy in others. That's why the great reforming saints have always advocated it, or its direct devotional ancestors, and it's why popes in recent centuries have tirelessly begged the Faithful to take up their rosaries and pray fervently and constantly for unity in the Faith.

Devotion to the Blessed Virgin reflects the Church's particular concerns in every age, Paul VI wrote, and "among these especially in our day is her anxiety for the re-establishment of Christian unity. Thus devotion to the Mother of the Lord is in accord with the deep desires and aims of the ecumenical movement; that is, thus it acquires an ecumenical aspect... [D]evotion to the Mother of Christ and the Mother of Christians is a natural and frequent opportunity for seeking her intercession with her Son to obtain the union of all baptized people within a single People of God... [W]e wish to express our confidence that devotion to the humble handmaiden of the Lord, in whom the Almighty has done great things, will become, even if only slowly, not an obstacle but a path and a rallying point for the union of all who believe in Christ" (*Marialis cultus*, 1974).

In fact, it was during just such a campaign at the turn of the eighteenth century that the Rosary was given the final touch and achieved its present form, in the ministry of the great modern apostle of the Rosary, St. Louis-Marie Grignion de Montfort. Like the other great reformers of the past, he chose the Rosary as his primary weapon against the more subtle heresies of his day. And he was the one who suggested saying the *Gloria Patri* at the end of each decade.

St. Louis-Marie Grignion de Montfort (1673-1716) had an intriguing number of connections with the Rosary, and with its use against public disorders in particular, from before he was born. He was a

Dominican tertiary himself. He was educated at the Dominican house at Dinan, which had been founded in thanksgiving just after the Battle of Muret by a Breton knight named Alan de Lanvallay. Alan had fought with Simon de Montfort in the Languedoc—once, Alan said, he had found himself hopelessly surrounded by Albigensians but was delivered when he called upon Mary for aid; a shower of a hundred and fifty stones fell from the sky and routed his enemies. That school is where Blessed Alan de Rupe got his education, too, two hundred and fifty years before St. Louis-Marie Grignion de Montfort enrolled there, and the house at Dinan had a little shrine in its oratory dedicated to Bl. Alan de Rupe. As a priest St. Louis-Marie liked to celebrate Mass there.

> His family name recalls that of Simon de Montfort, the hero of Muret, but they come from different places. Simon was from Montfort l'Amauri, in the Ile de France north of Paris, and St. Louis-Marie was from a town in Brittany about fourteen miles south and west of Rennes, called Montfort-la-Cane—Montfort the Duck, because once a year during Mass on a certain date a wild duck waddled into the village church of St. Nicholas followed by her ducklings, left one at the altar, and took the rest back out. This phenomenon, memorialized by a carving of a duck's leg in the sixteenth-century reredos of the altar, was supposed to commemorate a flight of ducks that attacked a man bent on compromising the virtue of a local girl who invoked St. Nicholas's aid. The annual offering by the mysterious duck and her successors went on for nobody knows how long, but at last it stopped, evidently in the seventeenth century. The village is now called Montfort-sur-Meu, after the little River Meu that runs through it.

In fact, if you take a broader view of it, St. Louis-Marie's whole career runs remarkably parallel to that of St. Dominic himself. After he completed his schooling and was ordained, Louis-Marie worked for five years as the chaplain and general manager of a hospital at Poitiers, but he extended his ministry to fill the needs that he saw in the population far beyond its walls. He heard thousands of confessions; he taught catechism in the market sheds of the city; he helped the laity form religious associations; and he preached.

By 1705 Louis-Marie knew that preaching was his true vocation. He asked permission from his bishop to become an itinerant preacher—priests are "incardinated", of course; they belong to a particular bishop, and they're assigned to a specific parish that they can't leave without permission. But this particular bishop saw the need, too, and he agreed, so from then on Louis-Marie worked as a preacher, walking all over France and attracting immense crowds of listeners wherever he went. It was providential that he came along when he did, because France at that time was torn by a particularly slick and slippery heresy, Jansenism.

T he heresy got its start in the writings of Cornelius Jansen, Bishop of Ypres (1585-1638). He wrote most of his books and essays as exercises, to clarify his own thoughts, and he never intended that the public should ever see them. One of them, though, he thought worthy of publication: the *Augustinus*, a massive work of three volumes that took him twenty years to write.

The point of the *Augustinus* is to expound a certain doctrine about grace and its workings in the soul that Jansen claimed to have discovered in the writings of St. Augustine—a doctrine little known among the learned, Jansen said, but that would astonish everybody once he revealed it. But grace is a tricky subject, and Jansen got it wrong. He wasn't the first to make the particular mistakes that he did; they'd been forwarded by a man named Michel de Bay (Michaelus Baius) a few years before, and they'd been formally condemned as errors then, too.

On his deathbed, Jansen handed that manuscript over to his chaplain with the command that he put it through the Church's review process to be checked for accuracy. "If the Holy See wishes any change," he wrote on his will half an hour before he died, "I am an obedient son". The manuscript was reviewed and found erroneous, but even so Jansen's friends published it in 1640. Basically, Jansen asserted one of the same things that the Albigensians had asserted, that human nature, since Adam and Eve, is corrupt and depraved, so people can't avoid evil. But he also asserted that they can't avoid grace, either.

The *Augustinus* naturally attracted a good deal of attention, because this kind of thing makes religion so much easier; it puts all of the responsibility on God and none on humans. A whole movement—Jansenism—developed out of these mistakes, claiming that the thing to do is to just sit quietly and await that irresistible grace, the direct action of the Holy Spirit in the soul. That particular heresy is called Quietism; and the Jansenists thought that, after quietly awaiting the Spirit, without praying, without even making the effort to receive the sacraments, they'd suddenly become endowed with extraordinary graces.

They became convulsionaries; they rolled their eyes and fell on the floor, they barked like dogs, or they babbled like infants. They compared themselves favorably to the Apostles at Pentecost; they claimed to be faith healers; they preached, under the presumed direct inspiration of God himself, an endless torrent of invective against the Church in general and anybody in particular who opposed them or even tried to talk sense to them. They prophesied the end of the Church, and the end of the world itself. In short, they astonished themselves and each other with the depth of their sanctity and the violence of its expression.

These things have been seen time and again in the Church, of course; they're part of why St. Paul had to write again and again to the Corinthians, to explain what spiritual gifts are and what they're not. The particular excesses that the Jansenists fell into were a sort of revival of the Messalian movement that started in the fourth century and survived in some areas until the ninth. This sect, too, was based entirely on the good feelings that come from belonging to a group, from flouting the norms of social behavior, or of just releasing emotions, and they also mistook these emotions for the action of the Holy Spirit. And of course to them the vehemence of those emotions were a mark of perfection, of being one of the inspired elect. But Quietism, whether among the first-century Corinthians, the fourth-century Messalians, the seventeenth-century Jansenists, or anywhere else, is a psychological event, not a spiritual one.

The human soul's union with God through prayer happens primarily through the sacraments, and it happens in a mysterious way—that is, you don't usually feel it; it doesn't necessarily reflect itself in the emotions. Still, "many, lured by the delight and satisfaction procured in their religious practices, strive more for spiritual savor than for spiritual purity," St. John of the Cross explained. "Besides the imperfection of seeking after these delights, the sweetness that these persons experience makes them go to extremes and pass beyond the mean in which virtue resides" (*The Dark Night of the Soul* 1:6:1). This is what St. John calls "spiritual gluttony"; and while some people feel good while going through spiritual growth, many feel nothing at all except a gradual improvement in their psychological balance over a long period of time, so gently increasing that its coming is not noticed except in retrospect. They have it easy, really; most people going through spiritual growth feel at some time or another exactly the opposite of sweetness and consolation: they feel abandonment and desolation.

All people who take prayer seriously will go through times when they seem to be wandering alone in the desert and feeling nothing of God. Still, these experiences of desolation or even of affliction are parts of the process of union with God, which often comes through the most profound spiritual torment and a feeling of being utterly abandoned by God. It's "bitter and terrible to the senses," St. John of the Cross explained. "These souls do not get any satisfaction or consolation … the soul thinks that it is not serving God but turning back". But the very reason for these feelings of dryness and desolation, he points out, is that God transfers his goods and strength from the senses to the spirit. The senses that feel everyday emotions are left behind, and "since the sensory part of the soul is incapable of the goods of the spirit, it remains deprived, dry, and empty … but the spirit through this nourishment grows stronger and more alert, and becomes more solicitous than before about not failing God" (*The Dark Night* 1:9:2-4).

THE HABIT OF HERESY

After all, the whole point of the Church's penitential practices, the whole point of prayer, the whole point of conversion itself is to turn the soul constantly away from the world of the senses and toward the world of the spirit, toward God himself. So the Quietist idea that the Holy Spirit will possess a soul with all kinds of outward signs, with high emotions and with extraordinary gifts like healing, tongues, or even convulsions, is wrong; it looks exclusively at the self, not at God, and it separates people from his Church.

> It's interesting that the old Messalians included both Christians and non-Christians in their congregations, because for them the emotional experience was the point, not any religious doctrine or discipline. In fact, when the Church's hierarchy pointed out that grace comes in an entirely different way, the Christians among the Messalians at first conformed outwardly to the cultural and liturgical norms of the Church, but eventually they just left the Church entirely in favor of their own prayer meetings. This still happens, but since Messalian times the Church has often adopted a policy of silent waiting whenever Quietism comes around; usually, the groups disperse when the leader dies or leaves, or when his followers come to see him as a fraud. In the meantime, the clergy often asks members of Quietist groups to perform some extra service in the Church to keep their attention focussed on the Church until they recover themselves, and to let them know that they're appreciated—low self-esteem being a major factor in attraction to this particular heresy.

The old Quietism of Messalianism had started out as a movement among the laity, and only toward its end did a few priests embrace the sect. But when Quietism arose again as Jansenism it deceived not just crowds of the laity but clerics, too, nuns, priests, and monks, from the beginning. All of them awaited the "baptism of the Spirit", and they divided the world into those (like themselves) who were favored by the Spirit, and those (like people who remained with the Church) who were rejected by the Spirit, just hopelessly uninspired commoners who could never understand. With this viewpoint, the Jansenists simply disregarded the constant reminders from the Holy See, and the barrage of orthodox preaching against the nonsense, as coming from people not nearly so holy as themselves.

Jansenism seems so silly, in retrospect, that it's hard to understand how it could have attracted such a large following and such a prominent one, but it did. Even some bishops embraced the movement, evidently mistaking it for a real spiritual renewal or thinking that some good could come of it. One man alone could hardly have countered the movement, but

Louis-Marie Grignion de Montfort didn't exactly preach against Jansenism; he preached the truth that stood against it, and thousands listened.

Like good people everywhere, the French wanted to do what is good. They wanted to know what Christ teaches, and they wanted to live in accordance with it. And like most people who live amid a whole cloud of variant teachings all claiming to be Christian, they were eager to hear precisely what was accurate teaching and what wasn't, as they have a right to hear.

So Louis-Marie simply reminded people of Christian doctrine. He asked his listeners to renew with him the vows of their Baptism. He reminded them that the sacraments were instituted by Christ himself, who teaches nothing unnecessary, and he encouraged frequent communion— the Jansenists, of course, thought that they, as spiritually elect, didn't have to bother with any of that. And he called their attention ardently to the Rosary. He preached it tirelessly; he begged his penitents in the confessional to take up the devotion. He set up shop in barns and in marketplaces and in tents, praying the Rosary until, one by one, hundreds came to join him. He had the most talented of his listeners paint fifteen huge parade banners, one for each Mystery of the Rosary, and he organized processions under them, drawing people to gather and pray the Rosary together.

There were enough miracles around his work to encourage the doubtful—he made the blind see, and he cured crippling illnesses; he multiplied food and drink to feed the crowds of his listeners. But chiefly it was the Rosary that did it. Wherever Louis-Marie passed in northern France, he left crowds of people wearing their rosaries around their necks or looped on their belts, the way they used to centuries before. Within a year, he had left whole cities holding on to their rosaries and standing firm against Jansenism.

Naturally, the Jansenists were furious. They attacked him with clubs; they slipped poison into his food. They denounced him to the bishops and to the police—he was going around committing miracles, they said, miracles that were far more persuasive than their own convulsions (cf. 3Kn 18:21-39). The Jansenist bishops themselves were infuriated when they saw St. Louis-Marie leading hundreds and thousands of people back to the steadiness of the Faith; other bishops just became angry when they saw him leading the people, whether they agreed with where he was leading them or not. One after another, they banned him from preaching in their dioceses or even entering them. St. Louis-Marie was absolutely obedient to them, as obedient as a stick in the hand. He didn't enter those dioceses again until he got permission to do so. But then he walked to Rome to get that permission from the Pope.

Clement XI Albani (1649-1721) was undoubtedly surprised to see St. Louis-Marie, who was evidently rather the worse for wear by then. But he was precisely the right pope for St. Louis-Marie to approach. He himself was a great preacher and a tireless confessor; even as Pope he spent long hours in the confessional, counseling thousands of penitents. Like St. Louis-Marie he was a great broadshouldered man whose prodigious strength and endurance seemed at odds with his profound gentleness and humility—after he was elected to the papacy it took the College of Cardinals three whole days to persuade him to accept.

And, also like Louis-Marie, Clement XI was clear on what Christianity is about and what it isn't. As Pope, he had already issued an Apostolic Brief, *Cum nuper*, and apostolic constitution, *Vineam Domini*, that condemned some of the propositions of Jansenism and severely rebuked those who held them, citing particularly their duplicity—Jansenists had a tendency to claim to be members of the Church while refusing her sacraments or taking them with smug mental reservations, and while refusing to observe the regular moral discipline.

Clement XI knew of St. Louis-Marie's work and, to everybody's surprise, he appointed him "Missionary Apostolic", free to preach anywhere in Christendom and answerable only to the Throne of Peter. St. Louis-Marie walked back to the north of France and started preaching again. Naturally, the Jansenist bishops refused to accept these papal directives, or at least refused to implement them; and even this laxity was enough to confirm the Jansenists' own idea that the Holy See has no right to declare matters of faith, except of course insofar as the Jansenists themselves chose to agree. But St. Louis-Marie stood on his right, and he brought people back to the Church through the Rosary in even greater numbers. By the time he died in 1716—the year that Clement XI extended the Feast of Our Lady of the Rosary to the universal Church—Jansenism was not quite dead, but its forces had been wrecked as surely as the Turkish fleet, sunk under the weight of thousands of converted souls.

Like the conversions from Albigensianism, these conversions of whole regions happened quickly, but they never happened *en masse*; conversion never does. Conversion still comes individually to each and every person who converts. When people gather together to pray the Rosary for some great and universal intention, the turning point comes to each of them one by one, and their conversions together bear the collective weight that tips the scales for the nation as a whole: "Turn back, each of you, from your evil way and from your evil deeds; then shall you remain in the land that the Lord gave your fathers… You shall be my people, and I shall be your God" (Jr 25:5, 30:22).

I n fact, after the great Battle of Lepanto, St. Pius V had remarked that the greatest benefit of asking for help through the Rosary wasn't so much that it averts the emergency at hand but that "with the spread of this devotion, the meditations of the Faithful have become more inflamed; their prayers more fervent; and they have suddenly become different people." And that, in turn, is why Leo XIII could say that "We are convinced that the Rosary, if devoutly used, is bound to benefit not only the individual person but society at large" (*Lætitiæ sanctæ*).

The many spiritual and military victories that have been won through devotion to the Rosary make it clearly evident that this form of prayer is particularly pleasing to the Blessed Virgin, Leo XIII confirmed (*Supremi apostolatus officio*, 1883). So it is especially suitable as a means of defense for the Church, and for all Christians, he said.

> Moved by these thoughts and by the examples of Our Predecessors, We have deemed it most opportune ... by adopting those prayers addressed to the Blessed Virgin in the Rosary to endeavor to obtain from her son Jesus Christ a similar aid against present dangers ... to which the Church is daily exposed... [S]o many souls, redeemed by the blood of Christ, snatched from salvation by the whirlwind of an age of error, precipitated into the abyss of everlasting death! Our need of divine help is as great today as it was when the great Dominic introduced the use of the Rosary as a balm for the wounds of his contemporaries... [S]eek the intercession with God of that Virgin, to whom it is given to destroy all heresies.

EVA ❀ AVE

PROMISES

THE CHANGES THAT THE ROSARY WORKS IN people are specific, and if you know what to look for they're obvious. Bl. Alan de Rupe reported that Mary, in apparitions to himself and to St. Dominic before him, made a total of fifteen promises about the spiritual benefits that the Rosary brings to a person devoted to it. Of course, these are not taught officially as articles of faith by the Church— nothing coming from a latter-day apparition ever is, even if the event of the apparition is itself declared to be worthy of credit.

Nor are these promises certified by any indulgences officially promulgated by the Holy See. They don't mean that the Rosary itself is enough to assure salvation, because it isn't; praying the Rosary is no substitute for a full sacramental life in full communion with the Church (Rv 3:20; Mt 26:26-28; Jn 6:22-60), and in any case nobody can be assured of salvation (Sr 5:4-7; Mt 24:40-41).

But thinking about these promises and what they mean is a worthwhile exercise because they bring with them a lot of information about meditative prayer and its effects. And they lead to consideration of larger issues, too; the Rosary is the easiest and surest way to attain the skill of meditative prayer, but everything that these promises say about the Rosary specifically is true of meditative prayer generally. Some of these promises are self-explanatory, but others include some vocabulary that can be confusing these days, or statements in reference to unfamiliar theological concepts.

WHOEVER SHALL SERVE ME FAITHFULLY BY PRAYING THE ROSARY SHALL RECEIVE SIGNAL GRACES. Besides Jansenism, more heresies have sprung from misconceptions about grace than just about anything else, and more misunderstandings than heresies. But its nature and functions can be easily understood in general, and so can the ways in which grace works through meditative prayer.

Grace can be defined as the favor of God. It's not just a passive kindliness, though; grace is an action, the action of God's merciful—or gracious—disposition toward Mankind. In its broadest sense, the idea of grace would include the outreach of love through which God created the Heavens and the Earth, and humankind, too, and through which he keeps it all in existence. But that *sustaining* grace stands as an unchanging background to the subtle and complex ways in which God reaches out to touch individual human beings with distinctive graces intended to help them attain salvation.

Of course, it's entirely possible to understand that God does reach out to people in this way, but it's not possible to understand completely how he does this, nor even why. After all, his ways are not our ways, and his thoughts are not our thoughts. In the final analysis, grace is a mystery. But even so, you can't get very far studying any aspect of Christianity without studying grace, if only because Christianity is a revealed religion: God transmitted it to humans through a whole series of positive acts of love— revelation is itself an act of grace. The revelations to the prophets, the coming, teaching, and suffering of Christ, and in fact creation itself are all acts of grace, in the largest sense of the term. So every branch of Christian theology studies grace in at least some of its aspects.

Theology as a whole is divided into doctrinal theology and moral theology. *Doctrinal* theology focusses on things that people need to know about God, such as the fact of his existence, those things that we know about his nature, and so on, all of which was revealed by just such graces, through the prophets and by Christ himself. This revealed doctrine says quite clearly that God's people are to live in a certain way if they are to attain salvation, which is everlasting and unobstructed closeness to God after bodily death; so *moral* theology concentrates on what people need to do to attain salvation, which was also revealed by grace in revelations like the Commandments, the Sermon on the Mount, and really all of the moral codes of Christ and the prophets.

Moral theology includes the field of *spiritual* theology, which deals with the development of a person's spiritual life; spiritual theology is divided into three specific fields. It includes *ascetic* theology, which studies what humans can do to open their spiritual lives to the outflow of graces from God; *mystic* theology, which studies specifically how God reaches out in grace to call people to further development in spirit; and *pastoral* theology, which studies ways to arouse other people to a fuller possession of God's grace.

PROMISES

All major Christian writers, the Evangelists, St. Paul, St. Augustine, St. Thomas Aquinas, and many, many others, have written extensively about grace. They wrote for different purposes, they all define their terms differently, and they all say different things about it, but none contradicts the others. Grace, as the endless action of the inexhaustible love of an infinite God, is an inexhaustible subject, too, and seen from these various viewpoints it seems to work somewhat differently. But to see its connection to meditative prayer it's best understood as essentially God's favor pouring down on a specific human being.

In this sense, grace is a participation in the divine life. God can bestow it on a person or withhold it, as he wills; that divine life belongs properly only to the Father, the Son, and the Holy Spirit, and it need not be shared with any creature. That's why the Septuagint uses the word χάρις, "gift", to translate the Hebrew words that point to the divine disposition that generates grace, like חן (khen), which means "goodwill". The word is related to words meaning to bless or to be compassionate.

The authors of the New Testament elevated that same Greek word to indicate the outreach of God, an act by which he expresses his goodwill, in all of its forms and nuances—that is, for Christians, χάρις simply means grace (Jn 1:14, 16; 2Cr 12:9, etc.). Our word "grace" is from the Latin *gratia*, basically a direct translation of χάρις that's also the source of our words "gratitude" and "gratuitous"—we still use *gratis* by itself to mean free. Grace is a gift, a personal act of self-giving on the part of God. So it has to be absolutely free, because God can't be compelled to do anything.

Still, the fact that grace is a gift means that human beings can receive it; we are made in such a way that we can receive that gift. That's why Scripture and Sacred Tradition both insist that Man, made in God's image and likeness, is by nature good. The complication is that human nature includes free will, which is the way that God wants it; he doesn't force people to love him. So he offers agreements, covenants, between himself and humankind, contracts to which both parties have to agree, and to which both have to contribute. There have been three, in all.

The first expression of a covenant between God and Man, of course, was offered to Adam and Eve. God gave them an immense number of special graces. He gave them bodily immortality, and freedom from pain and suffering; he gave them integrity, which means that their emotions, and even their passions, were controlled by their intellect. He allowed them an intimate union with himself, so that they could see God and live with him on friendly terms. Their part of this original covenant was simple, almost symbolic, mere token obedience: they had only to refrain from eating the fruit of one particular tree, and they could keep all of those immense gifts.

Adam and Eve refused by disobedience. And because their supernatural gifts were conditional on their sustained love of God, demonstrated through meritorious obedience, God in his justice took those gifts away from Mankind. In his mercy, though, God offered another, and a greater, Covenant (Gn 3). Through the promise of this New Covenant, those people who accept God's laws of their own free will can accept his offer of sufficient grace to regain all of those supernatural gifts after crossing the threshold of bodily death, which is itself the wages of sin. In fact, it was specifically to offer all of these graces that God's love committed itself to the New Covenant, having as its price on his part Christ's blood (Jn 4:9; Rm 8:32; 1Cr 6:20, 11:25). This Covenant is offered to everybody, because God wants everybody to be saved (Mt 28:19, 1Tm 2:4). But salvation isn't a free gift; it's conditional, as the benefits of all covenants are conditional, on both parties' fulfillment of the terms of the covenant.

Sometimes confusion arises about the gratuity of salvation, because redemption is a free gift of God; but there's a difference between redemption and salvation. Both have to do with the reconciliation of God and Man, but Christ's redemptive work is not the same as his salvational work. His coming in fulfillment of the Old Covenant, and his establishing the New Covenant, is in general his work of salvation, because the saving of humanity is what it's all about. He didn't have to do any of this, of course; he did it out of love, and out of mercy. So, in that broad sense, salvation is a free gift of God.

But the New Covenant that Christ established as part of that salvational work lays out the terms under which people are to live if they are to see God—if they are to be saved. So, in that individual sense, salvation is not free; being saved or lost depends on what you do as well as on what you believe (Ex 32:33; Mt 24:42-51, 25:14-46; Rv 20:12, 22:12, etc.). But before the New Covenant could accomplish anybody's salvation, people had to be redeemed (from the Latin *redemptio*, a buying back) from the sin of Adam and their own sins. Christ suffered and died to do that, to take our punishment on himself (Is 53:2-6; Rm 5:15-21) and to undo what Adam did (1Cr 15:21-22). That was his work of redemption. It doesn't mean that there's no such thing as sin since the Crucifixion, and it doesn't mean that you can presume that you're forgiven for your sins. Christ's redemptive work opened the narrow gate for us, but each of us has to walk the steep and rocky path beyond it for ourselves, working toward our own salvation in fear and trembling (1Cr 3:11-15, 10:12, Phl 2:12, Sr 5:5-9).

Humans are joint heirs with Christ "provided that we suffer with him so that we may also be glorified with him" (Rm 8:17). That is, God regards obedience to the Covenant as Man's fulfillment of its terms; and he will offer all of the necessary help, the necessary graces, that each person needs to fulfill that Covenant. But the sufficient grace that God always offers doesn't guarantee individual salvation—that is, it's not necessarily efficacious, as the theologians say. It can't be, because we all have the free will to reject it, and it can't work if it's rejected.

That's why we can earn punishment by rejecting God's laws, but we can't earn the gift that is grace (Eph 2:8; Ps 48:8-10) by embracing those laws. This is what St. Paul meant when he wrote that the wages of sin is death, but the gift of God is life everlasting (Rm 6:23)—notice that he didn't say that the wages of righteousness is life everlasting. He meant that, as God is the Father of us all, we can earn punishment and even total disinheritance, just as a child can earn that rejection from his human father; but we can't earn the Father's love and we don't need to, any more than a human child needs to earn the love of his human father. Yet we are all bound to obey that Father, as children are bound to obey their fathers on Earth, so that we won't lose that love by rejecting it.

That is, we can't earn the love that God has for us, a love that is the basis for all good things that humans have, on Earth and in Heaven; but meritorious obedience is a condition of the full possession of that good, which includes God himself. And because God does not force people to do things against their free will, the human response to grace has to be free: like Adam and Eve, people are always free to accept God's Covenant or reject it (Sr 15:11-20), to turn toward God or away from him. A person has to accept grace when it comes, and in fact people have to ask for it and work to retain it.

There are more than one kind of grace, and there are several ways to ask for them and for all that you need to maintain them. The grace of Christ, the gift of participation in his own life that God gives us, is infused by the Holy Spirit into the soul at Baptism, healing it of sin and sanctifying it. "As the body derives its life from its union with the soul, so does the soul derive its life from its union with the Spirit of God through sanctifying grace," St. Irenæus and St. Clement of Alexandria explained. This particular kind of grace, *sanctifying* grace, is the grace described by St. Paul when he said that "If then anyone is in Christ, he is a new creature; the former things have passed away: behold! they are made new. All of this is from God, who has reconciled us to himself through Christ" (2Cr 5:17-18).

Sanctifying grace is the kind of grace that the New Testament often refers to by the Greek ζωή, which simply means "life". This conveys the sense that sanctifying grace is vivifying, and that it's an habitual gift. It's a stable disposition, supernatural in the sense of being above unsanctified human nature. It's an ordering of the life of the spirit that disposes it to live and act in accordance with God's call—the soul's vocation. That's why this constant and indwelling grace is often called *habitual* grace.

Habitual grace, sanctifying grace, is not part of human nature; it's supernatural, literally above nature. Yet it's so intimately merged into the good Christian, Juan González Arintero, O.P., said, "that without it he is dead—reduced to the level of the old Adam... In our human understanding, the life of grace has as its properties [those characteristics that flow from its nature,] charity and the infused virtues and habits that always accompany it and disappear with it" (*Mystic Evolution*). And indeed you can lose habitual grace, just as you can lose any natural habit or life itself, if you neglect the acts that strengthen it. But on the other hand the ability to perform meritorious acts is strengthened by *actual* graces.

Actual graces are God's interventions at the beginning of the process of conversion and at certain points along the way to final salvation. Actual graces, particular acts of help from God, help us perform the good acts that habitual grace prompts us to do. God grants actual graces according to the terms of the Covenant, in consideration of the merits of Christ. Actual graces come if you have asked for them, and they pass when their work is completed. So it's important to keep yourself always disposed to receive actual graces, and to ask for them constantly. These graces sustain the soul across the abyss step by step; ceasing to ask for them puts the soul in the position of St. Peter on the sea (Mt 14:28-31).

You can ask for actual graces by stepping forward to receive the sacraments of Confirmation, Reconciliation, the Anointing of the Sick, Matrimony, Ordination, and above all the Eucharist; these sacraments confer the actual graces that they signify. You can also ask by prayer: by the prayer that consists of simply doing some virtuous act motivated by the love of God—the works of mercy, for instance (Tb 12:12; Mt 25:31-46), or the act of vocal prayer—or by prayer of the heart, which is either contemplative prayer or, more usually, meditative prayer.

These actual graces give holiness and excellence to faculties like the intellect and the will, which everybody has as part of human nature, and to any natural talent, which people may have without reference to whether they use it for good or for bad. Actual graces elevate these natural resources to the high purpose of everlasting life. They're the little flashes of divine light that guide each of the Faithful through daily life as a parent constantly touches a toddler to keep him from stumbling (Ps 118:133; Pr 16:9).

Actual graces are really the most delightful graces, and the most interesting, because they're so quick, so economical, and so exquisitely fitted to each person individually, and to each act of each person, different as all people are. Look at the prophets, the Apostles, and the saints. Think of St. Peter and how he differed from St. Paul—and how he even differed with St. Paul, from time to time. Think of the fatherly St. Augustine and the cantankerous St. Jerome. Think of Ignatius of Loyola and Ignatius of Antioch, Teresa of Avila and Thérèse of Lisieux, Dominic Guzmán and Dominic Savio. How different they all are, and how utterly different their works were. Yet they were all motivated by the same sanctifying grace, and they were all sustained in their diversity by constant touches of actual graces that were precisely what each of them needed to raise their wills to consonance with God's will, and to elevate their highly individual minds to his purposes.

In general, three kinds of actual grace particularly touch meditative prayer. The *illuminating* grace that illuminates the intellect is the kind that suggests good thoughts (Ps 18:9). This prompting can come through external means, as when a sermon, a Bible reading, or consideration of the life of Christ moves a person to reflect seriously on sin and salvation (1Pt 2:20-25). This is the kind of grace that Christ conferred through the Apostles and continues to confer through their successors; it's the reason for his repeated command to convert people, to teach, to make all humans of every nation into disciples (Mt 28:19).

Usually, this illuminating grace's action through the mind and the senses only helps prepare the way for a more important actual grace that doesn't depend on external means (Ps 118:34). This is *immediate illuminating grace*, the action of the Holy Spirit directly elevating and penetrating the mind, prompting the soul to action and showing it, in a supernatural light, the eternal truths of salvation. This is what hit St. Paul in an instant (Ac 9:3-9), but the two-stage process of this illuminating grace is more usual; it's what he was talking about later when he said that he and his disciple Apollos had planted and watered through their preaching, and that God had given the increase (1Cr 3:6)—"instruction and admonition help somewhat externally", St. Augustine explained, "but the person who grasps with the heart has a seat in Heaven" (*Third Tract on First John*).

The illuminating and immediate illuminating graces that elevate the intellect also pave the way for the third kind of actual grace, the kind that strengthens the will. St. Augustine called this grace eagerness for the good, the inspiration of delight, or the heavenly delight—delight being, of course, the soul's joy in this particular gift of God and the closeness to him that it implies. Like the graces of the intellect, this grace can come directly or through indirect means, but it's more than just helpful for salvation: it's indispensable because no works of salvation are even conceivable without the deliberate choice of the will, and this grace is the touch of God that elevates the human will to a more nearly perfect concordance with his own.

PROMISES

With these graces, habitual and actual, the soul is empowered to live the moral life. By ourselves, we can often recognize an obligation without being able to fulfill it, or we can see an ideal without being able to reach it. But grace connects us with a power beyond ourselves, the active love of God that enables us to respond to those obligations and to attain those ideals.

This is how grace assists virtue on a supernatural level. Virtue, so called from the Latin *virtus*, "power", is basically the habit of doing good. But you have to fight for the good habits of natural virtue, and you acquire them only through constant practice of their acts—to be just, you have to make the effort to act fairly, always; to be prudent, you have to act prudently. To develop the habit of temperance you have to restrain your appetites in accordance with right reason, and to acquire fortitude you have to become habitually strong in pursuit of the right. In the same way, to acquire supernatural virtue you have to co-operate freely with God, working constantly to climb toward perfection.

With habitual and actual grace, God gives—to everybody who asks—the grace to achieve what he expects of us, constantly, against all of the obstacles that block our path back to him, at every step of the way. This is the promise of grace, and the promise of the sacraments, of prayer itself, and of meditative prayer in particular.

I PROMISE MY SPECIAL PROTECTION AND THE GREATEST GRACES TO ALL THOSE WHO PRAY THE ROSARY. This repeats the promise of great graces, which is the greatest fruit of meditative prayer, but it's different in that it offers Mary's special protection as well. That raises the question of patronage, of the idea that a certain saint will extend special protection to the group that particularly asks the aid of that saint's prayers in connection with their work, their institution, or their interests.

The doctrine at the foundation of the practice is the communion of saints, the spiritual union between the Church in Heaven and the Church on Earth. A good many of the Church's prayers ask the intercession of all the saints, but since earliest times Christians have focussed their prayers, individually and in groups, on some particular saint with whom they have a particular association. Sometimes the saint was the Apostle who announced the Gospel to that locality, or the first Christian to do so; that's how St. Patrick became patron saint of Ireland and St. Francis Xavier of Borneo.

Sometimes it was a local person, known well to everybody else in the parish, who had been martyred. Later, it might be a saint whose life and work here on Earth had a particular application to a certain group who vowed to live that way, as St. Francis and St. Clare are asked to watch over the orders they established.

Or it might be that a certain trade or profession sees a special bond with a saint who did that kind of work, or that those suffering from a certain spiritual or physical ailment would turn for help to somebody who had the same problem in this life. That's how St. Cecilia became patroness of musicians and St. Thomas Aquinas patron of schools and universities; St. Apollonia, whose teeth were all extracted by her torturers, of toothache (and of dentists), and St. Lucy, whose eyes were put out, of ocular ailments.

The Church understands, Paul VI remarked, "that certain outward religious expressions, while perfectly valid in themselves, may be less suitable to men and women of different ages and cultures" (*Marialis cultus*, 1974). But these patronages are strong enough to hold the devotion of those regions and groups that focus their devotions this way, and they are reinforced by enough graces to maintain them—if that saint doesn't obtain answers to those particular prayers, his patronage fades, over time. A patron saint whose intercession succeeds, though, is often spoken of exactly as people would speak of an earthly patron who saw to their special needs with donations from superior resources, except that the saint doesn't supply money but graces.

Sometimes these saints are considered honorary presidents of an organization, but sometimes they're simply thought of as members in good standing; and, as monarchs sometimes wear the uniform of a certain regiment, the saints themselves are given marks of rank. The practice goes back at least to Constantine's day, when Christ himself was shown in the uniform of the armies who conquered in his sign, but it lasted a surprisingly long time. St. Andrew, patron of Amalfi in the part of Italy ruled by Spain, was made a Knight of the Order of the Golden Fleece by Felipe III of Spain, and his statue in Amalfi still wears the insignia of that order.

St. Anthony of Padua was commissioned an admiral in the Spanish navy by Felipe's successor in 1731, and in fact had been a general in the Portuguese army since 1710. He served in a captaincy in the army of Brazil from 1751 until 1810, when he was commissioned a major. His monthly salary, about forty dollars, was paid to him—by way of a Franciscan convent in Rio de Janeiro—for use as alms until 1911, when the Brazilian government revised its rules about payments to Church institutions. Even during the First World War, St. Anthony was honorary commander of the Kaiserjäger Corps of the Austrian Tyrol, and saints like George, Demetrius, or Martin of Tours are still sometimes shown in the uniforms of the armies that they protect.

Specific saints can take an interest in certain groups, but Mary's intercession—and hers alone among saints—is universal, and it's incomparably powerful, as you can read in the Gospels. The prayer of one who serves God willingly is heard; his petition pierces the skies (Sr 35:16-18; Jn 9:31), after all; and Mary's will is in perfect accord with God's, so Mary's prayers are heard perfectly. Grace is strength, and Mary is full of grace.

That's why she's been chosen as patroness of so many confraternities, parishes, cities, and nations, and it's why the Litany of Loreto addresses her as Tower of David, Virgin Most Powerful (Cn 4:4). Her strength in grace is why the Hours of the Feast of the Most Holy Rosary quoted verses like Jt 13:22, "The Lord has blessed thee by his power, because he has brought our enemies to nought." From the beginning of her vocation, Mary herself was aware of the power that it involved: he has shown might with his arm, and he has scattered the proud in the conceit of their hearts, she said; he has put down the mighty from their thrones, and has exalted the lowly (Lk 1:49-52). The difference in this world before and after the moment at which Mary said "Let it be done" is almost unimaginable, and it's all because of the power of the graces that she brought down with her *fiat*.

And those particularly powerful graces that Mary conveys by way of the Rosary are the reason that Gregory XIII replaced the Feast of Our Lady of Victory with the Feast of Our Lady of the Most Holy Rosary, just after the Battle of Lepanto.

THE ROSARY SHALL BE A POWERFUL ARMOR AGAINST HELL; IT WILL DESTROY VICE, DECREASE SIN, AND DEFEAT HERESIES. The Rosary works its wonders in hearts and in the world at large in two ways. On an earthly level, it works because it makes you think; it makes you pay attention to Christ and to his mother. On a higher level, it's understood as a particularly effective way to ask for graces. Either way, the exercise of the Rosary makes it harder for Hell to touch you because it keeps you in touch, daily and deeply, with God. It decreases sin and destroys vice because "a soul that truly loves God with all its heart will by its own volition avoid whatever displeases Our Lord and strive to please him in all things," as St. François de Sales used to say.

It defeats heresies by the same two-pronged attack. Just thinking about what most heresies teach punctures them pretty quickly; and it's not easy for somebody to mislead you about what Christianity is if you know your Bible and Sacred Tradition well enough to meditate meaningfully on the Gospels, the prophecies that foretell them, and the Epistles that apply them. Cultivating the habit of meditative prayer strengthens the virtues, chiefly faith (which ties you closer to God), hope (which keeps your eyes on the goal of final reunion with him), and charity (which is the love of God)—all of which make it harder for any eroded version of Christ's teachings to pull you away.

PROMISES

The deepened intimacy with God that the Rosary nurtures is also how it destroys vices other than heresy, too—or, you might say, how it heals vices. St. Augustine described vices as wounds, and "wounds mean nothing but the absence of health. When a cure is effected, that doesn't mean that the evils that were present … go away from the body and exist someplace else; they cease to exist completely. Because the wound or disease isn't a substance; it's a defect in the fleshly substance… In exactly the same way, what we call vices in the soul are nothing but deprivations of natural good. And when they're cured, they aren't transferred to someplace else: when they cease to exist in the healthy soul, they can't exist anywhere else" (*Enchiridion* 11). We tear those wounds in our souls by turning away from God; the Rosary heals them by turning all aspects of the soul toward God. Naturally, because a vice is simply the habit of sin, and a sin is nothing other than an act that expresses a vice, healing the vices prevents the sins.

T HE ROSARY SHALL CAUSE VIRTUES AND GOOD WORKS TO FLOURISH; IT WILL OBTAIN FOR SOULS THE ABUNDANT MERCY OF GOD; IT WILL WITHDRAW THE HEARTS OF MEN FROM THE LOVE OF THE WORLD AND ITS VANITIES, AND IT WILL LIFT THEM TO THE DESIRE OF ETERNAL THINGS. This promise of conversion has a triumphant ring to it, but triumph can only come after battle. And just as the Glorious Mysteries themselves make no sense unless they follow the Sorrowful, the grace of conversion does not come easy, in the general course of things.

It's not easy to tear oneself away from the things of this world, and it's still harder to endure those growing-pains of the spirit, the symptoms of the healing of vice and the growth of virtue. When humility urges you to ignore pride, that vice kicks and screams against the goad; sloth drags you back to your previous ease when fortitude calls you to move forward toward the right. Even the bodily appetites cry like hungry babies when you begin to discipline them.

That's why the Church has always mandated fasting and abstinence as the right and left hands of prayer, ever since Christ prescribed them to his followers— ever since Josaphat did, for that matter (Mt 6:16; Ac 14:23; 2Pr 20:3). Fasting means eating less food than normal, usually limiting yourself to one full meatless meal a day and two smaller ones that together don't equal the full meal; abstinence means avoiding certain kinds of food (usually meat), or eating simpler food; but always eating enough to sustain your strength for your duties.

The sacrifices of fasting and abstinence make atonement for sin (Jr 36:9; Jl 1:14; Jo 3:5), so they move you closer to God, but more than that these exercises turn you away from this world, or at least help you see the transient material pleasures of this world in their proper perspective (Mt 6:19-20). The sacrifice doesn't necessarily have to be restricted to food; with the permission of a confessor, a person might move beyond the letter of the law and set aside a certain kind of entertainment, luxurious clothing or jewelry, or any other licit pleasure, or take on extra works of mercy (Is 58:6). Giving up the little luxuries that you've grown accustomed to is the only way to build your ability to give up illicit pleasures altogether, and to set aside permissible ones when you need to, as when you're praying for some particularly great or important grace (2Kn 12:16-22; 1Es 8:23; Es 4:16; Ps 34:13; Is 58; Mt 17:20).

St. François de Sales explained this with a parable about a child who weeps compassionately seeing his mother bled by the surgeon's lancet but who will not give her the piece of candy that he's holding if she asks for it. So do some people, he says, meditate on the stroke of the lance that pierced the heart of Jesus, with all kinds of emotional tears and lamentations, but then they put away their rosaries and go on as they were before, refusing to give up those sweets that we love more than his heavenly grace. "Ah, this is the friendship of children: tender indeed, but weak, willful, and useless" (*Introduction to the Devout Life* 4:13).

It's in the nature of children to grow, but growth hurts; and with conversion everything in your previous life has to pass away so that everything can be made new again. Christ said metaphorically that conversion meant to take up your cross and follow him, and those who heard him knew exactly what kind of agonizing death to self he meant. Even in recent times—even today—there are missionaries and laymen all over the world who face agonizing death from hatred of the Faith, but most people today are more likely to face three crosses that Leo XIII pointed out in 1893, in his encyclical *Lætitiæ sanctæ*, three particular challenges that the modern age seems particularly squeamish about, and for which the Rosary seems to be a particularly powerful cure.

First among these evils is distaste for a simple and laborious life, Leo XIII said. He saw that society was threatened by a growing contempt for the homely duties and virtues that constitute the beauty of humble life. This is what causes children to so readily withdraw themselves from the natural obligation to obey their parents, he said, and it's what makes everybody increasingly impatient of any kind of treatment other than the indulgent and the luxurious.

This contempt for the simple life provokes the workman to desert his trade, to shirk honest toil, and to become discontented with the fair return that such toil would earn him; it even makes him pine, "with unthinking hopefulness", for an upheaval in the order of things that would bring about an equalization of property. So, he said, people's minds become unsettled; they openly trample human rights underfoot, and, when their unrealistic expectations are at last betrayed, they attack the public order and openly conflict with those charged with maintaining it.

"For such evils as these, let us seek a remedy in the Rosary," Leo XIII recommended. The Joyful Mysteries in particular bring home to people's minds object lessons of how easy, how abundant, and how sweetly attractive the honest life is—how much we have to learn, he said, from the daily life that was led within the walls of that humble house at Nazareth! He pointed to the life of the Holy Family as the perfect model of domestic life, in which we can see simplicity and purity of conduct, perfect agreement, and unbroken harmony, mutual respect, and mutual love that find their vitality and their charm in devotion to service. Here we can see honest and patient labor earning what is required for food and clothing in the sweat of the brow, a family content with little, seeking to diminish its desires rather than to increase the sources of its wealth.

Better than even that, he said, in the Joyful Mysteries we see that supreme peace of mind and gladness of soul that never fail to accompany the possession of a tranquil conscience. These five examples of goodness, modesty, humility, and hard-working endurance, expressed as they are in kindness to others and diligence in the small duties of daily life, gradually take root in the soul and in the course of time bring about a happy change of mind, and of conduct. Then, he concluded, work will become light and robed with joy; gentler manners will prevail, and home life will be loved and esteemed. And if this improvement goes out from the individual person to the family and to the community at large, it will lift human life to that same standard, and no one will fail to see the great and lasting improvement in society as a whole. In other words, devotion to the Rosary will cause virtues and good works to flourish.

The second great evil that Leo XIII saw on the horizon at the turn of the twentieth century was a repugnance for suffering; people seemed increasingly eager to escape anything difficult or painful to endure. This, he said, robs the greater number of people of the peace of mind that is the reward of those who do what is right despite the troubles that they will encounter along the way. Instead, they nurture unrealistic fantasies about a civilization in which everything unpleasant is removed and everything pleasant is supplied without effort. These expectations lead to lives of irresponsibility, spent in the unbridled pursuit of pleasure, and even those who don't succumb to them become demoralized and cowardly when faced with the hardships in this great battle that is life on Earth.

In this battle, he said, example is everything. And he pointed again to the Rosary, particularly to the Sorrowful Mysteries, as a powerful weapon that renews our courage. If from our earliest years we have trained our minds to meditation on the Sorrowful Mysteries of Our Lord's life, we shall learn how Christ began to do and to teach so that we might see in his example everything that we need to learn how to bear our own burdens of labor and sorrow. In meditation on these Mysteries we can grasp the fact that he embraced the most difficult sufferings with the greatest generosity and goodwill, even when he was overwhelmed with sadness, bound, flogged, and insulted, and nailed to a cross. And here, too, he said, we meditate on the grief of his Holy Mother, whose soul was pierced by the sword of sorrow—indeed, who became our "Mother of Sorrows" in fact as well as in title. Witnessing these examples of fortitude, not with bodily sight but in faith, who would not feel his heart inflamed with the desire of imitating them, he asked.

Then Leo added a reminder that a person who deserves to be called a Christian must not shrink from following in Christ's own footsteps, not in empty endurance of pain but in that patience through which he, "for the joy set before him, endured a cross, despising shame" (Hb 12:2). This is the patience obtained by grace; and that grace is well asked through meditative prayer on those Sorrowful Mysteries, which will obtain for souls the abundant mercy of God.

Ninety years after Leo XIII exhorted Christians to remember the meaning of suffering, John Paul II renewed that message in an encyclical of his own, *Salvifici doloris* (1984). He based this letter on a reminder that redemption itself was accomplished through the suffering of Christ, and salvation comes to each of us by that same path (Rm 5:15-21; 8:17). A person suffers whenever he experiences any kind of evil, which is a lack, a limitation, or a distortion of good, he explained. So, in the Christian view of things, evil always refers to some good, but the suffering caused by any evil inevitably raises the question *Why?*—a question that Mankind always raises to God as Job did, even though the suffering itself comes not from God but from this world.

Suffering does have a clear meaning when it's connected to a specific fault, which is why Job's friends tried to convince him that he must have done something terribly wrong to deserve that kind of suffering. But Job maintained his innocence; and in the end, John Paul explained, the Book of Job teaches that not all suffering is connected to a particular fault, and not all suffering has the character of punishment. Some suffering, like Job's, is in the nature of a test; some is intended to teach (2Mc 6:12; Pr 13:24; Hb 12:6). So suffering "creates the possibility of rebuilding goodness in the subject who suffers... [S]uffering must serve for conversion". Whether voluntary or not, suffering can be turned into penance, and "the purpose of penance is to overcome evil", the evil that causes the suffering in the first place.

The desire to overcome evil and heal the wounds that it inflicts can be directed to act outwardly as well as inwardly, as when it prompts works of mercy like those of the Good Samaritan (Lk 10:25-37). In this way, suffering not only refers to a definite good but causes good to come into being. "[S]uffering, which is present in so many different forms in our human world, also exists in order to unleash love in the human person," John Paul said. This love unleashed establishes the fundamental moral values of society, such as the value of human solidarity and of Christian love of neighbor, that combat hatred, violence, cruelty, contempt for others, or simple insensitivity. The suffering of others makes Christians put into practice all that they have learned about love from Christ himself.

So Christ, who in himself carries the fullest meaning to that question *Why?*, taught Man to do good by suffering and to do good to those who suffer. "In this double meaning," John Paul concluded, "he has completely revealed the meaning of suffering." And like Leo XIII and so many of his other predecessors, he suggested that devotion to Mary is the surest and easiest way to find valid answers to that age-old question. "Together with Mary, Mother of Christ, who stood beneath the Cross, we pause beside all of the crosses of contemporary Man," he wrote; and he tied his own letter to the apostolic constitution *Gaudium et Spes* of Vatican II, which reaffirms another concern that had afflicted Leo XIII: "in the past it was the exception to repudiate God and religion to the point of abandoning them, and then only in individual cases; but nowadays it seems to be a matter of course to reject them".

This is the third evil that Leo XIII foresaw strengthening and multiplying to destroy souls and fill nations with ruin: the rejection of God and religion, the "forgetfulness of future life". In addressing this crisis he opened whole horizons of prayer and beatitude that had perhaps already been lost to many people, and he touched on the whole purpose of prayer itself.

When he looked out across the world on the eve of the First World War, Leo XIII noticed a significant difference—in fact, an epochal difference—between his own time and ages past. In former days, even people who loved the things of Earth and loved them far too much didn't aggravate their sinful attachment to it with contempt for the things of Heaven. Even the right-thinking part of the pagan population regarded this world as a stage on the journey, not as a destination. But now, he said, even with the advantage of Christian education people pursue the false goods of this world as if nothing beyond them existed, and as if nothing that they did or failed to do here had any further consequence.

"We may doubt if God could inflict upon Man a more terrible punishment than to allow him to waste his whole life in the pursuit of earthly pleasures," Leo wrote, "and in forgetfulness of the only happiness that lasts forever." Meditation on the Glorious Mysteries of the Rosary, he said, sheds the clearest light on the good things that are hidden to sense but visible to faith, those lasting and unsurpassable goods that God has prepared for those who love him. This is how we can learn that death is not an annihilation but a passage to life; and this is how we can feel the consolation of the assurance that "our present light affliction, which is for the moment, prepares us for an everlasting weight of glory that is beyond all measure, while we look not at the things that are seen, but at the things that are not seen" (2Cr 4:17-18). That is, devotion to the Rosary will withdraw the hearts of Men from the love of the world and its vanities, and it will lift them to the desire of eternal things.

As Leo XIII predicted, this forgetfulness of the life that is to come has proved to be so persistent and so pervasive in modern society that the Congregation for the Doctrine of the Faith prepared a *Letter on Certain Questions Concerning Eschatology*—that is, the study of the End of Time—some ninety years after Leo sounded his warning (May 17, 1979). In so doing, they amplified the admonition that the pope had proclaimed about just how this situation needs to be addressed (*Testem benevolentiæ*, 1899).

The Congregation noted the Church's growing concern for integrating the Christian Faith into a wide variety of cultures around the world, and it remembered that the profound changes in so many of those cultures demand extreme attentiveness from those responsible for communicating the truths of the Faith. Teachers—which includes all of the laity, who must bear witness to the world—must be extremely sensitive to anything that might induce the Faithful to gradually devalue or extinguish any element in the Creed. All of the Church's doctrine is necessary if the Faith is to remain coherent, accurate, and fully connected with all of the Church's practices, they said.

The Congregation also saw some urgency in reminding the Church's professional teachers, lay and clerical alike, that many Christians today refrain from thinking about their destiny after death. Many theological controversies outside the Church may even make some Christians think that teachings about everlasting reward and punishment have been dropped entirely. Certainly some of the Faithful are asking themselves questions such as whether there really is anything after death, whether anything remains of us after we die, and whether only nothingness lies before us. More than that, when they ask they may not find any answers.

Yet the answers are simple, embodied in the most basic precepts of the Faith. "All who are commissioned to transmit these points must have a clear idea of them," the Congregation proclaimed; they must "be firm with regard to the essence of the doctrine". The tendency to ignore the nature and conditions of life after death tills fertile ground for heresy; people who aren't clear on the basic premises and perspectives of the Faith have, for all practical purposes, deleted those premises from their spiritual life. That can only be repaired with prayerful study and with prayer itself; but people who don't clearly understand what's at stake for them may not bother to pray at all, and if they do pray it's hard to see how they could pray well.

In its largest sense, the purpose of prayer is to glorify God; that's what the prayers of the angels are for, and those of the saints who stand before him. But the angels and saints don't need anything other than that immediate presence of God. For those of us here below, specifically, the whole point of prayer—any kind of prayer—is to make us better, so that we can attain that kind of closeness with God after death. It's a quest for increase in all of the virtues, including faith; it's a campaign to make everything that we do, our thoughts, words, and deeds, more agreeable to the will of God. That's how human prayer glorifies God: by drawing us nearer to him while we're here on Earth, and by working toward that ultimate and everlasting prayer of glorification when we have passed all of these tests and trials. So prayer requires a constant remembrance of future life, of everlasting life, which will be either inseparably with God or irreparably apart from him.

That quest for the immediate and everlasting presence of God radically reorganizes people's lives on Earth. If you are directed at that goal, and if you understand that your success in reaching depends on the way you conduct yourself here and now, obviously, your life is going to be vastly different from the lives of people who aren't aiming at any such goal, or who think that they can do as they please and get there anyway. A society made up largely of people who direct their lives purposefully to that goal will, therefore, be radically different from a society made up of people who have forgotten God, who have rejected the Covenant, or who ignore their responsibilities under its terms.

And when people forget God and the things of God, Dom Vital Lehodey wrote in his classic *The Paths of Mental Prayer*, the final destination of the voyage, the rocks to be avoided, and the virtues to be practiced along the way, are all clouded over; faith sleeps, hope is without desire, and charity is without fervor. This is why people are lost instead of saved; it's why lives are trapped in a tangle of disorders of career, marriage, parenting, and all the rest. "This," Dom Vital said, "this is why the Earth is laid desolate" (*cf.* Gn 6:12-13). Constant prayer is the mechanism of progressive conversion, which is the movement of the whole person toward the perfection necessary to attain everlasting life. Meditative prayer is the shortest route to perfection, St. Ignatius of Loyola and many other saints have affirmed; it's first and foremost among all of the medicines that heal the vices and the weapons that defend the virtues.

The habit of meditative prayer keeps the soul on course because, in a sense, meditative prayer is the process of replacing human thoughts with divine thoughts. As time goes on, that habit changes everyday patterns of thought and behavior for the better. "I voyaged on this tempestuous sea for almost twenty years," St. Teresa of Avila recalled in the book of her life, *El Libro de la Vida* (8); "I should say that it is one of the most painful lives, I think, that one can imagine [but] if the soul perseveres in prayer, in the midst of the sins, temptations, and failures of a thousand kinds that the Devil places in its path, in the end, I hold as certain, the Lord will draw it forth to the harbor of salvation".

Dom Vital suggests that people at the beginning of their spiritual lives should propose to themselves the healing of whichever vice afflicts them most—the governing of some particular passion, victory over some temptation, or the correction of some bad inclination. When that particular evil is corrected, perhaps after years of constant prayer, turn to the next, and so on. This is how meditative prayer, well practiced, purifies the soul. It strengthens the soul, of course, by drawing down the graces that strengthen the soul's union with God and its detachment from the temptations of this world. It's not easy, because it really does demand the conversion of one's whole life; but "we shouldn't mistake difficulty for impossibility," Dom Vital cautions. "When we manage to think about our work, our occupations, and a thousand temporal affairs, can it be possible that the only things we can't think about are the things of Heaven and our own eternal interests?"

THE SOUL WHO RECOMMENDS HIMSELF TO ME BY PRAYING THE ROSARY SHALL NOT PERISH. Of course, if souls could perish, life would be easy; but souls live forever, either in the ineffable bliss of Heaven or the unspeakable pain of Hell. "Perish" here can't be taken literally. It comes from the Latin *perire*, which literally means to pass away entirely, into nothingness. Figuratively, it means to be ruined, to be lost, which is why we refer to things like fresh produce as perishable: it won't vanish into nothingness, but it can be irredeemably lost if you don't take proper care of it. In that sense, the opposite of perishing is being preserved; and in the spiritual sense, the opposite of perishing is being saved.

So the promise has to do with preservation of the soul. That can only come from prayer; as St. Alphonsus of Liguori said it: "He who prays shall certainly be saved. He who does not pray shall certainly be damned" (*Way of Salvation*). It's a lot to say, but it pivots precisely on the very nature of prayer: prayer is the act of deliberately turning the soul, the heart, and the mind to God, which means that the soul, heart, and mind must turn away from sin. The more and the better you pray, the more and better you turn away from sin. That, logically, is how prayer preserves the soul.

Any form of prayer works toward preserving the soul: the sacraments—which are all prayers of the highest form—the liturgical prayers of the Mass that support and surround the Eucharist, and the individual prayers of each person alone, which can be vocal, meditative, contemplative, or all three. But meditative prayer is particularly powerful because it includes good resolutions that reshape the soul, and it obtains the graces needed to fulfill them. It is as odious to the Adversary as it is salutary to us, St. Nilus of Sinai wrote; the whole war that Satan wages against us has no other aim than to make us abandon meditative prayer.

As a form of meditative prayer, the Rosary has the additional strength of enlisting the help of Mary. St. Alphonsus of Liguori affirmed that it is impossible for a faithful client of Mary's to be lost. "To some this proposition might seem exaggerated at first glance, but," he said, "we must not understand it as referring to those who take advantage of the devotion so that they might sin more freely... It is to be understood of those clients who are faithful in honoring, and in recommending themselves to, the Mother of God; it is, as I say, morally impossible that these should be lost" (*Glories of Mary*). St. Anselm of Canterbury, the Scholastic Doctor, went even further, concluding that it's impossible for one who is not devoted to Mary to be saved, either (*On the Blessed Virgin*). Many other saints over the centuries—St. Bonaventure, St. John Chrysostom, St. Hilary, and St. Ignatius of Antioch in the first century—said exactly the same thing, and they said it more than once.

That's because Mary is indispensable to the plan of salvation that God implemented on Earth; she is the mother of Jesus of Nazareth, so, without her, there would be no Jesus of Nazareth. Repudiating Mary is repudiating Jesus, and with him the whole plan of salvation—which is why the heresies that repudiate Mary always substitute some fundamentally rearranged scheme of how people attain salvation. They have to. Without Mary, Christ's coming, teaching, suffering, and rising just couldn't have happened as they did.

For this reason, St. Alphonsus of Liguori pointed out, the Devil does everything that he can to help sinners lose devotion to Mary. "When Sara saw Isaac with Ishmael ... she wanted Abraham to drive away both Ishmael and his mother Agar: 'cast out this bondwoman and her son,' she said (Gn 21). She was not satisfied with turning the son out of the house; she insisted that the mother go as well, lest the son, coming to see his mother, would continue to visit the house... The Devil, too, is not satisfied with a soul's turning out Jesus Christ unless it also turns out his mother; otherwise, he fears, the mother will, by her intercession, bring back the Son" (*Glories of Mary*).

Staying with Christ through thick and thin is the persistence that he himself asked for, and devotion to Mary nurtures a special kind of persistence, the grace of final perseverance. That's the grace of being in a state of sanctifying grace at the time of death. The idea is that perseverance in grace and in the virtues, no matter how long it lasts, falls short if you give up before death; some "receive the word with joy, and the Devil immediately takes it away from them because they don't persevere", but "he who perseveres until the end, he shall be saved" (Mt 10:22; *cf.* Lk 18:1-8, 35-40).

The sacraments, of course, are the indispensable means of maintaining that devotion to God, and so are the many forms of prayer. In fact, the ability to persevere until the end isn't really within the power of the human will by itself, but the interesting thing is that it isn't even within the power of God alone. Everybody has the free-will choice of accepting the Covenant and living by it, or rejecting it; and, since God has established the terms of the Covenant, he will not save you if you don't want to be saved, or if you don't particularly care one way or the other (Rv 3:16-20). Having voluntarily structured the Covenant in terms that people can understand, and having voluntarily set its terms as a limit to his own infinite power, God cannot make the Covenant into a lie by rewarding those who reject it; and that means that people have to stay within its terms, too, as God does.

For that, people need perseverance. St. Augustine explained that perseverance itself was not given to Adam, but only the ability to persevere through his own free will; "but now, through Christ, people can receive not only the possibility of persevering but the virtue of perseverance itself" (*On Admonition and Grace* 11).

WHOEVER SHALL PRAY THE ROSARY DEVOUTLY, APPLYING HIMSELF TO THE CONSIDERATION OF THE SACRED MYSTERIES, SHALL NEVER BE CONQUERED BY MISFORTUNE. GOD WILL NOT CHASTISE HIM IN HIS JUSTICE; HE SHALL NOT DIE AN UNPROVIDED DEATH. IF HE BE JUST, HE SHALL REMAIN IN GOD'S GRACE AND BECOME WORTHY OF LIFE EVERLASTING. Notice that, like Christ himself, Mary is on record as saying that the truly faithful won't be conquered by misfortune: she doesn't say that they won't have any misfortunes. And she's speaking of spiritual misfortune, not promising that a set of rosary beads is some kind of lucky charm. Still, the habit of the Rosary is promised to serve as an armor against vice, and vice is the cause of all human unhappiness, so there's something of earthly benefits in this promise, too.

This promise also uses the phrase "worthy of life everlasting", which stands as a reminder of the importance of "works", of what you do, what you refuse to do, and what you omit to do, in your earthly life. It's not intended as an assertion that anybody can merit Heaven on his own; God does not have to save anybody, for any reason. But then God has made that grace conditional on careful adherence to his Covenant. He put it all in comprehensible, manageable terms suited to human nature and to the human condition, even coming as a man to teach that Covenant. That's why St. Augustine remarked that compared to his own faults God's punishment was inconsiderable, and it's why so many saints have claimed that the greatest sufferings on Earth are really only a token in comparison with the supreme happiness of Heaven.

Notice also that this promise says "if he be just"; the Rosary is not enough. It yields its benefits only in the context of a full sacramental life in the Church, and that life, in turn, is fertile ground only when those seeds fall on a converted heart. But, as the next promise indicates, the Rosary offers help in keeping people in that full sacramental life, too.

W HOEVER SHALL HAVE A TRUE DEVOTION TO THE ROSARY SHALL NOT DIE WITHOUT THE SACRAMENTS OF THE CHURCH. It's unlikely, of course, that anybody who habitually prays the Rosary would stray very far from the sacraments, in any event, but this promise speaks of an extraordinary grace. Things would have to happen in the right order here on Earth to ensure that a person would have access to the sacraments just before the moment of death.

The sacrament principally referred to here seems to be the Anointing of the Sick, because its administration *in extremis* is customarily referred to as "dying with the sacraments". This sacrament used to be called Extreme Unction specifically because it was given to those at the extremity of life, but before that it was referred to as the *sacramentum exeuntium*, the "sacrament of those who are exiting", for the same reason. Its modern name is really a restoration of ancient Christian practice (Mr 6:13; Jm 5:14-15), because the emphasis of the rite is on life and on healing, not on death, and for that matter on spiritual healing more than on the healing of the body.

The sacrament consists of anointing the body of the sick with blessed oil—pure olive oil in the Latin Rite, but elsewhere and in other times mixed with a little wine in memory of the parable of the Good Samaritan (Lk 10:34) or with a little water to recall Baptism. The priest prays certain prayers given in the *Rituale Romanum*, grants the recipient absolution and remission, and, if possible, combines this sacrament with the Eucharist. Thus freed from sin and the punishment that it merits, the person is ready to die and be taken straight to Heaven.

The following promise is similar, but it adds a reference to ways of obtaining grace other than the sacraments themselves.

T HOSE WHO ARE FAITHFUL TO PRAYING THE ROSARY SHALL HAVE, DURING THEIR LIVES AND AT THEIR DEATHS, THE LIGHT OF GOD AND THE FULLNESS OF HIS GRACES; AND AT THE MOMENT OF DEATH THEY SHALL PARTICIPATE

PROMISES

IN THE MERITS OF THE SAINTS IN PARADISE. This twofold promise first recalls the particularly elevated forms of actual grace that St. Paul, St. Augustine, and the other Apostles and Fathers of the Church spoke about and wrote about, the ones that come directly from the workings of the Holy Spirit in the soul to illuminate the intellect and the will. The most interesting part of it, though, is the mention of participation in the merits of the saints.

Merit is a person's entitlement to reward for a good act, an act of virtue (Gn 15:6). It's the complement of a person's entitlement to punishment for a bad act—for a sin, an act of vice. And just as a sin in itself deserves punishment, a good act in itself has merit, in the sense that it has some inherent property that makes it fit for reward. This idea of punishment for sin and reward for meritorious acts—the whole idea of divine justice—structures the relationship of God to Man, the Covenants that one offers and the other accepts, and, thereby, it structures both Scripture and Sacred Tradition. Most of the Old Testament is a record of the great graces that God gave to Israel as a reward for their fidelity to them, and much of the rest is a record of the punishments that he allotted to them as the wages of sin.

Of course, God chose Israel by grace; being as yet unborn when God called Abraham, they hadn't done anything at the beginning to earn all of those graces. Nobody could earn them—even Adam didn't earn the great gifts that God gave him, any more than he earned his existence or his life. God gave him those, in the literal sense, gratuitously (from the Latin root *gratia*, grace), and after the Fall he chose Israel gratuitously to be the nation through which salvation would come to all people. Yet all of the rewards and punishments that God gave Israel along the way resulted from their actions within the terms of the Covenant between God and Israel.

The same justice gives shape to the New Testament, too. Its main message is that the promised salvation has come, available for the whole world through Jesus Christ (Lk 2:10-11; Jn 1:12-13, 3:16; Hb; etc.), but available specifically to those who would yield the fruits of his kingdom: he promised people punishment for their sins (Mt 25:31-46), and he promised them rewards for their meritorious acts. He promised a reward to those who love their enemies (Mt 5:46) and forgive offenses (Mt 6:15), give alms (Mt 6:1-4, 10:42), persevere in persecution (Mt 5:11-12, 44), and, in general, who take on his discipline and follow him (Mt 11:29). So God's gifts are free, like the talents that were given to the servants (Lk 19:11-26), but using them willingly and well merits a reward; human effort can increase the good that those gifts do and the fruit that they produce. God takes human efforts into account in the Christian Covenant that he offers, and by the fruits of those efforts he knows those people who are his own. So human efforts to serve him have a value. Those acts are meritorious; they have merit, and they earn merit for those who do them. St. Paul summed it up in his letter to the Romans: "God will render to every one according to his works" (Rm 2:6; *cf.* Mt 25:31-46; 1Cr 3:8; 2Cr 5:10; 2Tm 4:8; Jm 2:26; Rv 22:12).

Because God has put Mankind in an order of things that's directed to a supernatural end—salvation—and since he has made salvation attainable through the redemptive work of Christ, it's perfectly understandable that his mercy continues to work in favor of people who willingly serve him in the Covenant. On the other hand sin, a deliberate act of rejecting that Covenant, deprives a person of entitlement to God's graces. But by embracing the gift of faith and building on it, turning from sin and putting yourself in a state of grace through the sacraments, you can become able to merit special graces for yourself, and, in fact, for others. That's why people in the Church can pray effectively for other people. Looking at it the other way around, you can see that people here on Earth can participate in the merits of those who have gone before us marked with the sign of faith.

Many of the blessed whose sanctity is known only to God must have earned more merit than they needed under the Covenant to attain their place before God. The canonized saints won their merits by constant hero-ic acts of virtue and in some cases through martyrdom itself; those rewards are known to be "superabundant", more than the saints really needed to attain Heaven. Certainly Mary's merits are greater than those of any other saint, and Christ's are greater than anybody can imagine; because he is God, his merits are enough to achieve salvation for everybody, if salvation were a free gift like redemption. Together, these merits are inexhaustible.

These superabundant merits are at the disposal of the Church because Christ gave the Church the authority to bind and loose on Earth and in Heaven (Mt 16:17-19), the power to decide when and how sin is forgiven and punishment is remitted (Jn 20:19-23). And the Church, as the Communion of Saints, is one spirit, one body; no particular member is an island, entire unto himself. That's how those merits constitute what's called the "Treasury of the Church" or the "Spiritual Treasury". Through the ministry of the Church, the superabundant merits of Christ, Mary, the other saints, and those good persons not known to us by name are applied, for some just and reasonable motive, to remission of the punishment that's due for sins that have been forgiven. That is, drawing upon those merits, the Church can grant an indulgence to her members—other members of the Body of Christ.

In this promise, Mary is affirming that her superabundant merits, and those of Christ himself over which she has control, will be applied on behalf of those who pray the Rosary persistently and well. In fact, the Rosary car-ries particular indulgences, and its part in applying the superabundant merits of Mary and all the saints is made somewhat clearer in terms of the following promise.

I SHALL DELIVER FROM PURGATORY THOSE WHO HAVE BEEN DEVOTED TO THE ROSARY. One of the primary purposes of the Rosary, and of all of its predecessors and all of the pious practices out of which it was ultimately formulated, is to make up for sin. These prayers are all meritorious acts; they earn merit for the person who does them properly, from the motive of charity and while in a state of grace. Those merits can be applied to any intention that you have for your prayers, and they can be supplemented by the indulgences that have been attached to the devotion.

An "indulgence" is not a license to sin, and it's not a way to get off the hook for sin entirely. There are three main factors to consider in the matter of indulgences: sin, forgiveness, and punishment. A sin is a violation of God's law, an offense against God, and a repudiation of his Covenant. Forgiveness is an act of God by which he removes guilt for sin; punishment is the consequence of sin, just as reward is the consequence of acts of merit.

Of course, God can forgive sins, and he can remit punishment; but forgiveness and remission are entirely different acts. Sin deserves punishment even after it's been forgiven (2Kn 12:13-14, for instance). It's the same as it would be in an earthly courtroom: at the trial of a person who robbed you or assaulted you, you could forgive the defendant from the depths of your heart, but his crime would still deserve punishment, and you would still deserve some kind of restitution. As the offended party, you would have to forgive the miscreant and then say that you didn't want any restitution or punishment, before the criminal would be entirely free. But the important point is that forgiving the offense and remitting the punishment are two different things. Christ gave his Church the power to do both, to grant absolution from sin and remission of the punishment, the *penance*, due in justice (Mt 16:17-19).

> It's important, here, to have the terms straight: "penance" comes from the Latin *pænitentia*, meaning sorrow or regret. "Repentance" comes from that same Latin root, and so does "penitentiary", a place to which people are sent to develop sorrow and reform their lives. "Penalty" looks like it might come from the same root, but it doesn't; it comes from *pœna*, meaning punishment, as in the phrase *sub pœna*, "under punishment", meaning that the court orders you to do something under the compulsion of punishment.

Absolution is generally given through the sacrament of Reconciliation, also called "penance" or "confession", but the Church, exercising her authority to bind and loose, has also assigned certain other acts for the absolution of minor sins, like the Confiteor said privately, the absolution given by the priest to the congregation just after this prayer is said at Mass, or the proper use of holy water, or certain other sacramentals, to name only a few.

But however absolution is attained, there's still the question of making satisfaction for the sin. That means punishment; but the punishment can be endured during life on Earth, instead of after death, again because the Church has the power to bind and loose. So, after the sins are forgiven in Reconciliation, the priest assigns some penance. Within certain universal guidelines, he himself can establish the penance that will suffice for the particular commission of the particular sins that you've confessed; he takes into account any mitigating circumstances, what you tell him about whether this sin is a chronic problem with you, and so on. The token penances like five Our Fathers or five Hail Marys that are sometimes assigned in this sacrament are accepted by the Church, and therefore by Christ, as sufficient reparation for your sins—their merit supplying the defect caused by your sin—and the slight discipline of obeying your confessor and of saying them properly is accepted as sufficient punishment.

Still, the penance can be quite severe, for a serious sin—people used to have to walk to the Holy Sepulchre in Jerusalem and back, for some sins, or stand in front of the Church every Sunday with a sign around the neck detailing the particular thing they'd done. Today, penance might include some additional reparation of whatever wrong you've done to somebody else, beyond the token penance. Or the priest may assign you some spiritual exercise that will help strengthen you against the temptation to commit that sin in the future. But whatever the penance, it suffices for the temporal punishment due to your sin. It's called *temporal* punishment (from the Latin *tempus*, time), because it's the kind that doesn't last forever.

That is, temporal punishment includes punishment in this life as well as the punishment of Purgatory (Mt 5:26, 12:32, 18:34-35; 1Cr 3:13-15). So to understand temporal punishment it's important to understand what Purgatory is, and what it's for. And to understand that purpose, it's important to understand something about the different kinds of sin. Sins severe enough to constitute a complete repudiation of God and his Covenant are *mortal*, meriting the condemnation of the soul to the everlasting torment of Hell; that's why mortal sins are to be avoided at all costs, even at the price of death, and why they need to be healed through the absolution and remission of Reconciliation as soon as possible, if you commit them despite your best efforts to avoid them. Minor sins, those that constitute only a minor turning away from God, are called *venial* sins; they aren't enough to consign you to Hell forever, but they do lead the way for mortal ones, and all by themselves they delay you on your journey to reunion with God. With the penalty of venial sins unpaid, you have to go through purification—*purgatio*, in Latin—before you can reach Heaven, because nothing impure is admitted to God's presence (Mt 5:8, Rv 21:27). Through the ministry of the Church (Mt 16:17-19), you can undertake this purifying temporal punishment here on Earth through penances properly assigned and willingly performed, or you can endure it in Purgatory after you die.

Accepting the punishment of penance here on Earth is generally reckoned as much easier. St. Paul, like Christ himself, compared the punishment of Purgatory to fire. Saints since Perpetua in the second century have reported insights and even visions of what that suffering of purgation is like, and their accounts make any earthly sacrifice seem trivial by comparison.

> St. Vincent Ferrer (1350-1419) saw his own sister in Purgatory, surrounded by flames, in unspeakable torment; St. Stanislaus Kostka (1550-1568) reported a vision in which a drop of sweat from a woman in Purgatory burned a hole through his hand. The vision of St. Antoninus, which came to him in 1285, is still used, unofficially, in any number of parochial grade schools to convey some idea of what it's like.
>
> A certain monk, St. Antoninus said, suffered so much from disease that he begged God for the favor of death. Instead, God gave him the favor of seeing his own guardian angel, who was allowed to offer him a choice: the monk could spend one more year on Earth, suffering as he now suffered, or he could take three days in Purgatory. The monk eagerly accepted the three days in Purgatory, upon which he died. But when his guardian angel visited him in Purgatory, the monk complained that the deal had been for three days there, and he felt that he must have been there for several years already. No, the angel told him; you've only been here about an hour.

So the Church, loosing on Earth what will be loosed in Heaven, assigns penances, mild or severe, to take the place of this indescribable torment, to free you from it. Or she can remit this temporal punishment, which she does most normally through an indulgence. In granting an indulgence, the bishop (mostly the Bishop of Rome, the Pope) does not offer his own personal merits in place of what God demands from the sinner; he acts in his sacramental capacity, as successor to the Apostles, drawing on the spiritual Treasury of the Church to apply the superabundant merits of the saints to this particular case. He has to apply these merits responsibly, so he has to keep in mind God's justice as well as his mercy, which is why no indulgence is automatic and none is free. You can only gain the benefit of an indulgence if you are in the state of grace (that is, if you've been absolved of all your sins), if you have the intention of gaining the indulgence (you can't get an indulgence unknowingly or accidentally), and if you perform the required acts properly and well, from the motive of charity—the love of God.

The Pope often assigns an indulgence to certain devotional acts and practices, like the Rosary. These concessions of grace naturally accumulate over the centuries. So, from time to time, the Apostolic Penitentiary (the office through which the Pope handles these matters) gathers together the lists of acts required to gain these standard indulgences. The Penitentiary publishes this information in a handbook, an *Enchiridion of Indulgences* (from the Greek ἐγχειρίδιον, handbook), that's revised and regularized every so often. The indulgences for practices that have fallen into disuse— or, like walking to Jerusalem, into impossibility—can be revoked or replaced with more feasible exercises available to all of the Faithful.

Like everything else in the discipline of the Church, the administration of indulgences underwent a thorough systematization and clarification after the Second Vatican Council. The apostolic constitution *Indulgentiarum doctrina* (January 1, 1967) promulgated by Paul VI Montini, in fact, is one of the best brief reviews of the workings of indulgences, as well as distinguishing their proper functioning from the abuses that have arisen in the past. Certainly, anybody who's thinking of taking up a devotional practice in reparation for his own sins or those of others ought to read it.

One of the puzzling aspects of indulgences that Paul VI clarified in this constitution was the old manner of measuring partial indulgences by the days or years that they equate. This practice dated from the Middle Ages, when certain penitential acts were said to carry three hundred days' indulgence or seven years' indulgence, or something of the kind. This was often misunderstood to mean that if you performed this act you would have that much time taken off your stay in Purgatory. This misunderstanding, in turn, led to a lot of derision about indulgences in general—how can anybody know how long you'll be in Purgatory for a certain sin, and who knows how time is measured in the afterlife? But those are the wrong questions, based in an error.

The time equivalencies listed in the old editions of the *Enchiridion* meant that the act—substantial but comparatively easy—would be accepted through the ministry of the Church as equivalent of that much time spent in the more severe penances that were customary in ages past. Now that those penances are no longer customary, that standard of measurement has become less meaningful, which is why it was so often misunderstood. So, as part of a continuing disciplinary development to make indulgences possible for everybody, regardless of physical strength and ability, Paul VI abolished that standard.

In any case, those equivalencies only pertained to partial indulgences. There are also *plenary* (Latin *plena*, full) indulgences, those that remit punishment for all sins forgiven. A plenary indulgence only puts you back at zero, so to speak, taking away the punishment due to your sins to date; it doesn't do anything like removing responsibility for sins in the future. There's no such thing, in Christianity, as an act that assures your salvation, period; you have to work constantly at your own continuing conversion, and you have to keep on making recompense for your sins, even after Reconciliation.

These plenary indulgences understandably demand more effort on the part of the penitent, including more time of spiritual preparation. So Paul VI was particularly careful to clarify and regularize them, and to make them available to more of the Faithful. He reduced the number of plenary indulgences available. He also abolished a great number of "real" (Latin *res*, a thing) and "local" (Latin *locus*, a place) indulgences, to emphasize the fact that the indulgence is attached to what you do, not what you do it with or where you do it.

As to the Rosary, the current *Enchiridion of Indulgences* assigns it a plenary indulgence if it is recited in a church or public oratory, or in a family group, a religious community, or a pious association; a partial indulgence is granted in other circumstances. The *Enchiridion* quotes the definition in the Roman Breviary, which says that the Rosary is a certain formula of prayer consisting of fifteen decades of Hail Marys with an Our Father before each decade, and in which the recitation of each decade is accompanied by pious meditation on a particular mystery of our Redemption. It also notes that the name "Rosary" is also commonly used to refer to only one-third of the whole formula, five decades said in sequence, and it allows that this suffices for this plenary indulgence.

> The new *Catechism of the Catholic Church* (§ 1032; *cf.* 2Mc 12:44-46) reminds us that any meritorious act contributes to the Treasury of the Church; and because you can apply the grace and merit of any worthy act of charity to any proper intention, you can say the Rosary to gain the indulgence on behalf of the souls in Purgatory; your prayers may be enough to free some of them from their torment and open the gates of Heaven.

T HE FAITHFUL CHILDREN OF THE ROSARY SHALL MERIT A HIGH DEGREE OF GLORY IN HEAVEN. It may seem that Heaven is an absolute state of being; after all, it's Heaven or Hell, ultimately, with no middle ground—Purgatory is only a state of transition. But Christians have always understood that not everybody in Heaven stands on an equal footing. Angels have their varying ranks among them (Tb 12:15; Ez 1), and Mary, of course, outranks all other saints, canonized or not, but even within the ranks of the saints there are levels and distinctions.

The general idea of rank in Heaven—and in Hell, for that matter—pivots on divine justice. A judgement can't be just, St. Thomas Aquinas reasoned (*Summa, Suppl.* 87) unless it's based on relative merits and demerits. For God's justice to work in each individual judgement, each person has to know his own sins and merits, because it would hardly be fair to reward or condemn a person for things he doesn't know about. So when we face judgement "a kind of divine energy will come to our aid, so that we shall recall all of our sins to mind," St. Augustine said (*City of God* 20).

And for God's justice to shine forth in his judgement, everybody has to see plainly everybody else's merits and demerits, too. "For all of us must be made manifest before the tribunal of Christ," St. Paul explained, "so that each one may receive what he has earned by means of his body, according to his works, whether good or evil" (2Cr 5:10; *cf.* Mt 25:31-46; Rv 22:12; Jm 2:26). So at the Last Judgement, everybody will know his own sins and his own good works, as well as everybody else's, and they will be seen with wondrous speed—instantaneously, St. Augustine thought. That incidentally gives you some hint of how great the angels' knowledge must be, and how great Adam and Eve's was before they had that gift taken away by sin.

But the important point is that nothing bad is allowed in Heaven (Mt 5:8; Rv 21:27), but once you're admitted there you might very well deserve greater reward because you've run a better race than certain other people; everybody's history is different (Mt 11:11, 19:30, 20:20-28; 1Cr 15:41-42; Rv 4:4). On the other hand, if divine justice condemns you to Hell, that same divine justice won't allow the penalty to exceed the offense; so just as not everybody commits exactly the same sins, not everybody gets exactly the same punishment. It's all unspeakable torment, of course, and the joy of Heaven is indescribable no matter where you stand, but there are differences in rank within those final dispositions of the soul.

YOU SHALL OBTAIN ALL THAT YOU ASK OF ME THROUGH PRAYING THE ROSARY. Christians know that everything comes to us from Almighty God. "We know, though" Pius XI Ratti wrote (*Ingravescentibus malis*), "that everything comes to us from Almighty God through the hands of Our Lady." That has always been the teaching of the Church, and it's why Mary has the title "Mediatrix of All Graces". Scripture—the Gospels especially—shows explicitly that Mary has unparalleled powers of intercession, but this title reflects a fact beyond this that's implicit in the Bible. Christ is the source of all graces; Mary is the source of Christ on

Earth; therefore, Mary is the channel through whom all of Christ's graces come to us.

Any grace granted in response to prayer comes to the recipient through the mediation of Mary, whether the intercession is asked or not, because she brought Christ, and redemption, to Mankind. "From the moment that the Virgin Mother conceived the Divine Word in her womb," St. Bernadine of Siena explained in a sermon, "she obtained a kind of jurisdiction over the temporal manifestations of the Holy Spirit, so to speak, so that no creature can obtain any grace from God that is not dispensed by his tender and compassionate mother".

Mary stands always between Mankind and her son in the reality of their wants, their needs, and their sufferings, John Paul II explained (*Redemptoris mater*); she acts as a mediatrix, not as an outsider. "She knows that she can point out to her son the needs of Mankind, and in fact she has the right to do so… And that is not all. As a mother she also wishes the messianic power of her son to be manifested… And this maternity of Mary in the order of grace … will last without interruption until the eternal fulfillment of all the elect", he concluded, quoting the apostolic constitution *Lumen gentium* of Vatican II.

ALL WHO PROPAGATE THE HOLY ROSARY SHALL BE AIDED BY ME IN THEIR NECESSITIES. The promise naturally refers to spiritual necessities, but it seems to intimate also that those devoted to the Rosary will have what they need of earthly goods that work to their salvation or to the salvation of others. Earthly things are necessary to one's own spiritual life, to the fulfillment of duties, and to the pursuit of his vocation.

Jacob and Solomon asked for the necessities of life (Gn 28:20-22; Pr 30:8), and Christ told his followers to do so every day (Mt 6:11). St. Paul even prayed for deliverance from the enemies who sought to kill him (Rm 15:30), which was what he needed at the time. The criterion for making this kind of prayer is the purpose; we don't ask these temporal blessings as our goods, St. Augustine said, but as our necessities (*On the Sermon on the Mount* 3:16). That is, we're not supposed to ask for earthly things as ends in themselves, but only because we need them to do our work here below, to meet the obligations that we have to other humans, and to do whatever higher work God calls us to, the work of our vocation.

In any case, the Christian call to asceticism is a call to turn away from idolatry of material goods and from luxuries, not from necessities. Still, it's probably important to measure God's providence against an accurate estimation of just how slight our necessities really are—Christ himself got shelter when he needed it at his birth (Lk 2:7), but it was not a shelter that most people would choose. St. John the Baptizer got sustenance when he set forth to preach the Kingdom (Mt 3:4; *cf.* Ex 16:31), but it was not food that many people would eat by preference. On the other hand, these austere necessities were sweetened by occasional treats like gifts of frankincense or wild honey.

I HAVE OBTAINED FROM MY DIVINE SON THAT ALL ADVOCATES OF THE ROSARY SHALL HAVE THE ENTIRE CELESTIAL COURT FOR INTERCESSORS DURING THEIR LIVES AND AT THE HOUR OF DEATH. Devotion to Mary leads to friendship with God, but also to friendship with all of the other saints. That's because people are holy insofar as their hearts and wills are consonant with God's will.

But notice that Mary claimed to have secured this as a special grace. In general, the intercession of the saints is an integral part of the plan that God established for the salvation of everybody, and their merits do contribute to the Treasury of the Church as God wills them to. All of the saints are understood to pray incessantly for the salvation of everyone here below, too (Jr 15:1; 2Mc 15:14; Rv 5:8, 8:3). But the particular intercession of any particular angel, or of any saint other than Mary is not, strictly speaking, necessary for your salvation; not all angels and saints work specifically for the salvation of any individual person. They will help you individually if you ask (Tb 12:12; Eph 6:18-19), though; and Mary is saying here that asking her aid through the meditative prayer of the Rosary is asking the aid of all of the saints, canonized or unknown, and of all of the angels, in response to Christ's command issued at her request.

A LL WHO PRAY THE ROSARY ARE MY CHILDREN, BRETHREN OF MY ONLY SON, JESUS CHRIST. It's hardly possible to meditate regularly on Christ's coming, suffering, and triumph without drawing closer to him. But this promise centers on the ways in which the habit of meditative prayer changes a person and the ways in which a person acts. It seems to echo Mt 12:47-50 and Jn 19:26-27, both of which refer to Mary's universal motherhood—"Whoever does the will of my Father in Heaven, he is my brother, and my sister, and my mother." This is the middle term of the promise: those who are devoted to the meditative prayer of the Rosary will do the will of God, and those who do the will of God are Christ's brothers and sisters, children of his mother. That makes sense, because that's exactly what meditative prayer is supposed to do for you: connect you with the graces that you need to fulfill your part of the Covenant.

But this promise also implies that it's possible to see the results of these graces in a person's life, and that leads to the implications of the next promise, which are somewhat more complex.

PROMISES

DEVOTION TO MY ROSARY IS A GREAT SIGN OF PREDESTINATION. Like many theological terms, "predestination" is defined one way by Christianity and other ways by heresy. The definition derived from Calvinism and related heresies is that God predestines people by creating some people saved and other people damned; but that's not accurate. Christ said explicitly that he came to save all nations (Mt 24:14, 28:19; *cf.* Lk 2:10-11; Jn 3:16-17; Rm 5:18; 2Cr 5:14-15; 1Tm 2:3-6, 4:10; Hb 2:9; 1Jn 2:1-2), and that he draws all people to himself (Jn 12:32); it's up to each person individually to respond to that attraction by moving toward him, of your own free will, or moving away from him—draw near to God, and he will draw near to you, as St. James put it (4:8). Sin, the movement away from him, is always a matter of free human choice, as it has been since Eve. And of course what you do—your "works"—has just as much to do with your ultimate salvation as what you believe—your faith.

Still, Bl. Alan de Rupe recorded this promise quoting Mary as using the term herself, and it's entirely possible that she would. Predestination as the Church has always understood it is, admittedly, complicated, but basically the word means what St. Paul said it does (Eph 1:11): it's the purpose of God, who works out all things according to the counsel of his will. Or, as St. Augustine put it, predestination is the way that God disposes within himself all that he intends to accomplish (*On Perseverance* 17:41). So, in terms of human salvation, predestination is the ordination of God—the way he puts things in order—by which certain people are led to the attainment of salvation. This presupposes two factors.

First, predestination correctly understood means that God knows infallibly which people will end up with him and which won't. So it's crucial to understand the *destination* part of it as meaning exactly that: destination, not destiny. It refers to where you're going; it neither says nor implies that you have no choice in the matter, nor does it say or imply that your acts won't make any difference in whether you get there or not.

God's foreknowledge of where you will end up also means that he knows the precise means by which you will attain that fate. He knows all of this because God, by definition, knows all things, and it doesn't matter whether they've happened yet or not.

Why, then, does he create some people knowing that they'll end up in Hell? Isn't that the same as creating them damned? No. People are by nature good (Gn 1:31; Ps 8:5; Hb 2:6); God does not create some people with one nature and others with another, because that would mean that there were two different species, two different kinds, of human being on Earth, and there's only one (the idea that there are two, one kind of person created saved and born booted and spurred to rule the others, created saddled and damned, is Calvinist heresy, which obviously caught on because it appealed to the rich). And God wants all people to be saved (1Tm 2:4), so he's not going to design you in such a way that this is impossible.

But although God made you, as Francisco de Osuna puts it, "your own free will has formed you" (*Third Alphabet Book*). So even though God knows what decision each of us will make, he doesn't force us to it, and we're free to change our minds. And he established the Church—not just the hierarchy and the clergy but every member of the laity, too—duty-bound to make every effort in persuading you to choose life.

That brings up the second factor in God's foreknowledge of your destination, the act of will on his part by which he decrees that these people will be saved in exactly the way that he has planned for them. But, again, he won't force a decision on you. His providing—his providence—means that no matter who you are, and even if God knows that you will ultimately be lost to him, he still creates you with everything that you need to attain salvation. The whole tragedy of damnation is that you could have made it. Because of the configuration that he gave your distinct personality, and because of the particular set of gifts that he gave you, he may need to press you rather firmly toward the right decision, or you may require comparatively little urging to choose the right path and stay on it. But everybody can do it.

God has left most of the immense responsibility for this pressing and urging to his Church; he entrusted the terms of his Covenant and its maintenance to his Church, and Christians are in business to reach out to everybody, and to bring them into the fold, persuading them by teaching, preaching, discussing, and above all by setting a good example (Jn 13:35). So while he knows that his people will not succeed in reaching everybody, he does not ordinarily interfere to bypass the Church that he established as the channel through which the teachings of his Son—and his Son himself, in the Eucharist—are brought from Heaven to humans here on Earth.

On the other hand, the terrible responsibility of reaching everybody in time is what spurs the Church's great missionary activity, domestic and foreign. To a large extent, if one lamb is lost, all of the sheep have failed to keep him with the flock. As more and more people succumb to the attractions of wandering off into the wilderness, the more energetically those in the fold have to call after them. And the general decline in morals and religion in the industrialized world today only intensifies the Church's concern for the safety and well-being of all people, which is why the popes speak with such increasing urgency about these matters these days.

So, St. Augustine explained, predestination is God's "foreknowledge and preparation of his gifts by which those who are delivered are most certainly delivered" (*On Perseverance* 14:35). And while the Church can confidently say that certain departed persons—the saints—are with God, she has never in her long history said that any particular person is in Hell, and she never will. That would violate the cardinal virtue of hope, it would testify to lack of faith in God's mercy and in the efficacy of the prayers of others, and it would cry out against Scripture as well as against Tradition (Mt 7:1-3).

But there are certain symptoms that indicate disorder in a person's spirit, signs that indicate that help is needed, and there are certain signs that a human being is living in close friendship with God, which indicate that the chances are good that the person will end up with God after death. There's no guarantee, and the friendship has to be maintained day by day, moment by moment; just as a disordered life might be retrieved by final repentance, a life in intimacy with God may be lost through final sin.

On the other hand, there are signs that the Covenant is working. One of these great signs is devotion to Mary. As you grow in holiness, as you adjust your own will to accord with the will of God, your will comes closer and closer to perfect accord with the will of Mary, too. And because Mary participates fully in the radiance of divine love that comes from God—because she is the channel through which that love came to us—a person striving to participate ever more intensely in that love comes to love Mary more and more as time goes on. A genuine love of Mary is an unmistakable visible sign of a genuine love of God, and no one can be saved without a genuine love of God. There has never been a saint who didn't love Mary; there has never been a heretic who didn't revile her.

E VA ❀ AV E

THE SKILL OF VOCAL PRAYER

CHRISTIAN PRAYER IS COMMUNICATION between a human soul and God. Therefore, it consists of two complementary halves. There's *active* prayer, in which the human is making the effort, and there's *passive* prayer, in which God reaches out to a human. Passive prayer is a mystic phenomenon, an event over which human beings have no control, because it's an action on the part of God. But God did promise to answer active prayer, and everybody can practice active prayer—in fact, everybody assuming the name of Christian must pray actively (Mt 26:41; Mr 13:33; Lk 18:1; 1Th 5:17).

Active prayer, in St. John Damascene's classic definition, is the elevation of the human mind and heart to God (Πηγὴ γνώσεως, *De fide orthodoxa*, 3:24) and to divine things. Now, your mind and heart work all of the time, and their workings determine the quality of your life. The attitudes of your mind and the habits of your heart, your desires and the ways you decide to handle them, shape your relationships with the people all around you, and they determine your personality. Human beings are the only beings in Creation, except the angels, that can control the workings of mind and heart; and in fact your interior dispositions are largely of your own making.

When you are alone with yourself, when you have time to reflect about your life, you begin to carry on a kind of conversation with yourself. The young think about the present, the mature think about the future; the old about the past, and everybody thinks about himself. But people carry on this interior conversation in two different ways. People who converse with themselves selfishly see no farther than what they want and how to get it—

pleasures of the senses, material goods, revenge, and all of the other appetites common to Man and to animal. The person whose interior conversation remains at this Earth-bound level, talking to himself only about himself, doesn't look to the higher part of his human nature, the part that's common to Man and to angel.

So his thoughts never move out of himself; those desires and appetites that he nurtures within the narrow confines of his own interest rankle and fester within him. He may invent all kinds of plot to attain those desires, and he may succeed at them; he may become wealthy, honored, and accomplished. But instead of rising toward his higher self, he can only fall back to the lower part of himself, the part that he has made the center of his universe. This is progress in the wrong direction, and it can't end well. Because a person who thinks this way desires only the inferior part of life, he can only end by hating life—if he doesn't get everything that he wants, he sinks into hopelessness, anger, and frustration; and yet if he does get everything that he wants, everything that he has is inferior.

This is unhappiness; and it grows directly from the disordered self-love that fails to look to the higher part—the greater part—of human nature. "Because the wicked do not know themselves rightly, they do not love themselves rightly," St. Thomas Aquinas explained (*Summa* 2:2:25:7). "They love what they think themselves to be... [T]hey have no wish to be preserved in the integrity of their interior selves, nor do they desire spiritual goods for that interior self; they do not take pleasure in their own company by entering into their own hearts, because whatever they find there—past, present, or future—is evil and horrifying; nor are they agreeable even to themselves, because of the gnawings of their consciences". Or, as Reginald Garrigou-Lagrange, O.P., said it more succinctly, "if life is not on the level of thought, thought descends to the level of life" (*The Three Ages of Interior Life* 1:2).

But on the other hand a person can elevate that interior conversation with himself by making it serve as a kind of mirror in which he sees himself clearly, warts and all, but goodness, too, because human beings are by nature good (Gn 1:31; Ps 8:5; Hb 2:6). A person who looks for the real goodness in himself, and who seeks to strengthen and purify that goodness by healing the vices that wound it, is going to start using that interior reflection to look outside of himself. He will eventually feel his own weakness and inadequacies, and he will understand the need of opening himself up to put his confidence not just in himself, but in God too. That is, a person who looks to the goodness in himself will eventually look to the higher good of the Eternal God. He will occasionally see things in the light of a brief spark of faith. He will start to pray.

A person who prays begins to love himself properly, as a friend loves a friend. "Every friend wants his friend to live," St. Thomas Aquinas continued; "he desires good things for his friend, he does good things for him, he takes pleasure in his friend's company; he is of one mind with his friend… The good love themselves in this way". Such people take pleasure in entering quietly into their own hearts, he says, because they remember past good, recognize the good of the present, and hope for good in the future.

They strive to heal the vices of the soul and to avoid sin, because sin pushes them away from the greatest and highest good that is God; they strive to attain and maintain the state of grace and charity, which is the love of God and of all creation for the sake of God. Such people struggle constantly against sin and the bonds that tie him to sin, but they are at peace because the whole soul aims at one goal, a goal that stands outside of themselves, and higher than his Earth-bound life: ultimate reunion with the ultimate good, God himself (Rm 7:21-23; 2Cr 4:16-18; Eph 3:14-19; 1Cr 13:4-13).

So the way in which you manage the workings of your mind and heart determines your happiness, and the effort to turn those workings toward the good tends to bring you to active prayer, the human effort to elevate mind and heart to God. Life tends to fall into order when people start making this effort because the human soul is not a last and final end in itself, and it is certainly not self-sufficient, any more than the worldly things around us are last and final ends and self-sufficient. The last end of the human soul is the ever-living God; God made us not just to show forth his goodness, but to know, love, and serve him.

That is what prompted St. Augustine to complain to his Maker, "our hearts are restless until they rest in you" (*Confessions* 1:1). Once you face that primal need in your soul, it calls you more and more insistently; the more you pray, the more you want to pray. Some great souls find that call virtually irresistible, which is why so many saints have to forcefully restrain themselves from slipping off into recollection when duties call; and even then they could not bear to be separated from God. They offer those dutiful efforts to him, as the active prayer of work.

No matter what form it takes, active prayer is the application of the heart and mind to God in adoration and praise, in begging pardon for sins, in giving thanks for gifts and graces received, or in asking God for suitable gifts and graces in the first place. Of course, it also includes raising the mind and heart to God not just to gain these things but to make use of them in union with God. We have to pray, but not because God doesn't know what we need (Mt 6:8); we pray to give our needs definite form and to concentrate our whole attention on whatever it is that we want to communicate to God.

THE SKILL OF VOCAL PRAYER

Christians have always seen a hierarchy in the forms of active prayer, beginning with the most basic, and the easiest, which is vocal prayer. It's called that from the Latin *vox*, voice, or more directly from *voco*, meaning "I call", the same root as the word "vocation", which is God's call to you. Vocal prayer is how you call back to God, or call out to him. Much of the Church's prayer is vocal; alone or as part of a congregation, you simply talk to God. Or you talk to saints and angels, asking them to talk to God on your behalf, or you say the standard prayers written by Jesus or those written by devout Christians and approved by his Church. Vocal prayer can be *exterior*, when you articulate the words with the voice and lips (which is why this is sometimes called the "prayer of the lips", which is part of the "prayer of the body", along with other physical movement like genuflection, bowing, or making the Sign of the Cross); or it can be *interior*, in which you speak to God with your heart and mind but don't pronounce any words that another human being could hear.

In itself, repeating the vocal prayers is a good and holy thing to do, if they have full attention and devotion—how can you expect God to listen to you, St. Cyprian asked, if you're not even listening to yourself? But it's meditating on the Mysteries of the Rosary that bears the best and greatest fruit. Through this meditation, Leo XIII explained, "Christ stands forth clearly in the Rosary. We behold in meditation his life, whether his hidden life in joy, his public life in excessive toil and sufferings unto death, or his glorious life from his triumphant resurrection to his eternal enthronement at the right hand of the Father... In this way, the sublime mysteries of the Faith may be more deeply impressed in the minds of Mankind, with the happy result that we may imitate what they contain and obtain what they promise" (*Fidentem piumque animum*).

Anybody can practice both vocal and meditative prayer, but both forms of prayer are really skills. "Prayer cannot be reduced to the spontaneous outpouring of interior impulse," the *Catechism* of Vatican II points out; "it takes effort" (§§ 2650 *ff.*), as even the most spontaneous act requires a decisive effort, however slight. And because prayer is a deliberate act, you can learn how to do it, and you can learn how to do it better. It also means that there are right ways to pray, and wrong ways, which is why the Apostles themselves asked Christ to teach them how to pray (Lk 11:1). That's also why there are so many good books about the skills of prayer that help the soul climb up to God, like the sixth-century *Ladder of Divine Ascent* by St. John Climacus or the *Ladder of Meditation* that Johann Wessel Gansfort wrote in about 1450. In fact, there are thousands of approved books on prayer, but they're all remarkably consistent. You can hardly tell, from what they say and the way they say it, whether these books were written in the fifth century or the fifteenth, the first or the last. That's because the skills of Christian prayer, and the techniques that Christians use to acquire them, haven't changed since the beginning.

The general rule in preparing to pray is *sancta sancte*: do holy things in a holy manner. The first step is to assume a suitable posture that will help you pray better (Mr 14:35; Lk 22:41; Jn 17:1). Most kneel, but others sit, or stand. Some people prostrate themselves—prostration used to be very popular, in the late Roman Empire, and it persists in some of the Orders. A few people still maintain more difficult postures that also have a long history behind them, standing or kneeling with their arms outstretched like Christ on the Cross, or with their hands raised up like Moses at the battle with the Amalekites (Ex 17:11). Some, like Louis the Saint, genuflect repeatedly during prayer, and others walk back and forth as they pray; but staying still is generally preferred.

"The effort of bodily prayer can be of help to those who have not yet been granted real prayer of the heart," St. John Climacus wrote, "but this is not always possible when other people are present"—the idea being that your posture is not supposed to provoke admiration in others, or embarrassment. In private prayer, in your own room alone or in the bosom of your family, you're free to assume whatever respectful posture reflects your inward sentiment. If you pray in a public place other than a church, nobody should know that you're praying (Mt 6:5-6). In liturgical prayer, stand when the congregation stands, kneel when they kneel; when in Rome, do as the Romans do, as St. Ambrose put it. But however you dispose your body suitably for prayer, vocal prayer itself happens in the mind and in the heart, as well as in the voice.

The skills of vocal prayer are basic: say the words, and remember what the words mean, to whom you are speaking, and why. When you pray the vocal prayers established by Christ and his Church, Walter Hilton wrote in his *Ladder of Perfection*, "stir your affections and collect your thoughts so that you may pray them with greater care and devotion... [P]ut away all burdens, and by God's grace you will transform this duty into a delight, this obligation into freedom... This form of prayer is more helpful than any other spiritual exercise to a person at the beginning of his spiritual life."

The process of putting away all burdens, or of detaching yourself from the cares of the world and going into that private interior room that Christ talked about (Mt 6:6), is usually called becoming *recollected*—the terms used by various teachers almost always differ, so when you read about these things be sure that you define them as they do. Using "recollection" in its usual sense as the gathering together of your self before God, three things are necessary, St. Alphonsus of Liguori said: solitude, silence, and the recollection—

the remembrance—of the presence of God.

Christ himself gave the example of seeking solitude for prayer (Mt 14:23), because God does not speak in those places where time is squandered in loud laughter and idle talk, St. Alphonsus said. On the contrary, he quoted the prophet Osee (2:16): I will lead her into the desert, and speak to her heart. "This is the reason that the great saints felt an irresistible yearning to leave the noise and bustle of this world and retire into solitude," St. Alphonsus explains; "this is why the mountains and the forests and the caves were ineffably dear to them."

There aren't many caves available for prayer, these days, but there are churches everywhere; even in major cities there's usually an oratory in the business district. There's no better place for prayer than before the Blessed Sacrament, after all. And it may be easiest and most convenient to go there for the time that you set aside every day for prayer, St. François de Sales advised in his introduction to the devout life; no one, father or mother, husband or wife, can very well object to your spending an hour in church (*Introduction à la vie dévote*, 1609). More important than the place, though, is the time itself; be sure to set aside some special time, St. François said, maybe before dinner or early in the morning when your mind is less distracted, and fresher after a night's rest.

Going to a quiet and private place is probably necessary at the beginning, so that you can learn how to detach yourself from the things and movements around you. But basically the solitude is a matter of the spirit, and of the mind. You can't expect to go immediately from absorption in the duties of family and career to absorption in God, from the busyness of daily life to the business of prayer. You have to settle down, first, and empty your mind and heart of all of the clutter of daily life. That's not to say that you suspend reason or thought: quite the contrary. It's just that, as Francisco de Osuna put it, when a prince is to move into a house, the owner takes out all of the furnishings and cleans the empty house thoroughly. The prince will bring with him everything that he needs to make that house a suitable dwelling. And he'll bring better furnishings than were there before. So your mind and heart are still your own, and still built as they were built before, but they're uncluttered and clean.

Whichever way you develop the skill of detachment, once you've found that solitude you still have to focus your whole attention on God, to achieve that silence of the mind and heart that precedes prayer. This is not easy; the human mind naturally takes any quiet time as an opportunity to think about all kinds of things that it brought along with it. Nobody's immune to this; in fact, it seems from the records that the greater a person's desire to pray well, the greater the ferocity of the distractions that keep him from it.

THE SKILL OF VOCAL PRAYER

Brother Lawrence of the Resurrection, who eventually became a notably gifted mystic, "at the beginning of his conversion often passed the whole time of prayer rejecting distractions and falling into them again," his superior, M. l'abbé Joseph de Beaufort, recalled; and virtually every great saint who wrote about prayer said the same thing.

But distractions are not your fault unless they make you give up praying. The will to pray can only be suspended by a distraction that you freely consent to, without sufficient effort to reject it. The effort to reject distractions will usually work, but there are times when it won't. The idea is to push ahead anyway—do what you would do it you were walking down the street and the wind blows a cloud of dust into your eyes, Francisco de Osuna advised: close your eyes and keep going anyway. Unfortunately there doesn't seem to be any trick that makes it easier to fight distractions, and no definite technique that automatically excludes them. It takes willpower, and it takes discipline.

When you think about it, everybody has that discipline at least to some elementary degree. The ability to reject distractions and put aside personal preferences is what keeps the adult at work and the student at the desk. It's basically a matter of foregoing a lesser, and a less lasting, pleasure in favor of a greater and more durable good; it's an everyday reflection of setting aside worldly concerns for the sake of God. But even if the love of God is great and growing, even if a person may know intellectually that prayer is more important than any earthly concern, earthly concerns still call, and the love of earthly things still clamors for attention.

Two bits of advice appear in virtually every book of prayer from patristic times to the present: abstinence and persistence. Abstinence means voluntarily giving up perfectly legitimate pleasures like favorite foods or entertainment. The self-imposed discipline of abstinence is the only way to gain control of your appetites, and appetites impair your ability to pray in two main ways. For one thing, the appetites for forbidden things are the cause of sin. Abstinence helps you develop resistance to sin by exercising your ability to set aside tempting things little by little, starting with those treats that you have under your control already, the permissible ones. Eventually, you gain control over all of your appetites, and you gain the strength to refuse sin.

Increasing your ability to turn from sin increases the efficacy of your prayers, of course, but it also brings along with it the second benefit of abstinence, the ability to reject distractions during prayer. Appetites are what distract you from prayer—you'd rather indulge in something else that presents itself to your consideration—and abstinence puts those attractions in their place. A fasting man prays austerely, St. John Climacus noticed, but the mind of the intemperate is filled with unclean fantasies. "Fasting ends lust, uproots bad thoughts, and frees a person from evil dreams," he wrote: "Fasting makes for purity of prayer."

This is why the Church mandates acts of fasting and abstinence during Lent, but the fight doesn't stop according to the calendar. "One of the things that the spiritual combat requires is perseverance in the mortification of our unruly passions," Dom Lorenzo Scupoli wrote in the sixteenth century, "for in this life they are never utterly conquered; they take root in the human heart like weeds in fertile soil. This is a battle that we cannot escape; this is an enemy whom we cannot evade. The fight against the passions will last a lifetime" (*The Spiritual Combat*).

That, in turn, is why persistence in prayer is so important. Some people have compared the process of prayer to the idea of getting across to the other side of a swamp. Nobody would toss a pebble into a swamp and then give up because a single pebble is not a causeway. You have to toss thousands, maybe millions of carefully aimed pebbles into that swamp before even one shows above the surface; and then thousands more before they add up to a way to walk safe and dry across that swamp (Ps 9B, 12, 21, 39, 76, 101). And even if "you are occupied during your whole meditation fighting off distractions and temptations," St. François de Sales said, "you will have made a good meditation. The Lord looks at the good intention that we have, and at the effort that we make, and these he rewards."

The skill of remembrance of the presence of God can extend to fill a person's whole days and nights, lasting through work and recreation as well as the time set aside for prayer. Some people receive a similar mystic gift, which is called "continued awareness of the presence of God", without exerting much effort, but constant mindfulness of God is a habit that can be developed, and having that habit makes recollection a lot easier. Brother Lawrence of the Resurrection developed the "practice of the presence of God" into a whole devotional technique in its own right, which he practiced in conjunction with the Rosary. The books and letters that record his thoughts on the subject are among the most valuable manuals of working toward that skill, which is really part of any prayer.

Remembering the presence of God is a necessary part of recollection, St. Alphonsus of Liguori explained, because it helps us avoid sin, spurs us on toward virtue, and helps bring about an intimate union with God—"there is no more excellent means of quieting the passions and resisting temptation," he said, "than the thought of the presence of God." It strengthens our resolve to avoid sin because we're naturally less willing to offend some superior who's looking at us, whether parent, magistrate, or general; how much more will we be unwilling to sin as long as we remember that God sees all that we do, even when we're alone. But there's a more direct connection between meditative prayer and remembrance of God's presence, because the motive of meditative prayer is the love of God, not primarily fear of his displeasure. You have to keep the pot on the fire, or it cools off, St. John Chrysostom advised; in the same way, a soul can be set afire with the love of God, but the thought of his presence has to be maintained or that fervor, too, will cool.

St. Alphonsus offers four suggestions for keeping the thought of God always on your mind. The most beautiful way, he said, is to behold God within yourself; "it isn't necessary to ascend to Heaven to find God; we only need to recollect ourselves, and we find him within us." St. Teresa herself said that she never knew what it meant to pray well until she entered into her very self; "I found this practice very profitable for my soul," she said. This way seems to require some proficiency at recollection already; but there are others.

You might simply remember that God is omniscient, that he sees and knows everything, and act accordingly, tuning your conscience to his will. Another way is to picture him as present with you wherever you go; think of him as the Babe of Bethlehem, or as the Crucified. After all, Christ came as a man to make the Covenant of God comprehensible to Men; so contemplating his humanity is a good way to capture God in your heart. "Other visible things may move us to love God and contemplate him, but the sacred humanity of Christ overwhelms us and almost compels us to do this," Francisco de Osuna pointed out.

So you might remember the Creator whenever you see one of his creatures—consider the rising and the setting of the Sun, St. Alphonsus says, or a garden of flowers. These are all just so many reflexes of the beauty of the Creator, and if they're interpreted that way they point the soul in the right direction for prayer. Brother Lawrence of the Resurrection was converted, at the age of eighteen, when he saw a tree in winter. All of a sudden it struck him that God in his providence would make it bring forth flower and leaf again in due time. That tree made such an impression on him of God's goodness that it stayed with him for the rest of his life, and frequently refreshed his awareness when he thought of it.

The best help in detaching yourself from worldly concerns and fighting distractions to prayer, of course, is prayer itself—ask for the help that you need. In particular, it's often very difficult for people to look past the beauty, or really just the appearance, of creatures, which constantly presents itself for consideration.

St. Louis-Marie Grignion de Montfort urged the use of a small chain worn around the neck, arm, ankle, or waist, perhaps with a little cross hanging from it—or presumably a holy medal—as a reminder of servitude to God. "They are a surety and protection against enslavement by sin and the Devil," he said, "for we must of necessity choose to wear either the chains of sin and damnation or the chains of love and salvation" (*True Devotion to the Blessed Virgin*). Others recommend developing the habit of saying, "Lord, these eyes are for your service," whenever you're distracted by seeing something untoward, or "Lord, these hands are for your service," whenever you're tempted to sin more actively.

One other ancient practice that can be helpful in handling the distractions that come from created things is the old Hebrew custom of the *brachah* (BROCK-ah), which takes its name from *brakha* (ברכה), which is the first word of blessings—it means, basically, "blessed", and it's the source of the prophet's name, Baruch.

The Talmud specifies that formulas of blessing should begin with a praise of God, like "Praised art thou, Adonai, our God, King of the Universe," or "Blessed art thou, Lord, God of all creation," and then specify exactly why God, in this case, is to be praised. The *brachah* for the kiddush cup at Passover Seder, for example, is "Blessed art thou, Lord, God of all creation, who has created the fruit of the vine." Pious Jews use different *brachot* (the plural of *brachah*) for different foods and drinks, different times of day, and for little events like washing the hands, putting on a new garment, or seeing anything extraordinary in creation.

Pious Christians sometimes adopt the custom of saying a *brachah*, which can be made up on the spot and said silently, whenever they're distracted by anything in creation—an exceptionally beautiful person, an exceptionally ugly person ("Blessed are you, Lord, God of all creation: you vary the aspects of your creatures"), a mountain or a sunset, a big house or a fancy car, a child, a scholar, or a king. This practice acknowledges the material being that catches your attention but refers it to its source, to God. That makes it much more difficult to admire these things improperly, or even to despise them improperly; and eventually it keeps them from being any kind of a distraction from awareness of God's presence.

A *brachah* helps you see the beauty of the physical world as part of the glory of God, and as such admirable but trivial in comparison to God himself. It makes people beautiful, not with a purely animal beauty like that of a beautiful horse or a beautiful bird, but with a purely human beauty, a beauty like the beauty that the Fathers of the Church attributed to Mary—beauty that doesn't call attention to itself but carries the eye of the beholder to remembrance of God.

However you do it, the idea of becoming recollected is to take yourself out of your day-to-day world and put yourself in the presence of God. Vocal prayer is a great, a necessary, mechanism toward achieving this state, but it may take years of work to get there; and in the last analysis the ability to pray well is a gift from God—a gift that can be asked for, but a gift none the less. So it's a great mistake to abandon vocal prayer because you can't get past distractions day after day, or even if you can't seem to get better at prayer your whole life long.

On the other hand, the first blush of spiritual development as a fruit of prayer will probably seem so unusual—because you haven't experienced anything like it before—that it's easy to slip off the steep path of devotion and slide into mere enthusiasm. That's why St. Paul had to write so often to the Corinthians, and it's why cults and demagogues still attract followers today. So it's also a great mistake to abandon vocal prayer in the belief that you're ready for meditative prayer without it. People who feel a little fervor at the beginning of their conversion and are tempted to turn from vocal prayer are flirting with Quietism; and, Walter Hilton added, "they rely on their own ideas and emotions in spiritual matters for which they have not yet received the necessary graces. By such indiscretions ... they fall into strange fancies and misconceptions, or into obvious error, and by their foolish notions they obstruct the graces that God would give them. All of this is caused by pride, and by presumption; and it happens because they consider the little grace that they have received as so great and extraordinary that they fall into vainglory and lose even the little that they have received."

St. Ignatius of Loyola summed up the same three requirements in his *Spiritual Exercises*, in the "third manner" of prayer. "As soon as I recall that the time to perform the exercise has come, before I begin it," he advised, "I will call to mind where I am going and before whom I am going to appear, and I will briefly review its subject matter."

> Before entering the prayer, I would briefly recollect myself in spirit, either seated or walking back and forth, as I find better... Then I will raise my mind and think how God Our Lord is looking at me, and other similar thoughts... One should pray mentally by saying with each breath that is expelled a word of the Our Father, or of whichever other prayer that is recited. This is done so that one word of prayer is said between one breath and another. Between the two breaths, one reflects on the meaning of that word, on the person to whom the prayer is being addressed, or on one's own lowliness... One will continue, using this same procedure and mea-

sure of time, through the words of the Our Father, and the other prayers, the Hail Mary, the Soul of Christ, the Creed, and the Hail, Holy Queen.

Like the age-old practice of the monks, and for that matter of the laity before the industrial age, this method can be practiced during any kind of manual work. When vocal prayers are prayed during work, as the monks sang psalms while cooking, gardening, cleaning the house, or working in the shop, it's already the first step of meditative prayer.

But there must come a time at which you set aside some time for prayer alone; not for prayer during work, but for prayer alone. Simply set aside that time for prayer, go to a quiet place away from all possible distractions, and focus your mind and heart on God. Then take up your rosary, and begin counting off the vocal prayers. "Believe me," St. Louis-Marie Grignion de Montfort said, "if you really want to reach a high level of prayer, in all honesty and without falling into the traps that the Devil sets for all those who pray, pray your Rosary every day, or at least pray five decades of it."

Of course, none of the papal documents about the Rosary, none of the liturgies in the Missal, neither the Breviary nor the *Enchiridion of Indulgences* mentions the custom of counting the constituent prayers on beads. None of the Church's official texts about the Rosary mentions beads at all: the Rosary is a set of vocal prayers that accompany meditative prayer. Presumably, a person who could keep track of the vocal prayers without any physical object could still pray the Rosary properly.

Undoubtedly, very few people have that ability; and, even if you do, the idea of the beads is to take as much mental effort as possible away from mechanical tasks like counting, so that you can free your mind more completely for meditation. For all practical purposes, you need some mechanical way to count the vocal prayers, and rosary beads have stood the test of time. Since Bl. Alan de Rupe established the standard form of the Rosary, the beads used to count the vocal prayers during the meditation have had a distinctive, and standard, form to accord with it.

Today, the standard set of rosary beads in English-speaking countries consists of five "decades", each of them being a group of ten beads (hence the name). The decades are set off from one another by single beads between them. The five decades are brought together into a circle, a chaplet, by a larger bead, called the "center". The center is often ornamented, and sometimes it's made into the shape of a medal. A shorter string of smaller beads is attached to the center, and there's a cross or a crucifix on the end of that short string.

A set of rosary beads, like a blessed medal, holy water, or even a consecrated church building itself, is what you call a *sacramental*. That word sounds like the word "sacrament", and of course they both come from the same root, the Latin *sacrare*, from which we also get words such as *sacred, sacrifice,* and *consecrate*. All of these words have to do with being set apart religiously, somehow, dedicated to the service of God. But there's an immense difference between a sacramental and a sacrament. In some ways, they're direct opposites—or, rather, they work in two complementary ways toward the same goal, the bestowal of grace.

The seven sacraments are visible acts of worship established by Christ: Baptism, Confirmation, the Eucharist, Reconciliation, Matrimony, Ordination, and the Anointing of the Sick. The Church teaches that, in a sacrament, Christ gives grace directly to the person receiving the sacrament, provided that the recipient is "properly disposed" to receive it—that is, you have to be in the right relationship to God. The sacraments always have to be properly administered, but their effects depend not on the doer but on the deed itself.

On the other hand, the effect of a sacramental depends not on the deed but on the doer; not on the thing, but on the person who uses the thing properly. A sacramental produces grace, but indirectly, through the intercession of the Church: sacramentals arouse us to the acts of virtue that draw God's graces to us. No sacramental can ever substitute for the sacraments; you don't need any sacramental for salvation. But sacramentals can inspire you to greater devotion. Proper use of sacramentals brings other benefits, too: actual graces, protection from evil spirits, health of body, and material blessings. Through the prayers of the Church for those who use sacramentals properly, you can also obtain forgiveness of venial sins, as well as remission of temporal punishment. But with any sacramental the power to do good is in you, not in the sacramental itself.

Rosary beads don't have to be made of jewels like the beads of Lady Godiva, and they don't have to be made of crystal or precious metal. A rosary can be made of the simplest materials—wood, clay, glass, anything durable enough to stand up to years of daily wear. It's suitable to have a rosary as beautifully worked as you can manage, because that's appropriate to something made for God's service; and, like all sacramentals, it's supposed to be properly blessed, formally set apart to the service of God as the altar of the Temple and Jewish sacramentals were made holy (Ex 29:36-37; *cf.* Nm 21:6-9) and as the Church has always dedicated her own altars and every person, place, or thing that she reserves for sacred purposes (Lk 24:50; Hb 9:21-23; 1Cr 10:16). There's a special rite for the blessing of rosaries in Chapter 45 of the *Book of Blessings*.

Thinking that you need one kind of set of rosary beads over another, though, is the vice of superstition, the vice of treating something inconsequential as if it had some power to effect change. "You will hardly meet anyone who does not have some weakness in this matter," Saint John of the Cross said. "They weigh themselves down with overly decorated images and rosaries; they will now put these down, now take up others; at one moment they are exchanging, and at the next re-exchanging; now they want this kind, now they want another ... like children in trinkets... They want the rosary beads to be made in one style rather than another, or of this color or that metal rather than the other, or of this or that particular design."

None of this really matters, St. John reminds us. "One set of rosary beads is no more influential with God than is another; his answer to the Rosary prayer is not dependent upon the kind of rosary beads used. The prayer he hears is that of the simple and pure heart, which is concerned only about pleasing God and does not bother about the kind of rosary used, unless in regard to indulgences... I saw someone ... who prayed with beads made out of the bones from the spine of a fish. Certainly, his devotion was not for this reason less precious in the sight of God" (*Ascent of Mount Carmel* 3:35:7; *Dark Night* 1:3:1).

For that matter, beads aren't really necessary for counting the usual numbers of vocal prayers, anyway. God designed us with a rosary included; and a good many people use their own ten fingers to say a Rosary whenever they have to wait in line or are stuck in traffic. Far from being irritated by these enforced removals from the tasks of the day, many of them welcome these opportunities for meditative prayer, glad to toss a few more pebbles into the vast swamp of the world's problems.

No matter what kind of sacramental object you use to keep track of the vocal prayers of the Rosary, the process of saying them is the same as it's always been. The idea is to hold a bead while you say the appropriate prayer vocally, and then move to the next bead, until you've finished. The beads in their number and arrangement tell you which vocal prayer you should say at that moment. When the Rosary is prayed publicly, the leader and the people pronounce the prayers loudly enough to keep everybody in pace with everybody else, and, if it helps you achieve recollection, you can say the prayers aloud when you withdraw to your inner room to pray.

But generally, as Durandus of St.-Pourçain explained in the fourteenth century, the prayers of the Rosary are said quietly, "so that we may withdraw into ourselves and concentrate on the meaning of the words that we're saying ... because in prayer we speak with God, who scrutinizes not only our words but our hearts as well; and [we do this also] to emphasize the fact that the efficacy of the prayer has more to do with the devotion of the heart than with the tone of the voice" (*cf.* Mt 15:8; 1Kn 1:12-13; Jt 13:6-7).

St. Bernard of Clairvaux taught his monks the importance of mental attitude at vocal prayer by saying that while they were reciting their prayers in the oratory an angel stood by each of them, writing in a record-book. Some of the angels wrote with gold, which signified that those vocal prayers were said with attention and devotion; others with silver, which meant that the prayers were pronounced with some attention but there was something imperfect about the devotion. Some angels wrote with ink, which meant that the words were there, and carefully spoken, but without any devotion at all; others wrote with water, because the words were carelessly, hastily spoken with neither attention or devotion. And some angels just stood there, their pens in the air, waiting, because their monks were knowingly entertaining distractions while they recited the prayers—so they weren't praying at all.

The standard vocal prayers of the Church, the ones used in praying the Rosary, are all of a very high order, rhetorically as well as theologically. You could structure a whole catechism of Christianity using the phrases of these prayers as your headings, and in fact the Council of Trent and the Second Vatican Council did exactly that. The Fathers of the Church, the great saints, and the great theologians have drawn infinite insights from each phrase—each word—of these prayers; they have written whole books about each of these prayers, whole libraries full of books, over the centuries; and all of them are different, but all of them substantive and valid, leading through meditation to some new facet of truth.

Thinking about the rhetorical structures of these prayers and learning about the words themselves pay substantial dividends in meditative prayer. The meanings of these words, and of the forms in which they're presented, are far richer than you might see, at first glance.

אמת

THE SIGN OF THE CROSS

L IKE ALL OTHER PRAYERS, THE ROSARY MAY BE PREFACED WITH THE SIGN OF the Cross. The Sign is used to sanctify the time of prayer, to help you recollect yourself, and, as a prayer in itself, to raise your heart and mind to God whenever you pray it. Unlike the other vocal prayers of the Rosary, though, it includes an element of bodily prayer, because it involves gestures, just as genuflection, bowing, or the gestures of the Mass do.

To make the Sign, you touch the fingertips of your right hand first to your forehead, saying, "In the Name of the Father" (*In Nomine Patris*); then you touch them to your chest, saying, "and of the Son" (*et Filii*); then to the left shoulder and then to the right one, while saying, "and of the Holy Spirit, amen" (*et Spiritui Sancti, amen*). Often, in praying the Rosary, people hold the crucifix that's on the rosary and touch it to the forehead, chest, and shoulders as they say those words.

T he words, however brief, are still the words of a vocal prayer, and as such they ought to be considered as they're spoken, and spoken with reverence. They are, after all, invoking the Name of God. That brings up the question of what a Name, with a capital N, really is. That's not really very well understood, these days—in fact, it's virtually forgotten. But it's the whole point of the Sign of the Cross, and the Name echoes through the Rosary and through all of the Church's prayers, as it resonates through Scripture itself. It's the object of a good many ancient devotions, and it has always commanded the highest respect of the Faithful.

Thou shalt not take the Name of the Lord thy God in vain (Ex 20:7), for instance. Nowadays, we mostly figure that the second commandment means that we shouldn't say "God" or "Jesus" as a swear word when angry, and of course we shouldn't. But the Name of a thing is not just what you call it. The Name is the essence of the thing, the essence of its being.

That's why you can't really understand our Christian liturgy, or even the Bible itself, unless you know what a Name is. Look at the very beginning of Genesis: "And God said, 'Let there be light'. And there was light" (Gn 1:3). God created light by pronouncing its Name.

Because the Name is the essence of a being, the study of Names developed into a science among the Hebrews. Every Name in the Old Testament is significant. Abraham and Sara both changed their names when they were called by God to be the parents of nations, and the forebears of Christ himself. The old name Abram, אברם (Avram), which means "Mighty Father", was made universal by the addition of a letter; Abraham, אברהם ('brhm), means "Father of a Multitude". Sara's original name, Sarai, שרי (Sarai), means "my princess", which is specific; God told her to make it universal, too, by dropping a vowel and calling herself simply Sara, שרה (Sarah), "princess". And because Sara laughed when God told her that she would have a son, God told Abraham to call the child Isaac, a word that carries the idea of laughter. Joseph named his first-born son Manasse, which in Hebrew means, "to cause to forget"—"because," he said, "God has caused me to forget entirely my sufferings" (Gn 41:51).

Of course, in the New Testament, Simon, Son of John, became Peter, Πέτρος, the Rock on which Christ's Church is built (Mt 16:18). The Pharisee Saul (שאול, sa'ul; Σαῦλος in Greek) began to call himself *Paulus* (transliterated Παῦλος; Ac 13:9), which means little—and the change of that initial letter also transferred him from the Hebrew of the Old Covenant to the Latin of the Roman Empire, as appropriate for the Apostle to the Gentiles. And the angel Gabriel named the Savior at the Annunciation: "Thou shalt call his Name, 'God saves'" (Lk 1:31).

Notice that the angel didn't say, "Thou shalt call the child 'God saves'", nor did he say, "Thou shalt name the child 'God saves'". Nor did the angel say what the Name is. Just what the Name "shall be called." Isaia (9:5) also gives a whole list of what the Name shall be called, and Psalms are full of phrases like, "May your Name be praised." But none of these Bible verses mentions what that Name might be.

This is because knowing the Name of something gives you a certain control over its power—if you know the Name of something you grasp its inmost being. When God wanted to give Adam dominion over the animals, "he brought them to the man to see what he would call them; for that which the man called each of them would be its Name" (Gn 2:19; *cf.* Mr 5:1-9; Lk 8:26-30). This kind of control through knowledge of the Name works for people, too. In many native American tribes, a new mother, having brought her baby into this world, whispered his Name in his ear and never spoke it again, so that no one could possibly gain ultimate power over him. Even in the fairy tales, the miller's daughter blew Rumplestiltskin into oblivion by pronouncing his Name.

This helps us to understand why we aren't allowed to take the Name of the Lord in vain. "The true Name of God is none other than the essence of his Godhead," Gunther of Paris explained in the Middle Ages. By invoking the Name, a person wields tremendous power (Ex 23:13); through the Name of God, we can invoke Christ's great promise: "Whatever you ask the Father in my Name, I will do" (Jn 14:13). But Christ never told us what that Name is, exactly, either. Any number of people seeking a shortcut to spiritual or material success have made guesses about it, and their writings gave birth to a whole discipline of "white magic"—a vain discipline, and not a discipline that's very challenging intellectually, but a discipline, such as it is. The idea was to figure out the Name of God from Scripture, where it was thought to lie hidden among the Hebrew or Greek characters, and then, as often as not, to use the Name to ensure the fulfillment of all desires.

> You can still find "seals" for sale inscribed with occult symbols that supposedly represent the Name in the angelic language or something; they mostly come from the *Clavis Salomonis*, the "Key of Solomon" written in Mantua by the military engineer Abraham Colorno (b. 1530) in about 1580. Nobody knows why Colorno wrote it. He was a part-time archæologist, and he may have been asked to translate the text by his patron, Duke Guglielmo Gonzaga, or he may have done it on his own as a joke on Guglielmo, who—judging by his kind but empty face in his portrait by Rubens—probably fell for it.
>
> In any case, Colorno's book isn't really bad. It draws most of its prayers from Psalms, and many of those that are original to it are really rather fine. The worst of them is merely silly. But if the *Clavis* isn't bad, it's not that important, either, theologically. It offered no really new insight into any devotional practice, it didn't have anything substantive to say about the Names of God, and unfortunately it was taken far more seriously than Colorno can have intended. It quickly spawned a rash of "Little Keys of Solomon" that are still around today.
>
> Most of these "Little Keys" are more than a little nasty. Some prescribe animal blood, excrement, and other horrors. Colorno himself was horrified at their proliferation, which was falsely traced to him. He later wrote a book especially to deride all forms of magic—white, black, or indifferent—but it was too late. The "Little Keys", bizarre parodies of Colorno's *Key of Solomon*, had already spread all over Europe. They incidentally popularized a lot of symbols, everything from the six-pointed "Star of David" to the emblems still used by fortune-tellers, but they were mostly used then as they're still used today, in nocturnal rituals by those who still try to guess the Name of God and then use it to compel God to do their will.

That's a dangerous undertaking, and it's not the way religion works: Mt 26:39, and Ex 20:7, above all. And it's pointless, anyway; no one Name could encapsulate the essence of God, because God is infinite. Therefore,

THE SIGN OF THE CROSS

God evidently has infinite Names.

Only very few of these Names have been revealed to Man, and only on very, very special occasions. Even when Moses asked God in the burning bush, "Who shall I say sent me?" the answer he got evidently convinced the Israelites, but it was held in such reverence that it was written down only as the Tetragrammaton (from the Greek τετρα-, four, and γράμμα, letter). The Tetragrammaton consists of the four Hebrew consonants, יהוה (Yod, He, Vau, and another He). Sometimes these four letters are pronounced as if they spelled "Yahweh", but to this day no one knows for certain what these four letters mean or how they are supposed to be pronounced. This is just the way the Israelites wanted it; in Hebrew tradition, any Name of God is too holy for mortal lips.

So the rabbis substituted other words whenever they came across those four letters in a reading. Sometimes they said something like, "The Holy One, blessed be his Name," but more often they said "Adonai", אדוני, which means "Lords"—the plural form is intended to signify God's greatness or, perhaps, to raise the word to an abstract level. In fact, some Jews are so careful to avoid speaking the Name that many substitute "Hashem" (השם, "the Name") when they read the Tetragrammaton, or use the compound "Adoshem" (אדושם, from the first syllable of "Adonai" and the second of "Hashem")—substitutes for substitutes, just to be safe.

Just to be sure that nobody forgot to say "Adonai" when he read aloud, rabbis inserted the vowels from "Adonai" into the four consonants given to Moses. In the sixteenth century, a Latin translator took these letters literally and wrote the new word, "Jehovah". It's a useful word, now commonly used now to refer to God the Father, but it doesn't occur in the Bible. It's nothing more than a mistranslation, and it's only about four hundred years old.

In Christian liturgy, we ask things "in the Name of Jesus", but, like our Jewish fathers in faith, we don't pronounce the Name itself. "Jesus" is derived from Ἰησοῦς, the Greek form of Joshua—in Hebrew, יהושע, "Yehoshuah", meaning "God saves", which is also where Isaia got his name. Nobody who knew Our Lord as a man called him יהושע: they used the Aramaic form of Yehoshua, ישוע, which would be pronounced "Yeshu" or "Yeshua". Other modern languages use some other variant, like *Jesús, Jesu, Gesù, Iosa*, and many others.

We see the name "Jesus" most often abbreviated in the sign atop the crucifix, INRI. Pontius Pilate, Roman governor of Judea, posted above the Cross a sign in Hebrew, Greek, and Latin that said, "Jesus of Nazareth, King of the Jews" (Jn 19:19-20). The Latin phrase is *Iesus Nazarenus Rex Iudæorum*. The whole inscription is too long to be written over every crucifix, and the initials of the Latin phrase carry the meaning clearly to the Universal Church; the initial letter of a word, or a Name, is generally understood to contain the essence of the word itself.

You also see the three letters IHS, but people have forgotten what they mean, so there are lots of fanciful interpretations of these letters. Some say that they stand for "I Have Suffered". Others say that they signify the Latin phrases *Iesus Hominum Salvator*, "Jesus, Savior of Men", or *In Hoc Signo*, "In This Sign (of the Cross you shall conquer)", which is supposedly a Latin version of the Greek words Ἐν τούτῳ νίκα that Constantine the Great saw in 312, blazoned across the sky with the Cross just before the Battle of the Milvian Bridge, which made him put the Cross on the battle-standards of the Roman legions. The truth, as usual, is both simpler and stronger. The three letters IHS aren't English letters, and they aren't Latin. They're simply an abbreviation, the first three letters of the Greek version of "Jesus"—in capital letters, ΙΗΣΟΥΣ.

But it was the Hebrew form of the name Jesus that had the greatest effect in recent history. During early Christian times, the Jews had developed methods of meditative prayer, but naturally they didn't meditate on the passion and triumph of Jesus Christ. They contemplated the Name of God, the Tetragrammaton of four Hebrew letters, using it as a focus for meditations on God's greatness, his goodness, and his providence. After they were exiled from the Holy Land, though, the Jews held, sadly, that the integrity of the Name had been shattered, the י ה (Yod He) being separated from the ו ה (Vau He), and that the two halves would not be reunited until the Messiah would come in glory.

Starting in about the fourteenth century, Christians took up this study of the Cabala—so called from the Hebrew word קבלה, "received", which carries the meaning of tradition or heritage. Scholars like Athanasius Kircher, Pico della Mirandola, and Pico's student, the scholar whom Erasmus called "that incomparable worthy", Johann Reuchlin, all used the same techniques of Scriptural study as their Jewish counterparts, and the resulting books were so similar on both sides that you can't always tell very easily whether the author is a Christian or a Jew. But the Christian cabalists took this study of the Name to the next logical step.

They noticed that the Hebrew word for the descending glory of God is Shekhinah, שכינה; this is what the pillar of fire is called in the Old Testament, and it's what the descending Spirit at Christ's baptism is called, as are the tongues of fire at Pentecost, sometimes. It starts with the letter ש (Shin), so that letter was understood as representing the essence of the descending Spirit of God; and the Christian cabalists saw that putting the

שׁ between the two halves of the Tetragrammaton, the יה (Yod He) and the וה (Vau He), makes it possible to pronounce that unpronounceable Name: and it spells יהשׁוה (Yod He Shin Vau He)—which is the Name Jehoshua, Jesus.

That is, the combination of the Name of the Father and the Name of the Holy Spirit produces the Name of Jesus; and more than that, it makes that unpronounceable Name pronounceable, just as the action of the Holy Spirit made God incarnate in Jesus. Reuchlin wrote a whole book about this "wonder-working Word" (*De Verbo Mirifico*, 1494), but it was not a new idea—St. Jerome himself had noticed this, and remarked that because שׁ, the Shin, the Shekinah, was the agent through which the Son became flesh and dwelt amongst us, it wasn't so surprising that the Names combined this way, and made the Name of the Son audible to humans.

But this cabalistic name-play lay more or less dormant until around the year 1666—which the numerically minded saw as the Millennium plus the Number of the Beast, and therefore probably the end of the world anyway. Then a revival of this "combinatorial art" hit the Jews of Europe like revelation. Thousands and tens of thousands of Jews, having based their prayer life on contemplation of the two separate halves of the Tetragrammaton, saw the fragments of that Name united in Christ, and converted.

So it was true, then, that at that Name many a knee must bend. Today, devotion to the Name isn't taught as much as it used to be. But since earliest Christian times, it's been the custom to bow your head when you say "Jesus"—in whatever version—or when you hear someone else say it. Since the thirteenth century, the Dominicans in particular have preached devotion to the Holy Name.

At the Council of Lyons in 1274, the Holy Name Society was born, devoted to promoting reverence for the Names of God and of Jesus and to discourage abuse of language for perjury, blasphemy, and profanity. By 1564 the Society was approved by the Pope and richly indulgenced, and by 1882 it expanded to the United States. Devotion to the Holy Name was so successfully promoted by the Franciscan saints Bernadine of Siena and John Capistran that the Franciscan Order was given a feast of the Holy Name in the sixteenth century. In 1721 the feast, celebrated with a special Mass in early January, was extended to the whole Church.

By the end of the eighteenth century, the laity had taken up the devotional practice of saying aloud the Divine Praises to make up for all of the times that the Holy Names had been used profanely:

Blessed be God.	Benedictus Deus.
Blessed be his holy Name.	Benedictum Nomen sanctum ejus.

Blessed be Jesus Christ,
   true God and true Man.
	Benedictus Jesus Christus,
	   verus Deus et verus homo.

Blessed be the Name of Jesus.	Benedictum Nomen Jesu.
Blessed be his Most Sacred Heart.	Benedictum cor ejus sacratissimum.
Blessed be his Most Precious Blood.	Benedictus sanguis ejus pretiosissimus.

Blessed be Jesus in the Most Holy
   Sacrament of the altar.
	Benedictus Jesus in sacratissimo
	   altaris Sacramento.

Blessed be the Holy Spirit,
   the Paraclete.
	Benedictus Spiritus Sanctus
	   Paraclitus.

Blessed be the great Mother of God,
   Mary Most Holy.
	Benedicta magna mater Dei,
	   Maria sanctissima.

Blessed be her holy
   and immaculate conception.
	Benedicta sancta ejus
	   et immaculata conceptio.

Blessed be her glorious Assumption.	Benedicta assumptio ejus gloriosa.

Blessed be the Name of Mary,
   virgin and mother.
	Benedictum Nomen Mariæ,
	   virginis et matris.

Blessed be St. Joseph,
   her most chaste spouse.
	Benedictus sanctus Joseph,
	   ejus castissimus sponsus.

Blessed be God in his angels
   and in his saints.
	Benedictus Deus in angelis suis,
	   et in sanctis suis.

The prayer was most popular, or at least most frequent, in homes for retired sailors, where it was usually required of the pensioners. The version most often used in English adds the following petition:

> May the Heart of Jesus, in the Most Blessed Sacrament of the altar, be loved, adored, and praised, with grateful affection, at every moment, in every tabernacle of the world, even to the end of Time.

The Name of Jesus, then, is understood to be a worthy object of contemplation, of reverence; it is not to be taken in vain. The Name—which we do not know—is the essence of the Savior, the central and most sacred reality of him. That's why we can't know it as long as this mortal clay weighs us down. It's also why the Psalmist (112:3) says "from the rising to the setting of the Sun is the Name of the Lord to be praised". Which is exactly what Christ meant when he said simply "hallowed be thy Name."

By invoking the Name of the Father and of the Son and of the Holy Spirit, the Sign of the Cross affirms the Christian's faith in the Holy Trinity. The doctrine of the Trinity isn't in the Bible, but even sects that profess the Bible as the sole and only rule of faith subscribe to that teaching. They have to; if you know the doctrine you can make some sense of the Bible, but the Bible doesn't tell you the doctrine explicitly. The doctrine itself is embodied in Sacred Tradition, which is really the living presence of the Holy Spirit in the Church.

Sacred Tradition is not just custom, the habitual way of doing things; it's not just a matter of doing and teaching things without giving them any thought because they've always been done that way and taught that way. In fact, Sacred Tradition has nothing to do with the way something is done at all; outward signs like priestly vestments and the language of the liturgy are only expressions of Sacred Tradition, not its substance. Things like the habits of nuns, dress codes for students, and particular sacramentals are matters of custom, not Tradition.

Tradition is higher than all of that. Tradition is doctrine, the full body of doctrine conveyed by the prophets and completed by Christ, and while it never changes it is marvelously responsive to the particular problems of every time, place, and culture. The Epistles in the Bible, the papal encyclicals, and other written forms of authoritative teaching are all particular applications of Tradition to specific problems; but they are not Tradition itself.

In fact, the Bible encapsulates only a small portion of the whole doctrine of Christianity. Scripture is irreplaceable and incomparably rich, and you can't pray the Rosary without it—the Church couldn't celebrate any of her liturgies without the Bible. No Christian can get along without it. But the Bible can't change its mode of expression as times and cultures change; even "updated" translations have only so much material to start from. So the Bible can't be taken out of its context of Sacred Tradition; it was drawn from Tradition, which was entrusted to the living institutional Church. Cut off from Tradition, the Bible is a dry letter, rootless and subject to all kinds of disconnected interpretations.

> The Bible shows in two ways that it is drawn from Sacred Tradition entrusted to the living Church, and that it does not include all of Christ's teachings. It says so directly when the author tells you so (Lk 1:1-4, 10:16; Jn 13:18-20; 14:16-21; 16:12-14, 21:25; Rm 10:17; 1Cr 11:2; 1Th 2:13, 4:2; 2Th 2:14-15; 2Tm 2:2; Hb 13:22; 1Jn 1:3-4, 2:7, 3:11; 2Jn 12; 3Jn 13-14; etc.), in passages that refer to all of the things taught, not all of the things written.
>
> And it says so indirectly, and perhaps even more forcefully, when it shows that not all of the revelation, and not all of the history, of the Jews was written in the Old Testament. St. Stephen mentions in Acts that Moses was forty when he killed the Egyptian, for instance (Ac 7:23-24), and St. Jude tells about the struggle between Satan and St. Michael (9); St. Paul recounts the teaching of rabbinic Tradition that

the rock in Ex 17:1-7 and Nm 20:2-13 followed Israel in the desert to give them water (1Cr 10:4), as well as mentioning of the names of the magicians who opposed Moses, which aren't recorded in the Old Testament (*cf.* Ex 7:8 *ff.*; 2Tm 3:8). St. Matthew mentions a prophecy about Christ (Mt 2:23) that isn't in the Old Testament, either. These facts, these parts of revelation, were conveyed only by Tradition.

The same holds true for the New Testament, too; its authors say, directly and indirectly, that the Bible does not contain all that constitutes Christianity. The authors of the Epistles report direct quotations from Jesus that aren't in the Gospels, like Acts 20:35. Any one of these verses alone proves that while *sola scriptura* is an easy creed, it makes very little sense—no sense, in fact, since it's contradicted by the very book that it holds as the sole rule of faith.

So the basic guideline in understanding the Bible is this: the Church does not hold doctrines because they're in the Bible: they're in the Bible because the Church has always held them to be true, since long before she wrote and assembled the Bible.

In focussing exclusively on the Bible, it's easy to forget that the Church was born with Christ, that the Church was with him when he walked among us as a man, and that she walks with him still. The Church knew him and his inner circle at the beginning, and she remembers them now; her memories, kept alive by living Tradition, have endured without break or interruption from that day to this. Disputing the Church's teachings on what Christ said, or even her memories about details like whether he had any siblings, shows a peculiar view of history. Christ is no stranger to his Church, and neither is his mother. The Bible is not an archæological artifact, and it did not drop down from Heaven, printed and bound, at the feet of King James I or Martin Luther one day long after the events described in it had transpired. The Bible was written and assembled by the Church, and the Church has kept it alive every day since. Christianity is the living Sacred Tradition, and the Bible encapsulates only part of it.

Basically, the doctrine of the Trinity is that in the unity of the Godhead there are three persons, the Father, the Son, and the Holy Spirit. The Son is begotten of the Father by an eternal generation, and the Holy Spirit proceeds by an eternal procession from the Father and the Son. But because God exists in Eternity, outside of time-bound considerations like "before" and "after", they are all co-eternal, co-equal, uncreated, and omnipotent: none is inferior to another, and none owes his existence to an act of any other. "There is nothing created, nothing subject to another, in the Trinity," St. Gregory Thaumaturgus explained in the third century; "nor is there anything that has been added as though it didn't exist before, but entered after; the Father has never been without the Son, nor the Son without the Spirit; and this same Trinity is immutable and unchangeable forever" (Ἔκθεσις τῆς πίστεως, c. 265).

The mystery of the Trinity is the foundation of all of Christ's teachings, which is to say that it's the foundation of all of the Church's teachings. But it's a mystery, in the fullest sense of the word, something that cannot be known by the human mind. Because we exist within the limits of time and space, because we can only know what we receive through our senses and interpret through reason, we can't grasp a full knowledge of the Trinity, and our language can't express it. It's the essential nature of God, and his thoughts are not our thoughts, nor are his ways our ways; his nature isn't our nature, either.

As far as we can see, one nature has one person; no single being comprises more than one person. (The multiple personalities exhibited by persons suffering from certain mental disorders, of course, are exactly that: *personalities*, varying expressions of one and the same *person*.) For that matter, one nature has one person and one body; but God is not restricted by nature to the constraints of the nature that he created, and, as a spirit, isn't restricted by physical bodies at all. Our ideas about existence are trapped in the dimensions of time and space; God's existence fills Eternity.

Naturally, the doctrine of the Trinity is the basis for the divinity of Jesus. As Christ, he is the Messiah, but as God he is more than that, too. He said that he would come to judge all people (Mt 25:31), and in Jewish theology final judgement is a power of God's, not specifically of the Messiah's. He has dominion over the angels (Mt 24:31), which no prophet has and which isn't described in prophecy as a power of the Messiah. All of the Apostles recognized Jesus as the Messiah, but when St. Peter realized beyond this that Jesus is the Son of God, Christ approved of what he said and elevated him above the others (Mt 16:16-17); this, Jesus said, was a special revelation to St. Peter.

Even those who condemned him knew the difference. The Sanhedrin asked him first if he was the Messiah (Lk 22:67), and then they asked him whether he was the Son of God, which was different. His answer to that question brought him the charge of blasphemy (Jn 19:7), which wouldn't have attached to the claim of being the Messiah—claiming to be sent by God is different from claiming to be God. That's the reason that the Jews gave for demanding his death: the idea of a saving God was not always clear in their understanding of prophecy. St. John wrote his Gospel particularly to clarify the point (Jn 20:31) that Jesus of Nazareth, the Messiah, is truly the Son of God, the second person of the Holy Trinity.

O f course, the crucial fact about the Sign of the Cross is precisely that it is the Sign of the Cross. Today, it's hard for anybody to think of Christianity without the symbol of the Cross, but it was extremely difficult for people in the early Church to think of that symbol at all. The early Church had a lot of explaining to do about why her God and Savior had been crucified, and for the first few centuries she did avoided any display of that particular fact.

Crucifixion wasn't abolished until the early fourth century, and until then everybody knew perfectly well that crucifixion was the most shameful death, more repulsive than any modern mode of execution. So it wasn't really until about two hundred years later, after everybody who had seen a crucifixion had died, that Christians abstracted the cross into a symbol of their Faith, and then it was usually as a golden ornament patterned with jewels, not as a realistic representation of Christ crucified. It wasn't until 692, after the Third Council of Constantinople, that churches were ordered to use crucifixes instead of ornamented crosses, and it wasn't until about the year 1000—when so many people thought that the world would end, and started thinking about penance—that the crucifix became a fairly standard Christian image.

Half a millennium later, the crucifix had become the primary symbol of Christianity. Although it is, really, a kind of devotional artwork, "high-church" Anglicans and some Lutheran sects still retained it when they discarded all other devotional images. Even many of those radical Protestant sects that allowed no figural sculpture at all retained the plain cross itself. Today, virtually every Christian building displays a cross, and any number of Christians wear one around the neck or carry one in the pocket. But unquestionably the most common representation of the Cross of Christ is traced not in wood or metal but on the flesh of his followers, every time they make the Sign of the Cross.

In point of fact, the gesture of signing oneself with the Cross is older than Christianity itself. Ezekiel was supposed to deliver the faithful of the Old Covenant, those who mourned the iniquities of Jerusalem, by tracing on their foreheads the letter t, which at that time was shaped like an X, and which was transliterated as the Greek tau, T, in the Septuagint. A divine commandment specifying the Cross (†) would have been incomprehensible, but the letter T amounted to the same symbol, and as the last letter of the Hebrew alphabet it signified a finality, too. Christians never forgot this prophetic mark of salvation (Rv 7:2-8), but it took them a long time to work up the courage to show the Sign in public. As late as the fourth century, St. Cyril of Jerusalem had to exhort his catechumens not to be ashamed to confess the Crucified through the Sign. "Let the Cross be our seal, made boldly with our fingers on our foreheads and in everything else: over the bread that we eat and the cups that we drink, in our coming in and our going out, when we lie down before sleep and when we awaken, when we travel and when we rest" (*Catecheses* 13:36).

But eventually the efficacy of the Sign overpowered people's reluctance to be branded in public as Christians. By St. Cyril's day, signing the Cross on the forehead with the finger or the thumb was well on its way to being universal, evidently as a form of greeting, like a military salute. St. Jerome mentions that the Sign was often traced on the lips, too (*Epitaph for Paula*), and Prudentius (348-405) mentions that it was made over the heart (*Cathemerinon* 6:129).

Liturgically, the Sign of the Cross has been made on the forehead, lips, and heart before the Gospel readings at Mass since patristic times, then as now to serve as a prayer to clarify and purify the mind so that the Word may be understood, the lips so that it may be proclaimed, and the heart so that it may be lived.

The current fashion of signing not just the forehead but the whole body dates from the days of the Monophysite controversy in the fifth century. Monophysites usually assert either that Christ is only God and that his human appearance was only a kind of apparition, or that he was only a man who had a special closeness with God. But in the fifth century certain heretics adopted the third possible position; they seem to have asserted that Christ is a unique being who had some of the characteristics of both God and Man.

But they insisted that he had only one nature; so, when they made the Sign of the Cross, they used only one finger. Christians countered that sign of heresy by making the Sign of the Cross with two fingers, either adding the index finger to the thumb or using the first two fingers. And to make sure that everybody saw the difference they made the Sign larger.

After that, the symbolism of the details started to vary, depending on the point of faith that was denied by the current crop of heretics. If heretics at a certain time and place were denying the doctrine of the Trinity, Christians made the Sign with three fingers extended; when some Greek-speaking heretics disputed Christ's salvational work, some Greek-speaking Christians started making the Sign with their fingers contorted into a complicated pattern representing the letters IXΣ, an abbreviation of the phrase Ἰησοῦς Χριστὸς Σωτήρ, Jesus Christ, Savior.

There are still several different ways to make the Sign of the Cross, depending on who you are and what you intend to do, and for that matter where you live. In some cultures, people who bless themselves kiss their fingertips after the "Amen", but that's not, strictly speaking, part of the Sign of the Cross. It evidently got its start in the Spanish liturgical custom by which the celebrant would trace the Sign on the altar-cloth and then kiss the cross he'd traced, or the thumb with which he made it.

In the Greek-speaking Rites, the touching of the shoulders is the opposite of the sequence followed in the Latin-speaking Rites, making the Sign by touching the forehead, the chest, then the right shoulder, and then the left. Evidently the Sign was made this way throughout Christendom until Latin became the predominant liturgical language, at which time it changed in the West. People have tried to come up with some kind of symbolic reason for this—the mediæval *Myroure of our Ladye*, for instance, says that the sequence of left shoulder to right signifies that Christ descended into Hell ("left" in Latin being *sinister*) and then rose to sit at the right hand of God. But evidently this has no symbolic purpose whatever; it simply happened because spoken and written Greek move in a different conceptual order from the one followed by Latin.

There are special forms of the Sign used to bless something other than yourself. When priests or deacons bestow a blessing on people, or when parents bless their children, as some still do every evening before bed or every morning before leaving the house, the Sign of the Cross is traced with the right hand in the air over the persons, places, or things blessed; usually, the first two fingers are raised and held together while the others are closed beneath the thumb, which is an ancient and universal sign of benediction and of teaching. Sometimes the Sign is traced with holy water, and sometimes with chrism, as when bishops ordain priests or confirm laymen; sometimes blessed oil is used, as in the Anointing of the Sick.

By the middle of the ninth century, there were dozens of different ways, and complicated ways, of making the Sign of the Cross, all of them intended to convey some particular assertion of some particular doctrine or other. So Pope St. Leo IV issued a general instruction to the clergy. "Sign the chalice and the host with a right cross, not with circles or with a varying of the fingers, but with two fingers stretched out and the thumb hidden within them, by which you symbolize the Trinity. Take care to make this sign rightly, because otherwise you bless nothing." The laity took up this mode, too, when they saw the priests everywhere doing it this way, and it's remained the standard ever since.

Whichever gestures are used to form it, the Sign of the Cross involves an element of bodily prayer, and it shouldn't be made hastily. St. Bernadette Soubirous once gently rebuked a hasty sister novice at Nevers. "You make the Sign of the Cross badly," she said sorrowfully. "You must watch out for that, for it's important to make it well." For her part, having seen the Blessed Virgin cross herself, St. Bernadette habitually made the Sign of the Cross with a majesty and grace that impressed even those who did not know who she was, or those who despised religion itself. One eyewitness who had come to Lourdes to jeer at the visionary came away saying that if the Sign of the Cross is made in Heaven, it can only be made as this girl makes it.

A☙Ω

THE APOSTLES' CREED

THE APOSTLES' CREED, THE *CREDO*, CUSTOMARILY BEGINS THE ROSARY, IN the Latin Rite of the Catholic Church. Like the Sign of the Cross, it's recited as you hold the cross or crucifix that's attached to the chaplet itself by a short string of beads. This short string of prayers is really preliminary to the Rosary itself, which consists of the meditations on the Mysteries, so rosaries in other Rites of the Church might not have it. But these preliminaries give you a little time to recollect yourself and to think again about the basic teachings of your Faith.

These are the words of the Apostle's Creed.

I believe in God
the Father Almighty
creator of Heaven and Earth;
and in Jesus Christ,
his only son,
our Lord,
who was conceived
by the Holy Spirit,
born of the Virgin Mary,
suffered under Pontius Pilate,
was crucified, died,
and was buried.
He descended to the dead;
on the third day
he arose again from the dead.
He ascended into Heaven,
and is seated at the right hand
of God, the Father Almighty.
From thence he will come
to judge the living and the dead.
I believe in the Holy Spirit,

the holy catholic Church,

the communion of saints,

Credo in Deum,
Patrem omnipotentem,
creatorem coeli et terræ;
et in Jesum Christum,
filium ejus unicum,
Dominum nostrum,
qui conceptus est
de Spiritu sancto,
natus ex Maria Virgine,
passus sub Pontio Pilato,
crucifixus, mortuus,
et sepultus.
Descendit ad infernos;
tertia die
resurrexit a mortuis.
Ascendit ad coelos,
sedet ad dexteram
Dei Patris omnipotentis.
Inde venturus est
judicare vivos et mortuos.
Credo in Spiritum
  sanctum,
sanctam Ecclesiam
  catholicam,
sanctorum
  communionem,

the fogiveness of sins,	remissionem peccatorum,
the resurrection of the body,	carnis resurrectionem,
and life everlasting. Amen	vitam æternam. Amen.

This prayer was written down so long ago that nobody remembers how it came about. St. Ambrose mentioned in a sermon (*Sermon 38*) that the Apostles themselves put it together, which is why it has that name. Later sermonizers, starting with St. Jerome's friend Rufinus of Aquileia in his *Commentary on the Apostles' Creed* (*c.* 400), broke the prayer down into a dozen clauses and attributed one to each of the Twelve, but this was just a way to help people memorize the Creed and the names of the Apostles, not an exposition of an historical fact. It seems that it would be fairly easy to compose a homily or a treatise on the Apostles and their teachings this way, using the names and clauses as headings and then elaborating on each.

But precious few sermons or treatises were composed this way, evidently, because the matching of clauses to individual Apostles doesn't seem to make much sense theologically—St. Peter, as Prince of the Apostles, is said to have contributed the first clause, but really it would make more sense if he were said to have written "and in Jesus Christ, his only Son, Our Lord" (Mt 16:13-17), which is attributed in the usual scheme to St. James. And in any case some Apostles have two clauses attributed to them, to make twelve divisions.

Even so, this correspondence of Apostles to clauses was a continuing theme in art, for more than a thousand years after Rufinus, lasting even beyond its appearance as an organizing principle in the calendar pages of the *Grandes Heures de Berry* in 1409. But none of the Fathers of the Church, none of the popes, has taken seriously the idea that all twelve of the Apostles themselves gathered together at some unnamed place and time, composed the Apostles' Creed. After all, if they had put down such a fundamental statement of faith on paper, it certainly would have ended up in Acts, or in some other book of the New Testament, and it didn't. But no matter how the Creed came to be composed, and no matter who first put it down in writing, it deserves the name Apostles' Creed because it does give a clear, accurate summary of the Faith that the Apostles received from Christ and that has been kept intact in their Church from that day to this.

The actual written records of the Creed itself are among the oldest in the Church's archives, some of them dating from the pontificate of Pope Victor, who reigned from 189 to 199. *The Apostolic Tradition* written by St. Hippolytus at about the same time notes that this Creed was given to catechumens by the bishop during their training, and then given back to him—recited—as a kind of test of knowledge and a proclamation of loyalty before Baptism. Of course, in those days you could still be flayed alive or thrown to the lions for saying things like that; so stating the Apostles' Creed before witnesses meant irrevocably that you had turned your back on the pagan state religions and cast your lot with Christ.

So it was a serious matter, and it was carefully guarded. Persecutors made bad use of the Creed whenever they got hold of it, twisting its brief statements of faith into all kinds of treasonable plots. And in any case the Church was at first unwilling to throw it open to the general public, simply because it does sum up so well the central mysteries of the Faith (Mt 7:6).

E ven if it would be difficult to press the points made by associating the clauses with individual Apostles, the rhetorical structure of the prayer is of a very high order; it's not really inferior to the language of the Bible itself.

In its general structure, the Creed is divided into three main parts. First, it describes briefly what we know about God the Father, the First Person of the Holy Trinity. Then it recounts the main points that we know about the Second Person of the Trinity, Jesus Christ, and tells some of the key events in the history of his time walking among us. The third part speaks about the Third Person, the Holy Spirit, and his continued working in the Church. So it follows the pattern of creation, redemption, and sanctification that structures God's relationship to Man. Within each of these parts, specific articles follow, in their proper order.

The expansions on the brief articles of the Creed that you find in the catechisms are recommended reading before you start praying the Rosary, or as refreshers if you have been devoted to it for a while. Most Christian sects profess exactly this same Creed—although many don't—but they define the terms very differently. So there are a few words that require particular attention.

The very first of them is "I". Most of the Church's formal prayers are communal, asking God to deliver *us* or saints to pray for *us*, but this one is a personal profession of faith. You have to accept the Faith personally, all by yourself; the whole Church in Heaven and on Earth stands ready to help you, but nobody can do it for you. So the "I", the first word that you say when you begin the Rosary, usually, asserts that you are a distinct person with your own identity, and that you have come to accept the Faith of your own free will; that you have a personal relationship with your God, a relationship that isn't going to be exactly like anybody else's, because you are not exactly like anybody else.

"I believe" is a phrase that we use today to express opinion or doubt, but look at the Latin: *Credo*. It looks like our word "credit", and they're from the same root. When you say, in this prayer, that you believe in God, you're saying that you put full faith and credit in his existence; that there's no doubt about it.

Another phrase that might cause a little confusion now is "he descended into Hell". To us, the word "Hell" connotes a place of unending torment, full of filth and stench, devils and irredeemable sinners, and so it should. But notice that the Latin doesn't say that, exactly; it says *Descendit ad infernos*. That means more literally "he descended to the place below": *infernos*, you can see, is related to our word "inferior", which means something below something else, either in location or in quality.

This lower place, this subordinate state of being, the *Catechism* of the Council of Trent explained, isn't just the everlasting torment that the Bible calls *Gehenna*; "these abodes are not all of the same nature". Among them, it says, is also the fire of Purgatory, in which the souls of just people are cleansed by temporary punishment, and also an abode in which the souls of the just were received before the coming of Christ. There, without experiencing any kind of pain, and supported by the hope of redemption, they waited in peaceful repose. When he died, Christ's soul—still united to his divine nature—passed among the dead.

"Hell, then," the *Catechism* of the Council of Trent explained, "here signifies those secret abodes in which are detained the souls that have not yet obtained the happiness of Heaven. In this sense, the word is frequently used in Scripture. Thus the Apostle says, 'At the Name of Jesus every knee shall bend, of those that are in Heaven, on Earth, and below' (Phl 2:10)"—*infernos*, again. But it does not mean that Christ plunged himself into the everlasting lake of fire or anything.

Theologically, Christ's descent has to be understood in light of his whole advent, passion, and resurrection. St. Thomas Aquinas, in his great Sum of Theology, the *Summa Theologica* (3:49:5:1), explained it this way, back in the thirteenth century. Before Christ came and accomplished all of his work, nobody could enter Heaven. But when his soul left his human body, it passed to the abode of the dead, where it stayed as long as his body—which was also still united to his divine nature—lay in the tomb. Then, at the Resurrection, his soul rejoined his body, and he rose from the dead.

This is why the Bible, the Apostles' Creed, and so many other statements of faith say that Christ "rose from the dead". He was among the dead, and then he rose. Now, while he was among the dead, though, he brought deliverance to those who were united to his passion, his work of redemption, during their lives but before he was born. These were the people whose faith in the coming of the Redeemer was sparked by the charity, the love of God, that takes away sins. He delivered those just and holy souls who had died with faith and charity, and in the hope of his coming, releasing them from the penalties that had disbarred them from Heaven—Christ has risen, St. Peter explained, "having loosed the sorrows of Hell" (Ac 2:24). At the Ascension, these blessed souls accompanied him to stand before God, to partake fully of the vision of God that is beatitude.

> In art and in pious literature, this sequence of events is often called the "harrowing of Hell", meaning that Christ raked the place over and took out those who deserved salvation, even though they'd had to wait for it. In depictions of the scene, Christ is often shown breaking the gates of Hell and letting out the patriarchs and prophets, the first among them being Adam himself.

It also might be puzzling to hear that Christ sits at the right hand of God. We speak of a "right-hand man", and people used to say that they'd give their right arm for something that they want. In Latin, the word is *dexter*, which is where we get words like "dexterous" and "dexterity", which indicate cleverness, aptitude, or some other good quality. And it's no coincidence that "right" means good, proper, and morally acceptable as well as the opposite of left. Left, on the other hand, is *sinister* in Latin, the root of all evil words like—well, like "sinister".

Because most people on Earth are right-handed, this symbolism is universal; anything good, or supremely favored, is on or at the right hand (Gn 48:14). Rachel wanted to call her son Ben-oni, "Son of Affliction" (Gn 35:18), but Jacob named him Ben-jamin—Son of the Right Hand. And in fact Jamin, Yamani, and similar names, all referring to the right hand, are still popular in levantine and African countries. The right hand means power, and specifically it means the power of salvation (Gn 48:1-22; Ex 15:6; for example), which is why the Right Hand of God is so often shown in art directing Noe to build the Ark, holding back the hand of Abraham from the sacrifice of Isaac, handing the Law to Moses, and taking Ezekiel up to Heaven. And it's why the Hand is shown at the Ascension, reaching through the sky to grasp the outstretched right hand of Christ.

Sitting at the right hand of the Lord, whether the lord in question is Pharaoh, the King of Israel, or the King of the Universe, means that you have the Lord's full confidence and some share in his power. That's why this seat is the seat of highest possible honor throughout ancient literature, including the Bible. But because God the Father exists outside of time and space, and because he's a spirit, he doesn't have a right hand, *per se*. The great English mystic Julian of Norwich says that the expression in the Apostles' Creed "doesn't mean that the Son sits on the right-hand side as one man sits beside another in this life, because there isn't any such thing as sitting, as I see it, in the Trinity. But he sits at his Father's right hand: that is to say in the highest honor of the Father's joy."

One term that pinpoints the importance of knowing the meaning of the words that you say in vocal prayer is the reference to the "holy catholic Church". Now, the word "catholic" is not capitalized here, because it's not part of the Church's name. The Church doesn't have a name. It doesn't need one because Christ founded only one; because it's unique, the Church needs no other name but "Church". The word "catholic" comes from the Greek word καθολικός, meaning "universal".

The word is applied to the Church for two reasons. First, as St. Ignatius of Antioch pointed out, because the Church is to all nations and all times and places. Second, as St. Augustine said, because the Church and the Church alone contains all of Christ's teachings, without omission. So "catholic" is just an adjective, not a proper name; when you see it capitalized, as in "Catholic Church" or "Catholic Faith", it's because those are just rhetorical titles for the Church that Christ founded and for the Faith that he imparts. That's why some separated sects still use the word to refer to themselves, and why so many of them say the Apostles' Creed while denying that they belong to the Church.

The universe seen through the perspective of the Creed is different from the universe that can be seen without it. It outlines a uniquely Christian understanding of God and Man, Earth and Heaven, sin and salvation, and the relations among them all. That was revolutionary when the Creed was first proclaimed, and it's always revolutionary when it's put before those who refuse the Covenant on which it's based. "In making this profession, we are aware of the disquiet that agitates certain modern quarters with regard to the Faith," Paul VI admitted (*The Credo of the People of God*, 1968).

> They do not escape the influence of a world being profoundly changed, in which so many certainties are being disputed or discussed. We see even Catholics allowing themselves to be seized by a kind of passion for change and novelty... But ... the greatest care must be taken, while fulfilling the indispensable duty of research, to do no injury to the teachings of Christian doctrine. That, as is unfortunately seen in these days, would be to give rise to disturbance and perplexity in many faithful souls... [As] once at Cæsarea Philippi the apostle Peter spoke on behalf of the Twelve to make a true confession, beyond human opinion, of Christ as the Son of the Living God, so today his humble successor, pastor of the Catholic Church, raises his voice to give a firm witness on behalf of all the People of God, to the divine truth entrusted to the Church to be announced to all nations.

147

THE OUR FATHER

THE OUR FATHER IS THE PRAYER SAID ON THE NEXT BEAD AFTER THE CREED is said on the crucifix, and on the large beads between decades. It has always been the framework of the Rosary, and it's always prayed at Mass, because Christ himself told us to say this when we pray. Christians generally learn it first of all vocal prayers, and maybe with familiarity it becomes something that we don't really notice all that much—it's so simple, and it sounds perfectly natural and even spontaneous, or we just recite it as we've always recited it, all our lives.

But when you start to think about it, it's difficult to even begin analyzing the perfection of this little composition. Every word of it must have come as a surprise to those who heard Christ teach it; and it's no less a marvel today. Look at this, Tertullian said: it is a summary of the whole New Testament. It is a condensation of all of the beauties of the Psalms and Canticles, Thomas à Kempis added—it surpasses all of the desires of the saints. Clearly, we cannot be our Master's disciples, St. John Chrysostom advised, unless we pray as he did, and as he told us to.

And the Our Father contains all of the duties that we owe to God, St. Louis-Marie Grignion de Montfort pointed out. Moreover, he added, God will listen more readily to the prayer that we have learned from his Son than to prayers that we, with all of our human frailties and limitations, have written for ourselves—not that I disapprove of the prayers that the saints have written, he said, but these cannot possibly approach the perfection of the prayer uttered by the Incarnate Wisdom himself; each word is a tribute that we pay to the perfections of God. And he makes an important point, there; the Our Father is a remarkable piece of work from a rhetorical point of view, one that has never been surpassed in the world's literature. The text of it is given twice in the Gospels, partly in Luke (11:1-4) and fully in Matthew (6:9-13). Because the Lord wrote it, it's often called the Lord's Prayer, but we usually refer to it by the first two words in English, and in Latin it's named the same way: it's called the *Pater noster*.

Our Father, who art in Heaven,	Pater noster, qui es in coelis,
hallowed be thy Name.	sanctificetur Nomen tuum.
Thy kingdom come;	Adveniat regnum tuum;
thy will be done	fiat voluntas tua
on Earth as it is in Heaven.	sicut in coelo et in terra.
Give us this day our daily bread,	Panem nostrum quotidianum
	da nobis hodie,

and forgive us our trespasses	et dimitte nobis debita nostra
as we forgive	sicut et nos dimittimus
those who trespass against us.	debitoribus nostris.
And lead us not into temptatation,	Et ne nos inducas in tentationem,
but deliver us from evil. Amen.	sed libera nos a malo. Amen.

The Our Father may have become a matter of rote memory because this English version that most of us memorized came out of sixteenth-century English translations, which is unfortunate. That version came from the Anglican *Book of Common Prayer*, in its editions of 1549 and 1552, which Henry VIII imposed on England. The king, "perceiving now the great diversity of the translations ... willed them all to be taken up, and instead of them hath caused a uniform translation of the said *Pater noster, Ave,* Creed, etc., to be set forth, willing all his loving subjects to learn and use the same and straitly commanding all parsons, vicars, and curates to read and teach the same to their parishioners", so that was that. By the time the Rheims translation of the New Testament came out in 1581—or for that matter when the King James Version came out in 1611—everybody in the English-speaking world had been using Henry's translation for a whole generation, and they were used to it.

By now it's probably impossible to shift. But the words of it have shifted a lot in meaning during the past few centuries, and the meaning of the prayer is really clearer if you compare it, phrase by phrase, with the Latin of the Vulgate, and analyze the words and the structure of the prayer a little more deeply.

Our Father,
Pater noster,

The very first word of our English version, "Our" Father, establishes a whole new economy of salvation and sets up a whole new society on Earth. When you pray, he said, say, "*Our* Father"—and people who have the same father are all brothers and sisters, aren't they. The whole world is one family, he said, in that single word; this was astonishing to his hearers. No previous teacher had ever put things that way.

"This is why, when a Christian prays, even if he prays alone, his prayer is in fact always within the framework of the communion of saints in which and with which he prays, whether in a public and liturgical way or in a private manner," the Congregation for the Doctrine of the Faith explained. "The Christian, even when he is alone and prays in secret, is conscious that he always prays for the good of the Church in union with Christ, in the Holy Spirit and together with all the saints" (*On Some Aspects of Christian Meditation*, 1990).

"It is clear from this word 'Our'," St. Thomas Aquinas wrote, "that we owe our neighbors two things. First, love, because they are our brethren; all are the children of God. 'For how can he who does not love his brother, whom he sees, love God, whom he does not see?' (1Jn 4:20). And we owe them respect, because we are the children of God: 'Have we not all the one Father? Has not the one God created us? Why then do we break with one another?' (Ml 2:10). 'Love one another with fraternal charity' (Rm 12:10); and this is to be done for the sake of its fruit: 'He became the cause of eternal salvation to all who obey him' (Hb 5:9)."

Of course, the second word was just as big a surprise. Christ could have told us to call God Our Lord, or Our Creator, but he didn't; he said that we're to call God Father, which is rendered in Latin as *pater*, the root of English words like *paternal* and *paternity*. But in fact the word that Christ used is the equivalent of the Hebrew and Aramaic *Abba*, אבא, which is really something more like "Papa" or "Daddy"—the title that a child uses. Biblical scholars still haven't found any other use of this word in reference to God in the whole of Judaic literature.

who art in Heaven,
qui es in coelis,

The part about God's being in Heaven might be a little confusing, too. God is everywhere. He himself asked Jeremia, "Do I not fill the heavens and the Earth?" (Jr 23:24). But Christ specified that prayer is addressed to God in Heaven to distinguish our heavenly Father from any earthly parent, and to raise our sights to where they should be. As St. Paul remarked (Cl 3:1-2), we're supposed to seek the things that are above, where God is, rather than things upon the Earth.

And Christ may also have intended to point out that God isn't going to be restricted to any specific place on Earth, like the Temple of Jerusalem, but dwells within each of us. He may also have wanted to correct certain folkloric interpretations of allegoric passages like Jb 36:29-33, which keep being taken too literally age after age. When we say, "Our Father who art in Heaven," St. Augustine explained (*On the Sermon on the Mount* 5:17), "this means that he is within the saints, and the just; for God is not confined to local space. The 'heavens', naturally, are those sky-high bodies of the material universe, but those are bodies; they cannot exist unless they exist in a place. If God were believed to be in the heavens as if he were dwelling in the upper parts of the material universe, then the birds would be of greater merit than Man; they'd be living closer to God. It isn't written that God is closer to people who live on mountains, but it is written that the Lord is near to those of contrite heart" (*cf.* Ps 33:19).

THE OUR FATHER

hallowed be thy Name;
sanctificetur Nomen tuum;

One part of this familiar phrase that's always confusing is the word "hallowed". It looks like part of our word "Hallowe'en", and there's a reason for that. It's an old English word meaning blessed or holy; Hallowe'en is All Hallows Eve, the night before All Hallows—All Saints—Day. In the Latin, you can see that "hallowed" corresponds to the word *sanctificetur*, which looks like our word "sanctify". And in fact it just means "may your Name be praised as holy; may your Name be respected."

Notice also that the phrase "hallowed be thy Name" is in the *passive* voice, in English—who's doing the hallowing? It's also in the *subjunctive* mode: it means "may thy Name be hallowed", a statement of wish or desire, which means something entirely different from what the indicative "thy Name is hallowed" would mean; that would be a statement of positive fact. The important word in the Latin is *sanctificetur*, which is a *reflexive*: a verb of which the subject and the object are the same person or thing. In fact, these passive, reflexive, subjunctive structures in English and Latin represent the reflexive structures in Aramaic, Jesus's own language. Subject and object are one and the same, in that grammatical structure, so the "Name" stands for God himself. That points twice to the importance of the Name; but it also makes the petition mean, "May God himself sanctify his Name"; continue to glorify your Name among us.

And look at this petition's location in the prayer: it's the first. It comes before asking for bread, certainly, and even before asking God to bring us into his kingdom. That's because of charity, which is the virtue of the love of God. Pure charity loves God above all else, and loves all creation because God loves it. So charity moves us to direct our whole attention, our whole hearts, our whole minds, and our whole souls to the love of God, above all other loves and desires. So, to put his prayer into good order, Christ put this petition immediately after the salutation, showing us that before asking for anything for ourselves or others—even before things that are well and truly necessary—we ought to ask for those things that glorify God, and to put before him a heart that loves him above all else. That's why the very first thing that we're supposed to ask is that God's Name be more known and better known in this world, and praised more, and praised better.

After this first petition, which refers to the nature of God himself, Christ put two others, subordinate to this first one because they refer to his relationship with us—to his lordship over us and the obedience that we owe him—not to any intrinsic part of God as "hallowed be thy Name" does. So they're properly mentioned after that first petition, not before it.

thy kingdom come;
adveniat regnum tuum;

The same grammatical structure as in "hallowed be thy Name" shapes "Thy kingdom come". It's subjunctive, too, a statement of wish or desire.

The puzzling part here, though, is probably "kingdom". Today, we think of a kingdom as a certain territory that happens to be ruled by a king or a queen. But here the word means that office itself, not a piece of land; it does not refer to any terrestrial country, no earthly paradise. The Latin for "kingdom" in this case, as you can see, is *regno*, and the farther back you take that word the clearer it gets. The ultimate root of *regno*, back in the first Indo-European language of the world, sprouted many branches: the Sanskrit root *raj-*, meaning to reach for, to take control of; the Greek ὀρέγω, which means approximately the same thing; the Latin *rex* (king), *regulus* (a princeling or minor ruler) and *regula* (the wooden straightedge or a pattern); the German *Reich* (empire or dominion) and *recht*, which is exactly like its English cousin "right", in the sense of being entitled to something as well as the sense of being correct, just, and the opposite of left; also our words "regent", "rule", "regular", and even "regulate".

All of these words have to do with order, and more than that they all have to do with acts of affirming order or establishing order; and they all have a connotation of justice, or "rightness" about them. *Regno* itself means public order, really, whether it's maintained by a Senate, a President, or a King. So this petition means, send us your kingdom, establish your rulership among us; may you establish your rule here on Earth, or unite us all under your rule in Heaven—but however you do it, we want you to establish your kingdom over us.

thy will be done
fiat voluntas tua

Children often have a problem with this phrase. Some, trying to make sense of the unfamiliar words, figure that "thy" is something that's going to be done: *thy* will be done. Whatever "thy" is, it's going to be done.

"Thy", of course, is an old word that we've replaced with "your"; but there's more to it than that. Many languages have two ways to refer to the second person ("first person" means the speaker, naturally—*I, me, us, our*—"second person" means the person spoken to—*you*—and third person means the person spoken about—*he, him, she, her, they, their*).

Nowadays, in English, we only use "you" and "your" to indicate the second person. But we used to have two ways to do it, a formal way and an informal way, as Spanish has *Usted* and *tu*, French uses *vous* and *tu*, and

THE OUR FATHER

German has *Sie* and *du*. We used to have the formal *you* and *your*, and the informal *thou*, *thy*, and *thee*. If you wanted to give a present to a person who outranked you, you'd say, "I would like to give this to you"; but if you were going to give something to a person with whom you lived intimately— a friend, a child, a spouse—you'd say, "I'd like to give this to thee."

The formality of the *you* forms in English is why the Society of Friends—the Quakers—refused to use them; all Men are created equal, in the Friends' view, and they were as good as their word, when it came to talking about that precept in this world. So, with the Quakers, it was always *thee*, *thou*, *thy*, and *thine*. The familiarity of those forms is why Christ used the parallel forms himself, when he said things like "thy Name" and "thy will". He's reinforcing the ideas of love and intimacy that he initiated when he told us to call God "Father".

The word *fiat*, "let it be done", is important, too; it's the same one that God uses, in the Genesis of the Vulgate, to create things: *Fiat lux*, let there be light, let light be made, let light be, in actuality; bring forth the first-born of creation (Pr 8:22-36). This is an active word, a word that makes things happen in reality. This phrase is a prayer of co-operation with God to change things for the better; and the preface for this phrase in the Lord's Prayer, of course, is Mary's statement of absolute submission to God: let it be done unto me according to thy will, *fiat mihi secundum voluntas tua* (Lk 1:38).

And you can see that the Latin *voluntas*, meaning will or willpower, is related to our words "voluntary" and "volunteer", words that refer to what somebody wants—somebody's will. In Heaven, the Celestial Jerusalem of Revelations, everything is in perfect accord with the will of God (Mt 5:8, Rv 21:27), which is why Christ rounded off these first three petitions with the next phrase.

on Earth as it is in Heaven.
sicut in coelo et in terra.

Because of the rhythm in which we chant the Our Father, we sometimes tend to tie this phrase only to the one before it: thy will be done on Earth as it is in Heaven. But really this phrase hangs on all three petitions that we've presented so far: hallowed be thy Name on Earth as it is in Heaven, thy kingdom come on Earth as it is in Heaven, and thy will be done on Earth as it is in Heaven.

Life on Earth, obviously, isn't anything like life in the Heavenly Jerusalem. Crime, sin, indifference, barbarism, ignorance, illiteracy, and all kinds of other disorders show us every moment just how much we lost in the sin of Adam and Eve. That first small step away from the will of God— committed in the exercise of our own free will—made this world what it is, and it brought about all of the distress and disorder that naturally follow from that step.

Christ repeated over and over that his followers are supposed to work their way back to that heavenly city and that while we're doing this we're supposed to do all we can to establish that kind of arrangement on Earth. Treat each other as you would be treated; forgive those who hurt you, and pray for those who hate you; turn the other cheek; give not only your cloak but the shirt off your back, if need be. Pray always. Live together in the love of God, in charity, seeking to know the will of God, and to do it.

That makes this world radically different from a world that does not know these teachings and all the others like them; imagine a world in which people genuinely lived like this. This simple phrase, "on Earth as it is in Heaven", is one of the richest fields for meditation on this world and what you might do about it; and it's a point of meditation that can bring the whole of Christianity to bear on the solutions of the disorders in your own life, spiritual, emotional, and physical. In fact, ever since Christ reminded Pilate that his kingdom was not of this world, the kingdom of Heaven on Earth has always been understood to be a matter of interior conversion; it's up to us to change the exterior reality of life here below to conform to that inner Heaven.

"The word 'Heaven'," St. Cyril of Jerusalem pointed out, means the spiritual world in which the souls of the blessed, and the angels, stand immediately in the presence of God, but it "also means those who carry in them the image and likeness of the heavenly Man—because God is dwelling in them and working in them" here on Earth. "Effectively, then," he added, "this is what you mean by this phrase: as in the angels [in Heaven] ... so let it be in me on Earth, O Lord... Therefore, do not let sin reign in your mortal body" (*Catecheses* 5; cf. Lv 26:11-12; 1Cr 15:49; 2Cr 6:16; Rm 6:12).

Give us this day our daily bread;
Panem nostrum quotidianum da nobis hodie,

"How beautifully the Divine Wisdom has ordered the sequence of this prayer," Tertullian exclaimed. "After the heavenly things—the Name of God, the will of God, and the kingdom of God—he left room for petitions about earthly things." Following the graceful rhetorical structure that he established in the first few petitions, Christ turned to the requests that are even more subordinate to the nature of God, his lordship, and the obedience that we owe him. This phrase requesting bread has stayed clear through the ages, but it's so simple that you might not think about what it implies. Christ is telling us to ask God for everything that we need, even the basics; "this too is Wisdom, to know whose is the gift" (Ws 8:21).

He also uses the plural here, "give *us* this day"; he doesn't tell us to say, "give me". Christians are inseparable; we are supposed to love our neighbor as ourselves, and pray for them as for ourselves. United in one body, with Christ as the head, no Christian can forget any of the other members (1Cr 12).

In the Greek, this phrase contains an interesting kind of wordplay. The phrase in Matthew is τὸν ἄρτον ἡμῶν τὸν ἐπιούσιον. If you divide that last word as ἐπ- ιούσιον, it means "coming" or "daily"; but if you understand it as divided ἐπι- ούσιον, it means "transubstantial".

In any language, phrases like "this day", of course, and "our daily bread" remind us that we need to pray always, every day, and that we depend every day on God to sustain us in the struggle that ends only with death. There's no easy, once-and-for-all assurance of salvation, just as there's no earthly food that you can eat once and never be hungry again—not even the food that God rains down on us from Heaven (Ex 16:4; Jn 6:31-60).

And he said "bread"—not meat, not sweets, not even fruits or vegetables, but bread, understood as the simplest and most basic food, the staff of life. This is perfectly consistent with everything else that he did, when it came to physical necessities; he dealt in what you really need, not in what you'd like. Even when he came among us, he came to a stable, not to a palace.

So, he says, ask God for what you need, for enough bread to get by, because after all this is his gift, and he really doesn't need to supply it to you. It was Man's first sin that got him banished from the Garden of Eden, anyway, where he had all possible creature comforts; only after he sinned did he need clothing, shelter, medicine, tools, or weapons to secure his livelihood, and only then did he need to secure a food supply for himself. Only then did Man need to produce his bread by the sweat of his brow (Gn 3:17).

Many saints, notably St. Jerome, have noticed that three petitions in this prayer point to Heaven, and four to Earth, which might seem disproportionate. But this petition, the middle one, stands both in Heaven and on Earth. St. Bernard of Clairvaux summed it up well when he said that this central petition is pivotal to the prayer; it connects the heavenly first part to the everyday second part because the bread referred to comes from Heaven but is used on Earth. It's like the manna of Exodus, he said, or, rather, like the Bread of the sixth chapter of John. So, in the Our Father, the metaphorical meanings of bread outweigh the literal meaning, as metaphorical meanings usually do in the Bible—the word "metaphor" itself is from the Greek μετά, meaning with, and φέρειν, to carry. "Bread" here indeed signifies necessary, not luxurious, food, as in 4Kn 6:22, and earthly food; but it carries with it greater and higher significance: Christ told us specifically that we can't live on this earthly bread alone, but on every word that comes from the mouth of God (Mt 4:4). And more than that he told us that he himself is the Bread of Heaven: which is why he instituted the Eucharist (Jn 6).

and forgive us our trespasses as we forgive those who trespass against us.
et dimitte nobis debita nostra, sicut et nos dimittimus debitoribus nostris.

By a happy coincidence, the Latin *debita* of the Vulgate—obviously like our word "debt"—got translated into "trespasses". In the Greek, Matthew uses the word for debt in both halves of the phrase, but Luke puts the phrase something more like, "forgive us our sins, because we also forgive our debtors." "Trespass" isn't really out of place here, of course, because it straddles both meanings, sin and debt. It's from the Latin *trans-*, across, and *passare*, to pass—it means to cross that line, to step on somebody else's property, or somebody else's rights. It means to offend God's rights, or your neighbor's.

Each of the two Evangelists puts a different cast on the tenses of his verbs, too. Matthew uses the perfect tense, asking God to forgive us "as we have forgiven", which would remind you that judgement is nigh. Luke uses the present tense, forgive us "as we forgive", which reminds us that we have to live the Christian ideal every day, in preparation for judgement at the end of those days.

But in either case, this petition underscores Christ's other pronounce-ments—and he repeats himself so seldom that anything he says twice deserves particular attention. "For if you forgive people their offenses," he said just after this petition, "your heavenly Father will also forgive your offenses. But if you do not forgive people, neither will your Father forgive you your offenses" (Mt 6:14-15). And he mentioned later that those who "do not each forgive your brothers from your heart" will be handed over to the torturers (Mt 18:34-35).

This sums up the whole principle of moral theology, the application of Christ's teachings to daily life: salvation depends on the forgiveness of sin, and sin is forgiven depending on how you behave—salvation is not a free gift, and it does not depend on faith alone, nor on acclamation of Christ, nor on confession of his lordship alone. This petition is formed to affirm again that salvation depends on both faith (which prompts you to ask forgiveness) and on works (which require you to act in a certain way here on Earth). No other idea of salvation can stand compatible with this segment of the Lord's Prayer, nor indeed with any other part of it.

This petition is shaped rhetorically like a hinge, one half of it turning sym-metrically on the other. It opens the door to a new manner of praying that characterizes the Our Father from this point to its conclusion. Up to here, we've asked God everlasting and temporal goods, spiritual and physical necessities; but now we're asking to be freed from the evils of body and soul now and in the life to come.

In this phrase, Christ's continued use of the plural might sound a little presumptuous when we say it, because it takes for granted that we're all going to sin. It might sound like you're accusing everybody else, or at least imputing sin to them. But everybody sins, and everybody knows it (1Jn 1:8; Pr 20:9), and one person's sin afflicts everybody—we're all one body, and sin spreads disorder across the whole world, just as burning trash pollutes the air near and far.

Notice also that this phrase takes for granted the fact that God is a merciful God, slow to anger and quick to forgive. If he were just a furious avenger, there wouldn't be much point in asking for forgiveness. If we acknowledge our sins and confess them, Christ said (Lk 17:4; 1Jn 1:9), they will be forgiven; and he set up an apostolic Church empowered to do exactly that, carrying on his work of freeing people from the penalties of sin until he comes again himself (Jn 20:23).

And lead us not into temptation,
Et ne nos inducas in tentationem,

Of all of the phrases in the King James version, probably none has caused more confusion over the years than this one. As with everything else that appears to be a contradiction in Christian teachings, this confusion is based in a misunderstanding, and it can persist only in the unwillingness to probe with questions beneath the surface of the words (or in an unwillingness to answer, lest the faults in heretical teachings be discovered). God can't tempt people to sin; that would be duplicity, two-facedness; and God, as all perfection, can't lie. Besides, the whole point of revelation is to draw people closer to God; and for that we have to trust him, absolutely. If he dangled temptation before us, enticing us to do things that lead away from him, that would be God working against God; and a house divided against itself cannot stand (Mt 12:25). Obviously.

But look at the word *tentationem*. The first syllable of it is "tent", and that's the key. *Tentationem* basically means a stretching, a pulling tight, as when you pull ropes tight to set up a tent, or really as you stretch cloth to make the tent itself. Figuratively, it means pulling on something to test it; putting it under some stress and strain to see if it will hold up; it means putting something to the test. *Inducas* looks like "induce" or "induction", and in fact it means to lead somebody into a place or a situation.

So the phrase really means, "Don't lead us into a situation in which we will be put to the test." It refers to the great trials before the final judgement (2Th 2:1-8) or, really, the great trials that we'll all face before death, our own private Judgement Day at the end of our allotted Time (Mt 24:21-22). And it's one of those comparatively few things that Christ repeated: pray that you will not be put to the test, he said again (Lk 22:40; Mt 26:41), and he himself begged his Father to take away that cup of trial that was his to drink (Mt 26:39; *cf.* 20:22).

but deliver us from evil.
sed libera nos a malo.

Libera nos, free us, echoes through the Old Testament, especially in Psalms, and it sums up the last few petitions, bringing the Our Father to a close. This phrase is one of the most frequent refrains in the Church's prayer— free us from sin; free us from temptation; free us from evil.

In fact, the *Libera Nos* is a prayer in its own right. It's an *embolism,* which means an insertion or an interpolation. In fact, it's sometimes called *"the* Embolism", but most often just the *Libera Nos.* There are many older versions of it: the Alexandrine Embolism, the Antiochene, the Gallican, the Mozarabic, the Milanese, and the Roman itself. Some of these add a subsidiary list of petitions asking Mary, St. Peter, St. Paul, St. Andrew, or other saints to pray for our deliverance, but these petitions can only ask their prayers, because the saints can't deliver us from sin; only Christ can do this, and throughout the Church's prayers that phrase *libera nos,* quite properly, is reserved to the Savior alone. For everybody else, it's always been only *ora pro nobis,* pray for us.

Today the Church uses a fairly brief form of the Roman Embolism, with no subsidiary petitions asking help from the saints. It's always said after the communal praying of the Our Father at Mass, and it's been set to music many times over the centuries so that it can be sung on those feast days when singing it is appropriate.

Deliver us, we beg you, O Lord,	Libera nos, quæsumus, Domine,
from every evil,	ab omnibus malis,
and grant us peace	da propitius pacem
in our day;	in diebus nostris;
in your mercy	ut, ope misericordiæ tuæ adiuti,
keep us free from sin	et a peccato simus semper liberi
and protect us from every anxiety	et ab omni perturbatione securi
as we wait in joyful hope	exspectantes beatam spem
for the coming of our Savior	et adventum Salvatoris nostris
Jesus Christ.	Jesu Christi.

And the people answer:

For the kingdom,	Quia tuum est regnum,
and the power,	et potestas,
and the glory are yours	et goloria
now and forever. Amen.	in sæcula. Amen.

This congregational response is extremely old—it shows up in the *Didache*— and it has worked its way into some latter-day versions of the Bible, as Mt 6:13, but it isn't part of Scripture. It isn't part of the Our Father at all, as you can see not only from the fact that Luke doesn't give it but from the rhetorical structure of the prayer itself. It's a little embolism on its own, and as such it's used by itself after the Our Father by the Byzantine Rite of the Universal Church, without the Embolism of the *Libera Nos*.

The Our Father is what's called a *liturgical* prayer. It comes straight out of the Bible, like Psalms, and in fact straight from the lips of Jesus Christ himself; so it can be used in the Church's public prayers. Everybody at Mass always recites it, because Christ said, when you pray, say this. But there are also what are called *devotional* prayers, those that aren't used in the Church's public prayers but only in private devotions. Liturgical prayer outranks devotional prayer, which is one reason that you're not supposed to pray the Rosary at Mass. Your whole attention is supposed to be directed to the miracle of the Eucharist, and the Rosary should be said before or later, but it should not usurp the place of the Sacrament.

Still, devotional prayers are an integral part of Christian prayer life. Through the centuries, the Church, largely through the laity, has put together a good many devotional prayers that address some essential reason for which everybody prays, in a high and suitably noble form. These prayers are approved, they're good patterns of prayer, and they're a sound starting place for those higher forms of prayer that don't necessarily involve spoken words.

A ❀ Ω

THE HAIL MARY

J UST AS THE GREATEST OF THE CHURCH'S LITURGICAL PRAYERS IS THE OUR Father, the greatest of the Church's devotional prayers is the *Ave Maria*—the Hail Mary. It's largely composed of Bible verses, too— words proceeding from the mouth of God himself, by way of the Archangel Gabriel, and words that St. John the Baptizer prompted his mother to say. But it was assembled over the centuries by pious Christians as a way of asking Mary's prayers for their spiritual welfare. It's repeated on each of the ten beads of each decade.

Hail, Mary, full of grace!	Ave, Maria, gratia plena!
The Lord is with thee.	Dominus tecum.
Blessed art thou	Benedicta tu
amongst women,	in mulieribus,
and blessed is the fruit	et benedictus fructus
of thy womb,	ventris tui,
Jesus!	Jesus!
Holy Mary, Mother of God,	Sancta Maria, Mater Dei,
pray for us	ora pro nobis
sinners	peccatoribus
now and at the hour of our death.	nunc et in hora mortis nostræ.
Amen.	Amen.

Although it's composed mainly of Bible verses, the Hail Mary isn't used as part of the Church's public liturgies. Devotional prayers, holy as they are, don't rank anywhere near the Sacrament of the Eucharist or any other sacrament, which is why "it is a mistake to recite the Rosary during the celebration of the liturgy, although unfortunately this practice still persists here and there" (Paul VI, *Marialis cultus*). If you pray the Rosary at Mass, you're turning your attention from a higher form of prayer to a lower— you're turning from the Presence of Christ, in fact.

Like the Rosary itself and so many of the Church's other devotional prayers, the Hail Mary condensed out of Bible verses that were customarily used in the ordinary prayers of the laity. So it developed gradually, phrase by phrase.

Hail, Mary, full of grace; the Lord is with thee.
Ave, Maria, gratia plena; Dominus tecum.

THE HAIL MARY

This is of course Gabriel's salutation to Mary at the Annunciation, right out of Luke (1:28), although the Church added the name "Mary", as a way to identify the one to whom the prayer is addressed, which is just a matter of common sense.

The "Hail" is significant in its form. Latin has two principal words of greeting, *Ave* and *Salve*, which is related to our words like "salutation", "salutary", and "salvation". *Salve* is used for solemn occasions, and for taking leave of people, because it has to do with wishes for their health and well-being. If you were to send off a soldier to war or a friend on a perilous journey, or if you were to greet a great lord or lady solemnly, you'd use *salve*. But *Ave* is a greeting of happiness. It's more joyful, the kind of expression you'd use when you see someone dear to you, someone whom you're glad to see. That's why St. Jerome used *Ave* when he translated this verse into Latin, and in Mt 28:9, when Christ appeared after his resurrection to the Apostles, running toward them in his joy.

> The Middle Ages looked at *Ave* from all sides and took it apart, to get the full meaning of the Annunciation across by means of this single word. For example, the *Myroure of our Ladye* says, "this word *Ave* spelled backwards is *Eva*, for as Eve's talking with the devil was the beginning of perdition, Our Lady's talking with the angel was the beginning of our redemption. And so *Eva* is turned to *Ave*, for our sorrow is turned to joy by Our Lady."
>
> The author of the *Myroure* then goes on to give one of those fanciful etymologies so often used in the Middle Ages to get valid points firmly into the memory. It's not easily followed today, but it's a good example of the intricacy of mediæval thought. The name *Eva* means woe, the author says, and in the Middle Ages it did; the classical Latin word for woe, as in "woe is me," is *heu!*, but *h* is silent, and *u* turns into *v*, so even by Vergil's day the expression of woe was often spelled *væ* or *he væ!*, which is close to *Heva*, the Vulgate's name for Eve. Reversing this word, "to say *Ave*," the author continues, "is to say 'joy', or *a-ve*, which is 'without woe'." Therefore, the *Myroure* concludes, "meekly and reverently thanking this glorious Queen of Heaven and Mother of Our Savior for our deliverance, we say devoutly to her, *Ave, Maria.*"

Of course, Mary's name itself is significant—all names in the Bible are significant—but nobody seems to know exactly what its significance is. It's the same name as that of Moses's sister, which is usually written as Miriam. And just as Miriam of the Old Testament accompanied Moses—the prefiguration of Christ—on his work, so did Mary accompany Christ. Miriam prophesied, too (Ex 15:20). But the exact meaning of the name Mary is still elusive.

Some scholars have tried to establish it as an Egyptian name, as Moses and Aaron are Egyptian names, but although the name Meryt or Mery (cherished or beloved) was popular in Egypt before Israel left, it doesn't quite seem to fit, for philological reasons. Others have suggested that it's derived from Hebrew words meaning things like "drop in the ocean" or "bitter sea"—the root מר (mr), the source of our word "myrrh", occurs in a lot of Hebrew words referring to bitterness, and in words having to do with the sea, and it means "droplet" all by itself. In fact, "Star of the Sea" is one of the oldest titles of the Virgin, dating back past the time of St. Jerome. But the idea of calling Mary *Stella Maris* doesn't come from the derivation of her name; it comes from her protection of sailors, particularly from the miraculous preservations from shipwreck that she accomplished, which were often accompanied by apparitions of her, and which were surprisingly frequent in early Christianity.

Others have tried to derive the name from words referring to rulership. Some have derived it from מרי (mry), meaning rebellion. The tenth-century scholar Josephus Genesius looked back to the occurrence of a similar word in 2Es 9:17, כמרים, which means "their rebellion", and suggested that as the source of the name. It doesn't hold up, again for philological reasons (that כ is apparently just a prefix, not part of the word), but it's interesting in light of what Mary accomplished—overturning the social order of the western world. But it's unlikely in the extreme that Joachim and Anna would have named their daughter, the child of their miracle, a name proclaiming rebellion.

Most likely, the name is not related to מרי but to מרא (mara), meaning to be well nourished, sleek, or even fat. It sounds improbable at first, but in the countries of the arid Levant there's never been much difference between being well nourished and being thought beautiful. Daniel appeared fatter and, therefore, fairer in flesh after his imprisonment (Dn 1:15), and Proverbs predicts that the soul of the diligent, those who trust in the Lord, shall be made fat (Pr 13:4, 28:25)—metaphorically, that is, being given an abundance of rich graces; those same books go into some detail about the punishments that await the greedy.

But even the fat of the land is a Biblical byword for prosperity, abundance, and beauty, and even lush, well-watered plants are used in Scripture to denote the Lord's nearness and his favor, in contrast to the shrivelled and the dry (Ps 51:10, 127:3; Dn 4:7-11; Ez 17:24; Lk 23:31). The name in these senses is appropriate to Miriam, who helped lead her people into a promised land of milk and honey, and to Mary, who bore the Son who would eat butter and honey (Is 7:15)—she who was well nourished by the fullness of exceptional grace. And certainly the name Mary is appropriate to the Mother of God in its metaphorical meaning of "the beautiful", or even "the perfect one".

The phrase "full of grace" has been puzzled over for many a year. Some recent translations of the Bible substitute verbiage less puzzling, perhaps, but less emphatic, like "most favored one" or even "highly favored one". But there's something to be said for the direct translation of the Vulgate's *gratia plena*, full of grace. St. Luke's original Greek term is κεχαριτωμένη, which bears the sense of being gifted, or, in other words, graced. It's related to χαριτόω, to show grace to someone—it's like the English word "charism", in the sense of having to do with spiritual gifts. The same word is used in Sr 18:17 to mean precisely that, giving a gift.

Nobody else in the Bible is addressed that way, so Gabriel's reference is to unique gifts of grace. "When the angel cried, 'Hail, full of grace, the Lord is with thee; blessed art thou amongst women!', he told us by divine command how tremendous the dignity and the beauty of the Ever-Virgin Mary are," St. Jerome explained (*On the Assumption*). The Church has always understood the term to mean that Mary was endowed with as much grace as human nature can receive, comparable to the supernatural gifts that Adam and Eve were given but lost by original sin—a sin that Mary didn't share. This fullness of grace stands as a kind of complement to her sinlessness: the grace is a positive gift, and the sinlessness is the absence of anything that counters that gift.

In other humans, the two stand in varying proportions—whatever part of the soul isn't filled with grace is filled, so to speak, with the emptiness of sin. But in Mary the grace was as complete as grace can be in a human, leaving no room for sin; grace was bestowed on her, Pius IX Ferretti said, "in such a wonderful way that she would always be free from absolutely every stain of sin and that, all beautiful and perfect, she might display such fullness of innocence and holiness that none greater would be known under God" (*Ineffabilis Deus*, 1854).

Mary's unique closeness to God is expressed in the phrase, "the Lord is with thee." It refers to her sinlessness as the phrase "full of grace" does: indirectly. Sin is what keeps people from God (Mt 5:8); Mary, being without sin, has a unique closeness to God. Of course, her maternity of Jesus by itself puts her closer to God than any other human being possibly could be, but this phrase refers to something else; after all, Gabriel said it before Christ was conceived.

So she could not, as some separated brethren have taught, have been made sinless after the Incarnation; she must have been sinless before it, when Gabriel came to her, and in fact from the first instant of her conception. To be the mother of the Savior, Mary had to have, already, a highly intimate relationship with the Holy Trinity, a "sanctifying union", as it's called by some theologians. In fact, Catholic theologians regard her supernatural, sanctifying relationship with God himself as axiomatic.

Blessed art thou amongst women, and blessed is the fruit of thy womb, Jesus. *Benedicta tu in mulieribus, et benedictus fructus ventris tui Jesus.*

The second part of the salutation is also straight from Scripture. The first part of it is a kind of bridge between Gabriel's greeting and St. Elizabeth's (Lk 1:42). After all, Elizabeth's greeting starts with the words that end Gabriel's. We are accustomed to add this verse to the Angelic Salutation, Archbishop Baldwin of Canterbury wrote at some date before 1184, because Elizabeth "caught up and completed, as it were, the Angel's word".

In fact, by Baldwin's day the two verses had been customarily said together for at least seven hundred years. This was evidently the norm by the time of the Council of Ephesus, which sat in 431; the earliest written evidence was found in Egypt on an ostracon—a piece of broken pottery, used for notations throughout the ancient world—that dates from about 600. It has written on it, in Greek, a fragment of liturgy that includes the prayer, "Hail, Mary, full of grace; the Lord is with thee. Blessed art thou amongst women, and blessed is the fruit of thy womb; for thou didst conceive Christ, the Son of God, the Redeemer of our souls."

Long before Bishop Baldwin's day, too, bishops and synods all across the known world had already commanded that the laity should be taught the Angelic Salutation—including the greeting of Elizabeth—just as they were taught the Creed and the Our Father. That combination of verses was already integral to so many private devotions that the clergy were concerned that it be learned properly and accorded the respect that was due to it, as Scripture.

"Blessed art thou amongst women" is not, strictly speaking, an expression of Mary's holiness, because "blessed" doesn't necessarily mean holy. We capture several distinct meanings in that single word "blessed", which blurs some of what we read in Scripture and what we say in prayer. Here, it translates the Latin *benedicta* and the Greek εὐλογημένη, both of which come from roots meaning well spoken of, or praised. This is what Elizabeth said to Mary, and what Gabriel had said to her; and "blessed" carries this meaning in contexts like the Divine Praises. "Blessed" also denotes happiness when it translates the Latin *beatus* and the Greek μακαριοῦσι, which is what Mary said in the *Magnificat* (Lk 1:48). To use "blessed" to mean holy, speakers of English have to run a long and indirect route of connotations. Christians understand that true happiness is only possible in closeness to God, so closeness to God is a necessary step between us and happiness; but closeness to God is also holiness, because nothing unclean is permitted near him (Mt 5:8, Rv 21:27). "Holy" is far the better word to use when we mean holy; it directly translates the Latin *sanctus* and the Greek ἅγιος.

The Church added the name "Jesus" to this joyful call of praise, simply because it's common sense to add the name when the verse is taken out of its Scriptural context. Judging by archaeological remains, this was already customary by about the year 600, too.

Holy Mary, Mother of God,
Sancta Maria, Mater Dei,

Christians have always recognized that the Hail Mary as a whole stands in two halves: the praise and then the petition. The Jesuit scholar Herbert J. Thurston noted that some of the Faithful in Ireland, when told to say the Hail Mary as a penance after confession would ask, "Must we say the Holy Mary too?"—and this as late as 1900. But this second half of the prayer has never really stood on its own as a separate prayer, the way the Angelic Salutation did.

The "holy" in this first phrase of the second half, of course, comes from the Greek ἅγιος or the Latin *sancta*; it would be more normally translated by the English word "saint" (which means precisely the same thing), when it comes before a person's name.

The "Mother of God" merits a little more explanation, but it makes sense: Mary is the mother of Jesus; Jesus is the Second Person of the Trinity, God; so Mary is the Mother of God. But grasping this concept only partially sometimes makes people ask how God, who always was and always will be, God who is the First Cause of everything, the Creator, could have a mother. That, it seems, would put Mary as the First Cause. Of course, it doesn't mean that. That would be nonsense.

The misunderstanding was definitively settled by the ecumenical Council of Ephesus in 431. Like all ecumenical councils, this one was convened to counter certain specific attacks and confusions that were opposing the Church and her mission on Earth; this particular problem centered on a man named Nestorius of Antioch, who died in the middle of the fourth century. He was a priest and a monk, living a cloistered life in the monastery of Euprepius, when the Emperor Theodosius II called him to the capital to be Bishop of Constantinople. Nestorius was vigorous in his actions against Quartodecimans, Novatians, Pelagians, Arians, and all kinds of other heretics, but then he slipped into a heresy himself, the heresy that still bears his name.

Nestorianism got its start when Nestorius preached a sermon, toward the end of 428, against the use of the word θεοτόκος, "bearer of God" or, effectively, "Mother of God", in reference to Mary. This attitude stemmed from his background at Antioch, where the nature of Christ was taught by means of some very confusing language, but the idea seems to have been his own. He said, correctly, that Jesus has two natures, the divine and the human, but then he asserted incorrectly that Mary is the mother of only his human nature—"nobody can bring forth a son older than herself," he said. Nestorius taught, therefore, that Christ was born only a man, but a man who attained union with God as the reward of his Passion. That is, Nestorius taught that Christ was not a complete person, not his complete self, from the very moment of his conception.

Naturally, the Church opposed this view then as now: Christ's nature didn't change at some point after conception, any more than anybody else's does; you are what you are. There were riots in the streets about this point in those days, too, just as there are civil disturbances about it now, between those who maintain the Christian view of human nature and those who deny it.

Basically, of course, Christian teaching is that Christ does indeed have two natures, being true God and true Man, and that he had both natures from the instant of his conception, at the Annunciation. Nobody can bear a son older than herself in the natural order of things, but Mary's maternity of Jesus partakes of the supernatural order of things. It was ordained from Eternity, too, and Eternity stands outside of Time. Considerations like "older than", "younger than", "before", and "after", have absolutely no meaning when you talk about Eternity. "You don't know how to think about divine things," St. Augustine had already said (*Sermon 64 on John*; *cf.* Jn 1:1, 14-15). "He existed before his own flesh existed; he created his own mother. He chose her in whom he would be conceived; he brought forth her of whom he would be brought forth. Why do you wonder at this? This is God of whom I speak: 'the Word was God'."

When Nestorius started preaching his errors, other bishops and teachers of Christendom reacted instantly and in no uncertain terms. John Cassian, for instance, answered Nestorius's sermon immediately with seven books giving the Church's consistent doctrine of Christ's incarnation. A Tuscan deacon named Leo took a leading role in the Church's response to Nestorianism, and when he became Pope Leo I a few years later he maintained his opposition to this heresy in particular. Nestorius's chief opponent at the time, though, was St. Cyril, Bishop of Alexandria, who sent Nestorian texts, with his own refutations, to Pope St. Celestine I. The pope reviewed the documents, thanked St. Cyril, and summoned Nestorius to recant his errors within ten days of receipt of the pope's letter. St. Cyril drew up a list of errors that Nestorius was supposed to abjure. The Bishop of Antioch objected to them; and with all of the patriarchal sees—Rome, Alexandria, Antioch, and Constantinople—squaring off about the exact nature of the heresy and the exact formulation of its correction, the Emperor intervened and asked the Pope to summon an ecumenical council. It met on neutral but highly significant ground, in the church of St. John the Evangelist at Ephesus.

Mary evidently lived in Ephesus with St. John the Evangelist after Pentecost—there's still a little church there that's always been called the House of Mary, just outside the city at a place called *Panaya Kapulu*, in Turkish. Certainly Ephesus was a city devoted to Mary, so while the people took a great interest in the formulation of an accurate statement about the nature of Christ, they were especially eager to hear what the Council had to say about whether Mary might properly be called what they had always called her, Mother of God.

When the Council had formulated its teaching on the nature of Christ and pronounced it solemnly, affirming that θεοτόκος is indeed a proper title for Mary, the Christians of Ephesus poured into the streets chanting, "Holy Mary! Mother of God! Pray for us sinners!" After that, this salutation, and this petition, were often added to the praise of the greetings that Mary heard from Gabriel and from Elizabeth, her kinswoman.

Pray for us sinners, now and at the hour of our death. Amen.
Ora pro nobis peccatoribus, nunc et in hora mortis nostræ. Amen.

This petition to Mary is the same as the petition to any other saint, or to any of the Faithful here among us on Earth: pray for us. Nobody asks Mary to save us, as if salvation were hers to grant, nor to have mercy on us, as if judgement were hers. Prayers sometimes include phrases that ask her extraordinary help, or that beg spiritual alms from her by invoking her pity, but these, too, are to be understood in the full light of her position: greatest of the saints, by far, but by nature human, not divine. That's why the Church's great refrain of petition to her, in the Hail Mary, the Litany of Loreto, and in the other devotional prayers addressed to her, is simply *ora pro nobis*, pray for us.

By about the year 1300, the Angelic Salutation consisting of Gabriel's salutation and Elizabeth's joined to it by the phrase "blessed art thou amongst women", had been standard across Christendom for uncounted centuries, and it had been worked into any number of devotional practices. Some Christians repeated these praises alone, recalling and sharing the joy that Mary must have felt when she knew that the Savior was on his way at last.

Most people, though, took this opportunity to ask Mary to pray for them, so they added a petition for intercession to that repetition of praise. This could be something as simple as "pray for us", or something of considerable literary merit, like the petitions long attributed to Dante: "O Blessed Virgin, pray to God for us always, that he may pardon us and give us grace, so to live here below that he may at our end reward us with Paradise." As late as the end of the fifteenth century, there was no standard conclusion to the prayer, but nearly everybody in Christendom added some kind of petition to the Salutation.

The English *Kalendar of Shepardys* (*Calendar of Shepherds*) of 1495 seems to have been the first printed text to add the petition of Ephesus definitively to the prayer: "Holy Mary moder of God praye for us synners, amen," it said. In that same year, though, the terrifying Florentine preacher Savonarola—of all people—published a version of the prayer that's almost exactly like the one used today: "Holy Mary, Mother of God, pray for us sinners, now and at the hour of death. Amen," it adds to the Angelic Salutation and the greeting of St. Elizabeth.

Only a few years later, an anonymous Camaldolese monk inserted the word "our" where it is today, when he edited the order's breviary; but in fact he was not the first to publish the Hail Mary in its definitive form. Alan de Rupe, the Dominican who set down the Rosary itself in its definitive form, had already given the Hail Mary the shape that it has today, in the works that were not published until after his death. But the coincidence of all of these identical publications only shows that the prayer had already come to its final development, all across Christendom. The *Catechism* of the Council of Trent stabilized it in the form that has been standard ever since, and the Roman Breviary of 1568 published it officially for the use of the whole Church.

EVA ✦ AVE

AMEN

MEN IS THE WORD THAT USUALLY CONCLUDES EACH PRAYER THAT'S SAID in the course of the Rosary, although it's not really an integral part of any of those prayers; many people omit it until they come to the end of the Rosary, or to the end of the one-third of it that they customarily say. "Amen" is really a little prayer in itself. It comes from a Hebrew word אמת (emet), meaning truth or certainty, and the Israelites used it to mean "so be it". Some philologists have traced it back to an expression meaning something like "I'll drive my tent peg into that"; so it means that you understand the matter as solid, firm, and completely reliable. St. Jerome called this word the seal of prayer; it stamps your approval on what you've just said. It's recommended as another aid to concentrating on your prayers, because saying it is a positive act of affirmation. But all by itself, this little word is a canticle of praise, and confidence, and gratitude, and a profession of faith; it's a little song of joy and thanksgiving, all in one word.

It's basically the same word in Greek and in Hebrew as it is in Latin and English, the only difference being that in English it's pronounced with a long *a*, as in *able*. In Latin is that the *a* is pronounced as it is in *father*. Either way, it's generally supposed to be pronounced at the end of each prayer.

In the Old Testament, the word is used at the end of prayers, too, and it's used as a response to something that someone else has said, whether that person is human (3Kn 1:36) or divine (Jr 11:5). It's used in this way in the New Testament, too (1Cr 14:16), and as a seal on the person's own prayer (Rm 16:27), but Jesus used it at the beginning of what he said. This is evidently unique in Israel, certainly unique in Scripture; he used "amen" as a way to indicate the solemnity of what he was about to say, and to convey clearly a sense of his own authority to say it (Mt 5:18; Jn 1:51).

The Israelites used the word liturgically (Dt 27:15-26; Ps 105:48) exactly as it's used liturgically by the Church today and has been since the beginning. It's the universal word of unity, of single-hearted agreement with the Word of God. "Amen sounds well indeed," St. Ambrose said, "when all different ages and conditions of people join together in church like the harmonies of stringed instruments, singing the Psalms with alternate verses and then closing their song with the word, Amen."

But perhaps the most impressive use of "Amen" is also the most unusual, grammatically: the Bible uses it as a noun. God is "the God of Amen", Isaia said (65:16, *Iurabit in Deo amen*, in the Vulgate), the God of affirmation who, after granting a petitioner's request, dismisses him in grace, as the Catechism of Trent phrased it. "It is of little use, Lord," Ludolph of Saxony wrote in the fourteenth century, "for me to say 'Amen' and wish it to be so, if you do not say 'Amen' and command, 'So be it!' O, word of all power! Word wonderful in efficacy! My good Lord Jesus, Word of the Father, complete my prayer, complete my words … saying 'Amen!', saying 'So be it!'" And the New Testament sets the seal on this usage and on this understanding: in Christ, St. Paul wrote, is the Amen to all of God's promises (2Cr 1:20).

אמת

OPTIONAL PRAYERS

THE OUR FATHER, THE HAIL MARY, AND THE APOSTLES' CREED ARE THE basic prayers of the Rosary, but others are said before, during, or after the Rosary proper, according to the intention of the recitation and the customs of the particular age and locality. There are also certain standardized statements used to announce the Mysteries, but these also vary according to the place and the age in which you live, and none is really a part of the Rosary. Most of these additions are permissible, but the Holy See has not taken any official notice of many of them. The most that has been said about those that have come under official review is that adding them to the Rosary does not void the indulgences associated with the Rosary in and of itself.

In most countries, the *Gloria Patri*, sometimes called the "Little Doxology" or even the "Glory Be", is customarily said at the end of each decade, just before the next Our Father, although there's no bead for it. This prayer isn't an integral part of the Rosary as defined in the Roman Breviary and the Enchiridion of Indulgences. St. Louis-Marie Grignion de Montfort is sometimes credited with the idea of saying it after each decade, because he noted that "it is good" to do so in his book *The Secret of the Most Holy Rosary*. By his time, of course, the arrangement of beads in a rosary had become standardized, so there's no bead to count while saying this prayer; it's said after the last bead of the decade, before the next bead for an Our Father.

But it seems that St. Louis-Marie wasn't innovating when he suggested this; evidently he was remembering an ancient custom and reminding people of it. The Little Doxology has evidently been recited at the end of each decade since the earliest bead-counted devotions and in fact ever since monks started singing the Psalms. It's the oldest prayer in the Church, next to the Our Father. Today, it stands in the Rosary just as King David's doxologies stand at the end of his Psalms (71:18-20).

The Little Doxology goes like this.

Glory be to the Father,	Gloria Patri,
and to the Son,	et Filio,
and to the Holy Spirit,	et Spiritui sancto,
as it was in the beginning,	sicut erat in principio,
is now, and ever shall be,	et nunc, et semper,
world without end. Amen.	et in sæcula sæculorum. Amen.

This brief, simple prayer, one of the Church's most joyous hymns of gladness, is the summit of a whole mountain of theology. For one thing, it affirms the doctrine of the Trinity, of course, just as the Sign of the Cross does; but then it goes on to fulfill the Scriptural injunction to "give glory to the Lord" (Ps 28; Rv 1:6).

Glory, of course, is the awesomeness of God, the splendor on which no Man can look and live (Ex 33:20). It's described in the Old Testament as like lightning and thunder, or like a flashing fire, shrouded in cloud or smoke to shield people from its brilliance. But these images, even when they were really visible as in the Pillar of Fire (Ex 13:21) are, in a way, metaphorical. The visible glory is only a manifestation of the dominion—the lordship—of God, a way of impressing on people something of his majesty and power. Christ showed himself this way, with a face like lightning and raiment like snow (Mt 17:2; *cf.* Lk 2:9), which was taken as a manifestation of his divinity.

The *Gloria Patri* is called a *doxology* because it's a short song of praise to God. The word might sound like it's related to words like "orthodox", but it's not; the *-dox* in "orthodox" comes from the Greek δόξα, which means "a point of view", but the *doxo-* of "doxology" comes from a Greek word meaning glory, which is spelled exactly the same way, in the New Testament. The *-logia* part of doxology, of course, comes from λόγος, which means "word"; so a doxology is a word of glory, a word of praise.

In the Bible, it's customary to end a prayer with a doxology, as you can see in Psalms, and the Church has always practiced this, too. That same familiar doxology, "For thine is the power and the glory forevermore", is said at the end of the Our Father at Mass, as it has been since the *Didache*, the *Teaching of the Twelve Apostles* was written in about 140. And other liturgical prayers finish with the refrain, "To thee be glory forever".

These little doxologies are addressed to God without distinction of person, but some from earliest times are directed to Christ specifically, and the most important ones mention all three persons; so most of the Church's doxologies are also declarations of faith in the Trinity. The Great Doxology, for instance, is the *Gloria in excelsis Deo*, which is based on the song of praise that the angels sang at the Nativity (Lk 2:14) but follows this general divine praise with specific praise of God the Father and an invocation of Christ that mentions the Holy Spirit.

This Great Doxology is used today as it has been since before the sixth century, at Mass. The other doxology of the Mass, the one that ends the Eucharistic prayer, also pivots on the doctrine of the Trinity: after the consecration, the celebrant holds up the Body and Blood of Christ and proclaims that "Through him, with him, in him, in the unity of the Holy Spirit, all glory and honor is yours, Almighty Father, forever and ever. Amen."

OPTIONAL PRAYERS

Most doxologies are structured to convey some idea of the workings and interrelationships of those three divine persons, too: "Glory be to the Father through the Son in the Holy Spirit" is one of the earlier ones, recorded not only in the *Didache* but in the works of Origen and St. Clement of Alexandria, too.

But in the fourth century heretics in Antioch seized on this formula and claimed that it said that the Son is inferior to the Father. Of course, it doesn't mean that at all, but the Christians of Antioch didn't want to use prayers that were open to that kind of misinterpretation. So they looked back to the Bible, to the formula through which everybody is brought into the Church: baptize them in the Name of the Father, and of the Son, and of the Holy Spirit (Mt 28:19).

This left no room for doubt that the three persons are co-equal. Using the same form, the Antiochenes wrote the "Little Doxology" that the Church still uses at the end of Psalms whenever they're sung in praise of God—the *Gloria Patri* that we know today. From this practice, naturally, the Little Doxology was transferred to the Angelic Psalter, the Rosary, and carried over to the end of each decade.

And in addition to making important statements about the nature of God, the Little Doxology sums up the Christian view of the universe. Notice that in the second part of the prayer, it recalls that all glory has been to the Trinity since the beginning, and that so it is now, and always will be, world without end. That is, it refers to God as existing in Eternity, unlike the pagan gods that were still worshipped when this prayer was written in fourth-century Antioch. Those pagan gods were understood to have been born, but not as Christ was born—Christ, as the Nicene Creed says and the Little Doxology echoes, was born of the Father before all ages, and he came down from Heaven at a certain point in Time.

Pagan gods, by contrast, weren't said to exist in Eternity. They were understood as *sempiternal*; the myths that relate their birth tell that these gods came into being at a certain moment, not having existed before. That means that they depended on their existence for something that existed before them, something from which they could be born. But the God of Israel is bornless; he depends on nothing previous for his existence, nor on anything external to himself. He Is Who Is, as he said; he simply *is* (Ex 3:14). That's one important mark of his true and sole divinity.

The phrase "world without end" is really a paraphrase of the words *in sæcula sæculorum*, but it says the same thing. The Latin means literally "in the ages of ages", but the English conveys directly what this idiomatic expression says: that God exists in a world, a dimension, outside of Time, and that he will have no end as earthly things do.

THE SKILL OF VOCAL PRAYER

The prayer known as the Soul of Christ—the *Anima Christi*, in Latin—is often recommended as a preliminary to any exercise of meditative prayer, as a way to help you recollect yourself and to ask for help in managing distractions and weaknesses in your prayers. It isn't part of the Rosary proper, but it is included in a good many of the classic manuals for the devotion. It goes like this.

Soul of Christ, sanctify me.	Anima Christi, sanctifica me.
Body of Christ, save me.	Corpus Christi, salva me.
Blood of Christ, inebriate me.	Sanguis Christi, inebria me.
Water from the side of Christ, wash me.	Aqua lateris Christi, lava me.
Passion of Christ, strengthen me.	Passio Christi, conforta me.
O good Jesus, hear me.	O bone Jesu, exaudi me.
In your wounds hide me.	Intra tua vulnera absconde me.
Let me not be separated from thee.	Ne permittas me separari a te.
From the malignant enemy defend me.	Ab hoste maligno defende me.
In the hour of my death, call me,	In hora mortis meæ voca me,
and bid me come to thee,	et iube me venire ad te,
that with thy saints	ut cum sanctis tuis
I may praise thee	laudem te
for ever and ever. Amen.	in sæcula sæculorum. Amen.

Notice that this prayer is shaped like a litany; an invocation of a title or aspect of Christ is followed by a petition. It could well be prayed antiphonally before group recitations of the Rosary.

Each of the phrases is composed carefully so that invocation and petition make sense, theologically, and each is chosen to resonate with whole sections of Sacred Tradition and whole books of the Bible. A phrase about salvation in the Body of Christ, for instance, brings to mind the sixth chapter of John; a plea to be washed by the water from his side recalls not only the Gospels' accounts of the Passion but any number of psalms, too, like Psalm 50, the great *Miserere*. In fact, the pattern of this prayer follows fairly closely the pattern of creeds like the Apostles' Creed, except that the creeds state precepts of the Faith: the *Anima Christi* begs Christ's help in changing the self to accord with those precepts.

Stitch by stitch, this beautiful little prayer binds up the spirit's wounds in preparation for wholesome prayer. Yet like so many of the perfect little prayers of the Church, it's entirely anonymous. Bl. Bernardine of Feltre was generally thought to have been the author, but manuscripts of it dating from before his birth in the early fifteenth century make that attribution impossible. Pope John XXII d'Euse is also sometimes said to have been the author, but in reality all he did was enrich it with indulgences in 1330. So it must have existed in its present form by then. Certainly it was inscribed on the gates of the Alcazar of Seville by about 1350, and it shows up in Spanish devotional manuscripts from about a century before that.

In fact, it has always been a particular favorite in Spain, so well known there by the sixteenth century that St. Ignatius of Loyola specified it by name in the first edition of his *Spiritual Exercises* but didn't give its text, on the presumption that everybody in the world knew it already. The appearance of the prayer in the *Exercises* rekindled interest in it across Europe, so much so that St. Ignatius himself is sometimes credited with writing it, too.

It remained universally popular through the first half of the twentieth century—it was the favorite prayer of Pius XII Pacelli—and it's still a favorite prayer for after reception of the Eucharist.

The Hail, Holy Queen—*Salve Regina*, in Latin—is suggested as the final prayer of the Rosary, to be prayed after all fifteen Mysteries, or after the fifth Mystery if only one-third of the Rosary is prayed.

Hail, holy queen,	Salve, Regina,
Mother of Mercy;	Mater misericordiæ;
hail, our life, our sweetness,	vita, dulcedo,
and our hope!	et spes nostra, salve!
To thee do we cry,	Ad te clamamus,
poor, banished children of Eve;	exules, filii Hevæ;
to thee do we send up our sighs,	ad te suspiramus,
mourning and weeping	gementes et flentes
in this vale of tears.	in hoc lachyrmarum valle.
Turn then, most gracious advocate,	Eia ergo, advocata nostra,
thine eyes of mercy towards us;	illos tuos misericordes oculos ad nos converte;
and after this, our exile, show unto us the fruit of thy womb, Jesus!	et Jesum, benedictum fructum ventris tui, nobis, post hoc exsilium ostende.
O clement! O loving!	O clemens! O pia!
O sweet Virgin Mary!	O dulcis Virgo Maria!
V. Pray for us,	V. Ora pro nobis,
O holy Mother of God,	Sancta Dei Genetrix,
R. That we may be made worthy of the promises of Christ.	R. Ut digni efficiamur promissionibus Christi.

Some books add an additional petition that's often used when the Rosary is prayed publicly by a group:

> O God, whose only-begotten Son by his life, death, and resurrection has purchased for us the rewards of everlasting life, grant, we beseech you, that while meditating on these Mysteries of the holy Rosary of the Blessed Virgin Mary, we may imitate what they contain and obtain what they promise. Through the same Jesus Christ, Our Lord, Amen.

The Hail, Holy Queen is actually a hymn, and more particularly it's an antiphon, a prayer consisting of parts that would be chanted by two groups in alternation, or by a leader and by the rest of the group, or by one person in answer to the other person with whom he's praying. With three other hymns to the Blessed Virgin, the *Alma Redemptoris Mater*, the *Regina Cœli*, and the *Ave Regina Cœlorum*, this prayer was sung as part of the psalmodic devotions of the regular clergy in which the Rosary took root, and it was often sung independently of any other devotion at convents, monasteries, and schools.

In 1239, though, Pope Gregory IX dei Conti di Segni ordered that one of these four hymns, appropriate to the season, be sung at the end of the Office. Surviving manuscripts show that by that time the *Salve Regina* had already been assigned by the monks to the part of the Little Office that celebrates the Annunciation. So, logically, this particular hymn is particularly appropriate for the end of the sequence of Mysteries in the Rosary that begins with the Annunciation. The *Salve Regina* brings the whole cycle to a close.

The *Salve Regina* seems to have been written by at least two people almost at once. An eleventh-century Benedictine monk at the great monastery of Reichenau, Bl. Herman the Cripple, Hermannus Contractus, is sometimes cited as the author. He was a remarkable man by any standard; so afflicted by birth defects that he couldn't move without assistance, he still overcame his handicaps to become one of the leading intellects of his day. He mastered not only Latin but Greek and Arabic as well, and his learning shows through in his writings as much as his lovable personality does. He wrote standard works on history, astronomy, and mathematics, as well as a good deal of poetry and lyric hymns—he somehow managed to craft astronomical and musical instruments, too. He wrote an immense amount of devotional song, almost certainly the *Alma Redemptoris Mater* among them, and he either perfected the *Salve Regina*, making it virtually as it is today, or he wrote it from scratch.

But then again Durandus of St.-Pourçain (*Rationale*) made a case for a man who lived a generation before Bl. Herman, St. Peter of Monsoro (or of Mosoncio), Bishop of Compostela in Spain. That region has always been a center of Marian devotions, and the hymn figures as importantly in the liturgies and devotions of the Mozarabic Rite as in the Latin Rite and the old Gallican. There are other candidates, too. Some ascribe the hymn to Adhémar of Monteil, Bishop of Podium, who was said to have written it as the war-song of the First Crusade, about a generation after Bl. Herman died. That's why it's sometimes called the *Antiphona de Podio* or, in French, the *Antienne de Le Puy*. Others say that the composer of the *Salve Regina* was St. Bernard of Clairvaux.

The hymn has some connections with St. Bernard, but he probably didn't have anything to do with its composition. It was chanted every day in his honor at the cathedral of Speyer, and the legend arose there that while he had been serving as papal legate at Speyer he entered the church in procession as that hymn was being sung, and, prompted by a sudden impulse, added at the end the words *O clemens, O pia, O dulcis Virgo Maria!* But he probably didn't. A related legend from Speyer claims only that St. Bernard genuflected three times during that doxology—until Vatican II clerics were required to genuflect or kneel as they recited this part of their devotions—but he probably didn't do that, either, although somebody later set brass plates into the floor of the cathedral to mark the spots where he supposedly did.

For one thing, Speyer had its own local version of the hymn in St. Bernard's day, so an addition to it would not necessarily affect the other version that became standard. For another, nobody mentioned any of these incidents until at least four hundred years after they were supposed to have happened. Most of all, though, the structure of the lyric points to a single author for the whole thing, as it stands, rhetorically and musically.

I t's entirely possible that more than one person composed virtually the same hymn at nearly the same time because so many people around the year 1000 were writing this kind of hymn to the Blessed Virgin. In the West, the custom was that monks would gather after Vespers to sing songs of praise and joy to Mary, hymns that were called *Laudes*, praises. Everybody wrote these, clerics and laity both, and in fact the laity started to form special groups, the *Laudesi*, expressly for the purpose of getting together in the evening and singing these songs. Some of the *Laudesi* groups were made up of street urchins who gathered on some corner to make up songs about Mary; others were formed of school children, and still others of adults.

The customs of street-corner singing were roughly the same in mediæval Europe as they are in America today, except that in those days people sang hymns of praise and petition to God and the saints. But still, the mediæval groups were there to enjoy themselves, and they'd improvise. Individual members felt free to ornament the verses with other little verses of praise, as the spirit moved them, you might say. Sometimes they added little commentaries in song for each word, or interposed a word in between every two words of the text to come up with another text entirely, one that said virtually the same thing but was twice as long. In fact, this seems to have been the way the monks chanted their psalms, since the earliest days; it's why so many little verses were interposed among the verses of the psalms themselves, and where so many other hymns and devotional prayers came from.

Apart from generating an infinite number of songs in praise of Mary, these groups contributed immense benefits on the devotional life of the Church as a whole. The seven founders of the Order of Servites, the Order of the Servants of Mary, first got together as a *Laudesi* group. The custom of gathering in parish churches to sing at evening before the Blessed Sacrament eventually developed into the liturgy of Benediction, because the priests would expose the Sacrament for veneration and praise and then bless the group when the singing was over. In the Netherlands this simple but growing devotion was known as the *Lof*, meaning the hymn or the psalm; in France it was called as the *Salut*, which means both health and salutation; and Germany and England as the *Salve*.

Salve, of course, is the solemn greeting that you gave to someone revered; it's distinct from the other great word of greeting, *Ave*, which is a more joyful greeting, indicating that you've been desiring to see the person you're greeting. That's why Hermannus Contractus and the others who wrote these hymns of mercy to Mary so often chose *Salve* as the first word. It tells you immediately that the hymn is not particularly joyful, that it deals with a serious matter, crying out to a respected person for help in an unpleasant situation.

Because it was written as a hymn rather than as a prayer, the language of the *Salve Regina* is not quite so condensed and rich as that of some of the other prayers, but, still, each word is worth thinking about. It greets Mary as Queen of Heaven, a title by which she's also invoked in the Litany of Loreto, in the *Regina Cœli* and any number of other hymns, and in the Rosary itself, in the Mystery of the Coronation. Largely, though, the text speaks of Mary as Mother of Mercy; the phrase "poor banished children of Eve" plays on the age-old *Eva-Ave* theme of Mary as the New Eve.

Like the Hail Mary, the main body of the *Salve* has a symmetrical rhetorical structure. It consists of two parts, one of praise and one of petition. Each part is itself divided into two complementary halves: the first begins with praise of Mary, which is followed by an expression of our destitution; by recalling that we're Eve's children as well as Mary's, it explains why we call out to her from this vale of tears—an expression that's become idiomatic over the centuries. The second half implores Mary's loving care, and, finally, states the goal of all Christian prayer: salvation, and the everlasting sight of Christ himself in Heaven.

The *Salve Regina* became unquestionably the most popular hymn to Mary in Christendom. From the eleventh century to the nineteenth, people left endowments in their wills to support the singing of the *Salve Regina* after certain Hours, or on certain feast days. Composers since Hermann himself have written musical settings for it (Jean-Baptiste Lully wrote one of the most poignant and haunting of them, sadly neglected nowadays, for Louis XIV). Evidently the *Salve Regina* was the first Christian hymn sung in the New World—it was always particularly dear to the hearts of sailors, and Columbus taught it to the people he encountered on his first voyage.

For centuries, the *Salve Regina* was heard everywhere in Europe every time the bells rang, a reminder that brought forth songs of praise from Christians everywhere—and bitter complaints from Martin Luther. In fact, the Marian devotion that burst forth in this hymn across the Germanies almost washed away his plans for innovations in Christian doctrine. So he wrote his own "evangelical" hymn, *Salve Rex æternæ misericordiæ* (*Hail, King of Eternal Mercy*), in the same pattern and meter, based on a version of the *Salve Regina* that had been popular at Erfurt. That way, he thought, Protestants could use all of the musical settings for the *Salve Regina* that they loved, but the verse would no longer contradict Luther's own ideas about the economy of salvation. St. Alphonsus of Liguori reaffirmed the value of the original prayer, though, in 1750; he structured the first half of his *Glories of Mary* as a series of commentaries on its phrases.

In fact, any number of saints have used the phrases of the Hail, Holy Queen as points of departure for their books, homilies, and letters. "Turn back to us in love," St. Peter Damiano prayed with his congregation on the Feast of the Nativity of the Blessed Virgin. "Turn back to us in love. I know, O Lady, that you are most loving, loving us with a love that cannot be vanquished. In you and through you, your Son and God has loved us with the highest of all loves. Who can say how often you have held back God's anger when justice was ready to go forth from his throne? Turn back to us in your understanding love. In your hands are all the treasures of divine mercy; you alone have been chosen to dispense such graces. May your hand never fail when you seek to save the weak and pour out your mercy. Your splendor is not diminished but increased when sinners receive mercy and the just are taken up in glory."

I n 1917, the children of Fátima reported that the Lady asked that a simple prayer be added after each decade, after the *Gloria Patri*: *O meu Jesus, perdoai-nos e livrai nos do fogo do inferno; levai as alminhas todas para o Céu, principalmente aquelas que mais precisarem*, in the original Portuguese. In English, that would be "O my Jesus, forgive us and save us from the fires of Hell; please take all souls to Heaven, especially those most in need."

Like other utterances reported from credit-worthy apparitions, this brief prayer is surprisingly rich in its connotations and elegant in construction, and it resonates to two thousand years of Christian devotion. It's really only another version of the ancient Jesus Prayer, of course. But notice that it's addressed to "my" Jesus, emphasizing that he is yours, singular, your personal Jesus, one to one—the early monastic Jesus Prayers didn't approach him in this poignant tone of almost childlike affection.

Yet if the Fátima Prayer has something of the tears of childhood about it, it asks on behalf of all of us, save "us" from the fires of Hell. In that simple phrase it reaffirms two great theological truths, that Jesus has the power to forgive sins and that he is the Savior who can deliver us from the fires of Hell. But it begs his mercy for all people, principally those who most need it. Which may include the person who prays this prayer—who can know (Sr 5:5-9).

The Holy See has affirmed that saying this prayer after the decades does not affect the indulgences attached to the Rosary. But more than a thousand years before that, St. John Climacus suggested that the Jesus Prayer, in any of its forms, be repeated in those intervals of wakefulness that interrupt the night, sometimes. "Let the memory of Jesus be with you at every breath," he wrote. "Let the memory of death and the brief Jesus Prayer go to sleep with you and wake up with you," he advised, "for there is no stronger weapon in Heaven or on Earth."

Most recently, Leo XIII suggested a prayer to St. Joseph at the end of the Rosary, or the third of it usually said. We behold faith, the foundation of all Christian virtues, perishing almost everywhere, he wrote in 1889 (*Quamquam pluries*); we see charity growing cold, youth growing up corrupted in morals and in doctrine. We see Christ's Church attacked on all sides with violence and rage, and a vicious war waged against the papacy itself. The evils of our day have grown too great for human remedies, he wrote, sadly; the only course left open to us is to seek a total cure through the divine power. Particularly, the month of October has been dedicated to the Virgin Mary of the Rosary for this purpose, he said, but still another proposal remains to be made.

Leo then urged the Faithful to implore Mary's aid and to associate with this devotion a supplication for the aid of St. Joseph, her most chaste spouse. As guardian of Mary and Jesus, he stands closer to the Queen of Heaven than any other saint, and closer to God than any other saint but Mary. Jesus himself obeyed Joseph as he obeyed Mary, and he paid him every honor that a child should render to a parent.

OPTIONAL PRAYERS

"From this double dignity," Leo concluded, "arise all of his dignity, grace, holiness, and glory." Moreover, the holy household over which St. Joseph presided with paternal authority was the seed of the Church, which is why Pius IX had declared St. Joseph the Church's patron saint. If all Christians are brethren of Christ and children of Mary, then all Christians are the foster-children of St. Joseph; and this is the reason that all the Faithful, of all places and ranks, confide themselves to the guardianship of St. Joseph. "Accordingly … We decree that during the month of October a prayer to St. Joseph shall be added to the recitation of the Rosary." The text of the prayer itself followed the encyclical proper:

> Unto you, O blessed Joseph, do we fly in our tribulation, and, having implored the help of your holy Spouse, we now also confidently seek your protection. By that affection that unites you to the Immaculate Virgin Mother of God, and by your fatherly love for the Child Jesus, we humbly beg you to look down with compassion on the inheritance that Jesus Christ purchased with his blood, and in our need to help us by your powerful intercession.
>
> Do you, O prudent guardian of the Holy Family, watch over the chosen people of Jesus Christ. Keep us, O loving father, safe from all error and corruption. O great protector, from your place in Heaven, graciously help us in our contest against the powers of darkness. And as of old you did rescue the Child Jesus from the danger of death, so now defend God's holy Church from the snares of the enemy and from all adversity. Extend to each one of us your continual protection, so that, led by your example and strengthened by your aid, we may live and die in holiness and obtain everlasting happiness in Heaven. Amen.

THE TECHNIQUE OF MEDITATIVE PRAYER

T HE LEGEND MOST OFTEN REPEATED AS AN example of the way in which the vocal prayers of the Rosary unite with the meditations centers on a Spanish lady named Eulalia. It may refer to St. Eulalia of Barcelona or to the feisty twelve-year-old St. Eulalia of Mérida. They have the same name, of course, and they were both martyred during the persecutions of Diocletian in 304, too, so they're so easily mistaken for one another that it hasn't always been easy to tell whose relics are in which reliquary.

On the other hand, the legend may have nothing to do with either of them; it probably refers to a lady named Eulalia because that name, from the Greek meaning "good speaker" or "one who speaks well", is appropriate to the story.

The story goes that this Eulalia was in the practice of repeating, for the love of Mary, the Angelic Salutation as many times as she had heard there were psalms in the Psalter. To complete the whole hundred and fifty, though, she said them faster and faster each day, until at one point Mary herself appeared before her to slow her down. "I caution you, my daughter, that if you want the honor that you render me to benefit you more and to be more acceptable to me, then do not in the future say the words so rapidly. Let me tell you that when you greet me with the Angelic Salutation I experience a great thrill of joy, especially when you say slowly the words *Dominus tecum* (the Lord is with you), because it is then that I feel my Son within me even as he was with me, true God and true Man, was with me when he consented to be born of me for the sake of sinners. The delight that

THE TECHNIQUE OF MEDITATIVE PRAYER

I felt then cannot be expressed in words; and I feel that delight even now, when *Dominus tecum* is said to me in the Angelic Salutation."

When she heard this, Eulalia adopted the practice of saying only one-third of the hundred and fifty Salutations at a time, but saying them slowly, reverently, and with her full attention while she meditated on the glory of the Incarnation.

Prayer of any kind has to be simple, loving, and above all sincere; it's more the work of the heart than of the head. But emotion is not devotion; conversion is the turning of both the heart and the head to God, and heartfelt meditation is basically *discursive reasoning*—that is, you enter into a discourse of thought about the event. You hold in mind something that God has done, such as any of the Mysteries of the Rosary, and you reflect on exactly what it was and what it means, to the world in general and to your life in particular. "I remember the deeds of the Lord; yes, I remember your wonders of old. And I meditate on your works; your exploits I ponder" (Ps 76:12-13).

In the hierarchy of prayer, *meditative* prayer ranks slightly above vocal prayer. It's sometimes confused with *contemplative* prayer, but they're two different things. Contemplation is a high kind of prayer, too, but it's a loving gaze of the soul on some truth, which can be of the natural order, the intellectual order, or the supernatural order; and the point of contemplating a truth is to arouse delight and admiration in the person who contemplates it. It's perfectly legitimate—admirable—to gaze lovingly on God in joyful adoration, and contemplation makes people better by inflaming that love; but meditative prayer is more focussed, more structured, and more purposeful than contemplative prayer.

Meditative prayer is unlike vocal prayer, too. Christian meditation is an internal act, because it's the practice of thinking about God or some aspect or act of God; but it's more than simply thinking about spiritual matters. You meditate according to a particular technique (and there are many different techniques available), and you do it for the sake of spiritual improvement. "Meditate on these things," St. Paul advised Timothy, "give yourself entirely to them, that your progress may be made manifest to all" (1Tm 4:15).

The Rosary includes both vocal and meditative prayer. As Leo XIII reminded the Faithful back in 1896, faith, to be full and sufficient, "must display itself—for with the heart we believe unto justice, but 'with the mouth profession is made unto salvation'" (Rm 10:10). In the vocal prayers of the Rosary, he said, we have an excellent means to do this, "for by those vocal prayers ... we are enabled to express and profess our faith in God, our most watchful Father; in the future life; in the forgiveness of sins; in the mysteries of the august Trinity, the Incarnation of the Word, the Divine Maternity, and others" (*Fidentem piumque animum*).

183

THE TECHNIQUE OF MEDITATIVE PRAYER

To meditate on the mysteries of the Faith, you have to know what those mysteries are, and the best place to get that information is from the Bible. Reading the scriptural accounts of the events commemorated in the Rosary, and thinking deeply about what you're reading, is a necessary first step toward meditation. In the beginning, people who couldn't read, of course, got the information by hearing other people who could. The readings of the Mass give you the whole Bible in a three-year cycle, with the excerpts from the Old Testament, Psalms, and the New Testament matched up thematically and explained in the homily, so every member of the laity should know the Bible deeply. Monks went beyond this, of course; the Rule of St. Benedict prescribed about four hours of Bible reading a day.

Today the readings at Mass are still available to you, but you can refresh your memory of them by reading your own Bible at home; look for the *imprimatur*, which certifies that it's a complete and accurate edition, on the title page or soon after it. You may want to supplement your Bible readings with other texts. The homilies written by the Fathers of the Church on these mysteries are always worth reading, if you can find good editions of them in a language that you know—or, if none are available, you can always learn the languages in which they were written.

Apart from giving you the basic information, reading gives your mind something to focus on, which makes it easier to exclude distractions. Eventually, most people learn to meditate without the texts, but it takes some longer than others to retain all of the relevant information and to concentrate on it to the exclusion of all else, without reading about it as they meditate. "I spent fourteen years never being able to practice meditation without reading," St. Teresa of Avila said (*Way of Perfection* 17:3). "There will be many persons of this sort, and others who will be unable to meditate even with the reading but able only to pray vocally, and in this vocal prayer they will spend most of their time. There are minds so active that they cannot dwell on one thing but are always restless, and to such an extreme that if they want to pause to think of God, a thousand absurdities, scruples, and doubts come to mind."

St. Teresa's friend and confessor, St. John of the Cross, advised that when you can't meditate, don't force anything; "learn to remain in God's presence with a loving attention and a tranquil intellect," even though you seem to yourself to be idle. There are plenty of processes and other skills that can serve as substitutes for meditation, in those cases, and God will answer conscientious efforts in his own good time, and in his own good way. "For little by little," St. John said, "the divine calm and peace with a wondrous, sublime knowledge of God, enveloped in the divine love, will be infused into the soul" (*Ascent of Mount Carmel* 2:15:5).

"I don't say that we shouldn't try; on the contrary, we should try every-thing." St. Teresa cautioned. "What I am saying is that this is not a matter of your choosing but the Lord's... Be sure that if you do what lies in your power, preparing yourselves ... and that if he doesn't give it to you (and I believe he will give it if detachment and humility are truly present), he will save this gift for you so as to grant it to you all at once in Heaven" (*Way of Perfection* 17:7). These are gifts to be sought and asked for, but in the general course of things knowledge of the mysteries has to be worked for, through reading and hearing.

When you know what the Mysteries of the Rosary are, you have to know how to pray meditatively on that knowledge. There's no single right way to meditate, but there are plenty of wrong ways to do it, and if it's done badly or improperly it will work to your spiritual damage, not to your improvement. Naturally, the techniques of meditation were first written down by monks, and for monks, but their works are of immense use to any Christian who wants to master any of the approved techniques of meditative prayer.

> There's a difference between manuals of prayer and devotional books. Devotional books are intended to stir the affections, but the affections are only one part of prayer; so the language of devotional books tends to be poetic and expressive, and their effect highly emotional. Manuals of prayer, by contrast, are designed to teach you the techniques that you need to pray better; they teach you a kind of self-discipline that lets you use all of your faculties and talents to the full when you reach out to God. Their language tends to be clear—if sometimes highly symbolic—and analytical, and they draw more frequently from Scripture, and more profoundly. A few books, like the great *Life of Christ* by Ludolph of Saxony, manage to combine both strategies, but in general devotional books are intended to excite you; manuals of prayer are designed to explain skills and techniques to you.

One of the earliest comprehensive manuals is the *Ladder of Divine Ascent* by St. John Climacus: like most later books on the subject, it's concerned primarily with helping monks and nuns climb to perfection, but its advice is really universal. One or two manuals on meditative technique have been attributed to St. Bernard of Clairvaux, too, notably the *Ladder of the Cloister* and the *Meditations*. But these are evidently indications of St. Bernard's methods, not actual records of them; the *Ladder* was written down by

THE TECHNIQUE OF MEDITATIVE PRAYER

Guiges du Chastel (Guigo de Castro), the fifth prior of the Grande Char-treuse, or by his successor, the ninth prior, who was also named Guigo, and the *Meditations* were written down by one or the other of them or by some-one else whose exact identity remains mysterious. St. Bonaventure was real-ly the first to write down the techniques of meditative prayer in a form that anybody, inside the cloister or outside, could understand and use. A great number of good authors—many saints among them—have followed after him, just as there were so many who came before.

It's important to distinguish Christian skills and techniques of meditation from those of other religions; they're completely different, just as the aim of oriental meditation is directly the opposite of the aim of Christian medita-tion. Today, some Christians propose using oriental methods as a way to prepare for genuinely Christian meditation; others try to use those tech-niques to generate experiences like those described in the writings of great Christian mystics like St. John of the Cross or St. Teresa of Avila.

But by their nature mystic phenomena can't be induced. Mystic phe-nomena, from the fairly commonplace, gentle ones like answers to prayer to the rarer and more spectacular ones like levitation or the stigmata, are by definition the outreach of God to the human person. And God cannot be compelled to move toward any human person; he doesn't owe anybody any payment for prayer, least of all delights that can be felt with the bodily sens-es. No matter how hard you try, no matter what you try, you can't see God, or an angel, and you can't levitate; you can't prophesy by your own effort.

That's why these extraordinary phenomena, the ones that are available to the person's senses, are always *gratiæ gratis datæ*, graces freely given. Some of the Church's greatest saints have practiced the most fervent prayer, the most austere ascetic practices and penances, for years and decades, without any extraordinary mystic experience at all; other people, like St. Bernadette Soubirous or the children of Fátima, have had some of the most extraordinary graces on record without ever having given prayer or penance much thought at all. St. Paul had a spectacular mystic experience while living in the most contrary attitude possible (Ac 9:1-9).

As a rule, none of the saints particularly wanted any mystic phe-nomena, and those who receive them either decline to discuss them (except under obedience) or beg God to stop sending them. The appetite for extraordinary phenomena like visions, ecstasy, and rap-ture belongs "only to a soul that amused itself with the gift instead of rejecting it and going beyond the gift to God," as Brother Lawrence of the Resurrection explained (*The Practice of the Presence of God*). This appetite is the spiritual gluttony that St. John of the

THE TECHNIQUE OF MEDITATIVE PRAYER

Cross described, the craving that he called a "spiritual sweet tooth";
it's not a real desire to bring yourself into accordance with God's
will. It's the hallmark of Quietism.

There are even some today who take theological concepts from religions
like Buddhism—the idea of an "absolute" that contains neither images nor
concepts, for instance—and place that on a plane with the majesty of God
revealed in Christ. To do this, they have to suppress the idea of trying to
express what God is, and deny that the things of this world can offer some
traces of the infinity of God. This is to abandon Christian meditation altogether, because it requires abandoning meditation on the works of salvation accomplished in history by God through the Old Covenant and the
New, as well as abandoning the whole idea of a unique God, the Holy
Trinity, which is love. So, because the word "meditation" means two utterly different things from oriental and Christian viewpoints—being opposite
in technique, aim, and even in the concept of God himself—it seems clear
that they work against each other.

Christian methods and techniques all differ somewhat from one
another, but meditative prayer basically consists of devout reflection about God or some aspect of God, aimed at strengthening the
will toward good resolutions and their accomplishment in acts. So it can be
said generally to fall into three parts: preparation, the meditation itself, and
a kind of conclusion to let you carry the fruits of your meditation into the
workaday world.

The preparation for meditative prayer is the same as the preparation for
vocal prayer or any other kind of prayer: solitude, silence, and recollection,
which is the remembrance of the presence of God. The meditation itself
consists of certain acts that employ certain faculties of the human mind and
heart. The idea is to build up, step by step, a view of the object of the meditation, a kind of understanding that will prompt the desired response in
the soul, in the will, and in the faculties used in the meditative process
itself. The acts of meditation are usually distinguished as reflections, affections, petitions, and resolutions.

Reflections, sometimes called *considerations*, are the acts of turning the
Mystery over in the mind, looking at it from every side to know it thoroughly and well, and analyzing it, looking at its constituent parts and seeing how they relate to each other, to prophecy, and to events yet to come in
the Gospels and in Acts. There are any number of practical manuals for
reflection, and any number of techniques, but it's important to notice that
reflection is not exactly prayer. It's an exercise aimed at prayer; it's a kind

of study in which the mind reaches out to grasp the Mystery and to understand it as far as the particular person can understand it by natural means. Imitate the bee, St. François de Sales advises, that never leaves a flower as long as it finds some honey in it.

The need to focus your attention on the Mystery you're meditating about is part of what rosary beads are for—they relieve you of the mental task of keeping track of the vocal prayers—and it's why some spiritual directors recommend reading relevant texts before meditating. It's also why so many Christians pray the Rosary while looking at pictures or statues of the Mysteries that they're meditating about.

Generally, it's the same with the Rosary as it is with the Stations of the Cross: having before you a picture, or a series of sculptures, or a text—the Gospel passages that recount the Mysteries, the Psalms that foretell them, or the saintly books that celebrate them—helps give your mind something to work on that at least puts it on the same track. Christian art has always been made to remind people of the great mysteries of the Faith and of the lives and works of the great saints. Paintings, statues, mosaics, prints, holy cards, medals, and all the rest of these images are ways of communicating those truths to the mind through the eyes, and recommending them as suitable objects of meditation. They're intended to give motivation, St. John of the Cross said; the devotion should be directed "spiritually toward the invisible saint in immediate forgetfulness of the statue" or other kind of image (*Ascent of Mount Carmel* 3:35:3).

Just as it's best to have a wide familiarity with Scripture when you read about the Mysteries in the Bible and in the writings of the saints—and to have the rhetorical skills necessary to analyze them meaningfully—it's best to have some understanding of the conventions of representation, symbolism, and composition that Christian artists have used to present these same episodes. Paintings are like poetry, after all, and so is music; the human mind gives structure and shape to all of these modes of expression through exactly the same mechanisms, which are most easily accessible through the study of the shaping of language—rhetoric. If you understand how texts are shaped to convey meaning, you can understand how images, sounds, and even buildings are meaningfully composed; it's all according to the same mechanisms and figures.

In pictures and other visual arts, the arrangement of the figures, their postures and gestures, the colors that they wear, and even the plants and animals and household items in the scene all carry meaning. All of these features are intended to point to some aspect of the Mystery itself, often by reference to a metaphor that an Evangelist, a writer of an Epistle, the Fathers of the Church, or the great saints made with words. The placement of all of these elements in relation to all of the others carries meaning, too.

All of this is intended by its makers to be self-explanatory, but times change; so today we have to study to understand the arts of times past, just as we have to learn how to read and how to recognize the rhetorical structures of the texts that we read. Knowing what these features meant at the time and place the image was made, and knowing how and why they're positioned as they are, helps you bring out their fullest meaning; and the basic skills of visual literacy give you the ability to use the Church's great art treasures as effective aids to meditation. Which is precisely what they're intended to be.

> Apart from paintings and sculptures, apart from manuscripts, Christians have used many other kinds of material object to help them concentrate on the lives of Christ and Mary as they pray meditatively, and particularly when they pray the Rosary. The Metropolitan Museum of Art in New York owns an astonishing little rosary that belonged to Henry VIII, of all people. It's a single wooden bead, slightly smaller than a tennis ball, that could be carried in the pocket. It shows virtually no signs of wear, but anybody who wanted to use it could open it up to see the miniature carved scenes of the Mysteries that it contains, none much larger than a postage stamp.
>
> In the Middle Ages, some of the Faithful organized their prayers with the aid of little illuminations in the margins of their prayerbooks, and later printed books illustrated with woodcuts, or just catchpenny prints of the Mysteries, served the same purpose. A good many people used painted "meditation cloths" that had somewhat larger images of certain key episodes in Christ's life arranged around a central picture of his face, which was generally that of the Man of Sorrows, drawn after the image on the Holy Shroud that's now in Turin. They were used for all kinds of devotion.
>
> Some of these composite pictures represent the Seven Sorrows of Mary—the prophecy of Simeon at the Presentation (Lk 2:33-35), the flight into Egypt (Mt 2:13-15), the loss of Jesus at Jerusalem (Lk 2:41-45), the meeting with him on the way to Calvary (Lk 23:26-31), standing at the foot of the Cross (Jn 19:25), taking him down from the Cross (Mt 27:57-61), and, related in the same Gospel passage, burying him in the tomb. Others represented the Stations of the Cross, or other episodes like the Annunciation, the Agony in the Garden, the Resurrection, and related events.
>
> You can still see the fifteenth-century prayer cloth that belonged to St. Nicholas of Flüe today, in Sachseln in Switzerland, but most of

them have perished, having been simply painted on woolen or linen fabric. It can be supposed that many of them are no great artistic loss, but those that showed some degree of artistry were not much cheaper than handwritten devotional books. They were sometimes bought with contributions from the whole parish and put up in the church so that everybody could use them. When the Rosary as we know it had developed, churches sometimes furnished a special chapel for publicly recited Rosaries, commissioning huge altarpieces that depict all of the images that you'd need to meditate on the Mysteries. Most masters of the Renaissance and after worked to supply these pieces—even Caravaggio did one. Sometimes they depicted the Donation of the Rosary to St. Dominic (from the Latin *dono*, to give) by itself, but the Italian master Lorenzo Lotto, in his Rosary altarpiece for the church of St. Dominic in Cingoli, showed the Donation before an immense rose tree on which hang fifteen rondels, each a picture of a Mystery.

With these kinds of aid, you can at least make your mind focus on the same material that you want to meditate about. But you have to make your mind focus somehow: "the soul is ruined and dissolute when it lets the mind and its thoughts flutter around carelessly, running off to wherever they want to go. When at last they come straggling home, worn out, dying of hunger, they drag behind them an even greater burden of desire and greed," Francisco de Osuna warned.

The Mysteries that you find most easily grasped and most rewarding will help you learn how to approach those that you find more difficult, and sooner or later you'll learn how to reflect profitably on any of them. The skills come with practice, as well as with study of the great manuals of meditation that the Church has produced for so long; but no matter which technique you use, reflection of meditative prayer calls upon all of your natural faculties: your imagination, your emotions, your intellect, and your memory.

"At the door of your memory," St. Bernard advised his monks, "station a porter called remembrance of your profession [the laity might appoint remembrance of baptismal vows]; and when your mind feels itself overwhelmed by the weight of shameful thoughts, let this porter reproach you by saying, 'Come now! Should you think of these things, you who are a priest, you who are a cleric, you who are a monk [you who are a Christian]? Is it becoming for a servant of God, a friend of God, to dwell upon such thoughts as these, if only for an instant?" (*Sermon* 32).

Imagination enters into meditative prayer in that a person who prays can keep the eyes of the mind and the eyes of the soul fastened on an image of

Christ, and talk to him as if he were before the eyes of the body. The *Introduction to the Devout Life* by St. François de Sales is a great help in acquiring the technique of imagination in prayer, but the *Spiritual Exercises* of St. Ignatius of Loyola are the classic way of learning to use your imagination as a tool for meditative prayer; you can usually find retreats that take you through the *Exercises* through a local Jesuit school or parish.

These exercises help overly imaginative people harness that particular gift to the service of prayer, but even people like St. Teresa of Avila, who claimed that she didn't have much of an imagination, can still profit from them. She herself pointed out the importance of choosing your subject strategically, drawing on the strengths of your emotions or other particularly strong faculties when you're beginning to practice this skill. "Since I could not reflect discursively in the intellect," she wrote,

> I strove to represent Christ within me; and it did me greater good—in my opinion—to represent him in those scenes where I saw him more alone. It seemed to me that being alone and afflicted, as a person in need, he had to accept me. I had many simple thoughts like these.
>
> The scene of his prayer in the garden, especially, was a comfort to me; I strove to be his companion there. If I could, I thought of the sweat and torment he had undergone in that place. I desired to wipe away the sweat he so painfully experienced, but I recall that I never dared to actually do it, since my sins appeared to me so serious. I remained with him as long as my thoughts allowed me to, for there were many distractions that tormented me.
>
> Most nights, for many years, before going to bed when I commended myself to God in preparation for sleep, I always pondered for a little while this episode of the prayer in the garden… I believe that my soul gained a great deal through this custom because I began to practice prayer without knowing what it was; and the custom became so habitual that I did not abandon it, just as I did not fail to make the Sign of the Cross before sleeping (*Book of Her Life* 9:4).

You can't hide your inmost feelings from God, anyway (Ps 138; Mt 6:4; 1Jn 3:20), so you may as well acknowledge them frankly during recollection and then ask for help in overcoming them or handling them wisely, within the terms of the Covenant that you've agreed to. If you're angry, recollect yourself and examine your anger; if you're happy, examine that, too—bad things are, after all, the source of a lot of earthly pleasure. Then sort out the feelings: St. Bernard called together all of his "intentions, thoughts, desires, affections, and my whole inner self—come! let us go up the mountain, let us see the place where the Lord sees and is seen. Cares, worries, anxieties, labors, pains, and duties—wait here until I get back" (*On the Contemplation of God* 1).

THE TECHNIQUE OF MEDITATIVE PRAYER

Affections, so called from the Latin *affectio*, feeling, arise naturally from reflections; they're the feelings that result from thinking about the Mysteries. They are extremely important in meditative prayer; the intellect can only go so far in framing your understanding of the Mystery. The affections of the heart are the pulse of prayer, the motivation to take what you've gained and put it into practice, for your good and the good of all the Church.

But the affections are not just devotional feelings; they're not just your immediate and subjective emotional response to the Mystery. Of course, meditative prayer provokes a lot of emotions; in fact, one of its benefits is that it inflames the love of God—"hot grew my heart within me; in my thoughts, a fire blazed forth" (Ps 38:4). But the emotions provoked by meditative prayer can be very tricky; if they're pursued for their own sake rather than being harnessed to good purpose, they can be an insurmountable roadblock to spiritual growth. People who pray the Rosary naturally feel captivated when they meditate on the Joyful Mysteries, and elated when they think about the Glorious ones. Some weep when they reflect on the Sorrowful Mysteries, and they might take this as a sign of contrition for sin; but interestingly enough it probably isn't. St. Teresa of Avila warns that tender persons are likely to weep over every little thing; "A thousand times they will be led to think they weep for God, but they will not be doing so" (*Interior Castle*).

It's evidently not at all unusual for meditative prayer, in the beginning, to relieve the immense stresses that have strained a person almost beyond endurance, and sometimes when that dam breaks a flood of tears pours out. But, happy or sad, these are "devotional feelings", St. Teresa explained (*Book of Her Life* 29), "that often occur and seem to suffocate the spirit because they can't be contained. These devotional feelings," she said, "should be avoided by trying gently to gather them within oneself and quieting the soul. This condition is like that of children crying so furiously that it seems they are about to be suffocated; their excessive feelings cease when they are given something to drink. So it is here. Reason should bridle these feelings because they could be caused by our own natural feelings... One should strive earnestly to avoid exterior feelings."

Reason, the activity of the intellect, serves as a tool for getting past the exterior feelings involved in meditative prayer because reflection on a Mystery goes beyond the examination of that great Truth in itself to the examination of that Truth in yourself. Reflection on the mysteries of the Faith is like reflection in a mirror, St. Bernard said; it lets you see dirt on your face that you wouldn't have known about otherwise, and it lets you make sure that you've washed it off. Meditative prayer includes trying to see if your conduct and your will conform to the Mystery and its implications, searching for the ways in which you've failed to align yourself with it, and thinking of the best ways to correct these faults. So reflection should culminate in a greater understanding of the Mystery and the ways in which it should guide your own development, while the self-examination should do something to stimulate your affections in regard to that Mystery.

Affections, by contrast, are the heartfelt insights that you get about precise areas of self-improvement. Reflecting on the Nativity, for instance, might strengthen confidence in God's providence and reduce the desire for worldly things beyond necessity; thinking deeply about the Carrying of the Cross will often fortify the will to endure the burdens of duty, and thoughts of the Assumption will often refresh confidence in the promise of the life of the world to come.

Besides prompting deeper self-examination, the affections of meditative prayer also bring to light the graces that God has already given you. Reflecting on the Flagellation might make you see that you've lost some of your taste for the impurities of thought, word, and deed that lash Christ like the whip; or the Finding in the Temple might remind you that you're less fearful in bearing witness to your religion. Either way, the self-examination that helps you understand the affections is probably going to provoke regret for past transgressions as well as thanks for past favors, and it almost certainly stirs up confusion about the present; but then it clarifies your resolutions for the future, too, and it helps you shape your petitions.

Petitions in prayer are a necessary part of Christian life—"ask, and you shall receive," Christ said (Mt 7:7), not "you shall receive whether you ask or not." Petitions in meditative prayer are those acts during and after meditation by which you ask primarily for the graces that your examination of conscience indicates that you need. But beyond that, the Rosary is an effective way to ask for any good intention, like the welfare of the Church in general, the good of your family and your country, and whatever else you or others may need (Mt 21:22). "Meditation shows us what we need," St. Bernard said, "and petition gets it for us. The first shows the way; the second leads us along that way. By meditation we learn the dangers that threaten us; by petition we escape them" (*Sermon 1 On St. Andrew* 10).

Sometimes you have to repeat your petitions over and over again, but that doesn't mean that you won't get what you're asking for: "when God delays granting our petitions, it's to make us value his gifts," St. Augustine explained, "not because he intends to refuse them. When we have desired them for a long time, we receive them with greater pleasure, but if they were granted without delay they would be less esteemed. Your desire to have them grows by asking and seeking; God withholds for a while what he does not wish to give at once, so that you may learn to want his great gifts with a greater desire" (*On the Word of the Lord*; *cf.* Lk 11:5-8, 18:1-8; etc.).

> The Sulpician method of meditative prayer—the one promoted by the Society of St.-Sulpice to teach the skills of prayer to seminarians—suggests presenting God with some reasons that he should give you what you ask. You might mention that it's his will that people should have that particular virtue and not the vice that wounds it, for instance, or that granting the petition will glorify him. Or that he shouldn't let a member of his Church, which he loves so dearly, remain so imperfect; that you receive the Eucharist frequently, and without this favor that you ask Christ will be glorified in you less than is becoming and proper.
>
> The most effective arguments, evidently, are those that present to God his own infinite goodness and generosity toward his creatures, the infinite merits of Christ, and his promises in Scripture (2Es 9:5-32; Dn 3:35-36). Some teachers recommend asking God to be as generous with the others as he has always been with you, which presupposes that you've counted your blessings, yourself. St. Alphonsus of Liguori asked Christ to "look not upon my sins, for Hell itself would not be able to expiate them; but look upon the sufferings that you have endured for me," which shouldn't be wasted (*Passion and Death* 6). And the very act of resolution—promising to use the graces that God gives you—is a powerful prayer in itself.

Resolutions are, of course, the promises that you make to yourself and to God to fix the things that you've found wanting in yourself. St. Vincent de Paul called good resolutions the principal fruit of meditative prayer, "good resolutions, and strong ones, with grounding them on a firm basis, being ready to put them into practice, and foreseeing obstacles so that you can overcome them."

Some teachers compare meditation to the needle, and resolutions to the thread. You have to have the needle to get any sewing done, but the needle itself just passes through the cloth: it's the thread that stays and holds the garment together. Nobody in his right mind would sew with only a needle, and nobody would meditate without drawing after the prayer those resolutions that mend his soul; nobody would try to sew up a tear with only a thread, either, just as good resolutions aren't much use without meditative prayer.

To keep from making your resolutions so general that they're vague or so specific that they're trivial, some teachers suggest linking two resolutions about the same thing: a general one like, "Lord, I have not done much about this until now; today I will become better by trying to be more patient," and a more specific one like the example given by St. François de Sales, "Well, then, I will not allow myself to be offended by the irritating words that somebody or other—my neighbor, my servant, or whoever it is who bothers you—says to me today. Instead, I will say and do thus and so to try to win him over." Sometimes you have to make the same resolution over and over again; nobody can expect to jump up perfect from only one session of meditative prayer. But if you pray the Rosary the practice of repeating the vocal prayers makes it easier to get into the habit of repeating resolutions, and petitions about them, again and again until those things are accomplished in you.

However you persuade God to favor you, sooner or later your examination of self is going to reveal that you can move on to another resolution and another series of petitions to ask for the graces that you need to accomplish it. At that point, a person devoted to meditative prayer will find that the things he wanted so desperately when he took up the practice just don't appeal all that much any more; desire for illicit sensual pleasures, or even for permissible but extravagant ones like fine houses, fancy cars, and expensive clothing have fallen away, but they've left no emptiness, and no sense of loss.

Of course, those undesirable desires will flood in upon your soul again through the least chink in your armor, at the first sign of spiritual laziness (Pr 6:10-11, 24:33-34), but this painless absence of illicit desires is really the consolation that brings the greatest sigh of relief, one of the most profound and tangible answer that can be received to any prayer; it's the most satisfying of gifts and the surest proof of God's loving care, if proof should be needed. It's also one of the subtlest of gifts; and looking back on the person who picked up those worn rosary beads when they were new, you might not recognize yourself at all.

The conclusion of a session of meditative prayer is in a way the reverse of the process of recollection; it turns you back into the workaday world, gently, so that you can carry with you the graces that you've received, and use them to attain the goals of your resolutions. "Watch out for disturbing your heart, lest you spill the balm that it has received through prayer," St. François de Sales advised his friend Philothea. "A person given a precious liquid in a porcelain vase to carry home walks with great care; he does not look from side to side, but he looks first of all straight ahead for fear of stumbling against a stone or making a false step, and secondly at the vase to be sure that it doesn't spill."

Generally, the conclusion of prayer includes thanking God for having heard you; the teachers agree with Osuna's recommendation that "to find thanksgiving and the voice of praise, which are the same thing, in your soul, you have to rejoice and be glad in the Lord who created that soul.

And then from joy and gladness go on to the thanksgiving". This may take the form of the psalms that remind the soul itself to "bless the Lord, and forget not all his benefits" (102:1-2) or even those that cry out in the hearing of others in gladness—Hear now, all of you who fear God, while I declare what he has done for me! (65:16). But the greatest and most perfect hymn of thanks is Mary's own canticle: "that is so perfect that it is often said ... that Our Lady invented the way of speaking used by all religious when they say *Deo gratias*, 'thanks be to God.' She attained the state of thanksgiving more perfectly than any other saint, as you can see in her canticle, the *Magnificat*; she was of course the cause for the abundance of thanks offered up to God every day ... *Deo gratias*".

But with this joyful thanks the conclusion should also include asking God to pardon the faults and any negligence that you may have committed in your manner of praying. St. Teresa of Avila used to apologize for the stench that Christ had to endure whenever she approached him, but she was mystically gifted to be more aware of those things than most people are. Anybody can develop the sensitivity to ask for the graces that he needs to pray better. Counting the graces already received is a good way to give thanks, Osuna says, and so is remembering them frequently every day. But the first of the ways to offer thanks, in his estimation, is by your deeds; this is to serve God through the talents and graces that he has given you, which makes some return to him and proves your gratitude. The martyrs took this so far as to offer their blood in return for his, he says, which isn't asked of most of us, but we can all offer ourselves, body and soul, heart and mind, and above all offering to him our good resolutions.

St. François de Sales also admonished his disciple Philothea that when she rose from prayer she had to put her resolutions into effect immediately, that very day. Unless you activate those graces that you have received, he said, meditation is worse than useless: it's harmful. Virtues that you think about but don't practice inflate your mind, he said, and you start to think that you really are what you've resolved to be. "By all means, then," St. François warned, "practice those resolutions". Seek occasions to practice the specific virtues that you've resolved to acquire; and make up a "spiritual bouquet", he said, a collection of two or three thoughts or insights that have touched you in prayer that you can carry with you all day and refresh yourself with their fragrance.

THE STORY OF THE MYSTERIES

O F ALL SPIRITUAL EXERCISES, MEDITATIVE PRAYER IS THE MOST PROFOUND for the learned, and the simplest for the unlettered, wrote Luis de Sarriá, known today as Ven. Luis de Granada (*Memorial of the Christian Life, Additions*, 1574). And then he quoted St. Bernard of Clairvaux: "To meditate on these things has been my wisdom, and here I have found everything that was necessary or profitable for me to know... I always bear these Mysteries in my mouth and always preach them, as you know; I am always meditating on them in my heart, as God knows. And of these things I always write, as everybody can see. For this is and always will be my loftiest philosophy: to know Jesus, and him crucified." What else is there to say, Ven. Luis concluded, but to ask all who truly desire to advance in spiritual life to use this holy practice, and to ask all masters and teachers of the spiritual life to require it of those subject to them?

Yet many of the Church's oldest meditative devotions—the alternation of the Our Father and Angelic Salutation or a certain large number of either prayer alone—raised another problem. Like people in monastic orders, lay people were still supposed to announce and meditate upon certain episodes in the life of Christ as they repeated these prayers. But saying fifty Our Fathers alternated with fifty Angelic Salutations, or a hundred and fifty Angelic Salutations alone, with each and every prayer tied to an episode in the Gospels—a worshipper had to have some kind of memory aid in front of him that listed the episodes. Otherwise, he could hardly be expected to keep track, even with beads to measure the prayers themselves.

Manuscript books were always the preferred form of devotional aid, but these were still expensive and scarce, and even when you could get them they were complicated. Probably the most famous early one was the fifteenth-century *Liber experientiarum* by the Carthusian Dominic of Prussia. As its name says, it was intended to help you experience the key episodes in the lives of Christ and Mary. But Dominic wanted to retain the number of the psalms, which had customarily structured these devotions for more than a thousand years. So he wrote down a hundred and fifty meditations, a different one for each *Ave*. St. Catherine of Bologna used essentially the same pattern when she wrote her *Treatise on the Seven Spiritual Weapons* at about that same time, but people were still looking for a simpler system of meditative prayer that they could draw from what they all knew about the Faith. And most people still couldn't read.

During the fourteenth and fifteenth centuries, though, two developments made this kind of devotion available to almost everybody. One was the invention of printing around 1440; all of a sudden, pictures and texts could be reproduced cheaply, which made it worthwhile to learn to read. Huge numbers of devotional books were produced in the next hundred years or so, and everybody from kings and queens to hewers of wood and drawers of water read them avidly. But, like the Breviary and the Lady Psalters, these devotional tracts were still very complicated and very demanding of time and attention.

Fortunately, the second development started at the same time: the hundred and fifty episodes customary in these vast meditative systems were steadily focussed more and more closely on the really crucial events of Christ's work. Appropriately enough, this ultimate stage of the process took just about a hundred and fifty years to accomplish.

The beginning of this stage of the Rosary's development happened in 1365, when a man named Egher von Kalkar, or Heinrich von Kalbar, or Henry of Kalbar or of Kalkar, became disgusted with his work as Procurator of the Holy Roman Empire and retired to the Carthusian monastery of Köln. He was not allowed to devote himself to recollection and prayer, though; the Order called on his talents and experience to restore regular observance to Carthusian installations throughout the Germanies, and to help ensure that they would not be damaged by the Great Schism, which happened to be tearing Christendom at the time.

Under obedience, Henry spent the next twenty years visiting Carthusian houses and reforming them. That work was important, of course, but what he saw as he traveled from one monastery to the next was even more important, in the long run. To penetrate the walls of the enclosures, the laxity of observance and corruption of morals had to reach tremendous proportions outside, among the secular clergy and the laity themselves, and Henry saw that no matter how bad things were in the Order they were worse outside. So he went beyond the call of duty. He preached, and he taught; and, single-handed, he prompted a spiritual renewal of the Germanies and the Low Countries, the effects of which are still with us today. His writings inspired other writers like Denis the Carthusian and Thomas à Kempis—people used to think that Henry himself wrote the *Imitation of Christ*—and St. Ignatius of Loyola found the writings of Henry of Kalkar a rich source of ideas for his own *Spiritual Exercises*.

Henry's *Monastic Exercises* indicates his strategy for helping the laity of the Germanies keep their faith intact and lively during this difficult time. Like so many others confronting massive disorders in the life and religion of their countries, Henry knew that the only way to really improve things was to turn the people to prayer, and chiefly to meditative prayer. He wanted to encourage people to bring out the beads that they might have put by and forgotten, but he could hardly teach everybody in Germany the way through all of those massive devotional tomes of the day, even if printing put copies within most people's reach.

So he studied all of those devotions, and the great psalmodic devotions of the Orders out of which the more popular versions had condensed. Then he took the process of condensation one step farther: he maintained the beads, the Our Fathers and the Hail Marys, and the traditional number fifty, but he grouped the fifty meditations that he recommended into five groups of ten Hail Marys each, and he divided each "decade" from the next by an Our Father.

These decades made it easier to remember where you were in the Rosary, just as dividing Scripture into chapter and verse makes it easier to find your way around the Bible. Henry of Kalkar's simplified meditative prayer became tremendously popular throughout the German states, and once again widespread meditative prayer brought a rain of graces to the lands where it was practiced, stirring a Catholic Renaissance that was to bear its ultimate fruit in the Council of Trent. But it still left a person with fifty episodes to remember, with the texts that describe and explain them.

Then in about 1480 an anonymous Dominican priest in Germany published a book entitled *Unser Lieben Frauen Psalter* (*Our Dear Lady's Psalter*), which retained the pattern of the decades that Henry of Kalkar suggested but focussed them on fifteen episodes in the life and work of Mary and Jesus, not on fifty or a hundred and fifty of them. Instead of meditating on a Mystery for the space of a single Hail Mary, people could meditate more deeply for the time it took to recite ten Hail Marys devoutly; and instead of circling the Mystery by meditating on a myriad of details, they would approach the details by focussing on the heart of the Mystery itself. The Mysteries suggested in *Our Dear Lady's Psalter* corresponded exactly to the events commemorated in the modern Rosary, except that the Assumption and Coronation of the Virgin were combined into a single meditation, and the Last Judgement stood at the end.

As had happened with every other development in the history of the Rosary, Henry of Kalkar and the author of the *Unser Lieben Frauen Psalter*—and the anonymous authors of any number of similar books that came out in that decade between 1480 and 1490—didn't really invent anything but only gave shape and system to the sensible pious practice of the laity. In that way, Henry's suggestion and the subsequent books on the Rosary were important steps in formulating all of the age-old practices into a simple, effective method of meditative prayer, the first to be universally available to all of the Faithful.

The transition to the simpler, deeper pattern of fifteen meditations was completed about a generation later, in 1521, when the Dominican Alberto da Castello published his *Rosario della gloriosa Vergine*. In this book, Da Castello set the pattern of one Our Father and ten Hail Marys for each of the fifteen key episodes to be remembered during their recitation, and he illustrated it richly with a hundred and fifty engravings, one for each Hail Mary, according to the old pattern. But he grouped the pictures thematically into tens; each picture illustrated a single aspect of the Mystery of the decade. In fact, Alberto da Castello was the first writer to apply the term "Mystery" to each of these episodes, and so they have been called ever since.

The term "Mystery" can sound somewhat—well, mysterious, but that's because theology tends to retain words in their ancient form; theology keeps its focus on the root of the term rather than on its everyday use, which naturally changes as centuries roll on and new languages grow from old ones. We use the word today to mean some kind of puzzle, something that makes no sense, or something that we need to know but that somebody keeps from us deliberately. The word that more accurately describes that sort of thing is *arcanum* in Latin, from *arca*, meaning "chest" or "strongbox", which is why we refer to such things as arcane.

We tend to use the two words interchangeably now because people who want to pretend that their arcana are actually unknowable by ordinary people almost always refer to them as mysteries. Certain pagan religions used these terms to describe esoteric doctrines like those of Pythagoreanism or any number of other gnostic sects, which were kept secret because knowing them gave members a certain distinctive *panache*—it was the idea of "I know something you don't know, and therefore I'm better than you". James I certainly meant it that way when he proclaimed his astonishment that ordinary people "will freely wade" in "the deepest mysteries of monarchy and politick government", and when he later told the ordinary people sitting in Parliament that none of them "shall presume to meddle with anything concerning our government or mysteries of State." Other pre-Christian sects like the cult of Dionysus at Eleusis referred to their ceremonies as "mysteries", because you had to be an initiate to take part in them, which reflected more or less that same occultist frame of mind.

But you have to use the term precisely; there's a big difference between something that's incomprehensible and something that's inconceivable, between something that can't be fully grasped and something that stands absolutely contrary to reason. In classical Latin, the word *mysterium* refers to something that really is unknowable, or, more on a purely human plane, to valuable knowledge that's kept private for good reason. Its Greek counterpart, μυστήριον, means those things, too, and in fact the ultimate source of both the Greek and the Latin terms is μύειν, which means "to shut", and which also happens to be the source of that other much-misunderstood word, "mystic".

The Septuagint uses μυστήριον to translate the Hebrew סוד (sod) in passages like Pr 20:19; Jt 2:2; Sr 22:27; and 2Mc 13:21, in which it means things that are properly kept private—secrets. Christians understand "mystery" in the same way, whether God or Man withholds the information. In the early Church, after all, laity and clergy both had to be circumspect when they talked to non-Christians, not necessarily from the insiders' feelings of superiority to the outsider, but because if people found out that you were Christian they would kill you. So the great truths of the Faith were called mysteries then, and they're called mysteries now (Mt 7:6).

But there's yet another level to the mysteries of Christianity, and it's by far the more important one; it's captured in the second sense of *mysterium*, the sense of something that humans simply can't know. That's the main reason that the key episodes in the lives of Christ and Mary are referred to as mysteries "truly and properly called mysteries", as the Council of Trent reminded us—*mysteria vera et proprie dicta mysteria* (Mt 11:25-27; Jn 1:17-18; 1Cr 2; Eph 3:4-9; Cl 1:26-27). We can't fully grasp the mysteries of the Faith simply because we're bound here on Earth by the limits of space and time, and the mysteries of God exist outside of those limits. Our senses, including our common sense, can only see so far, not by any measure to the fullness of God in his infinity and in his eternity (Jb 11:7-9; Ws 9:16; 1Cr 13:12). Yet reason and common sense can tell you that the mysteries of Christianity are true—not how they're true nor everything that their truth comprises, but that they're true.

We can know, for instance, that the doctrine of the Trinity is true, but we can't comprehend exactly how it's true. We can understand that Jesus of Nazareth was conceived of the Holy Spirit, born of the Virgin Mary, suffered under Pontius Pilate, was crucified, died, and was buried; but we can't grasp the full implications of those facts, any more than we can fully understand the meaning of his resurrection from the dead. "So, on some points that pertain to the doctrine of salvation, those that we cannot yet grasp by reason (although some day we shall), let reason be preceded by faith," St. Augustine explained to Consentius in about the year 410.

And although the full meaning of these mysteries is beyond human comprehension here below, God does want you to know something about these mysteries. He wouldn't reveal things to humans if he didn't want humans to know them (Jb 12:15, 22), and Christianity is a revealed religion. Very rarely, knowledge of the mysteries comes to a person all at once from Heaven, as it did to St. Paul on the road to Damascus in the first century, or to Alphonse Ratisbonne in the church of Sant' Andrea delle Fratte in Rome in the nineteenth. Usually it comes from teaching, chiefly in the Liturgy of the Word at Mass. So, St. Cyril of Jerusalem warned his students: "with what reverence, then, must you come forward from Baptism to the holy altar of God, and there to enjoy the spiritual and heavenly mysteries" (*Catecheses*).

It's not enough to just receive this knowledge as it's given to you, though; there's also the need to reach out for it by studying and taking hold of all of the information about the mysteries of the Faith that you can possibly grasp, even though much of that information has to be indirect—the parables of Christ, for example, and all of the metaphors, images, allegories, and prototypes of the Bible. St. Ambrose explained that "the divine mysteries are indeed hidden, and, as is suitable to the prophetic word, it is not easy for anyone to try to penetrate the counsel of God. But from certain facts, and from the acts of our Lord and Savior, we can know and approach that divine plan" (*Second Book on Luke*; cf. Mt 5:2; 1Cr 15:20, 51).

You can also derive knowledge of the mysteries from the other sources that the Church uses to try to convey the same ideas, like the lives of the great saints, and for that matter the order of creation that you see around you. "Although nobody, certainly, can do justice to God the Father," Origen wrote, "it is still possible for some knowledge of him to be obtained by means of visible creation, and from those things that the human mind naturally senses; and, moreover, it's possible for this knowledge to be confirmed by Scripture" (*Fundamental Doctrines*; cf. Ws 13:1-5).

Meditative prayer connects the two efforts, the heavenly and the earthly. It's a way of taking the facts that you have been given, and those that you have collected, and pondering them in your heart. As prayer, it calls down the graces that you need to understand it all: the illuminating grace that comes through the medium of sermons, books, and study, and the immediate grace that follows it, the direct workings of the Holy Spirit in the individual soul.

The Holy Spirit, living and working in the Church, holds all that we know about the episodes in Christ's career that form the Mysteries of the Rosary. Some of this knowledge was written down, of course, in the irreplaceable treasury of the Bible, and that written deposit has been articulated and clarified in innumerable books since. But Sacred Tradition preserves intact and complete all of Christ's teachings, even those that are not included in the Bible. So, just as the Bible can't be understood out of its context of Sacred Tradition, the Rosary can't be understood out of its context of Scripture and Tradition.

When you begin to pray the Rosary, you might read the Bible passage that's appropriate for each Mystery, to fix the facts of the matter clearly in your mind. You might think about how that passage relates to other Scriptural passages, too, which will help you draw out its full significance in the Cycle of Redemption.

Of course, there are infinite connections among any number of Bible passages and these key episodes in the lives of Christ and Mary. To make sure that your Biblical meditations make sense (2Pt 1:20), you'll want to consult at above all the writings of the Fathers of the Church, and at least some of the great devotional books written about the mysteries of the Faith like *The Glories of Mary* by St. Alphonsus of Liguori or *The Secret of the Rosary* by St. Louis-Marie Grignion de Montfort. They recount lots of insights by other authors whose works might be a little more difficult to find, these days.

In fact, you can find any number of devotional books that record the meditational insights of any number of people, including some of the great saints. But reading is passive; prayer by its nature is active. Remember that the point of reading and studying is to develop within yourself the skills of meditative prayer, so that you can extract your own insights from meditating on the Mysteries on your own. Developing these skills yourself broadens and deepens your prayer life as reading other people's meditations never can, and the insights that you draw forth from prayer, like the resolutions that you bring with you, are living parts of your relationship with God that will suit your situation far more precisely, and yield far more fruit, than anyone else's possibly could.

Still, these preliminary exercises are necessary, and they're one of the most important ways in which the Rosary calls you forward to deeper study of the crucial episodes in the three major parts of Jesus's life on Earth: his coming, his suffering, and his exaltation.

The modern terminology of Joyful, Sorrowful, and Glorious, the definitive pattern of the Mysteries of the Rosary, was established in 1573 by another Dominican, A. Gianetti, O.P. In his book *Rosario della Sacratissima*, he was the first to classify the fifteen Mysteries that way in print, but he was not the first to perceive this structure in Christ's redemptive work. St. Paul structures his "hymn" in the Letter to the Philippians in exactly that way, saying that Christ, "being made like unto Man," came among us as a man; that he "humbled himself, becoming obedient to death"; and that "therefore God also has exalted him ... in the glory of God the Father" (2:6-11).

This three-part cycle remained a constant theme in Christian devotions, century after century. St. Dominic, of course, patterned his wonderful sermons to the Albigensians in the same way, focussing on the Incarnation, the Redemption, and Everlasting Life. The Lady Psalter attributed to St.

Bonaventure began the first fifty meditations with the word *Ave*, Hail, the greeting of happiness at seeing a loved one; the second fifty with *Salve*, the salutation wishing health and sympathy meaning, "Be well, be in good health," "May you be freed from your difficulties"; and the third with *Gaude*—rejoice!—the cry of congratulations.

The three kinds of Mystery were reflected in art, too. When Guido Reni painted his great altarpiece for the Sanctuary of the Madonna of St. Luke in Bologna in the seventeenth century, he depicted the Donation as taking place in a sort of chapel, on the floor of which there's a mysterious three-part plant growing out of a silver urn, bearing little oval pictures of the fifteen Mysteries. One-third of the plant is made up of rose branches, its blossoms taking the form of medallions with the Joyful Mysteries. The central branches are thorns that bear medallions of the Sorrowful Mysteries, and the remaining third consists of palm branches bearing oval pictures of the Glorious Mysteries.

The focus on these fifteen Mysteries makes the Rosary the most profound method of meditative prayer, and approaching them through vocal prayer makes it the simplest. With the vocal prayers and the beads, it supplies a framework in which any Christian can attain the deepest recollection and the most meaningful meditation with relatively little skill in prayer. And by concentrating precisely on fifteen of the most pivotal acts of Christ's work and revelation, from the first instant of his earthly life through the fulfillment of his promise of heavenly bliss for the Faithful, it focusses all of the natural faculties clearly on Christ and his redemptive acts.

And of course the Mysteries are infinite. Nobody can exhaust the possibilities of meditation on them, and there are an infinite number of ways to approach each of them. Some of the Mysteries, nowadays, seem best approached by way of their symbolic value; others directly through the stark reality of the historical events that embodied them. Sometimes detailed textual analysis opens hidden features of their meaning for the modern reader, and sometimes we can see them most clearly if we look through all of the symbols and appurtenances that ornament our celebrations of the feast days commemorating the Mysteries.

The following chapters examine the Mysteries from several different viewpoints, or they offer samples of historical, anthropological, rhetorical, theological, representational, or other information that surrounds and explains the events themselves. They can't be complete or exhaustive, but perhaps they will help to show a variety of approaches to thinking deeply about these key events in the lives of Jesus and Mary here on Earth.

THE JOYFUL
MYSTERIES

THE JOYFUL MYSTERIES ARE THOSE THAT have to do with the fulfillment of God's promise of a Messiah: specifically, they cover the period of Christ's incarnation, his birth, and the completion of his childhood. They are the Annunciation, celebrated liturgically on or about March 25; the Visitation (May 31), the Nativity (December 25, Christmas), the Presentation (February 2, Candlemas), and the Finding of Jesus in the Temple, which is remembered on the Sunday within the Octave of the Epiphany.

EVA ❀ AVE

THE ANNUNCIATION

HUMAN HISTORY ITSELF IS THE BEST EVIDENCE FOR THE REALITY OF Christianity, but it can be difficult to raise your view to see it. Just as the improvements that happen to the individual heart come so gradually that their immensity can only be seen in retrospect, it's sometimes difficult to appreciate the immense difference between the world before Christ and the world after Christ.

The epoch between the two ages, of course, is the Annunciation, the most significant event since Eve ate the Forbidden Fruit. In fact, although the Annunciation is recounted in the first chapter of Luke (1:26-38), its roots go all the way back to Genesis, and its ramifications will extend all the way to the Apocalypse.

When Adam and Eve sinned, God retracted all of the supernatural gifts that he had originally planned to give to humans—freedom from illness and death, and freedom from the need to work to fill natural needs; knowledge, wisdom, and the ability to see God face to face and talk with him familiarly. But these gifts were *super*natural, above human nature; when God took them back he didn't obliterate human nature itself, nor even change it. He just left it as it was, which is good (Gn 1-3). And he promised a Messiah who would come one day to offer redemption from sin and make salvation possible (Gn 3:14-15) for those who lived in accordance with God's will (Gn 15:18; Ex 19-20).

That is, in response to sin, God offered a Covenant, a contract, to his chosen people, and through them to the whole world. This Old Covenant opened a way for humans to participate again in the divine plan of creation and to attain, after their own bodily death and resurrection, that same everlasting familiarity with God that Adam and Eve had lost. The whole cycle of life, sin, forgiveness, death, and union with God was established, through Abraham and the other prophets of the Old Testament.

But it all hinged on the person of the Redeemer, the Savior. The Israelites waited patiently for his coming, observing all of the requirements of that preparatory Covenant (and when they slipped, God sent more prophets to call them back to obedience). Year after year, century after century, they waited. Through prophecy, God gradually revealed more and more about who this Redeemer would be—most of the Old Testament is about the family into which he would be born—and what he would do.

THE ANNUNCIATION

St. Luke uses every mechanism of classical rhetoric to convey to his readers the epochal importance of the Annunciation, the moment of the incarnation of that Messiah (from the Latin *in-*, meaning in, and *carnem*, flesh). In particular, he structures his account symmetrically, to help you extract the fullest possible meaning from the facts. He stitches the events tightly to their precursors in the Old Testament by expressing them in similar words and phrases, and he even structures his own passages to stand as mirror images of each other.

In writing his Gospel, St. Luke combined the meaningful rhetorical forms of Hebrew literature so successfully with the Greek language of his narrative that some scholars have supposed that the book is a Greek translation of a Hebrew original. Certainly his information came from Hebrew, or really Aramaic, sources—directly from St. John, who can only have received his information about the Annunciation from the only human witness to the events described: Mary herself.

St. Luke begins before the Annunciation of Jesus, with the Annunciation of St. John the Baptizer (Lk 1:5-25), and he arranges both accounts in exact parallel. Both start with the narrative introduction of the parents, after which comes the appearance of the angel, whose name is given as Gabriel. He's the angel who came to the prophet Daniel (Dn 8:16, 9:21-22), and the prophecies that he imparted to the prophet call forth a whole system of comparisons with St. John the Baptizer and with Christ himself. But his name גבריאל (Gavriel) means "Man of God", which is appropriate to the angel who came to announce the birth of John, just as, in Jewish tradition, he announced the birth of Samuel to the aged and barren Anna (*cf.* 1Kn 1)—above all, appropriate to the angel who announced the incarnation of the Savior.

In both narratives, the parent whom the angel addresses, whether Zachary or Mary, is anxious about the announcement, although in significantly different ways. Mary looked at Gabriel calmly; St. Luke writes that she was troubled at what he said, but not that she was afraid when he appeared.

This is almost unique in Scripture. Unless the angels appear in disguise as in Gn 18 or Tb 5:5-6, they appear with faces like lightning, with raiment like the Sun, speaking with voices like deafening trumpets or the roaring of a multitude (Dn 10:6), and with the glory of the Lord around about them (Lk 2:9). Even the great prophets trembled and fainted (Ez 2:1; Dn 7:28), to say nothing of laymen (Lk 2:9); the understanding was that nobody could look on the glory of the Lord, even when it surrounded his messengers, and live (Ex 19:21, 33:20; Jg 6:22-23). The Fathers of the Church understood that Gabriel appeared in this way to Mary—"to me came the archangel Gabriel with glowing countenance, gleaming robe, and wondrous demeanor," St.

Augustine presents her as saying (*On the Annunciation* 3). But Mary was troubled at his word. Not at his appearance.

That indicates her sinlessness. Preserved from the darkness of original sin, and free from the poisonous effects of actual sin, Mary had natural gifts in the highest perfection, as Adam and Eve had. The Fathers of the Church record the Church's ancient memory of her astonishing beauty, surpassing the beauty of Rachel, more graceful than Rebecca, more queenly than Esther, yet it was a beauty that never attracted attention to itself, but that transported the eye of the beholder to the contemplation of God.

She evidently had those gifts of intellect that Adam and Eve lost, too; the Scriptural record of her role shows her to be an amazingly acute person endowed with remarkable poise and a firm certainty of mind. She spoke with prophets as a prophet herself (Is 8:3), and she must have been the source for much of the information that the Evangelists wrote into the Gospels, beyond those things that she alone among humans witnessed. Even on a more mundane level her counsel let her know exactly what to do at difficult junctures, as when the days of her confinement were fulfilled. Far from home, pregnant, about to give birth for the first and only time, and sheltered in nothing better than a stable, she got through it all. She was even calm enough in the midst of this epochal event to notice details like the resemblance between a manger and a cradle.

Her sinlessness also meant that she had no obstruction to seeing angels ordinarily. She must have been as accustomed to seeing them as she was used to her family, or the human attendants at the Temple. Yet on this occasion she was troubled by what he said. Origen, in a commentary on the Annunciation (*Sermon* 6), noted that Mary must have known that similar words had never been addressed to anybody else; otherwise, she, "who had knowledge of the Law, would never have been astonished at the apparent strangeness of the salutation."

Whether you attribute the fact to her daily familiarity with angels or to a purely natural knowledge of Scripture, Mary knew that angels do not ordinarily greet people this way, by hailing them politely, calling them full of grace, and assuring them of God's favor. The only precedent for the angelic use of the phrase, "The Lord is with thee" is the greeting to Gedeon (Jg 6:12), and that was to pull him out of obscurity to take on the mission of saving Israel; Mary must have known this precedent, and it can only have troubled her. No other angel in Scripture even says "Hail", a word that bears no significance but courtesy, spoken to a loved one whom we have longed to meet. This was undoubtedly something else that troubled her, because it sounds suspiciously like flattery, which comes not from God but from the Father of Lies.

THE ANNUNCIATION

That's one of the main reasons that pious Jews of the time, like the Church ever since, advise instant rejection of any and all apparitions. "When they come to you in the night ... to say, 'We are the angels', do not heed them, for they lie," St. Anthony of the Desert taught his disciples three hundred years after the Annunciation. "And if they praise your strict life, and call you blessed, do not hearken nor deal with them at all. Rather ... pray, and you will see them disappear." Bad apparitions, those sent by the Devil or bubbled up out of one's own imagination, can't do any harm unless they're accepted. Good ones, those sent from God, carry a message that God wants delivered, so much so that he supervenes the order of nature; they won't fail to convey what they are to convey, whether they themselves are rejected or not.

So Mary was ready to reject Gabriel and his message, which sounded so extraordinary, even to a person accustomed to seeing angels. Zachary, on the other hand, had fallen down in terror, before the angel could say anything.

In St. Luke's account, the angel reassures each parent by saying, "Fear not", which is followed in both cases by the announcement itself. Here, St. Luke is careful to set up a parallel that pulls together two separate chains of prophecy in their proper order. The annunciation of St. John the Baptizer shows him to be the next in a long line of prophets. Like Samuel, he was to be born of a barren woman, and moreover one past the years of childbearing; he was to adopt the ascetic life of a Nazarite, like Samson and Elias before him (Jg 13:2-14; 3Kn 17)—more than any other reference to the Old Testament, Gabriel's description of John as the new Elias links the Gospel to a universe of prophecy. The whole First Book of Kings reads almost like a detailed biography of John the Baptizer.

Mainly, St. Luke's account of the annunciation of St. John collects and systematizes the accounts of all of the births of the prophets and much of their prophecies, marshaling the bulk of the Old Testament to show its fulfillment in his account of the annunciation of Christ. He handles the two accounts like the two leaves of a hinge, really; after showing that St. John is the rightful heir to the office of prophet, he lays that account against the annunciation of the prophesied Messiah, showing that John is to be the last to carry the mantle of Elias. John's birth links the Gospel and the Old Testament, and the Savior's birth elevates and gives purpose to the miraculous births of the prophets. And the structure of the account properly subordinates St. John the Baptizer to Christ.

John was to be born of a woman long barren; Jesus was to be born of a virgin. John was to announce the immediate advent of the Messiah, and

209

Jesus is that Messiah. John was to prepare the way for the everlasting king-dom of God that Jesus was to establish. So if St. John the Baptizer is Elias returned, Jesus is the King that the prophets announced. Which is why homilists like the great seventeenth-century Bishop Jacques-Bénigne Bossuet, as well as innumerable painters and sculptors since the catacombs, have referred to the Visitation of Mary to Elizabeth as symbolizing the meeting of the Church with the Synagogue, the house of the prophets deferring to the house of the Redeemer—the passing of authority from one dispensation to the next.

At this point in the narrative, both Mary and Zachary ask a question about the announcement. Zachary argued, the way Abraham and Gedeon had argued with God himself (Gn 18:16-33; Jg 6:11-40), and for his insolence he was punished, struck dumb (Lk 1:20; Ez 3:26-27). Mary didn't argue; she was puzzled, but she didn't doubt. "How shall this be done," she asked, "as I do not know man?"

The Church has always understood this question in its plain meaning, that Mary had taken a vow of virginity. This is the only situation that would prompt that question from her: if she had taken a solemn and holy vow of virginity—and girls did, in those days—then how would she bear a son? God certainly wouldn't ask her to violate a holy vow, so the angel's announcement troubled her.

Mary's affirmation, essentially "I don't do that", is unequivocal, and the Church has always taken her at her word—you are a virgin, you are holy, you vowed a vow, St. Augustine said (*Sermon 310, On the Nativity of John the Baptizer*), which sums up the Church's teaching on the matter. The expression *semper virgo*, always a virgin, sounds through the earliest Christian documents about Mary, with no voice raised to the contrary; both the *Protevangelion* and the second-century *De nativitate Mariæ* record that Mary was presented at the Temple in Jerusalem at the age of three, at which time she made a vow of virginity; she then entered the Temple precinct and did not come out until her marriage to St. Joseph.

These texts, however old they are, are still apocryphal; but they do record early Christian memories on the matter, and they're consonant with prophecy. Isaia foretold that a virgin would conceive and bear a son; that's the plain meaning of his text (7:14), and—as St. Jerome explained to Tryphon—a woman who was not a virgin conceiving and giving birth wouldn't be a sign of anything (*Dialogue with Tryphon* 84)—at least, not of anything supernatural. These texts also accord with Biblical passages like 2Mc 3:19, which testifies to the presence of virgins in the Temple. In fact, the Presentation of Our Lady—her formal dedication to a life of virginity within the Temple enclosure—has been celebrated with its own feast in the calendar, on November 21, since at least the sixth century.

Mary's vow of virginity meant that she had voluntarily sacrificed the joy and honor of bearing children (Ps 126:3), voluntarily embracing the "reproach" of childlessness (Gn 30:23) for the sake of the Kingdom of Heaven. This can't have been easy, given the Israelites' love of children, but she had done it; so Gabriel's word that she would not have to make that sacrifice would probably have been enough to fill her with joy, as much as the angel's word to Abraham had overjoyed the patriarch on the mountain of Moria (Gn 22:1-12).

But when the angel announced Mary's miraculous child, she didn't say, as Abraham had said—and as Gedeon and Zachary had said—this is impossible. She only asked for clarification, which was a perfectly proper question. For her to fulfill the vocation that God was indicating for her, she would have to know fully who her child was and what he was to do. So Gabriel explained how it would be done that she would bear her son and remain a virgin. "The Holy Spirit shall come upon thee, and the power of the Most High shall overshadow thee" (Lk 1:35).

Given Mary's familiarity with Scripture, this must have overjoyed, her, too: it tells her explicitly who this son is to be, and it tells her implicitly what he is to do. The word ἐπισκιάσει, overshadow, pins the account directly to the account in Exodus (40:35) of God's acceptance of the dwelling-place in the Meeting Tent, over the Ark of the Covenant, when the cloud filled that Temple with glory. That Covenant was to be fulfilled, and fulfilled through her; she was to be the new Temple, the new Ark, of the New Covenant that her son, the Son of God, would establish to carry the Chosen People to their final glory (cf. Rv 11:19, 21:1-27). The Messiah, light from light, true God from true God, begotten not made, he who was born of the Father before all ages, was waiting for this moment to be born of woman (Ps 131).

That explained her part, but Gabriel went on to explain God's part a little further. Mary's son "shall be called the Son of the Most High", he had said, but now he added that because the Spirit would overshadow her, "therefore the Holy One to be born shall be called the Son of God".

All in all, Gabriel's explanation brought the whole of the Old Testament to bear on this moment, and on Mary's pivotal role in fulfilling it. But beyond that, by looking back to Exodus it points to the way in which her son would accomplish this; the prescribed blood sacrifices, the scapegoat victims, the passage of the High Priest into the Holy of Holies, even the details of the linens that he was to leave behind all find their fulfillment as prophecies in his career. All of this is most fully explained in St. Paul's letter to the Hebrews, but Gabriel's brief word ties prophecy and fulfillment together. It even hints at the Ascension, because Israel did not go forward to the Promised Land until that cloud lifted itself up from the Dwelling to rise above them.

Gabriel's answer to Mary's question also shows that Jesus was not conceived in the natural way but the supernatural. The angel's message to St. Joseph says precisely the same thing, that the child conceived in Mary is of the Holy Spirit. There can really be no question that, if the Gospel is true, Mary was a virgin when, and after, Jesus was conceived.

Her virginity (Lk 1:34; Is 7:14), a physical manifestation of her inner purity, remained perfect even though she became the mother of Jesus, which does not happen in the purely natural order of things; and she remained a virgin all the days of her life. Of course, heretics from the beginning have denied this, although it's difficult to see exactly what advantage this particular heresy is supposed to offer. It denies the divinity of Christ, which is the whole point of Christianity, and if he is not the Son of God then there's no sense in any of it. The claim that Mary conceived Jesus in a purely natural manner negates entirely the religion that the heretics claim to defend, so it seems motivated more as an insult to Mary than anything else—and insults certainly can't add anything to truth.

After definitive statements of the facts, which of course are fully consistent with Scripture, were outlined in answer to the heresiarch Cerinthus and to the Ebonites in the first century, the denials might have been expected to be laid to rest forever. But they arose again, and even today a good many people, evidently, are not quite clear on Christian teaching on Mary's virginity before, during, and after the birth of Christ.

Her virginity throughout life has been taken for granted as an article of faith since earliest times, and the earliest surviving liturgical texts for her feasts all praise her as "ever-virgin". Between the early doctrinal texts and the liturgical celebrations, the teaching is conveyed in patristic writings, too, unanimously: St. Athanasius, Didymus the Blind, St. Gregory of Nyssa, St. Germanus of Constantinople, St. Ambrose, St. Ephrem, St. Jerome, and of course St. Augustine all wrote extensively about Mary's continued virginity after the birth of Jesus. So Apostolic Tradition has always taught the fact as something that has always been known.

Mary's perpetual virginity is indicated in prophecy, too. "This gate shall be shut," Ezekiel prophesied, "and it shall not be opened; no one shall pass through it, because the Lord the God of Israel has entered by it" (44:2). There is absolutely no clear indication in Scripture that Mary had children after Jesus, and to assert independently that she did is only derogatory to Christ's own perfection. It's also an insult to St. Joseph: it accuses him of violating the one whom he knew by the angel's revelation to have conceived by the Holy Spirit. And it's certainly an affront to the Holy Spirit himself, whose shrine, as the Office of the Blessed Virgin says, was the virginal womb in which he formed the flesh of Jesus. Obviously, it's unbecoming that this shrine—dedicated as the immaculate Temple of the Messiah—should be misused by human intercourse, as the Fathers of the Church and indeed the sensibility of the Christian laity have upheld unanimously.

The Church's age-old teaching on Mary's perpetual virginity was articulated in 1555 by Paul IV Carafa in his constitution *Cum Quorundam*, and yet again in 1603 by Clement VIII Aldobrandini in *Dominici Gregis*—these last statements of doctrine were prompted by the Socinians, an heretical sect that started out in 1546 as a Bible-study group and ended by thinking that only they could understand Christianity correctly. Basing themselves on the Bible alone, and insisting that each member of their sect had the right to interpret it as he pleased, Lelio Sozzini and his nephew Fausto denied the Trinity and, therefore, Christ's divinity, saying that he was a perfect man, but only a man. And—quoting Scripture to prove it—they taught that Jesus was conceived by St. Joseph, and that Mary had other children after.

Their confusion turned on three passages in the Gospel that still trouble a good many people: Mt 1:20-25, which says that Joseph took Mary to wife and did not know her "until" she brought forth her first-born son; the fact that Jesus is referred to as her "first-born" son; and Jn 2:12, which refers to the "brethren" of Jesus.

The Socinians' objections are still repeated now and again today, but they don't accord with the Scripture that their advocates always claim as the sole rule of their faith. No matter what else the passage in Matthew conveys, it says plainly that St. Joseph was not the father of Jesus. St. Thomas Aquinas (*Summa* 3:28) answers most of the commonest questions that arise on the point, as he does for so many other articles of faith. Matthew 1:18 says that before Mary and Joseph came together she was found with child by the Holy Spirit, and therefore, some say, Mary and Joseph "came together" carnally afterwards. But Scripture also records that St. Joseph after finding out about the pregnancy—which he did before their marriage was consummated—thought he had to cancel the marriage and put her aside, which he would not have had to do if he knew that the child was his.

And St. Jerome, Aquinas points out, who himself translated the Gospels from Greek into Latin, explained that "before" (*ante*) points merely to a thing previously in mind; it does not confirm the reality of anything afterwards. In this verse, it simply indicates a point in time relative to that event that would be expected in the natural course of things, and that expectation didn't apply here. That is, the normal procedure would be to have the espousal and then the consummation; but St. Joseph's discovery of Mary's condition happened between the two points in the procedure, after the ceremony, and it prevented the next event in the sequence.

St. Matthew also relates (1:20) that Joseph was told not to fear to take Mary to wife, and, some believe, that means that they consummated their marriage. But, Aquinas says, St. Augustine noted that Mary is called Joseph's wife from the promise of her espousals, not from a statement of consummation, which is never mentioned in Scripture any more than it is known in Sacred Tradition—indeed, as he said, the idea is countered by Scripture. St. Ambrose added that the fact of her espousal is declared to witness to the reality of Joseph's marriage to her, not to insinuate a loss of her virginity, the preservation of which is established in the plain meaning of the whole passage, and others in the Gospels, like Mt 1:25, which says that St. Joseph "did not know her until she brought forth her firstborn son."

The Church doesn't deny that "know her" in this passage means exactly what it means in verses like Gn 4:1, about Adam and Eve knowing each other and conceiving Cain. But this passage does not imply that Mary and Joseph had normal marital relations after the Nativity—it's the "until" here that distracts people. In the Vulgate, the verse is *Et non cognoscebat eam donec peperit filium suum primogenitum.* The word *donec* used here means about the same thing as our word "until", but in classical Latin it also bears the meaning of "while", or "as long as", and even, post-classically, "at the time of day when". You have to derive its exact meaning from context.

St. Jerome explained. He was the translator who used *donec* in that passage when he translated it from the Greek original; and it's worth noting that, even though it would have been easier for him to simply change the phrase, he—like the rest of the Church—held to the original text. Words meaning *before* or *until* bear two different primary meanings in Scripture, he said. Sometimes these words indicate a fixed point in time after which something changes, as in Gl 3:19, which says that the Old Law was enacted on account of transgressions until the offspring should come to whom the promise was made.

But, he said, these same words can also be used to mean an indefinite time during which some state or fact continues and after which that fact or state remains exactly the same, as in Ps 122:2. That verse says that our eyes are on the Lord until he have pity on us; but it neither says nor implies that once he has mercy on us we turn our eyes elsewhere. This verse in the Gospel, he said—and nobody knew better than he—means simply that that Joseph did not know her carnally before the birth of Jesus, and it does not say that he did afterwards (*Against Helvidius* 5).

Another confusion comes from the fact that Christ is referred to as "firstborn", but "first" means that none came before him; it does not mean that anybody followed. It isn't even a biological term, but a designation in sacred and civil law. In fact, in Roman law, as in Hebrew law before it, the term "first-born" means the son who has the rights of the first-born, even if he had older brothers who were born before him but died. So the term "first-born" does not by any means signify only that this is the first of many sons. In Mary's case, of course, there were no children before Jesus, because there's no mention of any in Scripture and because everything in Scripture shows that there weren't—Mary's question to Gabriel, for example, and the prophecies about the Messiah being born of a virgin.

Perhaps the most persistent confusion, though, comes from the mention of the "brethren" of Jesus in Jn 2:12. "Brethren", of course, is another of those obsolete or archaic words that we really don't use any more, because our experience and understanding of family relationships are so different from those of other ages and other cultures. To us, the word usually means siblings born of the same two parents; but it also means children born to one parent and not to the other, depending on how the family is structured. St. Jerome recalls the persistent legend that Joseph was a widower with grown sons, but he rejects it as supported by no good evidence (*Against Helvidius* 9).

And again St. Jerome's unparalleled knowledge of the texts lets him make the clearest explanation: the exact meaning of the word *fratres*, which we translate as "brethren", depends on how the family is structured. Israel was not structured on the basis of the nuclear family, father, mother, and *fratres* as we understand the term; it was structured on the basis of the extended family, the tribe, the Twelve Tribes. Scripture speaks of "brethren", then, in four senses, he says: "those who are united by being of the same parents, of the same nation, or of the same tribe, and by common affection."

The fact that St. Jerome kept these words in his Vulgate is an unanswerable testimony to his accuracy. Nobody has ever been in a better position to shift the meaning of these passages than he, who was entrusted with the production of a standard translation of the Bible into the Latin that everybody in Christendom could understand. He could have made things easier by choosing other words, less open to misinterpretation but not quite so close to the meaning of the Greek originals. Of course, he aimed to make Scripture available and clear to everybody, not to hide facts or obscure the record; and the Church did not accept his work without thorough and universal review, so he could not have altered the text anyway. But the point is simply that he kept close to the original texts.

Like the rest of the Church, he agreed with St. Peter in understanding that the Bible cannot be interpreted outside the context of Sacred Tradition (2Pt 1:20-21); still less can you pick at a translation letter by letter. And St. Jerome also understood, like the rest of the Church, that these passages mean that

Mary was a virgin before the Annunciation, during the Incarnation, and after the Nativity, until—or, perhaps better said, all during her life up to the point at which—she was assumed body and soul into Heaven.

After Gabriel answered Zachary's impudent question, he punished the priest by striking him dumb for his insolence. But he didn't smite Mary, who merely asked for more information. So she was able to answer, and her response rings across history: Let it be done unto me, she said. She could have refused; Achaz did (Is 7:10-14). But God would not establish his New Covenant by force, any more than he maintains it by force. Each person since Adam has the power to choose the love of God or to turn from it. "When God, in the beginning, created Man," Jesus Ben-Sirach wrote (Sr 15:11-20) "he made him subject to his own free choice. If you choose, you can keep the commandments; it is loyalty to do his will. These are set before you, fire and water; to whichever you choose, stretch forth your hand. Before Man are life and death; whichever he chooses shall be given him."

So Mary's agreement was given freely, by her own choice. There seems to have been no need of the Annunciation at all, St. Thomas Aquinas pointed out, except for the purpose of receiving her consent (*Summa* 3:30). Of course, he adds, she had to know certainly who her son was to be, because there had to be a proper order to her bearing and raising the Messiah; she could not have raised him properly if she had suddenly found herself pregnant without knowing how it had happened or who her child was. Furthermore, St. Thomas added—quoting St. Augustine (*On The Blessed Virgin* 3)—there was the matter of faith: "Mary was more blessed in receiving the Faith of Christ than in conceiving the flesh of Christ." And, because faith comes from hearing (Rm 10:17), "her nearness to Christ as a mother would have been of no profit to Mary had she not borne Christ in her heart after a manner more blessed than in her flesh."

Now, maternity among humans always demands free consent, consent that ought to be given or withheld under the control of the will, in full accord with the moral laws of Matrimony. Maternity without this kind of uniquely human consent plunges humans to the level of the beasts that conceive blindly in the drive of the passions of their bodies. Human maternity is not simply a matter of flesh and blood, not simply natural but supernatural as well. So Mary's consent was a purely human act, and really an instance of the quintessential human act, self-control in view of the will of God. But Mary's acceptance of her vocation to be the mother of the Savior was also the act that marked the beginning of a second chance for creation, a way around the sin that had so corrupted God's original plan for the universe.

THE ANNUNCIATION

Mary's answer was the first human act to inaugurate a new order of life on Earth. St. Thomas of Villanova, reading about it in the Vulgate, noticed that the word she used when she said "Let it be done unto me according to thy will" was *fiat*, in Latin—that same word that God used to create the universe. *Fiat lux*, God said, let there be light, let light be made; let it be done. And Mary said exactly the same thing: let it be done. "Oh, powerful *fiat*!" St. Thomas wrote. "By this word *fiat* the world was made, and by this word the Most High founded the heavens and the Earth; but this *fiat* resounded not in the heavens, but in that which you, O Blessed One, O Happy One, said." Mary's simple phrase also stands as a kind of prophecy of her son's instruction that we should say, "thy will be done on Earth as it is in Heaven"—*fiat voluntas tua*, again. It's the battle-cry of the Church on Earth, but the waves of its repercussions roll even far-ther than that. "Never in human history did so much depend, as it did then, on the consent of one human creature," John Paul II remarked (*Tertio millennio adveniente*, 1994).

This is the instant that's usually represented in western images of the Annunciation, because it's the pivotal moment of Scripture and history. In many images, though, two events are shown happening together. The Annunciation proper is embodied in the figure of Gabriel, who arrives and extends his right hand in a gesture of salutation or teaching. In the other hand, he often holds a lily instead of the baton that the heralds of ancient Greece and Rome carried as symbols of their function—a visual reference to his message that Mary, the virgin most pure, will carry the Christ as the fragrant flower of dazzling whiteness encloses a golden heart deep within it. Often in the same image the Incarnation is represented in the figure of Mary, who stands or kneels in a posture of acceptance, with her head bowed and her arms folded across her breast, or with her face upturned and her arms spread, depending on the meaning of those gestures when and where the image was made.

Many artists include God the Father at the top of the picture, extending his hand, too, through the sky, or sending the Holy Spirit; sometimes the Spirit himself is shown in the form of a dove descending from on high, usu-ally in glory and sometimes on a beam of light that falls on Mary. Some images from northern Europe, from about the late thirteenth century to the end of the fifteenth, show a tiny baby Jesus, already fully formed, riding that sunbeam down to his mother; some even show him carrying a little cross. These were never officially permitted, because they suggest that Christ's body was formed in Heaven and delivered to Mary, rather than illustrating the fact that his body was formed in Mary's womb in agreement with his nature as True God and True Man. Still, countless Annunciations, some by major artists, kept showing the Baby descending that way. It took more than two hundred years to uproot that image from public art displayed in churches, and even longer to remove it from popular images.

It was even harder to stamp out an outlandish kind of Annunciation that showed that beam and that baby aimed at Mary's ear. Evidently this originated in early Christian times as a visual reference to Jesus as the Word of God (Jn 1:1-5), which also explains the beam of light in these pictures, but it was misunderstood very early on. By the fourth century popular piety had started to imagine that this was how the Incarnation actually happened, and natural history at the time supported the idea. People in the Dark Ages thought that the weasel (or the ermine) conceived through the ear rather than the regular way, which is why that animal frolics among the illuminations of so many manuscripts, particularly on Annunciation pages. A twelfth-century hymn, which apparently had a very short run, actually hailed Mary as *Mater Christi, quæ per aurem concepisti*— Mother of Christ, who conceived by way of the ear.

As late as the fifteenth century this peculiar idea was represented in public works like the tympanum right over the north door of the Marienkirche in Würzburg, and it must have still been part of popular piety in 1534 when Rabelais made fun of it in *Gargantua*. It was a violation of law and of faith, contrary to both reason and Holy Scripture; but even thirty years later the Council of Trent had to forbid these bizarre images explicitly, as they prohibited the ones showing the beam or the baby directed at Mary's abdomen, on the grounds of being offensive to taste and misleading to the ignorant.

They also formally discouraged the use of the unicorn in pictures of the Annunciation. People had romantic notions about unicorns, in those days; they had endowed the ponderous rhinoceros with the lightness and grace of a dainty horse, and they had come to think, for some reason, that nobody they knew ever saw one because unicorns were absolutely chaste and could only be captured by an absolutely pure virgin. With ideas like these, people started using the animal as a metaphor for Christ, which is why the designer of the great unicorn tapestries now at the Cloisters in New York showed the mythic beast captured in a little fence, the "enclosed garden" of Canticles that's also understood as a prophecy of Mary's intact virginity. After Trent, the enclosed garden remained in Christian art, but the unicorn was seen no more.

THE ANNUNCIATION

People sometimes ask why Christian artists so often represent Mary as reading at the moment of the Annunciation. In some paintings and manuscript illuminations you can read the actual letters of the text, but the book or scroll is always intended to be the Book of the Prophet Isaia, and particularly Is 7:14: Behold, a virgin shall conceive, and bear a son, and call his Name Emmanuel.

Pictures and sculptures of the event, like St. Luke's text itself, sometimes prompt the question of why an angel was sent, or why God himself didn't appear to Mary to announce the coming of the Savior. For one thing, if God himself had stood before her, it would hardly have been possible for Mary to refuse. When God himself spoke to Moses or to Abraham, it was to command, not to ask. And, St. Bede noted in a homily on the Annunciation, "it is a fitting start to Man's restoration that an angel should be sent by God to the virgin who was to be hallowed by the Divine Birth, because the first cause of Man's ruin was through the serpent sent by the Devil to tempt Eve by the spirit of pride." Just as Genesis itself contains the first promise of the Redeemer (Gn 3:14-15), Gabriel's annunciation makes that Redeemer's coming stand as a clear parallel the event that the Redeemer was to undo. If redemption were to happen at all, it had to happen in this way for its meaning to be clear.

Because its meaning is clear, the Annunciation, a joyful Mystery, still stands under the shadow of the Cross. Christ was born in the flesh to suffer and die in the flesh, although tactfully God instructed Gabriel to look past that when he told Mary what was to happen; so he spoke only of birth and ultimate triumph. The joy of the Feast of the Annunciation is shadowed liturgically, too. The Feast has not developed into a major holiday in secular culture because it necessarily falls in Lent—the early Church universally celebrated Christmas on the twenty-fifth of December, so the date of the Feast of the Annunciation was worked back from then to fall on the twenty-fifth of March. And the twenty-fifth of March, since long before Christmas was commemorated on its own feast day, happens to be the date that the early Church universally understood as the actual day of the Crucifixion.

The symmetry of St. Luke's account of this pivotal instant may well have prompted that understanding. Certainly it pointed clearly to this moment as the hinge of history that ended the Age of Law and initiated the Age of Grace. That's why the Annunciation stands as the era of our calendar; all human events since have been dated in their relationship to Mary's *fiat*. Before Christ there was only anticipation; but after this Year of Our Lord, fulfillment.

THE VISITATION

L ANGUAGE IS THE WAY IN WHICH THE HUMAN MIND WORKS. WE CONVEY information to one another in language, and we process that information in language unspoken within the walls of our own minds. The more skillfully you handle language the more easily and efficiently you can understand what goes on around you, in all its implications, and the better you can convey it to others. The study of these skills is rhetoric, the art of oratory. Rhetoric is the discipline of shaping sentences and texts so that they'll convey their full meaning; with grammar and logic, rhetoric was one of the basic parts of classical education that taught people how to analyze thought, dig out the truth, and communicate that truth effectively.

Among classically educated people—which would include everybody who wrote from Old-Testament times through the great days of Greece and Rome up to the Great War of 1914—the form of a text conveyed as much information as the words themselves. Just as you can search through Scripture to connect prophecy and fulfillment by finding similar words, you can connect verse to verse on the basis of the shape of the phrases, too, and in fact you can't really get the full meaning out of any passage unless you look at the form of its structure.

> So some working knowledge of the art of rhetoric is absolutely crucial for understanding the Bible or any of the other basic texts of western civilization. Unfortunately—tragically—rhetoric is no longer taught in elementary schools, but you can still find older textbooks on the subject. The best of these older textbooks date from around the time of the First World War, when educated people hurried to commit all of their knowledge to paper, to preserve it against the disaster that they all foresaw.

There are no better examples for the study of rhetoric than the texts in the Bible itself, particularly the Gospels, and each of the four has a particular rhetorical lesson to teach. St. Matthew, the onetime tax collector, is concerned with recording as many of Christ's words and deeds in the most particular terms; his account tends to be aimed at proving that the Messiah had come in the person of Jesus of Nazareth, and explaining his relationship to this world. That's why he's customarily symbolized by the figure of a man (Ez 1:10). St. Mark, the boy who was sleeping in the garden (Mr 14:51), gives more attention to the miracles that astounded Jesus's followers, rather than to his sermons; that's why his symbol is the lion, the symbol of power. St. John, the Apostle Jesus loved (Jn 19:26, 20:2, 21:7), exults in the spiritual glory of the Messiah as the Incarnate Word, the embodiment of the God who is love. That's why his symbol is the eagle.

St. Luke is symbolized by the ox, symbol of the Earth, symbol of strength, of the ability to pull great loads deliberately. He takes things analytically, step by step; his stated purpose is to draw out an orderly account so that the events he relates can be understood fully (Lk 1:3-4). St. Luke's Gospel and his Book of Acts are extremely rich texts, packed with quotations, allusions, and references that bear almost infinite analysis. But he doesn't plod along. He moves so much material so smoothly that the casual reader can slip past his meaning without noticing it.

St. Luke wrote the account of the Visitation of Mary and the incarnate Savior to Elizabeth and John the Baptizer in the first chapter of his Gospel (Lk 1:39-56). Mary and Elizabeth, like St. Luke, choose their words carefully; each phrase is loaded with significance from its use elsewhere in the Bible. And of course nobody wastes a word. St. Luke is careful to specify, for example, that to get to Elizabeth's house Mary went up into the hill country; that tiny phrase links the Visitation to a mountain of imagery that ranges from Genesis to Revelation, recalling as it does all of the prophets on high places (like Elias bringing rain to the long-parched land by praying on Mount Carmel, 3Kn 18:42-45) and most of all Sinai: the high holy place on which the tablets of the Old Law were written upon by the finger of God.

The tablets of Sinai—which were to be broken and then restored (Ex 32:19, 34:1-28)—are a foreshadowing of Christ, as the physical embodiment of the Law of God. In fact, the whole episode of the Visitation turns on the fact that this is the first time that the incarnate Christ is recognized by Israel as the fulfillment of the Old Law and the embodiment of the New Law in himself. That means that the implications of the Visitation are best understood if you remember the central image of the Ark of the Covenant in which those stone tablets were kept: they were carried toward the earthly Temple of Jerusalem in the golden Ark of the Covenant, and Jesus of Nazareth was carried on his journey toward the heavenly Temple in Mary—the Ark of the New Covenant (Ex 20:1-17, 25:10-22; Hb 7-11; *cf.* Jn 20:17).

> This parallel between Mary and the Ark of the Old Covenant is why the Ark appears frequently in or around images of the Visitation (or of the Annunciation) as it does in any number of mediæval manuscript illuminations, over the portal of the Virgin at Notre-Dame-de-Paris, and even in later works like the Lady Chapel in the oratory at Versailles. But dozens of other similarities surround this basic prophetic symbolism. The Ark of Moses was the throne of God, on

which his visible presence sat above the cherubim (Ex 40:34; Ez 1:4-28), which is why there are so many pictures and statues of Mary holding the Baby in her lap—or of Mary holding her dead son after the Crucifixion, as in Michelangelo's Pietà. And it's why she's called the Throne of Wisdom, *Sedes Sapientiæ*, in the Litany (*cf.* 1Cr 1:24, 2:6-11), just as she's called the Ark of the Covenant there.

After Christ's fulfillment of the Old Covenant was complete, the Ark of the Covenant was taken to Rome, as part of the spoils of the Temple of Jerusalem seized by the Emperor Titus when he destroyed the Temple in the year 70—you can still see the spoils paraded in triumph in the relief sculptures of the arch that Titus built in Rome to commemorate the destruction of the Temple. Roman generals dedicated the spoils of foreign temples to the temples of their own gods, as the Israelites themselves did (Nm 31:28-31) and as the Philistines tried to do with the Ark themselves (1Kn 5). But this time God did not smite the conquerors and return the Ark to Jerusalem. Titus put it in one of the city's temples, evidently the Temple of Jupiter Capitolinus, where it and the other furnishings stayed until later emperors, particularly Commodus, stripped all of the temples of their gold to make up the deficit they'd caused in public finance, and to pay for their endless, pointless wars.

But at the time of Christ the Ark was in the Holy of Holies in Jerusalem, and it contained the tablets of the Law and two other treasures: it held some of the manna, the bread from Heaven that sustained Israel on their way to Jerusalem (Ex 16:4-8; *cf.* Jn 6), the only manna that didn't decompose, and the flowering rod of Aaron, the walking-staff that he carried as patriarch of the House of Levi (Nm 17:8, 16-18; Hb 9:4).

These staves were important because Israel used to keep records of genealogy by carving or scratching marks on the staff of the patriarch of the tribe; the rod represents the family, the descent, of the whole tribe. At the beginning of Israel's life as an independent nation, God commanded the elders of the Twelve Tribes to make their marks on their staves and put them in the Tabernacle, before the Ark, so that he could show which would be the priestly house of Israel.

Aaron's flowered overnight, which indicated that he was the one who was to be High Priest, and that the House of Levi was to be the priestly house of Israel (Nm 17:21-25, 18:1-2). Now, in Latin, the word for a walking-stick like the rod of Aaron is *virga*, which happens to sound a lot like *virgo*, the Latin word for a virgin. And Aaron's rod bore fruit—almonds—without being planted; Mary bore Jesus without having marital relations. These kinds of association may have started people thinking about further similarities between the Arks of the two Covenants.

THE VISITATION

By the end of the first century, gospels—there are many more than the four in the Bible—started to relate that when Mary and the some of the other virgins dedicated in the Temple reached fourteen years of age, the High Priest ordered them all to go back to their families find husbands. Mary refused, having dedicated her lifelong virginity to God. That put the High Priest in a quandary; he couldn't make her break her vow, but then he wasn't prepared to receive an unlimited number of dedicated virgins into the Temple for their whole lives, either. So the High Priest went into the Sanctuary, and he prayed.

And a voice came out of the Ark, saying: as Isaia said (11:1), at the fulfillment of the Law a shoot shall sprout from the rod of Jesse, and from his stock a bud shall blossom, who will be the Messiah, the Promised One of God. And so the High Priest ordered that all of the unmarried men of the house and family of David, the son of Jesse, should bring their staves into the Temple. He placed them before the Mercy Seat, and the rod of Joseph burst into flower, and a dove alighted on top of it.

The High Priest commanded that Joseph be betrothed to Mary, and that he respect her vow; so Joseph returned to his own city of Bethlehem, and Mary went back to the home of her parents in Nazareth. The disappointed suitors of the family are often depicted as witnesses to their kinsman's betrothal. In the great picture by Raphael now in the Brera at Milan, one of them is shown breaking his sterile staff across his knee—a visual expression of his own frustration, but also a reminder, perhaps, that the priestly office of Aaron's Tribe of Levi had passed to the House of David, merging with the kingly office of the Tribe of Juda.

After the Annunciation, the Ark of the New Covenant revealed her character further in what she did, and in what she did not do. She did not get carried away by the epochal news that the Covenant was at last to be fulfilled, and that she was to be the one through whom it would be done. She didn't brag about the unique honor that she had received; she didn't even tell anybody else her great news. Instead of thinking of her own great honor and joy, she listened to what Gabriel said about her cousin—how many people would have even heard it, at such an occasion—and, when he had gone, she went out to help Elizabeth with the delivery of her own child of the miracle.

Elizabeth knew that the child she herself was carrying would be a great prophet; Gabriel had told Zachary (Lk 1:13-17), and even though he couldn't talk about it he could communicate (Lk 1:63), and she herself knew that her conception in old age was extraordinary—but she thought of it only in terms of herself (Lk 1:24-25). She had to be told what it all meant; she needed to either learn all of it from a prophet, or she had to be one herself. As it happened, she found out both ways: "And it came to pass, when

223

Elizabeth heard the greeting of Mary, that the babe in her womb leapt; and Elizabeth was filled with the Holy Spirit, and cried out with a loud voice, 'Blessed art thou amongst women, and blessed is the fruit of thy womb! And how have I deserved that the mother of my Lord should come to me? For behold, the moment that the sound of thy greeting came to my ears, the babe in my womb leapt for joy" (Lk 1:41-44; Cn 6:12).

Although he was only in the sixth month of his life, St. John the Baptizer recognized the Christ, who was himself only in the first days of his life; and he leapt for joy. He danced before the Ark of the New Covenant as David had danced before the Ark of the Old (Lk 1:41; 2Kn 6:12-14).

Some authorities see St. John's dance of joy as his reaction to a kind of baptism, his absolution from original sin. St. Alphonsus of Liguori takes it as a fact in his *Glories of Mary*, but he was only conveying a teaching that the Fathers of the Church had proclaimed long before. Pope St. Leo the Great understood the verse to mean exactly that (*Sermon 30*), and more than that "it is as though he is already crying out, 'Behold the Lamb of God! Behold him who takes away the sins of the world!'" (*Sermon 35*; cf. Jn 1:29)—that is, St. John not only received the Holy Spirit as his mother did at that moment; he was called forth to his vocation (Jr 1:5; Is 43:1; Lk 1:13, 15). The fifteenth-century Franciscan preacher and author of the Office of the Immaculate Conception, Bernardino dei Busti, O.F.M., explained succinctly: "Christ caused Mary to greet Elizabeth, and the word, proceeding from the womb of the Blessed Mother where the Lord lived, went out into Elizabeth, and came down to John; and he was thereby anointed as prophet".

In any case, the blessings that Christ's visit brought to the house of Zachary came through Mary's mediation—she was the one who brought him there, of her own will and in answer to a human need—so the Visitation sets the pattern by which Christ would bestow his graces from then on. And the meaning of John's sudden activity was clear to Elizabeth; the Holy Spirit let her know about Mary's pregnancy and its significance. She repeated Gabriel's salutation to Mary, and then she added, "How have I deserved that the mother of my Lord should come to me?" As Mary was the first to know of Christ's incarnation, and as St. John the Baptizer was the first to tell of him, Elizabeth was the first proclaim that Jesus is Lord.

She did this by acclaiming Mary. She used the form of acclamation that had been customary in greeting a woman coming in triumph (Jt 13:23-26), and specifically she echoed what David said when the old Ark approached (2Kn 6:9); both Elizabeth's phrase and the king's are graceful acknowledgements of unworthiness of such an honor. Elizabeth went farther; she referred to Mary as Mother of her Lord—the title of the Queen Mothers of Israel (3Kn 2:19-20; 2Pr 15:16), so she was also the first on Earth to declare Christ the King. But there was another side to Elizabeth's prophecy in this greeting: by hailing Mary as the Queen Mother, she was foretelling the acclamations of Israel when Jesus entered Jerusalem (Mt 21:9); she was foretelling the Passion.

Elizabeth brings her acclamation to a close with a verse of praise directed specifically at Mary herself: "And blessed is she who has believed, because the things promised her by the Lord shall be accomplished" (Lk 1:45). This is a necessary context for that troublesome passage, Lk 11:27-28: "Now it came to pass as he was saying these things that a certain woman from the crowd lifted up her voice and said to him, 'Blessed is the womb that bore thee, and the breasts that nursed thee.' But he said, 'Rather, blessed are they who hear the word of God and keep it'" (cf. Mt 12:46-50).

The woman in the crowd had echoed Elizabeth's greeting, but both of those acclamations refer to Mary's divine maternity, which none of us in the crowd can emulate. Christ's redirection of the praise doesn't deny that Mary is his mother, and it doesn't say or imply that Mary has no particular merit. It reminds us that Mary co-operated in Jesus's work of salvation by her own decision; it points to her conversion, to that particular facet of her participation in his work that everybody who would follow him has to imitate. And it establishes her as an example that anyone can follow, just as this last verse of Elizabeth's greeting does.

In the visual arts, the meaning of Mary's visit to Elizabeth is expressed wordlessly in any number of ways. In some icons and manuscripts from the East, all four of the principals of the scene are shown, with Jesus and St. John the Baptizer visible through the transparent abdomens of their mothers. Some western artists adopted that image, too, and for a while little wooden or ivory statues of Mary and Elizabeth, hinged to open and reveal their sons, were popular as private devotional images. Even the Emperor Charles V had two images of this kind, one evidently a painting with a little door in it, and the other a figure made of jewels.

But in general that kind of thing was too graphic to become a standard for Christian depictions of the Visitation in the West, and images of this type were always disapproved by the hierarchy or forbidden outright—in the Middle Ages the bishop of Zara in Dalmatia, on the frontier between East and West, burned a picture put up by the parishioners of the Church of St. John, explicitly because it showed a tiny John dancing in Elizabeth's transparent womb.

Normally the Visitation is represented as an onlooker would have seen it—that is, with only Mary and Elizabeth visible. Often they're shown joining their right hands, which is the ancient and meaningful gesture called the *coniunctio dextræ*, the universal sign of harmony, agreement, and alliance—it's what we do when we shake hands today, and why couples about to be married join their right hands, too. It's also why the Visitation is often depicted as an allegory of the passing of authority to the Church, personified by Mary and her Son, by the Synagogue, personified by Elizabeth—a Levite—and by her son, the last of the great prophets of the Old Law (Lk 1:5; Mt 11:13). And the symbolism of this meeting, the embrace, this handshake, is why Urban VI Prignano chose to extend the Feast of the Visitation to the whole Church in 1389, when he wanted to rally the Faithful in prayer for an end to the great Western Schism.

Often, too, Mary and Elizabeth are shown embracing in the kiss of peace, like Anna and Joachim at the Golden Gate. In some mediæval paintings and sculptures from Germany, Italy, and France, both women are shown great with child to symbolize their pregnancies. Generally, though, that's also seen as a little too emphatic, and it's not an accurate representation of what's in the Gospel; so more accurate images showing more delicacy of taste usually signify Mary's state by showing Elizabeth laying her hand lovingly on Mary's chest or abdomen, and in a few cases Mary returns the salute. And just to be sure that they get the message across, some artists add a couple of little rabbits, unmistakable symbols of fecundity and regenerated life, playing at the feet of the two women.

M ary understood Elizabeth's inspiration and, at last, she couldn't contain her joy any more. "Now," St. Augustine said, "Mary can sing and rejoice in all her youthful happiness. All Mankind can join with her in praise, in joyful chorus… Mary's canticle of praise silences the mournful wail of Eve" (*Sermon 18 On the Saints*). Her own answer to Elizabeth's song of greeting is called the *Magnificat* from the first word of the song in the Vulgate: *Magnificat anima mea dominum.* That's sometimes rendered as "My soul doth magnify the Lord", but that archaic translation starts the song with a puzzle: if God is all-present and all-powerful, who can magnify him?

But *magnificat* is a form of the compound verb *magna fico*, which is the root of our word "magnify" but also of "magnificent"; in Latin, it means to make great things, to do great deeds, or to say great things, or to praise someone by speaking of his greatness. This particular conjugation of it— third person singular, present tense—means "it praises", in the sense "it makes him out to be great"; Mary means that her heart speaks great things of God. More recent translations, like the Latin of the Vulgate itself, make phrase and the whole song a little clearer:

My soul proclaims the greatness of the Lord, and my spirit rejoices in God my Savior.	Magnificat anima mea dominum, et exsultavit spiritus meus in deo salutari meo.

THE VISITATION

For he has regarded the lowliness	Quia respexit humilitatem
of his handmaiden; behold:	ancillæ suæ; ecce:
henceforth all generations	enim ex hoc beatam me dicent
will call me blessed,	omnes generationes,
because He Who Is Mighty	quia fecit mihi magna
has done great things for me:	qui potens est:
and holy is his Name.	et sanctum Nomen eius.
And his mercy is from generation	Et misericordia eius a progenie
to generation on those who fear him.	in progenies timentibus eum.
He has shown might with his arm;	Fecit potentiam in brachio suo;
he has scattered the proud	dispersit superbos
in the conceit of their hearts.	mente cordis sui.
He has put down the mighty	Deposuit potentes
from their thrones	de sede,
and has exalted the lowly.	et exultavit humiles.
He has filled the hungry	Esurientes implevit
with good things,	bonis,
and the rich he has sent away empty.	et divites dimisit inanes.
He has given help to Israel,	Suscepit Israel
his servant,	puerum suum,
mindful of his mercy—	recordatus misericordiæ suæ—
even as he spoke to our fathers,	sicut locutus est ad patres nostros,
to Abraham and his posterity	Abraham et semini eius
forever.	in sæcula.

This canticle stands second only to the Our Father in its richness, its economy, and its perfection; it crowns the psalmody of the Old Testament and weaves tightly together countless threads of prophecy about the Child whom Mary was carrying. If she had done nothing more than sing this song, Mary would merit the highest rank among all of the prophetesses of Israel; with this ecstatic canticle she rises above Miriam and her simple antiphon (Ex 15:20-21), over Judith in her song of vindication (Jt 16:2-21); and she surpasses Anna and her canticle of thanksgiving (1Kn 2:1-10). In fact, she would outrank David himself, and Solomon, with this pinnacle of psalmodic composition.

Composers have evidently always recognized the superiority of Mary's song; no other passage of Scripture has been set to music so often. Evidently the *Magnificat* had been chanted in plainsong for more than a thousand years before Josquin des Prés wrote settings for it. After that, it was set in every possible musical style by Victoria, Gabrieli, Monteverdi, Vivaldi, the great Couperin and the great

Bach as well as the little ones, and virtually every other noteworthy composer down to César Franck. Most of them wrote more than one score for it—Palestrina wrote four in each of the eight modes of chant, and Orlando di Lasso wrote a hundred, of which about fifty survive. Franck himself was so enraptured by the lyric that he set out to produce a hundred musical settings for it, of which he finished about sixty.

At every moment, somebody, somewhere on Earth, is singing the *Magnificat*, and so it has been since the dawn of the Church. It has always been chanted every day in the Liturgy of the Hours, and as a prominent part of the devotions. In the sixth century, St. Cæsarius of Arles assigned it to Lauds, which is where it remains today in the Greek Rite, but the Latin Rite has always sung it at Vespers. Durandus said that this was done to recall the fact that the world was saved in its eventide, at the last moment, by Mary's assent to God's plan of redemption; others have supposed that it was sung then because Mary approached Elizabeth's house toward evening—as John was born of aged parents, St. Augustine mused, or as the Kingdom was to come under cover of night (*Eighty-Three Questions* 58; *cf.* 1Th 5:2).

Most probably, it was placed at Vespers because so many psalmodic devotions, like the Angelus, recalled the Incarnation at sunset, and because Vespers were celebrated with the most magnificent liturgy—magnificence being particularly appropriate for the song that proclaims the greatness of the Lord. So Mary's canticle on the rising of the Sun of Justice follows the setting of the Sun around the Earth, day after day, in constant praise until the end of Time.

The *Magnificat* is in many ways the answer to the canticle of Azaria (Dn 3:26-45), which acknowledges sin and begs for the fulfillment of the Covenant, and it echoes the song of Moses (Dt 32:1-43), which does so even more forcefully. And it stands as the fulfillment of the canticle that Isaia predicted would be sung by Israel when the Kingdom of Emmanuel would at last be established (Is 12).

But the most complete precedent for Mary's song is the canticle of Anna, the wife of Elcana the Zuphite, whose story is recounted at the beginning of the First Book of Kings. That song itself foreshadows a good many of the psalms that David and Solomon were to write later, so Anna's song and Mary's stand on either side of Psalms, like seed and fruit. Mary's great psalm is a kind of perfection of Anna's, and a synopsis of the psalms of her kingly ancestors. By virtually quoting certain verses of them all, it incorporates them into that same single message: salvation.

THE VISITATION

My soul proclaims the greatness of the Lord, Mary began. Like Christ's own response to the woman in the crowd (Lk 11:27-28), the first verse of Mary's canticle stands as a graceful answer to Elizabeth's praise (Lk 1:45). Mary deflects this praise of herself and accentuates Elizabeth's reference to God's promise by saying simply that her soul proclaims the greatness of the Lord, not of herself.

Then she goes on to explain the cause of her joy: her spirit rejoices in God her Savior, as David had said (Ps 34:9). Throughout the Old Testament, God is acclaimed by reference to any number of his aspects and acts—God of Mercy, God of Power and Might, Lord of Hosts. But Mary understood that God's principal aim in coming as the Messiah is salvation; so she shaped the beginning of her song (Lk 1:46-50) by recalling God's saving grace specifically, tying her utterance to those parts of Scripture that do the same thing.

In the following verse, Mary says that she's rejoicing because God has regarded the lowliness of his handmaiden—in Latin, that's *quia respexit humilitatem ancillæ suæ*. The word for handmaiden, *ancilla*, shows its ties to English words like "ancillary", meaning something that helps, but the other words are somewhat richer in meaning than their English cousins. *Respexit* means "he has looked upon", but it also carries the connotation of respect; he has recognized her lowliness and deferred to it, in some way. In fact, the word for lowliness here, *humilitate*, shows that Mary's not just saying that her station in life is humble. The virtue of humility is not lowliness as we'd understand that word in itself.

Humility doesn't mean abasing yourself from the place that God has given you: it means understanding that place precisely. Humility is not by any means denying the gifts that he gave you (so that you'll have what you need to fill that place), but having an accurate estimation of them. Mary is closer to God than any other human being can be; yet her very closeness to God means that she can see more clearly than anybody else just how immense the distance is between him and his creatures. So she isn't boasting in reverse, here, saying that all of these great things have happened because God has seen how much humility she has; she's marvelling that when God wanted to work such wonders he would reach down to a creature as lowly as she knew herself to be.

Sometimes that's overlooked, because in the next phrase Mary asks us to consider that from this moment all generations will call her blessed. Sometimes that sounds as if she's exulting in the fact that she will be understood as higher and holier than everybody else. But the Latin clears that up, as does the Greek: *ecce: enim ex hoc beatam me dicent omnes generationes*, she says, ἰδοὺ γὰρ ἀπὸ τοῦ νῦν μακαριοῦσί με πᾶσαι αἱ γενεαί. The Greek word for "holy" is ὅσιος, but St. Luke doesn't report that Mary said anything like that; he uses the word μακαρία, and that means happiness. St. Jerome translated it to mean exactly the same thing, too; *sancta* is "holy" in Latin, but in the Vulgate he used *beatus*, which also means happy. For that matter, "blessed" means happy; too. It's from the Old English *bletsian*, which is connected to our word "bliss"—when you "bless" somebody you make him happy, and in the Christian view of things the ultimate happiness is reunion with God.

In plain English, Mary's saying that from this day forward everybody will look at her and say that she must have been happier than anybody else every could be (*cf.* Gn 30:13). And in the next phrase she specifies the reason for that happiness: "because He Who Is Mighty has done great things for me, and holy is his Name." This reflects passages like Dt 10:21, but notice that in all her ecstatic joy, Mary didn't boast of her own deeds, as Judith did (Jt 16:8); she didn't claim any credit for herself, as Deborah did (Jg 5:1-31). She remembered Anna's admonition: Do not multiply to speak lofty things, boasting—*nolite multiplicare loqui sublimia gloriantes*, in the Vulgate (1Kn 2:3; *cf.* Mt 6:7). Mary referred all of her happiness to God, acknowledging that he had done all of the great things and refusing to claim any of them for herself.

She does this neatly by reminding us of verses like Ps 125:2-3: "Then they said among the nations, 'The Lord has done great things for them.' The Lord has done great things for us; we are glad indeed" (*cf.* Ps 113B:1; Lk 11:27-28). Her swift deflection of praise of herself is reflected in the symmetry—unfortunately lost in English—between *Magnificat anima mea dominum* and *quia fecit mihi magna*, between μεγαλύνει ἡ ψυχή μου and ὅτι ἐποίησέν μοι μεγαλεῖα. Both phrases turn on the same verb, *magna facio* or μεγαλύνω. So the shape of Mary's phrases says that her soul magnifies the Lord because the Lord has—literally—magnified things for her.

The next verse, "and his mercy is from generation to generation, on those who fear him" (Lk 1:50; *cf.* Ps 102:17), closes the first section of the canticle and leads to the second (Lk 1:51-53), in which Mary remembers what God has already done for Israel and—as she sings for her whole nation—what he has done for her in particular. The only word that might be a stumbling-block here is "fear", but notice that it's *timor* in Latin, from which we get the word "timid", meaning respectful; it's not *terror*, which brings with it an entirely negative flock of connotations. Fear of the Lord is closely connected to humility; it means, basically, recognizing his greatness and acting in accordance with it.

Mary undoubtedly learned the rhetorical techniques that she used to such advantage in this second section of the *Magnificat* by learning Scripture itself, but the Greeks were the ones who gave them their precise technical names. She selects her words with an eye to *parachresis* (pair-a-KREE-sis, from the Greek παρα-, for, and χρῆσθαι, to use), which is bringing another's words into your own context with new emphasis or focus, and *paradiorthosis* (pair-a-die-or-THO-sis, παρα-, for, and διόρθωσις, correction)—embedding famous words into your composition to give them a new twist.

For example, when she sings that "He has shown might with his arm; he has scattered the proud in the conceit of their hearts," she is pinpointing an image that instantly brings to mind the Canticle of Moses (Ex 15:1-18), celebrating the overthrow of Pharaoh's forces in the Red Sea: Your right hand, O Lord, magnificent in power, your right hand, O Lord, has shattered the enemy... O Terrible in Renown, Worker of Wonders, when you stretched out your right hand, the Earth swallowed them! ... By the might of your arm they were frozen like stone ... And you brought [your people] in ... to the sanctuary, O Lord, that your hands established" (*cf.* Ps 88:11).

Mary presents these embedded quotations in ways that configure the speech to convey meaning by its shape. One of the particular patterns or figures of speech that she used here is called *antithesis* in Latin (*anti-*, counter, and *thesis*, proposition) or ἐπάνοδος in Greek (ἐπί, upon, ἀνά, again, and ὁδός, the way)—both of which refer to something that reverses, that turns back or turns against itself, or sets up a contrast of opposite entities doing opposite things, as Anna of Elcana does in 1Kn 2:4.

Mary also uses the figure of speech called *chiasmus* (kee-AZ-muss), from the name of the Greek letter χ ("chi", which rhymes with "pie"). It's an X-shaped rhetorical structure, like Is 5:20; Mr 2:27; or 1Cr 11:8, all of which follow the pattern diagrammed as ABBA—Jn 15:16, "you (A) have not chosen me (B), but I (B) have chosen you (A)," is a perfect chiasmus.

The X-shaped structure of a chiasmus sometimes governs whole passages, shaping them into symmetry around a single point, as Nm 15:35, or really the whole Book of Ruth. You can see the figure clearly in Jn 5:8-11, in which statements progress toward the pivotal fact that it was the Sabbath and then move back again, in reverse order. Most forcefully, a chiasmus tells about a reversal, in which whatever is at the top ends up on the bottom, and *vice versa*.

Mary uses these figures effectively to represent the overturning of old ways and the establishment of new ones; but more than that she uses them to correct the problem of Israel's expectations. Everybody awaited the Messiah, but a good many Jews persistently thought that he was supposed to come in glory, ripping apart the sky and smashing the teeth of their enemies with a rod of iron (Ps 2, 9B, 34, 57; Ac 1:6). Mary wanted to convey the truth that the Christ was coming as the weakest and most fragile of all human beings, a baby; and coming in obscurity, born as all Men are born—born to a kingly family, of course, but born to them only after all of their earthly greatness had been purged away.

So Mary selects her words carefully to echo the prophecies of the Old Testament that speak of God's love for the poor and lowly, and she puts this twist on them to show that she understands the unexpectedness of this way of coming. She picked two particular metaphors from the Old Testament, and she stated them antithetically or chiastically, to convey this reversal.

"He has put down the mighty from their thrones and has exalted the lowly." she said. That phrase sets her remarks in the context of passages like Jb 5:11-13, Sr 10:14-15, and Ps 137:6, "The Lord is exalted, yet the lowly he sees", and "He raises up the lowly from the dust; from the dunghill he lifts up the poor to seat them with princes, with the princes of his own people" of Ps 112:7-8—which ties the phrase even more closely to Anna's acclamation of the Lord as the one who "raises up the needy from the dust, and lifts the poor from the dunghill; that he may sit with princes, and hold the throne of glory" (1Kn 2:8; cf. 2:4, 7; Ps 31:10, 33:10-11, 74:8, 146:6).

There's a subtle difference between the forerunning phrases and Mary's expression, though: there is no trace of boasting in her verse, and no sign of exultation in the destruction of the high and mighty as there is in the earlier canticles. She simply says, look at what the Lord has done; or, as her own son would say later in a series of antithetical verses of his own, beginning with "Blessed are the poor in spirit, for theirs is the Kingdom of God" (Mt 5:3).

Mary may have intended a reference here, however delicate, to the fact that hers was the kingly family of Israel, although at the time they were not the mighty on the throne. After the death of Solomon, the Davidic line had declined as the Twelve Tribes split apart and fell prey to foreign powers and political extinction. David's family fell into obscurity, although evidently they weren't impoverished.

By Mary's day, Solomon's reign was regarded as an ideal, a golden age (3Kn 3:12; Mt 6:29). But by then other families, Jewish and foreign, had managed to increase in power by supporting whichever Roman faction happened to have the upper hand at the moment. And, in the days of Joachim and Anna, Mark Anthony persuaded the Senate of Rome to recognize the head of one of these foreign families, a man named Herod, as King of Judea. This Herodian family set the political context in which Mary spoke and in which all of the Mysteries were played out, and they were not even distantly related to the kingly house of Israel.

The Herods are also an immensely confusing clan—not even the Gospels got it entirely right—so it may come as a help, and a relief, to have a single brief account of them here. The first Herod (d. 4 BC) was from Idumæa—°Ἰδουμαία in Greek—or Edom, southeast of the Dead Sea. The Edomites were Bedouins who were recognized by Israel as descending from Abraham, but through Esau (Dt 23:8), who was nicknamed Edom, the Red (אֱדֹם, in Hebrew; Gn 25:30-33), because he was red when he was born and because he sold his birthright for a dish of red food. So the Edomites were not numbered among the Tribes of Israel; they had a kind of secondary, semi-Jewish status (Gn 25:23). They lived a semi-nomadic existence, and they were semi-despised by Israel (*cf.* Dt 23:8-9).

As the first ruler of a foreign and unpopular dynasty, Herod was evidently very skittish about the security of his throne. When the Senate of Rome recognized his kingship over Israel, he instantly killed forty-five members of the Sanhedrin who opposed the idea, appointed a Babylonian as High Priest, and tried to kill the baby Jesus (Mt 2:16), the prophesied King of the Jews who was supposed to spring from the House of David, rightful kings of Israel. Still, with Rome's support, he impressed everybody enough to be known to history as Herod the Great.

Herod the Great had ten wives, not all of whom had any influence on history or Scripture. His first important wife was a woman named Doris; she was the mother of Herod Antipater, important in Jewish history but not mentioned in the Bible. Herod the Great's second notable wife was Mariamne; their son Aristobulus married Berenice, daughter of Herod the Great's sister Salome and a man named Costabulus or Costabarus, an Idumæan whom Herod the Great had made governor of Idumæa and Gaza. Aristobulus and Berenice of Costabulus begat two noteworthy children, Herodias and Herod Agrippa I.

Herodias of Aristobulus married her uncle Herod Philip, son of Herod the Great and Malthace, the wife whose line we'll come to shortly. This Herod Philip lived as a private citizen at Rome; by Herodias of Aristobulus he had a daughter, the Salome who danced (Mt 14:6; Mr 6:22). We know her name because Josephus recorded it for us (*Antiquities* 18:5:137-138), but the Evangelists probably left it out of the Gospels so that she wouldn't be mistaken for the Salome who was present at the Crucifixion and went to the tomb on Easter morning (Mr 15:40, 16:1). This was a different person entirely, the mother of James and John, the sons of Zebedee (*cf.* Mr 15:40; Mt 27:56, 20:20-23); she's sometimes thought to be Jesus' aunt, Mary's "sister" or close kinswoman (Jn 19:25). Some of the Herodian family converted (Ac 13:1), but evidently Salome of Herodias of Aristobulus wasn't among them.

In any case, Herodias of Aristobulus divorced Herod Philip the father of Salome the dancer and married Herod Antipas, Herod Philip's full brother, another son of Herod the Great and Malthace.

Herod Agrippa I (Marcus Julius Agrippa, *c.* 10 BC-44 AD), the son of Aristobulus and Berenice of Costabulus, was raised in Rome as a hostage, the childhood friend of the Emperor Claudius, who was exactly his same age. He was made King of Judea by Caligula in 37; this was the King Herod who imprisoned St. Peter and beheaded St. James, the one who died eaten by worms in a particularly embarrassing way (Ac 12:1-3, 19-23). He was also the father of the Drusilla mentioned in Ac 24:24, the woman who married the Roman governor Felix.

Herod Agrippa I had two notable children, Herod Agrippa II and Berenice. Berenice of Agrippa (Ac 25:13) was the one who went to Rome and had a flagrant affair with the Emperor Titus, or at least gave the appearance of doing so. Herod Agrippa II (27-100) succeeded to his father's throne at the age of seventeen; when he got to be about thirty St. Paul pleaded before him (Ac 26). After Titus destroyed Jerusalem in 70, Herod Agrippa II moved back to Rome—or was moved there as a hostage—and died there in the third year of the imperium of Trajan. He was the last of the Herodian dynasty to rule.

But this line that had sprung from Herod the Great and Mariamne is intricately—incestuously—intertwined with the line of Herod the Great and his third wife, a Samaritan woman named Malthace. By him she had three important sons, Herod Archelaus, Herod Antipas, and Herod Philip.

The Jews were not happy to have the son of an Idumæan and a Samaritan rule them (*cf.* Ez 36:5; Ab 1-9; Mt 10:5; Jn 4:9), but, after the death of Herod the Great, Herod Archelaus was installed as "Ethnarch" (from the Greek ἔθνος, nation, and αρχος, ruler; *cf.* Mt 2:22). He wanted to be King of the Jews, so he went to Rome, but the Emperor refused his petition (*cf.* Lk 19:12-27). Still, Rome let him rule for about nine years, until Christ was about ten years old, judging by Dio Cassius's account.

Things were so bad under Herod Archelaus that people started to think that his rule signalled the end of the world, but the only thing that his barbarism really meant was that he was an unbelievably bad ruler who couldn't do anything right. Rome deposed him, merged his dominions into the Roman province of Syria (which had always been the regional authority there; Lk 2:2), and exiled him to Vienne in Gaul, on the Rhône between Lyons and Grenoble (Vienne is where Pontius Pilate was supposed to have retired, too, later—you can still see his tomb there). This Archelaus married his own brother's wife, but he wasn't the Herod whom St. John the Baptizer rebuked for this same crime; that was Herod Archelaus's full brother Herod Antipas.

Herod Antipas married the wife of his brother Herod Philip—Herodias of Aristobulus—and apparently adopted her daughter (his niece, the Salome who danced), or thought of marrying her; he was certainly not immune to her charms, and the family did have the habit of indulging themselves this way (Mt 14:6-7). He ruled Jerusalem after Herod Archelaus was deposed, but not as King. St. Mark refers to him by that title (Mr 6:14), but it was only used locally; he was never recognized as King of anything by Rome.

This Herod Antipas was Tetrarch of Galilee, the one who beheaded St. John the Baptizer (Mt 14:1-11). He also tried to kill Jesus at least once before he managed to get him crucified by the Roman governor, Pontius Pilate (Lk 13:31, 23:7-13; Ac 4:27). Herod Antipas wasn't a very good ruler, either; he was also deposed and banished to Gaul, where he lived in Lugdunum (Lyons). He died while on a trip to Spain.

Herod Philip, third noteworthy son of Herod the Great and Malthace, figures in history only as the father of Salome the dancer and first husband of Herodias of Aristobulus. The fourth notable wife of Herod the Great was Cleopatra of Jerusalem, but she's only significant because her son, Herod Philip, who ruled Ituræa and Trachontis as Tetrarch, is almost always mistaken for Herod Philip of Malthace. He wasn't.

So the Herodian succession at Jerusalem is: King Herod the Great to the time of the Massacre of the Innocents; then Herod Archelaus the Ethnarch, until Christ's tenth year, more or less; then Herod Antipas the Tetrarch who presided over the Crucifixion; King Herod Agrippa I, who died of the worms and was succeeded by his son King Herod Agrippa II, who heard St. Paul's pleading.

Whether they have a political connotation or not, these verses of the *Magnificat* refer indirectly to Gabriel's announcement that Mary's son would attain the throne of David (Lk 1:32), but Mary's next acclamations of reversal carry her second metaphor, which has to do with food: "He has filled the hungry with good things, and the rich he has sent away empty."

Besides the similar verse in Anna's canticle (1Kn 2:5), this image shows up any number of times in Scripture, because Israel's food supply was never secure; God evidently wanted them to know that they were absolutely dependent on him. When they were faithful, they had good crops and pastures (Ps 106, especially verse 9), and when they weren't they didn't, so the image of plentiful food occurs in some chiastic passages that turn on faithfulness to the Covenant, like Ps 33:11. But the most revealing thing in the image of God's provision of necessary food is that in times of extraordinary need, when Israel's cause seemed hopeless, he intervened miraculously to save them with bread from Heaven. And that's also expressed in Scriptural passages that echo Mary's criss-cross verse—Ps 77:21-25, for instance, and most important of all Jn 6:31-58, which speaks of the Eucharist.

In the longer view of things, the chiastic form of this section of the *Magnificat* shows the whole plan of salvation. These early chapters of St.

Luke's Gospel are really one of the hinges between the Old Testament and the New. Passages like Gn 3:1-13—a passage that crosses and crosses again—tell how perdition came at the beginning through Eve; salvation comes at the end through Mary. Eve caused Man to be expelled from the earthly Paradise, but Mary opens the Way to the heavenly. "Eve, who consented to the serpent's seduction, was condemned to pains in childbirth and to death," St. John Damascene noticed, "but this happy woman consented to the Word of God… How could she possibly know the pains of childbirth… In her body she carried Life itself" (*Second Sermon on the Dormition*).

The third and last section of the song (Lk 1:54-55) is the shortest and the simplest. "He has given help to Israel, his servant, mindful of his mercy— even as he spoke to our fathers, to Abraham and his posterity forever." As Mary ended the first section with a reminder that God's mercy is from generation to generation on those who fear him, and as she began the second with a reminder of God's Covenant with Israel, she ended the third section, and the whole canticle, with a verse that combines those two facts into a single conclusion: the first explicit affirmation in the Gospels that God had indeed fulfilled his promise of a savior that he had made to Adam and Eve so long ago. At last, the House of David had supplied a dwelling-place for the Mighty One of Jacob (Ps 131; *cf.* 2Kn 22:51; Ps 97:3; Is 41:8-10; Mi 7:20).

So, in the end, the *Magnificat* is like the Visitation itself: outwardly simple, yet echoing to universal implications and effects. And just as the Ark of the Old Covenant called down blessings on the house of Obededom when it came under his roof (1Pr 13:14), the Ark of the New Covenant brought blessings to the house of St. John the Baptizer: "happy, blessed, is the house that is visited by the Mother of God," St. Alphonsus of Liguori remarked. Which is why the Feast of the Visitation is often called the Feast of Our Lady of Graces.

THE NATIVITY

D AVID THE KING FEARED BRINGING THE ARK OF THE OLD COVENANT INTO his own city—How shall the Ark of God come to me? he asked (1Pr 13:12-14; *cf.* Lk 1:43). So he diverted the Ark on its journey toward Bethlehem and let it rest a while in the house of Obededom the Gethite. Obededom received it joyfully and kept it in his house for three months; and God blessed him. In the same way, Mary stayed three months in the house of Zachary. Then, as the Ark went into Bethlehem with David (1Pr 15:1), Mary went into Bethlehem with David's direct descendant, St. Joseph (Lk 2:4-6).

The epochal meaning of this trip is made clear in the rhetoric of St. Luke's account, but its implications are best reflected, probably, in the history of the Church's celebrations of the birth that happened when the Ark of the New Covenant reached David's city.

St. Luke's account of the Nativity (from the Latin *natus*, born; Lk 2:7) is amazingly straightforward—to a point. There was a governmental decree that everybody should be taxed; everybody went to his own city to be registered. Joseph went to the city of David, the ancestral head of his tribe, with his wife. While they were there she gave birth, and evidently they had to stay in a stable, because the inns were full. And there were shepherds in the area, too.

The angel of the Lord stood by them—all of a sudden, Heaven bursts through the mundane details of a passage that sounds, really, like a report from the Commissioner for Judea. After this point, every detail takes on new meaning. Mary wraps the baby in swaddling clothes (Lk 2:7; *cf.* 1Pr 15:27; Mt 27:59); and they had to stay in a provisional shelter, a stable, not in a palace (*cf.* 1Pr 15:1, 17:1). At last, all prophecies were fulfilled; and the choirs of angels echoed the Canticle of Asaph (1Pr 16:7-36), another of the great prophetic songs of the Old Testament that foreshadow Mary's own *Magnificat*.

Now, although the birth of Jesus marks his first appearance among Men, its significance can get buried under a lot of the customs that have attached themselves to the Church's commemoration—or, on the other hand, that significance can be magnified out of all proportion. The Nativity doesn't mark the beginning of Christ's earthly mission; that mission began at the instant of the Incarnation, which has always been celebrated at the Feast of the Annunciation. Jesus's birth doesn't mark the beginning of his public ministry, either, nor is it part of his real work of redemption, the Passion.

That's why the Nativity wasn't always commemorated by the Church as a separate event at all. It was usually mentioned in the liturgy of the Presentation or of the Epiphany, but it didn't always have a separate feast of its own.

Irenæus, Origen, and Tertullian don't include a commemoration of Christ's birth in their lists of feast days, and St. Augustine omits it from his list of first-class feasts. Gregory Nanzianus may have tried in the year 380 to establish a commemoration of the Nativity in Constantinople, but the only real evidence for this consists of three sermons on the subject that he delivered in a private oratory; and at any rate after he was exiled the following year there's no contemporary evidence that a separate feast of the Nativity was kept in Constantinople.

The earliest surviving sermon that must have come from a specific celebration of the Nativity comes from Numidia in Africa, in the form of a sermon by Optatus of Mileve that dates from about 383. But as late as the fifth century, the Nativity was celebrated only in local observances, and it had no universally accepted date. The oldest existing calendars and lectionaries put the commemoration anywhere from January 6, at the earliest, to December 25 at the latest—a tract attributed to St. Cyprian puts it on March 28, and St. Clement of Alexandria notes that it was celebrated in his city on May 20. It wasn't fixed at December 25 for the whole Church until about 650 AD, and even then it was not a major holiday.

Today, of course, people outside the Church and even those outside any church look forward to Christmas as the greatest holiday of the year. But this is still not really the Church's way; the immense secular celebrations, the songs, the banquets, the presents, and so on, didn't become inseparable from Christmas until about the fifteenth century, when northern Christians had the leisure and the need for a big mid-winter festival.

Most of these observances had nothing, really, to do with the birth of Christ, but then they didn't have anything to do with pagan religious festivals, either. Northern pagans decorated trees before the coming of Christianity, but these were decorations for seasonal festivals, not directly part of pagan worship. And in any case the modern idea of the Christmas tree isn't a survival from pre-Christian times, not being recorded before 1605. It has its roots in the custom of hanging apples on a tree on December 24 as a reminder that the Tree of the Knowledge of Good and Evil was at last to be redeemed by the New Adam.

A "carol", from the Old-French *carole*, meaning dancing-song, is simply a song of celebration, and carols were used as processional songs at weddings, coronations, and all kinds of festivals, secular as well as religious—but today the only ones that survive are those sung at Christmas. *Noël* is simply an Old French cheer of joy, like our "hurrah". It came from the Latin *natalem*, and it was used originally to hail the birth of any child; but by the Middle Ages it started to fade in private life and was used only to salute the birth of an heir to the throne or the accession of a new king, or as a greeting at Christmas, which is all of these occasions in one. Even the custom of midnight Mass at Christmas is only the last vestige of the practice that once was normal at any feast that had a vigil.

It's the same with banquets and presents: the lord of the manor gave a load of firewood to the family whenever a child was born, and tenants were allowed to eat at their master's table for as long as it took to burn a great log (a "yule" log, from the old word for midwinter); special meals were served to the poor, and presents were given to children at the birth of their siblings.

All of these family customs naturally came together in the celebration of the birth of Christ, the universal brother, and there they survived after they died out as part of daily life. And since the Christmas season—Advent—stands at the start of the liturgical year, it was usually considered as the start of the calendar year, too. That's why Christians started giving New Year's presents, customary since Roman times, on Christmas: it was the first great feast of the year. The custom survived even after New Year's was moved away from Christmas when the calendar was reformed and standardized in the sixteenth century. But this secular enthusiasm only gradually came to be reflected in more elaborate liturgies at Christmastide; and none of it ever became obligatory.

T he holiest day in the Church's calendar is not Christmas but Easter, the Solemnity of Solemnities—after all, everybody is born, but only Christ rose from the dead, and that is the principal proof that what he taught is true (1Cr 15:12-19). For the early Church the miracle of the Resurrection far overshadowed the birth of Jesus, which was to all appearances a perfectly natural event. Still, the birth of Christ is a major landmark in human history, the pivot of immense consequences; and the very naturalism of the Nativity gives the event much of its significance.

A good many of the Israelites expected that the Messiah would come in glory, breaking the enemies of Israel with a rod of iron. Messianic prophecies since Jacob's metaphorical praise of Juda—that he is a lion's whelp, crouching as a lion in wait for his prey—were taken more literally as promising a lasting earthly dominion (Gn 49:8-12): "The scepter shall not depart from Juda, nor the staff from between his feet, until he comes to whom it belongs."

In fact, virtually all prophecies about the Messiah and his work could be taken this way, depending on how literally they were interpreted. The prophecies about Emmanuel in Isaia, for example, start (7:13) with a mention of the House of David and predicts his birth of a virgin of that family, but they also promise the destruction of Samaria and Damascus, Israel's earthly enemies at the time. They go on to predict that he will restore justice on the Earth, and that he will restore Israel to the homeland from which it has been exiled (8:23-9:6); his rulership (11:1-9) will bring about a new Paradise on Earth, a life without violence, permeated with an awareness of the God of Israel.

Of course, there was a body of prophecy, about equal to the one about the all-conquering Messiah, that told Israel that his reign would be pacific and that it would be manifested on Earth in a change of human hearts—Jr 24:7; Ez 11:19; Ml 2:2. Isaia (11:6-9 and 42:3), for instance, says almost literally that he would not lift a finger. But the Israelites preferred to think of being delivered from their oppressors here below, and they could probably make no sense out of prophecies like these, or those in Isaia that describe in detail the suffering and death of the Messiah at the hands of his enemies (Is 42-53). This couldn't become clear until after the Resurrection, just as Jacob's prophecy, "He washes his garment in wine, his robe in the blood of grapes" (Gn 49:11), was taken literally as a promise of princely wealth and extravagance instead of figuratively as a prediction of the Passion and Eucharist of Christ, which could not have been more clearly foreseen at the time Genesis was written.

Besides, the promise of a conquering savior was reinforced time and again in the Old Testament, largely because prophets arose to encourage Israel to hold fast to the Covenant whenever the Tribes suffered under earthly conquerors—so it was with Jeremia, Ezekiel, and Zacharia, all of whom promise the destruction of Israel's enemies. But as time went on, the concept of the conquering Messiah deepened and became richer. By the time Israel returned to Jerusalem and rebuilt the Temple under Zorobabel and the High Priest Josue, the Messiah was understood to be not only king but priest as well: a teacher as well as a ruler, one who would not only enforce the Law with judgement but proclaim it to the people, too (Sr 24:22-27).

And in the second century BC, during the persecutions by Antiochus Epiphanus—Antiochus Epimanes, the Mad—the prophet Daniel reminded Israel of the prophecies of Enoch and Esdras, particularly of their insight that the Messiah would be a man, or "one like a man". By about that time, the Jews may have thought that the Messiah had come already, or certainly that he was about to come, because priestly and kingly offices were united in a single man. The Maccabees, a priestly clan, had already led a rebellion that eventually gave rise to the last of the Israelite kings, the Hasmoneans.

But the Maccabees were not the highest priestly family, and the Sadducees, by whom the High Priest was elected, rose up in protest and split Israel in two; and, as usually happens to divided nations, the two halves split into any number of contesting camps. Each of these numberless factions seems to have expected the Messiah to descend upon the clouds, annihilate not only foreign enemies but all other sects of Israel itself, and establish his everlasting Paradise on Earth, ruling through them, the faithful and elect minority. They fully expected the Promised One to come, in power and immediately, and sweep them to victory over everybody who opposed them.

Members of all of these tussling sects could agree on only one thing: the prophecies on which they all hung their hopes leave no doubt that Jesus of Nazareth is the promised Messiah. Throughout all of their allegory and metaphor, these texts all point directly to the son of his particular ancestry. But people still puzzled over the fact that his kingdom is not of this world, principally; demanding a cataclysmic miracle, they seem to have overlooked the fact that the way Jesus came is more in tune with the way God has always worked on Earth. It was not by splitting the sky to command and conquer but working within the framework of the natural order of things, revealing fullness of grace gradually in the framework established by prophecy.

Adam, after all, was not dropped full formed and powerful out of the sky, nor called into being from nothingness; he was formed out of materials already created and already part of the Earth itself, just as the animals were brought forth from it rather than created *ex nihil*—the only distinction is that God breathed a soul into the body formed of earth. In a parallel way, the Messiah took flesh in the womb, as everybody else does, and he arrived as what is most beautiful and most fragile in human life, a baby, so that we would not be dazzled by his splendor but moved to love him.

So the Nativity has to do with the appearance of the long-awaited Messiah among Men. That's the real significance of Christmas: the Nativity was the first instant that human beings could look upon the person of the Redeemer; it was the first instant that the Savior made himself visible to Man—not the first instant that he came among Men in the flesh, but the instant that he made himself visible in the flesh.

The significance of the Nativity is conveyed not so much in the Gospel account of the birth itself but in the reports of what happened before it, and what happened afterwards. Before the Nativity, of course, God came among his people as the cloud of fire that dwelt in the Holy of Holies (Ex 40:34-38), above the Ark of the Covenant in which the tables of the Law, formed from stone by the finger of God (Ex 31:18), were kept.

Of course, for Christ to fulfill the Old Law and establish the New Covenant, it's crucially important that he was born, but his birth would not have counted for much unless he was recognized as the Messiah. That's why the Joyful Mysteries all emphasize recognition of Jesus as the Messiah; that's why Gabriel explained to Mary, why Elizabeth hailed her as Queen Mother, why Simeon prayed for dismissal, and why the doctors of the Temple were astonished, if not provoked, by his discourse to them.

According to the accounts of the Nativity in the Gospels, Jesus was recognized as the Messiah twice. The first people to know that he had been born the Messiah were the shepherds to whom the angels announced the fact: for unto you is born this day in the city of David a savior, who is Christ, the Lord—"Christ" being the Greek equivalent of the Hebrew מָשִׁיחַ (mashiakh), from which we get the word "Messiah". These shepherds were the lowly of Israel, but they were of Israel; and they were the first of the Chosen People to worship Christ.

His appearance to them, and their recognition of him, is what's called an *epiphany*, from the Greek ἐπί-, outward, and φαίνειν, to show oneself, to be made manifest. That's the term used to mean any event in which something unseen, or unrecognized, is seen and known for what it is; the apparitions of angels like the ones in Daniel and Tobit, or even the apparitions of the angels to the shepherds themselves, are all epiphanies, just as the sight of Jesus in his manger was an epiphany to the shepherds themselves.

That's why the Nativity used to be called the Epiphany to Israel; and it's another reason that the birth of Christ, with his recognition by the shepherds, wasn't celebrated on a separate holiday but subsumed into the commemoration of the Epiphany to the Gentiles—the Adoration of the Magi. Between them, the Adoration of the Shepherds and the Adoration of the Magi show that all nations will recognize the kingship of the Messiah, just as Isaia (2:2-3), Michea (4:2), and the other prophets predicted they would.

> The customary details in representations of the Nativity, from early Christian catacomb art to the Nativity scenes we put up today, carry the same meaning. The ox might seem to be there just to show that the setting is a stable, and the ass to show that Mary and Joseph had journeyed to get there, but in fact they're prophetic, too. Ox and ass are used in Scripture to mean two different or incompatible species of creature, two different nations—Jew and Gentile, in fact. Standing over the manger, they symbolize the dual recognition of the newborn Jesus as the Christ: the ox knows its owner, Isaia wrote, and an ass its master's manger (Is 1:3; *cf.* Ex 20:17, 21:33, 22:3-9; Dt 22:10; 1Kn 12:3; Lk 14:5; etc.). The sheep might seem to have come along with the shepherds, too, but of course they have a much more important symbolic function—see Ez 34:1-31; Jr 50:6; and of course Ps 23.

Preachers since before the Patristic Age have been drawing lessons from the two epiphanies and parallels between them. For example, the shepherds, Israel, were told of the Messiah's advent by supernatural means, but the Gentiles (that is, the Magi) figured it out by purely natural means, through their own science of the universe, such as science was at the time—showing that knowledge comes from above by grace or from right here on Earth by effort. The coming of the Magi also points to the fact that no matter where you start seeking the truth, no matter how you go about it, you will come to Christ as long as you seek that truth in good faith. The coming of the Magi also signifies the principle that St. Justin Martyr called the "Seed-Christ", the idea that, because Christ is God, everything created is in some degree his image, and that therefore he is already present among non-Christians; the work of the Christian is to look for the Seed-Christ in every human being, and to encourage it to sprout and bear fruit in full communion with his Church.

Other authors as early as Pseudo-Matthew have developed the theme of recognition beyond even the symbolic reverence from the ox and ass. Many highly figured accounts of the Nativity tell about wolves, lions, and panthers, as well as dragons that came up out of the Earth into the cave so that Ps 148:7 might be fulfilled. Apocrypha aside, the details of the Gospel account of the Nativity are just as prophetic, but although this is a joyous mystery of the Faith it carries with it the marks of the Passion: Jesus of Nazareth was born to suffer and to die.

That's why the first things that anybody did with his body were also the last: they wrapped it in linen and laid it in a cave—the *Protevangelion of James* and most other early Christian texts agree with St. Jerome and the other Fathers of the Church, as well as with St. Justin Martyr, Origen, Eusebius, and many others, all of whom report that the stable in Bethlehem was fitted up in a cave, which agrees with the site always venerated as the birthplace of Christ, now sheltered by a church built by Constantine's mother St. Helena.

In fact, the linen in which he was clothed at both points in his earthly career ties this Mystery to the ceremonies of the old Temple in Jerusalem itself, marking Christ as high priest and sacrifice at once, which became obvious at the Resurrection. It's also interesting that St. Ambrose (*Sermon 47 on Psalms*), St. Gregory of Nyssa (*First Oration on the Resurrection*), St. John Damascene (*On the Orthodox Faith*), St. Thomas Aquinas, and many others take the fact that Mary herself wrapped Jesus is a clear sign that she did not suffer from labor pains nor from the weakness that normally accompanies childbirth. Those are the consequences of Eve's original sin (Gn 3:16), which Mary didn't share.

T he commemoration of the Nativity on December 25, incidentally, coincides with the astronomical event of the winter solstice, which has appropriate symbolic value: it signifies that Christ was born at the time of the greatest darkness, and he, like the Sun, grew in strength to dispel this obscurity until he reached his full glory at Easter. That feast is set around the vernal equinox, when the material Sun has its greatest power, and the whole Earth reacts to its regenerative power by putting forth abundant new life: a natural resurrection.

This perfectly natural sequence of events is so obvious—indeed, unavoidable by anybody who lives on Earth—that the birth-festival of almost all salvational religions have been celebrated at or near the winter solstice. The birthdays of Mithra, Hercules, Bacchus, and any number of other forgotten saviors were all put there.

In fact, another important reason that Christmas wasn't particularly celebrated by the early Christians is that the winter solstice is symbolically the only appropriate time at which to commemorate the birth of Jesus—but so many pagan festivals were held at the time that Christians couldn't claim that day as their own. Only after paganism faded could Christians begin commemorating the Nativity on the date most appropriate to it. But even beyond its unparalleled symbolic value, December 25 was universally understood until the time of the Reformation as being the actual date of the birth of Jesus, and the view seems to have some documentary evidence behind it.

In the fourth century, St. Cyril of Jerusalem is supposed to have written to Pope Julius I, the pope who set the date of Christmas at December 25. The text of the letter still survives, and it asks the pope specifically to look at the census documents of Judea that had been kept by the imperial governor in Syria and sent to Rome by Titus. At the time, those documents were only about as old as our Declaration of Independence is now, and certainly the pope had access to them, because the civil government of the city had devolved into the hands of the Bishop of Rome by that time—ever since Constantine the Great had moved the imperial capital from Rome to Constantinople in 330.

Even before St. Cyril's supposed letter to the Pope, St. Justin Martyr and Tertullian referred to these census documents as still existing at Rome in their days, and after that St. John Chrysostom mentions them, too; and they all say that these records fix that date for Christ's birth.

So there may well have been written evidence that Jesus of Nazareth was really born on December 25, after all. Certainly Christ—like God the Father—used natural phenomena purposefully to indicate the full meaning of his actions. But whatever those documents said, they're definitely unavailable now, and they've been lost for centuries. So ever since the early Middle Ages, scholars and even rank amateurs have been trying to establish the exact historical date of Christ's birth from all kinds of other data, the way they try to fix the instant of creation or the date of the Flood.

There's not much point to these efforts, because if a date were significant, if it carried some information that we need to know for our salvation, it would be preserved as part of the Deposit of Faith, and probably recorded in the Bible. And in a scholarly sense it's risky to set up a modern chronology on the basis of data from ancient historians—who did not share our ideas about what history should be—and it's nearly impossible to reconcile ancient calendars. But enough information survives in early records to make guessing about it irresistible.

For example, the twenty-four classes of Jewish priests served in weekly rotation in the Temple. Zachary was of the eighth class, which was called Abia (1Pr 24:10). Rabbinic tradition holds that when the Temple was destroyed by the Emperor Titus (in the year we call 70 AD), on the ninth day of the Hebrew month of Ab, the first class, Jojarib, was in service. Working backward from this event, and assuming, from such early consular records as exist, that Christ was born in the year 749 from the founding of the city of Rome, Zachary would have been serving in the Temple from October 2 to October 9, in the year 748 AUC—*ab urbe condita*, from the founding of the city of Rome, as it's called, an event that happened in the year that we'd call 753 BC. Given the schedule of the conception of St. John the Baptizer and the Visitation in Luke, that would put the Annunciation in March, 749 AUC, and the Nativity would follow naturally in December; again, the dates are four years off because our calendar doesn't exactly match the ancient Roman one.

Others, notably St. John Chrysostom, arrive at the same conclusion working from the information that the Day of Atonement fell on September 24 while Zachary was serving in the Temple. That, incidentally, with the prophecy of Aggai (Ag 2:10-19; *cf.* Ps 117:22; Mt 21:42), apparently led some to think that the Messiah was born on September 24, but the idea never got very far. Chrysostom and the others compute that this date for the Day of Atonement would put the birth of St. John the Baptizer on June 24 and the Nativity six months later (Lk 1:36), during the night of December 24-25. St. Augustine agreed, taking St. John's own testimony to mean that he had been born about the time of the summer solstice, after which the days grow shorter, while Christ was born at the winter solstice—about December 24-25, again—after which the days grow longer (Jn 3:30; *Eighty-Three Questions* 58) .

Basically, though, the best testimony about the importance of the date of the Nativity comes from the Gospels themselves: the facts that the exact date isn't mentioned by any of the Evangelists, and that any number of contradictory arguments can be built on the information that Matthew and Luke offer can safely be taken as evidence that the actual date on which Jesus of Nazareth was born makes no real difference to his work of salvation.

THE PRESENTATION

ROPHECY IS OFTEN MISUNDERSTOOD, IN ITS NATURE AS WELL AS IN ITS proclamations. As a mystic gift, prophecy is bestowed by God as he wills (Jn 3:8). It falls on men, women (Nm 12:2), children (Jl 3:1-2), and, if need be, on animals (Nm 22:28-31; 2Pt 2:16). Nobody can achieve it for himself, and nobody can rightly ask for it (Nm 12:3; Jn 3:27, 34; 2Pt 1:21).

Prophecy is alive and well in the Church today, and it works in the same ways as ever, operating on several levels. In its everyday sense, it means the supernatural ability to tell what will happen in the future. It also means being able to reveal hidden things, whether of the past or of the present (1Cr 14); it means having Gifts of the Spirit like Knowledge and Understanding to an extraordinary degree.

One of the highest forms of the gift shows itself when prophets know future natural events that God sees from Eternity and commands according to his will (Ex 3:10; 1Kn 16:1; Mt 1:20-21); prophets can receive knowledge of these future events, favorable or otherwise. God may reach out to warn prophets about disasters that people might bring upon themselves, or to tell them about blessings that people might not get if they carry on as they are. But this doesn't mean that the events are inevitable. People can sometimes avert the disasters that prophets predict. This was true in Biblical times (1Kn 2:30; Jo 3:1-10; Mt 2:13-15), and it has been true of many of the predictions made by great saints like St. Vincent Ferrer, who understood that the prophecy of doom that he received was conditional, and who worked urgently for the rest of his life to effect the conversions needed to avert disaster. And it's true today, if you know whom to listen to, and how to listen.

So prophecy also means having a supernormal—if not supernatural—sensitivity to consequences. In that sense, a prophet is someone who can warn people that if they continue as they are they will meet with disaster, in fair punishment for their sins (Ab 10; Ml 1-3; Mt 14:1-12; Ac 5:1-11), with reward for their justice (Dt 7:12-24; Ac 3:22-26), or with certain trials of faith and charity (Jb; Lk 2:35).

The highest of all forms of prophecy occurs when prophets are moved to convey things that God has ordained according to the supernatural order (Ex 20:1-17; Is 7:14; *cf.* Lk 1:31). The consistency of what the prophets of the Old Testament said in this last way is really remarkable, unparalleled in the world's other religions—all the more so because the prophets of Judaism and Christianity don't come out of any schools centered around a human teacher, and although the gift has been acknowledged in ritual, prophets under the

THE PRESENTATION

Old or the New Covenant don't arise through any human rite or ceremony.

Still, although they said the same things, many of the prophets of the Old Testament didn't fully understand what they were saying or why they were moved to say it. That's why the Evangelists had to connect the points of prophecy with the points of Christ's words and acts (Mt 1:1-17, 22-23; Mr 1:2; Lk 3:4; Jn 1:23, 13:18), why the Apostles had to search back through Scripture to understand (Mt 22:29; Mr 12:24; Lk 24:13-32; Jn 12:37-38; Ac 8:26-35), and why St. Paul had to write to the Hebrews (Ac 17:2, 11; Hb 1:1-2). It's why Christ himself had to make the connections explicit, even after he died and rose again from the dead (Mt 13:14; Mr 12:10; Lk 4:21, 7:27; Jn 3:10, 5:39).

The Presentation of Jesus in the Temple, recounted in the second chapter of Luke (Lk 2:22-40), is one of those episodes in which the mysteries of prophecy are laid out most clearly before us. But you can't get a clear view of it unless you look at it in its context of law and liturgy, and until you focus on precisely what the event was about. The Presentation is not the Circumcision, which is mentioned briefly in a single verse (21) just before the much longer account of the Presentation. They're two utterly different events, with different meanings, and far separated in time and space.

The confusion may have been fossilized in some depictions of the two events, both of which are so often shown taking place in a splendid setting that looks like it must be the Temple itself. But in pictures of the Circumcision that magnificent house is supposed to be the house of the Virgin, in a kind of glorified state; the Presentation took place in the Temple. The events follow two different rituals fulfilling two distinct sets of laws, and they have two separate significations.

The Law of Moses defined a mother as untouchable or "unclean" for seven days after the birth of a son, just as she was during her menstrual period (Lv 12:1-2). That suggests that the birth process was not considered entirely completed, that there was something not quite settled about the matter, until the baby was circumcised and named on the eighth day (Lv 12:3). That's why Zachary wasn't freed from his punishment of muteness until this moment in the rituals following the birth of St. John the Baptizer (Lk 1:20, 59-64).

Circumcision was required by the Covenant with Abraham (Gn 17, 21, 34) and renewed by Moses (Ex 12:38-49) and Josue (Js 5:2-9); the ritual is what affirmed the personhood of the boy. In the case of Jesus of Nazareth, it also affirmed his nature, against all future doubts of monophysites of any sect: "the circumcision proves beyond the shadow of a doubt the fact of his humanity," St. Bernard explained (*Sermon 1 on the Circumcision*); it affirms that he is truly Man as well as truly God. Humans have genitalia because they have bodies, and those bodies are subject to death, so humans are equipped to reproduce. Angels and spirits don't have genitalia because they don't need them—they're not subject to death, so they don't need to reproduce, and they don't have any bodies to reproduce, anyway.

> The need to assert Christ's humanity is the reason that so many images of the Child seem to focus on that anatomical feature with an insistence that can seem rather immoderate to the modern eye. This signification of Christ's true humanity also underlies all of the representations of the Child nursing at Mary's breast: humans eat, apparitions don't (*cf.* Jg 13:16; Tb 12:19). "Mary did truly conceive a body that had God inhabiting it," as St. Ignatius of Antioch affirmed, "and God the Word was truly born of the Virgin ... and was in reality nourished with milk... He was condemned: he was crucified in reality, not in appearance, not in imagination, not in deceit. He really died". So nude representations of the dead Christ on the Cross or before the entombment—often composed in exactly the same emphatic ways as the images of the Infant—are intended to assert that, being truly Man, he truly died, and the similar images of him nude at the Resurrection assert that he truly rose in his human body.
>
> All of this, said Leo Steinberg, who wrote a whole book on the subject, "has been tactfully overlooked for half a millennium" (*The Sexuality of Christ in Renaissance Art and Modern Oblivion*, 1983). Still, this sacred nudity makes a fundamental point about the Faith, and the eyes of beholders in most Christian cultures on Earth have found it perfectly innocent (*cf.* Gn 2:25), especially in images of the Child. Those cultures that can't seem to distinguish nudity from pornography paint things over or employ plaster loincloths, but as St. Bonaventure wrote to a friend on the subject, "I would wish that you and I may ... detest no more than we ought, nor detest things that ought not to be detested."

Circumcision also affirmed the boy's parentage, and it marked his acceptance as a member of the nation of Israel—"he was circumcised because he was a true son of Abraham," St. Bernard continued. But despite its importance to Jewish society, this wasn't really a public ceremony. It had to take place at his mother's home because she had to remain at home for thirty-two more days after the eighth, making a total of forty days of isolation (Lv 12:4). So the Circumcision had to take place at the woman's home; she could not go out to the Temple or anyplace else.

After that fortieth day, though, the mother had to go out to the Temple, or to the Meeting Tent before the settlement in Jerusalem, and she had to

THE PRESENTATION

make certain token sacrifices (Lv 12:6-8). These offerings—a lamb for a sacrifice and a dove in atonement for sin, or two doves for the same purposes if she couldn't afford the lamb—were probably substitutes for the first-born son himself, just as the token bloodletting of circumcision was in part an abbreviated human sacrifice.

The period between the command to circumcise and the interrupted sacrifice of Isaac marks the transition between the two in Israel (Gn 17:1-14, 21:1-4, 22:1-13; although human sacrifice shows up as late as 2Kn 21:6-14). But the laws in Numbers (18:15) still speak specifically of these offerings as "redeeming" the first-born son, buying him back from God, as it were. Numbers also requires that any first-born son who wasn't of the Tribe of Levi—the priestly family—be freed from the obligation of direct service to God by the payment of five shekels (18:16).

The main purpose of the ceremony in the Temple, though, was the ritual purification of the mother, which is why this event is commemorated liturgically as the Feast of the Purification.

In a way, that's an unfortunate term, because it implies that the mother was somehow dirty. It's more accurate to think in terms of "touchable" and "untouchable" rather than "clean" and "unclean", because there are good and holy reasons not to touch something or someone, too, and under the Old Law these counted for more than the negative reasons like uncleanness or the possibility of infection.

In general, the concept of pure (טהור, tahor) and impure (טמא, ta-me) isn't fundamentally a moral distinction or a matter of practical hygiene: the "pure" is acceptable, and the "impure" is taboo. So the term that we unfortunately translate as "unclean" doesn't just refer to things or persons somehow compromised in cleanliness but also to those things or persons positively dangerous in a mysterious sort of way.

A person, an animal, a thing, or an act could be unclean by nature, as the Gentiles were (Jn 18:28), and camels, vultures (Lv 11:4, 13), or, most of all, sins like murder (Ez 36:17-26). They can also be unclean by condition, as lepers or corpses were unclean (Lv 13:6, 8; 22:4; Nm 19:11-22), and as permissible animals that had not been slaughtered ritually (Lv 7:26-27), things that had touched unclean persons (Lv 22:4-7), or people who have repudiated the Law by sin or otherwise compromised Israel's special status as a holy nation, a people set apart from the other nations of the world by their constant striving for holiness (Ex 19:5-6; Lv 11:44, 19:31; Jr 2:7, 23; Os 6:10).

But, like the unclean, the holy is untouchable (2Kg 6:6-7). In fact, the two sets of regulations in the Old Testament—those isolating the unclean and those setting the holy apart—are surprisingly similar, and the same root-word in Hebrew, חרם, is used to indicate both the sacred and the

249

abominable. People who touched sacred objects became "unclean" (Nm 19:1-10), just as those who touched unclean ones did.

Now, the important thing to remember is that the Hebrews' understanding of their own holiness as the Chosen of God meant that, to them, sexual intercourse wasn't dirty: it was holy, as it is in the Christian view of things. God ordered it and created Man with the ability to reproduce this way. In fact, he gave Man responsibility for generating human beings according to the natural order (Gn 1:27-28), a process in which God co-operates by endowing each human with a soul at the moment of conception, as he endowed Adam (Gn 2:7); human beings have never been created out of nothingness, any more than any other living thing of the Earth (Gn 1:11, 24, 2:7). So the Israelites recognized sexual intercourse as an act of immense consequence, an act by which Man fulfilled the commandment of the Creator, and called upon him to co-operate; and they regarded childlessness as a reproach, almost an uncleanness in itself (Gn 30:23; Lk 1:25).

That's why the act of procreation was regarded as holy; and holy acts had to be surrounded by rituals as a safeguard against abuse or defilement. So people who had had sexual intercourse incurred the same kind of taboo and had to be ritually readmitted to normal life among the community at large (Lv 15:16-24, 32-33). Therefore, a woman had to be "purified" after she had given birth—the fact of the child's birth, as far as anybody would reasonably expect before the Annunciation, proved that sexual intercourse had taken place.

T he most striking thing about the Presentation of Jesus in the Temple at Mary's purification is her initiative in it; this is another of the positive acts by which she participated in Jesus's work of salvation by her own decision. She hadn't borne Jesus as a result of sexual intercourse (Lk 1:34-37), so she didn't have to go through the ritual at all; she had no sin, so she didn't have to offer the dove in atonement, and she certainly didn't have to offer the lamb as a holocaust. She had to offer her son. But she was a faithful child of the Old Law—the New not having been established yet—and Christ himself had to be, or his sacrifice would have no power to fulfill that Law (Mt 5:17). So she went to the Temple to fulfill the Law, but beyond that she took Jesus with her, although there wasn't any specific regulation that required the parents to actually present the child at the Temple.

According to St. Luke, Mary and Joseph took Jesus to Jerusalem at some time after the fortieth day following his birth. At the Temple they encountered a man named Simeon, who has become over the centuries another reason that the Presentation is mistaken for the Circumcision. Because he held the Baby it's sometimes thought that he was taking the child to perform the operation, but of course the Child had been circumcised long before this.

In Christian art, Simeon is often shown in priestly robes, but his vestments only represent that he was a faithful adherent to the Old Covenant—the Presentation, like the Visitation and the Annunciation to the Shepherds, is another epiphany to Israel. And in any case Simeon was not a priest; he's referred to only as a just and devout man to whom the Holy Spirit had promised the physical sight of the Messiah, and who was prompted by the Spirit to go to the Temple on that particular day. Any other onlookers might have seen simply the infant son of a carpenter from Nazareth, but Simeon knew who this child was and what he had come among us to do. So this simple and holy man took the Baby in his arms and sang one of the great psalmodic canticles of the Bible, the *Nunc Dimittis* (Lk 2:29-32):

Now dismiss thy servant,	Nunc dimittis servum tuum,
O Lord,	Domine,
according to thy word,	secundum verbum tuum,
in peace;	in pace,
because mine eyes have seen	quia viderunt oculi mei
thy salvation,	salutare tuum,
which thou hast prepared	quod parasti
before the face of all peoples,	ante faciem omnium populorum,
a light of revelation to the Gentiles,	lumen ad revelationem gentium,
and a glory for thy people Israel.	et gloriam plebis tuæ Israel.

This is the last of the three great canticles of the New Testament, coming as it does after the *Benedictus* of Zachary (Lk 1:67-79) and the *Magnificat* of Mary. It's the shortest of the three, too, but it's rich in references to the pivotal events that fulfilled the Old Covenant and offered the New. Simeon's reason for asking God to let him die now in peace answers Isaia's prediction: in the birth of the Messiah "the Lord has bared his holy arm in the sight of all the nations; all the ends of the Earth shall behold the salvation of our God. Depart, depart, come forth from there, touch nothing unclean!" (Is 52:10-11).

St. John the Baptizer recalled this same universal promise as he preached repentance so that the rest of Israel might embrace the Lord as Simeon did (Lk 3:6); but Simeon also remembers passages like Is 42:6-10, in which God reminds Israel that they are a holy nation of the Covenant, formed to stand as a light to all nations, and Psalm 97. Both of these promises of universal redemption call Israel forward to sing a new song to the Lord for his wondrous deeds; the whole Earth, the sea and what fills it shall resound to his praise. So this prophecy and this psalm, incorporated by reference into Simeon's canticle, form a kind of bridge between his song and Mary's (Lk 1:46-55).

In the liturgy of the Hours, the *Nunc Dimittis* is followed by Christ's own quotation of Psalm 30 as he hung dying on the Cross: into thy hands I commend my spirit. This echoes another sublime harmony between the Testaments, but it's easily missed. St. Luke (23:46) alone among the Evangelists mentions that Christ quoted this Psalm, one that not only foretells his own sufferings but suggests what it must have been like for Simeon himself to keep faith, and to wait for the promise of the Spirit to be fulfilled. It was probably in recognition of his long and undoubtedly difficult wait, as much as for his sanctity and his instant song of joy at receiving Jesus, that the memory of the early Church placed Simeon among those first raised up at Christ's own Resurrection.

Mary and Joseph must have been surprised by having a stranger approach them and take the Baby in his arms. They undoubtedly understood what he meant when he sang the *Nunc Dimittis*, but Mary was troubled when Simeon went on to prophecy about Mary herself. "This child is destined for the fall of many in Israel, and the rise of many; he shall be a sign that will be contradicted. And a sword shall pierce your own soul, that the thoughts of many may be revealed."

This is the first specific mention in Scripture of Mary's heart, but not the last. St. Luke mentions twice that Mary kept all of the sayings and doings of Jesus in her heart (2:19, 51), and certainly after that heart was pierced by the sword of the Passion some of that knowledge, which she alone could have, came to form the basis of the Gospels themselves.

This immaculate heart, the heart that had never known sin, the heart that was privy to more, and more intimate, knowledge of the Messiah than anybody else on Earth possibly could be, soon became the focus of devotion to the Blessed Mother. In modern devotional art, the Immaculate Heart of Mary is represented by the emblem of a heart pierced by the sword of Simeon, or sometimes with seven swords, one for each of her sorrows; and the whole heart is surrounded by a wreath of roses. But the imagery of the devotion started very early. It was already expressed with some depth and maturity in the Fathers' commentaries on the Canticle of Canticles, which frequently refers to the heart of the bridegroom's beloved spouse. Like all Marian devotions, and like all specialized devotions to Jesus Christ, this one developed slowly, among the laity, and its focus sharpened century after century.

St. Bernard wrote a sermon, *On the Twelve Stars*, that encouraged devotion to the Heart of Mary, and parts of it have been incorporated into the liturgies of the Office of the Compassion and the Office of the Seven Sorrows. At about the same time meditative tracts based on the Hail Mary and on the great hymns like the *Salve Regina* show that the devotion was already strong. Especially from the thirteenth century to the fifteenth, visionaries like St. Mechtilde von Hackenborn-Wippra, St. Gertrude the Great, and St. Bridget of Sweden conveyed some theological clarification of the devotion in accounts of their own mystic experiences, and St. Bernadine of Siena's meditations on the Immaculate Heart have also been incorporated in the liturgy of the Hours.

By the sixteenth century devotion to the Immaculate Heart of Mary was universal in the Church, having strengthened immeasurably in response to the rising heresies of northern Europe, and particularly through the laity's increased fervency in devotion to the Rosary—no other devotional practice nurtures such sympathy with Mary's heart of hearts, and none brings a person into greater empathy with her joys, her sorrows, and her exultation than the Rosary. In the seventeenth century St. Jean Eudes completed the articulation of the devotion's sound theological basis, and he condensed and regularized all of the practices that had expressed it over the ages.

Through him, devotion to the Immaculate Heart of Mary came to center on two acts, both of which recognize the unique role that Mary plays in bringing souls to God: acts of consecration and of reparation. In consecration, people devoted to the Immaculate Heart pledge themselves totally and perpetually to God through Mary; they entrust to her care all that they have, and all that they are (Jn 19:26-27).

The idea of reparation to Mary for the sword that pierced her Heart in Christ's Passion and the sins of Mankind that pierce it again and again found new stimulus on May 13, 1917, when the apparition of Fátima asked the three children to sacrifice themselves for sinners—giving up treats, obeying their parents, and performing similar ascetic acts appropriate to their ages—and to "repeat often, especially whenever you make a sacrifice for them, 'O Jesus, it is for love of you, for the conversion of sinners and in reparation for the sins committed against the Immaculate Heart of Mary.'" On June 13 she said specifically that her Immaculate Heart would be a refuge for the little visionaries and a way that would lead them to God, and on July 13 of that year she asked specifically that Russia be consecrated to her Immaculate Heart.

The devotions stimulated by the apparitions at Fátima are tightly connected to the Rosary; the apparitions themselves happened while the children were praying the Rosary, and the Lady told them to "tell your beads every day, to obtain peace for the world and the end of the war." She even identified herself as the Lady of the Rosary. And, like the Rosary, devotion to the Immaculate Heart encompasses the entire holiness and love of the Mother of God, so it's really a kind of synthesis of all Marian doctrine and devotion.

The actual human heart of Mary, now glorified as an integral part of her body in Heaven, is the focus of the devotion, but, as with the Sacred Heart of Jesus, that devotion is metaphoric and symbolic—or, better said, it's a matter of metonymy, which means that the part stands for the whole. The phrase "The Immaculate Heart of Mary" is a title for Mary herself, which is why images of Mary with her Heart visible on her breast are sometimes referred to as pictures of the Immaculate Heart, just as she might otherwise be called the Blessed Mother, the Blessed Virgin, or, depending on the form of the particular image, the Queen of Heaven or the Immaculate Conception.

All of these titles are simply ways to focus on one or another aspect of Mary or to her relationship to Jesus and to humanity. The same guidelines apply, in this respect, to the Immaculate Heart of Mary and the Sacred Heart of Jesus; as Pius XII Pacelli wrote in his encyclical letter in 1956 on the centenary of the universal institution of the Feast of the Sacred Heart of Jesus, "When we adore the Most Sacred Heart of Jesus Christ, we adore in it and through it both the uncreated love of the Divine Word and his human love and all his other affections and virtues... The veneration ... paid to ... the picture of the pierced Heart of Christ ... is paid to the very person of the Incarnate Word as its final object."

So, when people meditate on the Immaculate Heart of Mary—they don't adore it—they are thinking of the innermost being of Mary, the Mother of Jesus; and that meditation, too, has the very person of the Incarnate Word as its final object.

There was also a prophetess named Anna in the Temple that day (Lk 2:36-38). Her name, of course, recalls the name of Mary's own mother, but they were not the same person. Mary was of the House of David (Lk 1:32), which is of the Tribe of Juda (2Kn 2:4), the kingly tribe of Israel, and this Anna was of the Tribe of Asher. That tribe didn't play a very important part in the history of Israel, so Anna wasn't there to signify that the mighty of the Chosen People recognized Jesus as the Messiah. Her lineage gave her a much more important prophetic role to fulfill.

Asher himself had been the son of Zelpha, the handmaiden of Jacob's wife Lia (Gn 30:13); and his mother gave him that name because "henceforth all women will call me happy"—almost exactly what the Hand-maiden of the Lord herself said when her maternity of Jesus was first acknowledged by Elizabeth (Gn 30:13; Lk 1:48). Anna's own name, of course, is derived from חנה (khanah), meaning "to be gracious", and it connects her to the other Anna, the wife of Elcana the Zuphite, who lived some eleven centuries before the Presentation. This Anna of old appears in the First Book of Kings; like Mary's mother, she suffered the reproach of childlessness (1Kn 1:6-7); and like the grandmother of Jesus she made a vow promising God that, if she were blessed with a child, she would dedicate him to divine service as a Nazarite.

A Nazarite isn't called that because he has anything to do with Nazareth; the two names aren't even related. The city is called Nazareth (נצרת) from the root-word נצר (n-ts-r), which means a sprout or a shoot, or a flower; a Nazarite is called that from the word *nazir* (נזיר, n-z-r), which means "dedicated", in this case, to God. The Book of Numbers outlines the regulations for the Nazarites (Nm 6:1-21); they drank no wine nor any strong drink, they had to let their hair grow uncut, and they had a special aversion to death: they couldn't approach any corpse or even be in the presence of the dead. A Nazarite who found himself made unclean by coming into the presence of a corpse had to shave his head and, on the eighth day, present himself at the sanctuary—the Temple or the Meeting Tent—and offer two doves, one as a sin-offering and the other as a holocaust, as well as a lamb.

In their asceticism, the Nazarites were the forerunners of Christian monks and nuns, and in fact there isn't really a definite break between the Nazarites of the Old Covenant and the regular clergy of the New. St. James the Lesser, the first Bishop of Jerusalem, was a Nazarite, and he kept strictly to those practices his whole life (Eusebius, *History of the Church* 2:23; cf. Ac 21:23-26). The Carmelites—the "Brothers of the Order of the Most Blessed Mother of God and Ever-Virgin Mary of Mount Carmel"—trace their history back to Elias and his companions on Mount Carmel; whether he formally took Nazarite vows or not, he certainly lived their life (4Kn 1:8; 3Kn 17:3-7, 19:5-9).

Like friars, monks, and nuns, some Nazarites were adults, of either sex, who took the vow for a specific period of time (1Mc 3:49-50), but some took solemn vows for life; but unlike normal Christian practice some Hebrew Nazarites such as Samson were dedicated by their parents to that way of life from conception (Jg 13:5-7). Anna's own son was dedicated in this same way, so, like St. John the Baptizer (Lk 1:13-15), the son of Anna of Elcana the Zuphite was a forerunner of Christ's. In fact, he was Samuel, the prophet (1Kn 1:20).

This Anna, wife of Elcana, called her son's name Samuel because she had asked him of the Lord. With her prayer fulfilled, she set out to fulfill her vow; and like Mary long after her she carried her baby to the Temple and offered him to God there (1Kn 1:21-25). But the most interesting parallel between the presentation of Samuel and the Presentation of Jesus is the canticle that Anna sang (1Kn 2:1-10). Now, Anna's canticle comes as something of a puzzle at first, really. It doesn't have much relation to her situation, apart from a general reference to childbearing by the barren in the second half of a single verse (5). The second half of the tenth verse contains an equally indistinct remark about the Messiah, but it's obviously a simple statement of faith in the promise and not a prophecy. As a whole, the Canticle of Anna is a magnificent psalm, but it has so little to do with what Anna was doing that some commentators have thought it to be a much later imposition, not part of the original at all.

In fact, in the Hebrew text of the First Book of Kings Anna's canticle breaks into the middle of a sentence, but it was moved a little in the Greek Septuagint to the position that it occupies today in the Latin Vulgate. Even so, it's surprising to find this canticle at this point in Scripture—until you notice that it sounds almost like a rough draft of the *Magnificat*. And the resemblance might not be accidental. The prophetess Anna who saw Jesus in the Temple more than a thousand years later must have known the earlier Anna's canticle, and she may have taught it to others. In fact, pious tradition says that Anna was a teacher of the young virgins who lived apart in the Temple, and that one of her pupils was Mary, daughter of Joachim.

Mary's obligation under the Law brought her to the Temple that day, and her initiative brought Jesus there. But the primary significance of the occasion doesn't center on her but on the Babe, and on what happened when he entered his Father's house for the first time. That's why the earliest liturgical commemorations of the event, in the East before the fourth century, weren't called the Purification but the "meeting" (ὑπαπάντη) of Jesus and Simeon. Because it wasn't considered a Marian feast in the West, either, it wasn't called the Feast of the Purification there until really the late sixteenth century—in fact, it's still considered a feast of the Lord, as the 1960 edition of the *Code of Rubrics* affirms. That's why it's often called the Presentation—he was presented. But before that, in the West, it was called Candlemas, because of a particular observance that grew up around the commemoration there.

In the early years, the Feast of the Meeting or of the Presentation was kept forty days after Epiphany, because the Nativity didn't have a separate holiday then; the birth of Jesus was celebrated together with the Adoration of the Shepherds and of the Magi, and the commemoration of the Purification naturally followed forty days after. When Christmas came into its own in the fourth century, the feast was moved to forty days after that, on the second day of February. As it happened, this was the same date as the pre-Christian Roman observance of the *amburbale* (from the Latin *ambire urbem*, to walk around the city), a rite of expiation and purification that involved processions around the city with lights, sacrifices of animal victims, and the singing of holy songs.

So by the time Justinian ordered the Feast of the Meeting celebrated throughout the Empire, the Latin Rite had long since added a penitential observance to the commemoration of the Purification. The Pope and the Faithful walked in procession around the city, singing psalms that beg forgiveness of sin; and they carried candles as they went.

Candles were a real luxury item in antiquity, and really right up to the time that artificial waxes came to be extracted in quantity from petroleum. In fact, wax candles used to be far out of the reach of even the well-to-do; even as late as the nineteenth century the use of candles was a mark of a princely house, and indeed of a particular festivity at a princely house. Sometimes people who kept meat animals formed fatty candles out of tallow, but most people used oil lamps, which could be filled with olive oil or other vegetable oil, or with rendered fat from animals. In many parts of the ancient world, there was simply not enough wax to make candles even for religious or festive use, which is why lamps are specified among the furnishings of the Meeting Tent and the Temple (Ex 25:31-40; 3Kn 7:49).

In early Christian times, though, the Romans used wax candles as a token of honor for religious rites, particularly funerals and commemorations of the dead, and in veneration of the Emperor or the gods. Lights at these ceremonies stand as a reminder of the presence of the divine, which is why candles are used at Mass and why people sometimes light them to set apart a special time for prayer or private religious observances—as pious Jews do at the Sabbath. Besides that, wax candles also carry an element of sacrifice about them because beeswax is so expensive, which is why people sometimes offer a votive candle as an adjunct to prayer.

Evidently it became customary for pastors to bless the supply of candles that their churches would need for the year on the second of February, which is why the Feast of the Purification came to be called Candlemas. Since about the twelfth century, there's been a special rubric for blessing the candles, and it's still done in many localities, or at least blessed candles are distributed to the laity then. After the Feast of the Purification was moved to accord better with Christmas, though, the penitential processions stayed on the old date.

After the two observances parted again, the Christian version of the *amburbale* celebrated at Rome and at Jerusalem kept two features of their old association with the Purification: both processions ended at a church dedicated to Mary, and both included the singing of the *Nunc Dimittis*. After all, Simeon did compare Jesus to a light of revelation to all people.

THE FINDING IN THE TEMPLE

BESIDES BEING THE MESSIAH FORETOLD BY THE PROPHETS, CHRIST IS HIM-
self a prophet, having come to tell people what would happen to
them if they agreed to God's Covenant and lived it, and what
would happen to them if they didn't. He, of course, knew perfectly well
what was going to happen to him, and he could tell people what was going
to happen to them, too (Jn 16:2-4). And he combined all of his prophetic
activities into a single function: that of teacher (Jn 1:38, 3:2). The Finding
of Jesus in the Temple (Lk 2:46) marks his first appearance as a teacher, but
its real significance lies in the fact that it didn't mark the beginning of his
career as the Messiah, the one sent to accomplish his Father's business.

He was beginning his thirteenth year—*cum factus esset Jesus annorum
duodecim*, the Vulgate says, "when he had completed twelve years". He
was a man, under Hebrew law. There wasn't any ceremony to mark the
occasion, in the time of Christ; the term *bar-mitzvah* (בר מצוה), "son of the
Law" or "subject to the Law) was used then only to denote a man of religious and legal responsibility, not the occasion of assuming those obligations as an adult. The ceremony, and the use of that term to denote it,
developed in the fifteenth century, a millennium and a half after Christ
himself had fulfilled the Old Covenant of the Temple, and in fact after the
Temple itself had been destroyed (Mt 24:1-2).

Still, the age was significant under the Old Covenant. Jewish Tradition
remembered that Abraham rejected the idols of his father at that age, and that
Jacob and Esau went their separate ways at the beginning of their thirteenth
years, Jacob to study the Law and Esau to take up the worship of idols. So it
was a pivotal time in a man's life, one at which he turned from false worship
to true, or at least the age at which he made that decision. Traditionally, it
was also the pivotal age for prophets: Moses at this age left his Egyptian family and began to rule his own princely household; Daniel began his career as
a prophet, and Solomon assumed the throne and began to prophecy, too.

All of these traditions put an immense weight of symbolism on Jesus's
age at the moment of this event, but even more meaningful is the fact that this
was the age at which a man under the Old Law took responsibility for his
own acts. A son of younger years partook of the merit of his father's acts, but
then again he also shared the blame for his father's sins or crimes; and the
father, as guardian of the boy, was punished for the transgressions of a son

under twelve years old. So by waiting until that moment, Jesus freed Mary and Joseph from suffering the penalties of his disputations with the doctors of the Temple: but consider what the point of those disputations was.

He was not exactly picking a fight with the doctors of the Old Covenant, but he was presenting himself to them as a force to be reckoned with. He was challenging their knowledge of Scripture, and their interpretation of it; and above all he was challenging their understanding. Now, the one thing that a student can do that's sure to provoke anger in some teachers is to be right when those teachers are wrong, or to understand the material better than those teachers—the one thing that anybody can do to provoke anger in just about anybody is to be right. The surest road to martyrdom is not to attack a person's beliefs but simply to offer, by words or just by way of life, teachings that are simple, clear, and obviously right.

People whose beliefs are incomplete or unformed, or perhaps hypocritical, feel themselves to suffer by comparison, and, unable to come up with any reason for being wrong, they usually strike out to eliminate the person who's right. "The truth breeds hatred," the Roman dramatist Terence observed (*Andria*), and he was right. Naturally, teachers and other professionals who have built prestigious careers by expounding faulty theories are particularly sensitive to the pinpricks of the truth, which is why Socrates was poisoned long before Christ was sent to the cross for being right, and why St. Joan of Arc was burned at the stake after him. None of the three committed any crime whatsoever, except the unpardonable offense of being obviously right and thereby—incidentally—making certain other people look foolish.

Jesus of Nazareth knew that his mission on Earth was to fulfill the Old Covenant and establish the New; and he knew that to do this he had to be put to death by the chief priests of the Old Law. So, as soon as that Law established him as a man, as a person responsible for his own independent acts—and as soon as that same Law sheltered Mary and Joseph from the consequences of those acts—he went forward on his own initiative to dispute with the doctors of the Temple. It would be extremely interesting to know exactly what he said; his discourse may have been like the one on the road to Emmaus (Lk 24:25-27). Whatever he said, he ran a serious risk when he said it.

The Jews at that time expected the messianic prophecies of the Old Testament to be fulfilled before their eyes. They had the prophetic texts themselves, and living Tradition, as well as certain supernatural promises that the time was at hand, like the promise given to Simeon (Lk 2:25-27). But they weren't sure when the Messiah would come, exactly, and they weren't sure exactly how. Already any number of teachers had arisen, "claiming to be somebody" (Ac 5:34-37), and they always caused trouble. The Book of Acts mentions two such revolutionaries by name. Judas the Galilean and Theodas. This Judas of Galilee was the one who joined forces with the Pharisee Zadduk to form the Sadducee faction, the Zealots, whose revolutionary program ultimately provoked the destruction of the Temple in 70.

Judas of Galilee may or may not have claimed to be the Messiah, but at least some of his followers claimed that he was; Theodas, who came along just before Christ, certainly did claim that title. The account of the times in Josephus (*Antiquities of the Jews* 17:6:4; 20:5:1) suggests that this Theodas was the eloquent and popular rabbi Matthias who had incited his followers to pull down the Roman eagle on the Temple—the two names mean exactly the same thing (one is Greek and the other is Hebrew, but they both mean "God's gift"). In any case, this Theodas, Josephus says, announced himself a prophet and said he'd part the Jordan River to lead his followers to the other side, but they were cut down by cavalry, and he himself was beheaded, before he could try it.

Of course, Josephus notoriously muddles his dates, so the Theodas of Acts and the Theodas of the *Antiquities of the Jews* may have been two separate "messiahs" thirty years apart, and the Matthias that Josephus mentions may have been yet a third; Josephus himself remarks that there were "ten thousand" such disturbances at the time (17:10:4). The priests of the Temple must, indeed, have been troubled to hear such things from yet another man claiming to be the Messiah, and they must have been astonished to hear it from a man so young. And whatever the details of his discourse those three days, its implication was clear: Jesus of Nazareth had to be either acknowledged as the Messiah or put to death.

> St. Luke underlines that meaning of the event by specifying that Jesus was "lost" for three days before being discovered in triumph over the propounders of the Old Law; that emphasizes the parallel between this trip to Jerusalem and his last one. Clearly, he was ready to "be about his Father's business", and get his mission over and done with. Christian visual art, since about the fourth century, illustrated the parallel, too, by showing the young Jesus standing before a column, like the one that appears later in scenes of the Flagellation. Often, the doctors are shown referring to scrolls while Jesus holds a volume—the ancient form of the book (particularly the Torah scrolls) being contrasted with the codex form preferred in modern times as Christ came forward to replace the Old Law with the New.

But Mary put a stop to it. Or, at least, she delayed it. At her word, Jesus returned with them to Nazareth and obeyed them. Mary's reason for imposing the delay isn't clear from the Gospel account. It may have been that she was unwilling to be parted from Jesus at that early age; it may have been that she could not have borne seeing him crucified at the age of twelve. Certainly, she knew why he had come and what he had to do—St. Luke's statement (Lk 2:50) that "they" understood not the word that he spoke is usually interpreted by the Fathers of the Church to mean that the doctors of the Temple didn't know what he meant, not that Mary and Joseph didn't; St. Luke is occasionally ambiguous in his use of a pronoun, here and in other passages like 23:28-31.

Even so, the Gospels are abundantly clear on the central points: that Mary did delay Christ's confrontation with the authorities, and, more significant than even this, that he obeyed her.

E VA ❀ AV E

THE SORROWFUL MYSTERIES

S ORROWFUL MYSTERIES ARE THOSE THAT HAVE to do with the passion of Christ, which consists of those sad episodes of his suffering (Latin *passionem*), beginning just after the Last Supper and ending in his death. They are the Agony in the Garden, the Flagellation, the Crowning with Thorns, the Carrying of the Cross, and the Crucifixion. All are commemorated liturgically during Holy Week, the week before Easter.

אמת

THE AGONY IN THE GARDEN

NOBODY EVER SAID THAT CHRISTIANITY IS EASY, LEAST OF ALL CHRIST himself (Mt 10:16-39). The war between what we want to do and what God wants us to do, between the desires of the flesh and the desires of the spirit, between the pleasures of the wrong and the difficulties of the right, is a perpetual contest that ends only with bodily death. The joy of reunion with God comes only after the pain of relentless struggle, a struggle so important that Christ put himself through the agony of it, sweating blood just to show us how difficult it's going to be, for each of us.

Because Christ asked nothing of us that he wouldn't do himself, his own agony, the Agony in the Garden, is recounted by St. Matthew (26:36-46), St. Mark (14:32-42), and by St. Luke (22:40-46), and it's indicated in several passages by St. John; St. Augustine wrote the classic harmonization of the Gospel accounts (*The Harmony of the Gospels* 4), which in fact fit together neatly into a consistent description of what happened, a description that also shows why those things happened as they did.

After the Last Supper, Jesus led his Apostles out of the city, across the Valley of Kidron to the Mount of Olives. They went into a garden on the slopes of the Mount, a place called Gethsemani, from שמן זית (Zayit Shemen), the Hebrew for olive oil. Christ told some of them to wait, and he went into the garden itself with St. Peter, St. James, and St. John, the three who had witnessed the Transfiguration (Mt 17:1; Mr 9:1; Lk 9:28; Jn 1:14; 2Pt 1:16-18). Apparently, these three were selected to witness the most intense manifestation of Christ's humanity, just as they had witnessed the most glorious manifestation of his divinity; and although they undoubtedly didn't make the connection that evening, their earlier experience outlines much of the significance of the Agony that followed. So to understand the Agony it's helpful to look at its reflection in the Transfiguration.

Like the Agony, the Transfiguration took place on a mountaintop; the site is not precisely identified in Scripture or in Tradition, but Origen, St. Cyril of Jerusalem, St. Jerome, and other authorities say that the Transfiguration took place on Mount Tabor, which is where Saul, just anointed King, met three men carrying bread and wine for sacrifice (1Kn 10:1-3). When Christ showed himself in his glory, Moses and Elias appeared with him and spoke with him (Mt 17:3; Mr 9:3) about his future death (Lk 9:30-31). The two are often said to represent the Law and the Prophets (*cf.* Mt 7:12; Lk 16:16), but they have a more complicated significance than this, too. Moses, obviously, is the foremost prefiguration of the Messiah, and his climb up Sinai to receive the Law, his own transfiguration there, and his descent to deliver the Law to the people below serve as a kind of outline of the career of the Messiah to come. It's also interesting to reflect on the fact that, although Moses died and was buried, his gravesite was unknown (Dt 34:6). This suggests, at least, that he was taken up to Heaven as Elias was (4Kn 2:11-14).

Elias himself links the Transfiguration and the Agony in the Garden to prophecy because he, too, despaired under a tree—in his case, a juniper—and he too was strengthened by an angel, after which he went to rest a while in a cave, to emerge and appoint a king over Israel, and a prophet (3Kn 19:4-9; *cf.* Ac 5:30-31, 10:39, 13:29-30; 1Pt 2:24). So the Transfiguration asserts Christ's divinity and stands as a foretelling of his Resurrection and Ascension; in this same way, the Agony prefigures his Passion.

Having come into the Garden, Jesus prostrated himself on the ground and begged his Father to relieve him of his Passion (Mt 26:39; *cf.* Mt 20:22); his stress was so great already, St. Luke says, that his sweat became like drops of blood, soaking his clothes and dripping on the ground. An angel came to strengthen him, St. Luke says, and he prayed the more earnestly, "falling into an agony"—καὶ γενόμενος ἐν ἀγωνίᾳ (Lk 22:43-44).

St. Luke's use of the word "agony", ἀγωνία, is highly significant. This is the one and only time that it occurs in the Bible, and it means a lot more than it may seem to signify; today, it's probably the most explosive word in the whole Gospel. That single word explains clearly what Jesus's suffering in the Garden was all about, and today, more than any other word in Scripture, it challenges us to examine our own lives and our whole culture, and to reflect on their relationship to the Christian ideal. More than any other meditation, perhaps, thinking about that word ἀγωνία and its ramifications opens the eyes to the connections between what Christians preach and what they must practice. That single word hammers home an essential point about what it means to be a Christian, yet it's a point so difficult for people to understand today that it might not come across no matter how plainly it's put.

Still—because virtually every word of the Gospel deserves this kind of close attention and calls for reform on this scale—examining the word ἀγωνία is a good example of the power of the Rosary to change viewpoints, to change lives, and to bring the individual heart into accordance with God. And it shows what a difference this kind of meditation can make in society as a whole.

"Agony" doesn't mean pain, nor torment. It means a struggle; and to the Greek-speaking world of St. Luke's day, ἀγωνία meant sport. Not as we might use the term loosely today to mean any kind of diversion, but sport in its essence: organized contention expressed physically, entering into some game of contending intellectually or physically brawling with another party to achieve some kind of goal while that party either tries to get there first or keep you from getting there at all, or both. It means tussling with some opposition to a goal, or striving for something against that opposition. By using this particular, unique word, St. Luke points to the importance of what you strive for, whom you strive with, and how you go about it.

To the pagans, watching athletes (from the Greek ἆθλος, contention) suffer, bleed, trounce people, and otherwise contend for human honors was as much an attraction as it is today; but the interesting thing historically is that between then and now sport was neither popular nor a normal part of life, and in fact it was prohibited. From the Fall of Rome until the time of the Communist Revolutions of 1848, Christians understood sport as utterly opposed to every moral principle that Christ taught. They didn't object to sport just because one athlete might inflict injury on another but because the essence of sport is contention, and contention is a vice (Mt 5:21-22, 38-39; Pr 17:14, 19; Mt 7:12; Rm 2:7-8; 1Tm 3:3; Tt 3:2; etc.).

The Fathers of the Church struggled mightily to close down the arenas and the hippodromes and to get the point across that sport is not compatible with a Christian way of life. It was as hard to make that point then as it would be now. Everybody went to the stadia routinely then, too, and nobody gave much thought to what they were doing and what they learned to do there; still less did they stop to think what sport was teaching their children. Many even failed to notice that what they heard in church was the dead opposite of what they heard at the arena.

That's why St. Augustine preached against sport, and why bishops constantly exhorted the Christian emperors to put an end to the Olympic Games and close the stadia; it's why Tertullian and Novatian wrote whole books about sport and its utter incompatibility with Christian principles. At long last the Church succeeded, at least far enough to close down public displays of contention in the stadia. Sport still erupted in informal events among the less-educated classes—ball games, the remnants of old Roman football, archaic kinds of polo, foot-racing, boxing, wrestling, and all of the sports we know today still happened, as did those sports like bull-running, horse-racing, or bear-baiting in which the contention was expressed vicariously through animals. But by the time St. Thomas Aquinas wrote whole articles on the vices that sport expresses (*Summa*, 2:2:37, 38, 41, 43, 65, 92, 116, 132, etc.), these activities were understood as aberrations, violations of Christian principles of life, and in fact as sins.

Preachers in the Middle Ages spoke unanimously against sport whenever it happened, and so did lawmakers, but in some cases the best that they could do was put some rules on it and contain it to a few outbursts a year. That's why football was tolerated only on Shrove Tuesday, and why Siena only runs the *Palio* twice a year and Pamplona only runs the bulls annually. Sport as an unquestioned part of life only got started again after the leftist revolutions of 1848, which did have the abolition of Christianity as part of their program. At first the revival of Roman-style sport met with universal opposition, but it took hold over the next few decades, and it seems to have crept up on moral theologians this time.

Still, astonishing as it may be to think of it at first, there's no way to define sport as anything other than strife—brawling—deliberately aroused and discharged, no matter how ritualized or rarefied it becomes, no matter how large or how small the field may be; any sport from football to checkers is the physical act of contending with other people, and contending for no real purpose.

Think of a football game in which all of the participants were acting according to Christian principles: seeing a person bent on taking a ball to a certain line—for some reason—they would do what they could to assist him; they could hardly stand in his way, and they would pick him up if he fell rather than knocking him down in the first place. In short, to take out the brawling is to take out the sport. Without the contention against other people, carrying a ball to a goal is obviously a matter of a useless thing taken to a meaningless destination; running to an arbitrary line, swimming to it or riding a horse to it, or jumping over something is pointless unless you try to vaunt yourself as higher, stronger, or faster than other people. Without the strife between contenders, nobody would buy tickets to watch any of it.

When you get it down to its nature, sport is the physical expression of the cardinal vice of anger, just as robbery through superior force expresses covetousness and as illicit sex is the expression of lust. No polite rules, no circumstances, no appliances or uniforms, no marching bands or referees, not even consent by the other party can change the essential natures of these acts; the beatings, the murders, in gladiatorial boxing matches were not made right because people paid to see them and called it entertainment. Sport is fighting, and it's fighting to prove that you're superior by knocking somebody else down, by beating him; and—no matter how much we'd like to justify our love of sports, no matter what particular denomination you belong to, no matter how puritanical it may sound to say it—there's no way to argue that Christians are supposed to act that way.

And when you think about what ἀγωνία is and what it means, when you search through the teachings of Christ, the Apostles, the Fathers of the Church, and the great theologians from that day to this—and most of all when you try to apply the Gospels in real life—it seems self-evident that every feature and aspect of sport is impossible in the light of moral theology or even of the Bible alone. Surprising though it may be, it has to be admitted that everything that sport teaches is contrary to Christian moral principles, as the Fathers of the Church said. Certainly people teach their children to do unto others as they'd want others to do unto them, and most punish their children for fighting or hitting, for seizing playthings that other people are holding or for refusing to release them if somebody else seizes them; but then they teach them to do precisely those things unto others in sport.

St. Luke's account of Christ's prayer in the Garden pivots on this highly charged word and turns it to new meaning for Christians. Jesus of Nazareth wasn't fighting against other people in a game for the fun of trouncing people, and he certainly wasn't trying to prove himself better than anybody else at anything. His ἀγωνία was a fight within his own human heart, the struggle with his own inclination to run from his duty (Lk 22:43).

This is precisely the point of St. Paul's analogy (1Cr 9:24-27; Eph 6:12; 1Tm 6:12; etc.): the Christian agony is an internal struggle; the Christian contends not with other people but with forces that deserve to be fought, like temptation, sin, vice, the world, the flesh, and the Devil. Sport is contention to no purpose except empty human honors; but I run as not without a purpose, he says, I fight as not beating the air; and, he may well have added, I don't beat upon other people for the fun of it.

I have fought a good fight, he says, not a fight like the pagans fight; I have run a good race: not like the races of these pagans, who contend for perishable and vainglorious honors; I seek an imperishable crown. I am not contending with other people for the possession of something not worth having, but contending against vice to reach God. The ascetic practices that keep you "in training"—fasts, abstinences, prayers of reparation, and other sacrifices and penances undertaken for the love of God—St. Paul actually refers to in jargon from the sport of boxing: ὑπωπιάζω μου τὸ σῶμα (1Cr 9:27); but here, too, he redirects the tussle inward, to the training of one's own soul, to the strengthening of the heart against itself.

So Christ, St. Paul, and the Fathers of the Church say explicitly that you should do precisely the opposite of what the pagan athletes were doing, and really the opposite of what athletes do today; so do the popes, although their remarks, too, are usually misunderstood or ignored. Just as it was in the waning days of the Roman Empire, sport is so much a part of so many people's lives today that it's nearly impossible to stand back from it and get a clear perspective; and there will undoubtedly be a good many objections to these teachings now as there were in the days of the Fathers. But all of the objections were answered long ago, in terms much more sweeping than these and by binding authority; moral theology defines all aspects and results of sport very differently from the way in which we think of them today.

The basic, inescapable point is that sport is strife, and strife is a vice; vice bears no good fruit. Some claim that sport is connected to physical fitness, but when you think about it that's not true. People can make themselves strong and healthy without fighting with each other, and obviously making yourself stronger specifically so that you can fight more ferociously is not motivated by respect for the body—the temple of the Holy Spirit—that God gave you. Naturally, the other excuses, and the values that sport teaches, also fall short when compared to the precepts of Christ. The "sportsmanship" of holding back on the strife counters the Christian ideal of not brawling at all, and the idea of being a good loser can't apply in Christlike interactions, in which there aren't supposed to be any losers—there isn't supposed to be any fighting in the first place. Once the essential nature of sport is recognized, even the customary prayers in the locker room take on a wholly different, and somewhat appalling, aspect, utterly opposed to the point and nature of Christian practice.

The Fathers' explanations of the inherent connections between sport and other vices, such as lust and sloth, might well be dusted off and examined again, too, as the writings of the pre-Christian Roman moralists; they contain even more surprises about sport and about how it affects the quality of life in this country now. But to meditate fruitfully on this Mystery it's probably enough to notice the full implications of St. Luke's word ἀγωνία; to reflect on the fact that this unique word has always been retained purposefully as the title of this Mystery; and to remember that neither St. Paul nor any other Christian moralist has ever encouraged people to come together in a ritual of strife with each other for no justifiable, or even substantial, prize. In that garden, Christ was struggling against his own human will to achieve the greatest and most meaningful prize in human history, the redemption of all Mankind; and his unspeakable agony stands as the example for our own internal struggle to attain salvation—the ἀγωνία that is, truly, not without a purpose.

After a time, Christ went back to the three Apostles, but they were already asleep (Mt 26:40; Mr 14:37; Lk 22:45; *cf.* Lk 9:32) . He woke them and rebuked them gently, but after he went again to repeat his prayers they fell asleep again; and when he repeated the same vocal prayers again, they fell asleep a third time. Some artists represent these awakenings in comparison to the waking of the Magi by the angel with his warning that Herod was seeking to kill Jesus (Mt 2:12). This comparison was especially popular in the twelfth century, which is why you can still see it carved into the capitals on the cathedrals of Chartres, where it's repeated on the old *jubé* and in the stained glass, and in the stonework of Autun. But the comparison of the three sleeping Magi with Peter, James, and John in the Garden seems to have been based on compositional similarities rather than any point of prophecy that it might make, and it faded in the West after the Middle Ages.

Yet Christ's repeated calls to awaken them are significant; repetition is one of Christ's favorite ways to emphasize anything. His triple call to watchfulness is a worthwhile message on the face of it (Mt 26:40-41; Mr 14:38; Lk 22:46), but the main point seems to be that the Apostles themselves evidently had no idea why Jesus had taken them out there after the Last Supper. All in all, one of the most remarkable things in the Gospels is the Apostle's inability to figure out Christ's living fulfillment of prophecy.

They followed him because his teachings made sense in themselves, and because he demonstrated his power with miracles that no other prophet could match; but they struggled to understand what those obviously right teachings meant in their lives, as all of his followers since have had to struggle. But it's still surprising that those closest to him didn't get very far in understanding what Jesus of Nazareth himself means in the great scheme of things. The whole story of the Apostles shows that they were not educated people and, unlike Mary, they had no extraordinary pre-lapsarian gifts of intellect and understanding. St. Peter himself didn't know who Christ really is until it was revealed to him (Mt 16:13-17), and none of the Apostles understood fully until the Holy Spirit infused the knowledge into them at Pentecost (Jn 14:26; Ac 2:1-4). They hadn't even seen Jesus's acts and words against the whole matrix of prophecy until he himself explained it all to them on the road to Emmaus and later opened their minds, infusing the knowledge into them (Lk 24:25-27, 45).

It's difficult now to understand how they could have missed it. Psalms, the prophets, and the whole panoply of sacrifices in the Temple outline the Passion as the mechanism through which redemption would be won and salvation made possible. In fact, the Agony in the Garden can be seen most clearly in light of what Isaia wrote about the Servant of God.

Sixteen chapters of Isaia's prophecies center on this figure, beginning with the fortieth and ending with the fifty-fifth; the text includes four poems. The first poem, beginning at 42:1, identifies the Servant as the one in whom God is well pleased (cf. Mt 3:17). This is the man who, endowed with the Spirit of God, will come to teach justice to all nations; and he will proclaim the kingdom of God in meekness, not shouting from the rooftops, not in battle or in conquest, but in meekness. He will not destroy the enemies of God's people; far from scattering those who oppress Israel, he will not even stir himself to pinch out the petty irritation of a smoldering wick.

Yet God has sent the Servant for the victory of justice; he will be the one who will free humanity from the blindness and bondage in which they live. This man will be set up as a covenant for the Israelites and for the Gentiles alike. This new covenant will come to pass when the old covenant is fulfilled; and the Servant will not only bring this covenant but will himself be the covenant.

In the second poem, which begins at Is 49:1, the Servant himself speaks. Of course, Christ, as the Second Person of the Trinity, was born of the Father before all ages, co-eternal with the Father and the Holy Spirit. So he didn't have to wait for the Incarnation to speak. As the Wisdom of God he spoke in the Old Testament, in the books of Wisdom and Proverbs; and in Isaia he speaks as the Servant. Here, in the second poem, he states that he was conceived for this work, which is to be a sword, an arrow, to accomplish the Lord's work (*cf.* Lk 2:34-35). This particular poem contains a surprising amount of details that correspond exactly to the Gospels' accounts of the coming of Christ. The Redeemer speaks of himself as a sword, as hidden at first, as Jesus lived in obscurity until his public ministry began. He says again that he is to be a light to all nations, a savior to everyone on Earth.

He speaks of making a straight path through the mountains (*cf.* Mt 3:3; Ps 25:12); and he mentions that he will stay with his people as a mother stays with her child—which takes on a double meaning because it's immediately followed with a prophecy of the Passion: "upon the palms of my hands I have written your Name" (*cf.* Jn 19:25-27). When his hand is lifted, the Servant concludes, it will be a signal to all nations; all Mankind shall know that I am the Lord, your Savior, your Redeemer, he concludes.

The third poem begins at Is 50:4; it most directly speaks of the Agony. The Servant has a well-trained tongue with which to rouse the weary. He himself has not rebelled, has not turned back from doing the will of the Father, even though he must give his back to be flogged and his face to buffets and spitting; he will respond to mockery and torture in silence, knowing that in the end he will triumph. Those who walk in their own light, not his, he warns, will be burned by the light of their own torches; they will lie down in the place of pain.

The fourth poem, beginning at Is 52:13, is rhetorically the most unusual of all, and really one of the most unusual passages in the whole Bible. Nearly all of the rest of Scripture follows fairly closely a traditional rhetorical form. Some passages take the form of a history, a midrash, a haggada, or a parable, but this is a song, a poem—a canticle, like the psalms. Poetic parts of Scripture can be identified as songs of thanksgiving, funeral songs, or liturgical poems. This poem has something of all of these three poetic forms about it, but it is not precisely any of them. That in itself tells you something about the unique mission of the Servant, and it points to those three important elements in his work: he will be given as an offering to God and as a gift to God's people; he will die; and he will establish, again, a New Covenant that will endure in his Church.

So this poem sings of the purpose behind the Servant's work expressed in the other three prophetic poems, but it chiefly establishes that the Servant should suffer and die for the sins of others. He shall give his life as an offering for sin, it says; through his suffering, my Servant shall justify many, and their guilt he will bear (53:10-11). And it describes in horrifying detail the Passion that is to come. The Savior will not do his work in glory, but in a way that revolts those who see it; he will be rejected by the people. Oppressed and condemned, he will be taken away, flogged for the sins of many, and pierced; he will suffer in silence, and he will be cut off from the land of the living—he will die—and he will be buried. Yet through his death his followers will know everlasting life; because he surrendered himself to death, he shall take away the sins of the many and win pardon for their offenses. And the will of the Father shall be accomplished through him.

The Apostles acted as they did in the Garden because they didn't know what the Father's will was; Jesus acted as he did because he knew. That's why he prayed so fervently while they slept, and it's why the angel came to comfort him. This angel is often represented in artistic representations of the Agony, holding a chalice as a visual metaphor for suffering, as Christ used the word as a rhetorical metaphor (Mt 26:39; Mr 14:36; Lk 22:42). Some artists make the point more immediately by showing the angel holding the instruments of the Passion itself.

In any case, it's worth noting that the angel sent to Christ is never shown embracing him, sympathizing with him, or even holding a towel to wipe away his bloody sweat: the angel is presenting to him the very cup of suffering that he's asking to have taken away. This is precisely what the metaphor means if you take the word "comfort" literally. There's nothing soft about comfort, or easy. The angel didn't offer him condolence, sympathizing with his pain; "condolence" is from the Latin *cum-*, with, and *dolentia*, pain or suffering. Nor did the angel "console" him; that's from *cum-* and *solor*, to solace, to sooth, and "pure pain, without any admixture of consolation, did he suffer," St. Thomas Aquinas affirmed. After all, his torment only increased from the angel's comfort: his sweat became as blood (Lk 22:43-44).

That's because the angel came to "comfort" him, which is from *cum-* and *fortis*, strength; "to comfort" means to prod somebody to go forward to do what's right, or at least to remind him to do it, whether he likes it or not. The last time that Jesus had complained—which he did also as an example—he received comforting words from Heaven, too: but people who heard those comforting words said that it was thunder (Jn 12:29).

So, when his hour came, he stood ready to do what had to be done. Thy will, not mine, be done, he said; and he showed himself to be as good as his word. Having taught his disciples to pray that God's will be done, he showed himself able to follow that will in obedience even to death. He didn't resist his enemies or beg them for mercy, and he didn't defer their plans supernaturally as he had done before (Lk 4:28-30). He simply said, "What you have to do, do quickly" (Jn 13:27).

The Passion of Christ was not easy, and certainly there must have been other ways for the Redeemer to accomplish what he had to accomplish— despite prophecies like Isaia's, the Israelites looked for a triumphal entry through the clouds and the immediate destruction of all of their enemies. But in the end the Messiah took true humanity on himself, and his triumph came only after indescribable suffering.

But why should he be reluctant to go forward to his Passion? Why should he have to go through the severest internal struggle, the agony, before accepting what he had to do? As he knew about his death, he knew about his resurrection. If he knew that everything was going to work to his glory, why didn't he go into the arms of his captors calmly, or even with cheerful assurance?

All of the basic questions about this Mystery revolve around the question of Christ's nature. Jesus of Nazareth is truly God *and truly Man* (Hb 2:18, 4:15). He is one person, but he has two natures; he has a divine nature, as the second person of the Holy Trinity, and he has a human nature. These natures are united in what's called hypostatic union since the instant of the Incarnation. The term is from the Greek ὑπό, under, and στάσις, state of being; hypostasis is the substance, the essential nature of a thing, regardless of its characteristics or "accidents" like its particular measure or color or any other individual descriptive features—it's the reality of the thing, the core and fact of its existence.

And just as his divine and human natures are united hypostatically, he is hypostatically united with the Father and the Holy Spirit. In the Gospel, the hypostatic union of Jesus and the Father is stated in his own declaration, "I and the Father are one" (Jn 10:30; *cf.* 14:10-11). In the Nicene Creed it's stated as *consubstantialem patri*: "one in being with the Father". So Christ is true Man, and he could suffer; and he is true God, so he knew that he would (Mt 17:12, 26:21-23; Mr 8:31, 14:18; Lk 9:22, 22:21).

People who deny either of Christ's natures are called Monophysites (mon-OFF-iss-sites), from the Greek μόνο-, one, and φύσις, nature—the root of our word "physics", the study of the nature of things. Monophysitism can go either way. Some sects focus exclusively on Christ's human nature: they deny that Jesus is truly God. They may say that he is a creature of God's, subordinate to him, that he was nothing more than an outstanding man who became somehow assimilated to God when he was baptized by St. John the Baptizer, or when he died.

Other sects focus exclusively on Christ's divine nature. They may deny that he is truly Man, teaching that he's a "spirit person", or that he was the archangel Michael, or that his apparent physical body was nothing more than a phantom, an illusion without substance. In hearing of the Trinity they may misinterpret the word "person" as if it could refer only to a human being, overlooking the fact that God is by nature different from humans, or they may use words like "nature" to mean condition or function.

Naturally, monophysites' teachings about Christ influence their teachings about the whole economy of salvation. Some sects claim that there's only one nature in Christ but two kinds of human nature, the saved and the damned. Others deny the resurrection of Christ and the resurrection of the body in general, and others deny the immortality of the soul altogether; but then oddly enough they almost all promise an everlasting bodily life in an earthly paradise.

In fact, monophysitic teachings are always rather a muddle. Any given precept contradicts the others, and they all require that members ignore the bulk of the Scripture that they claim as the sole rule of faith. The one thing that monophysitic sects seem to agree on, whichever way they go, is the displacement of Mary. If Christ is God but not Man, then Mary is not his mother; she gave birth to a phantom or an illusion. If he is Man but not God, then she doesn't rank any higher than any other prophet's mother. That's why a clear understanding of Mary's role leads to understanding of Christ's nature, and why an accurate knowledge of Christ's nature leads to an appropriate respect for Mary.

But monophysitism has its appeal; it makes religion seem simpler because it keeps people's view strictly limited to human experience, and it frees them from the effort of learning about God. Having eliminated all of the wonder of Christ's nature and of his work, it supplies pat answers instead of requiring people to meditate deeply and well on the mysteries of the Faith as outlined in the Bible. Monophysitic sects also free their members from struggling with moral principles. In denying Christ's nature either way, they split the life of the spirit from the life of the body, and therefore they almost always reject those precepts that have to do with physical life on Earth, like the Ten Commandments.

If Christ isn't God, then people don't have to take his moral teachings as revelation, or on the other hand if he isn't Man then those teachings don't necessarily apply to humans; as a disembodied wraith, Christ couldn't have practiced what he preached, so we don't need to, monophysites believe. But then, having rejected moral theology as all heresies must, they impose commandments of their own. The sixth-century monophysite Severus evidently insisted that it was against God's law to bathe, and present-day monophysitic sects often arbitrarily prohibit tobacco, which of course wasn't known to the Apostles, or even wine, the right use of which was commended by the Apostles and by Christ himself (Jn 2:3-10, 6:54-58; Mt 26:27-29; Mr 14:23-25; Lk 22:17-20; 1Tm 5:23).

It's hard to see how these beliefs can develop, considering that the Gospel tells so clearly of Jesus's birth, suffering, dying, and so many other things (like eating) that are related precisely to affirm that he is truly Man, and his miracles and his resurrection, which show that he is truly God, too—and his own explicit statements of the fact that he is both (Mt 1:1-16, 8:20, 29; Lk 4:41; etc.). Even the prophetic books affirm that the career of Jesus Christ on Earth was neither a sham nor an empty gesture.

But monophysite sects cut themselves off from Sacred Tradition, basing themselves on the Bible alone; and in that situation the Bible itself can't last long. To base a creed on Scripture without reference to the Tradition that it speaks of, or to the Church that wrote it and assembled it, people have to deny at least some aspects of the nature of Christ, the nature of God. Many of these sects deny that Jesus knew what lay ahead of him in his life.

One particular sprout from monophysitism still crops up today with a surprising frequency. Some monophysites deny specifically that any person of the Trinity is all-knowing or, in technical terms, omniscient, from the Latin omni-, all, and scientia, knowledge. People who deny this particular quality of God's are called agnoetæ (agg-no-EE-tee), from the Greek ἀγνοέω, to be ignorant of. The Christian understanding is that God—Father, Son, and Holy Spirit—knows everything and sees everything. But some sects in the past have based their whole existence on denying that God knows everything, and some still do: the idea follows logically from any number of other heresies. The fourth-century followers of Theophronius of Cappadocia said that even to know the past God would have to study and think about it.

The Arians were agnoetic by logical necessity, having denied that Christ is co-equal with the Father, and so were the Apollinarists, who denied that Christ has a human soul or an intellect; they taught that he was utterly devoid of knowledge. Nestorians, Adoptionists, and others taught that he had limited knowledge but acquired it, just as anybody else acquires knowledge.

This misinformation never made much headway, though, until the sixth century, when the agnoetic teachings of an Alexandrian deacon named Themistius started to spread confusion throughout the East and filter through to the West; at that point, Pope St. Gregory the Great formally declared the teaching anathema. But, like all subtractions from Christian doctrine, agnoeticism still shows up from time to time. Anybody who denies any of Christ's teachings must deny his nature, too, and that usually involves claiming that he didn't know what he was on Earth for. Luther, for instance, taught that Christ had extraordinary knowledge, but not omniscience, so really he was little more than a prophet; Calvin, Zwingli, and others denied his omniscience outright.

Today, some monophysites teach that because Christ has only a divine nature he knows all things and always did, but they seem to be a tiny minority of a tiny minority. Much more numerous are those who teach that he was some kind of angel or phantom who had more than human knowledge but nothing like God's omniscience, and those that teach that he has only a human nature, having no more knowledge than anybody else about the meaning of life.

THE AGONY IN THE GARDEN

Because all of these teachings put limits on the infinite God and deny at least one of his perfections, the Church has always taught that they are errors. But ironically, because many in the Church don't give the matter of Christ's natures a lot of thought these days—the matter having been clarified so long ago—you may even hear careless suggestions in Catholic sources that Jesus didn't know everything past, present, and to come. But wherever you find it, and like the rest of Scripture the Agony in the Garden stands against all of the doubts and diminishments of Christ's omniscience, and all of the reductions of his nature.

As God, Christ didn't come in glory, ripping open the sky to smash Israel's enemies with a rod of iron. As a man, he did a good many things that he didn't have to do, as examples to us. He didn't need Baptism, but he practiced what he preached, and he let himself be baptized (Mt 3:13-17). He didn't need to fast for his own sins, but he fasted to show us that we do (Mt 4:2). And many, many more of his followers, from that day to this, are called to take up their crosses and follow him. To their credit, they often do so cheerfully, singing hymns and praising God as they go. Naturally, they're afraid; like Christ, they know what's coming, resurrection as well as martyrdom; and like Christ they would prefer that the resurrection be accomplished without the martyrdom.

His last word on the subject, "not my will, but thine, be done" shows his resolution to put into practice the phrase from the Our Father, even to death. It's the final fulfillment of his mother's acceptance that it should be done unto her as God wills (Mt 26:42-43; Lk 1:38). In the end, this is probably the main lesson of the Agony: the struggle against your own inclinations, won at last as resignation to the will of God, and won through resolutions taken in prayer.

This is certainly the point that Guigo de Castro took away with him. "When we meditate on his blessed Passion, the representation of the chalice of his agony excites a more burning thirst in us," he wrote, "which is our longing to share his sufferings—we thirst, and we reach out to that chalice when we turn that longing into action... 'Rejoice, insofar as you are partakers of the sufferings of Christ'" (1Pt 4:13). This is the contest, St. Augustine said, the necessary and proper contention of the Christian: "take this away, and where is the combat? Where is the trial? Where is the victory, if no battle has preceded it?" (*Sermon 47 On Mark*).

By the time Jesus had resigned himself to his Passion, Judas was there with the authorities. Jesus didn't struggle, but St. Peter struck out and cut off the ear of one of the High Priest's servants, which Jesus replaced (Jn 18:10; Lk 22:51). With the arrest of Jesus, the Agony in the Garden was over. And the agony on the Cross was about to begin.

THE FLAGELLATION

T HERE WERE TWO OVERLAPPING JURISDICTIONS, WITH TWO DISTINCT CODES of law, in force over Judea at the time of Christ: Jewish law and Roman law. Some acts that were crimes under Jewish law were matters of complete indifference to Roman law, and Jewish law largely ignored much of Roman law. So miscreants could be tried under two different systems of law, for two different sets of offenses, and punished in two different ways.

The whole account of Christ's trial in St. John's Gospel (Jn 18) follows Jesus as he moves back and forth between the Jewish authorities like the Sanhedrin and the Roman government, personified by Pontius Pilate. Basically, the Jews wanted to punish Jesus for something, anything, but they didn't have the authority to impose penalties as horrible as they wanted to inflict on him, and the Romans didn't think that he'd done anything that was any of their business.

Both the Hebrew and the Roman codes prescribed scourging, though. It was imposed as a penalty in itself for certain smaller crimes including impiety and obstinacy, which is why the Apostles all felt the lash at least once (Ac 5:40-41), and why St. Paul was caned no fewer than five times (2Cr 11:24).

But even with whipping, some social distinctions applied. For one thing, there were two distinct forms of whip in use, depending not so much on which offense had been committed, but who had committed it. Soldiers, senators, and great ladies of good family who might commit some great crime, Livy mentions, were beaten with the lictor's rods, canes that would bruise the victim, but they wouldn't necessarily break the skin.

The Hebrews used rods, too, for serious infractions that didn't merit execution. It would be nearly impossible to beat a person to death with rods, particularly if law limited the number of strokes, which it always did. The Israelites restricted the number of strokes to forty (Dt 25:3). The Pharisees, who were anxious that the limit shouldn't be exceeded by executioners who lost count in their enthusiasm, insisted that no more than thirty-nine strokes should be given (2Cr 11:24).

Under Roman law, of course, slaves could be whipped at any time, for any reason, with anything that came to hand, and even to death. Scourging with a whip could also be imposed as a warning, without a trial, which is why Pilate tried to get Jesus released after that precautionary measure (Lk 23:16, 22; Jn 19:1). Both jurisdictional systems beat criminals who were condemned to death, too; Josephus says that those who were to be burned at the

THE FLAGELLATION

stake were flogged first, and the Gospels themselves show that people who were to be crucified were scourged, too. But the condemned who did not enjoy the protection of Roman citizenship were not beaten with rods: they were beaten with a cruel little instrument called a *flagrum* or *flagellum*.

The *flagellum* had a short handle and two or more thongs of leather, perhaps fourteen to eighteen inches long. At the end of each, the Romans would tie a little object called a *talus*, which means heel-bone; it was either really a knucklebone of a sheep or a little dumbbell of lead or bronze. The Hebrews used this kind of whip, too. They referred to the *tali* as עֲקְרַב, "scorpions" (3Kn 12:11, 14), because they stung.

Scourged not for his own sins but for ours (Is 53:5), Jesus of Nazareth was whipped with a *flagellum* (Mt 27:26; Mr 15:15; Lk 22:63; Jn 19:1), which is why this Mystery is called the Flagellation. It happened in the Prætorium of Jerusalem, the building housing the Prætor—the highest magistrate of the Roman towns, one who executed some of the functions of the Roman Consuls, to whom he answered.

Like most government buildings in the Roman Empire, the Prætorium had a special column, which would normally be in a courtyard. Some of these columns for flagellation were tall, so that the person would be stretched out full length, his arms above his head and his face to the column. Others, like the one in Jerusalem, were short, about three or four feet tall; but the short ones had a flaring base that kept his feet at some distance, doubling him over and stretching the skin on his back and thighs tight. Criminals to be flogged were always stripped naked, and Jesus was evidently blindfolded (Lk 22:64). Then the soldiers, at least one on each side, would lay on the strokes.

The straps of the *flagellum* would raise welts, just as the lictor's rods would; but the hard *tali* would rip into the skin and peel it off with each stroke, leaving it to hang in bleeding shreds. Naturally, the long strips of the *flagellum* would often whip the little weights around to the sides and even the chest and abdomen, too. The victim would be covered with wounds.

If there was no limit to the number of strokes—and for slaves and non-citizens there wasn't—the *flagellum* would lash again and again at the same wounds that it had opened already, cutting into muscle and laying open the bone itself (Ps 68:27). The victim would bleed to death or, more likely, die of shock, skinned alive. Horace (*Epodes* 4) writes of a victim so torn by the *flagri* that even the people whipping him were sickened by the sight of him.

But the Romans had enough practice in these arts to stop when they estimated that the condemned man could take not one stroke more without dying, or without being so disabled that he was not able to play his own part in the long, cruel pageant of his own execution.

There were also social distinctions in the mode of execution between the citizen and the subject, as between the master and the slave. The lictors carried the rods of scourging bound around a great axe, in the combination called the *fasces*. This was adopted as the principal symbol of the Fascists who claimed they'd restore Roman imperial-style order in Italy, of course, but it's so enduring a symbol of civil discipline that you still see it emblazoned in the decorations of our courts and legislative buildings, and even on some of our older coins.

Roman citizens condemned to death were scourged with the rods of the *fasces* and then beheaded with the axe, with one swift stroke. That's why St. Paul, as a Roman citizen, died that way. People who were not Roman citizens, ripped almost to death with the *flagellum*, were not beheaded. They were crucified.

THE CROWNING WITH THORNS

W E KNOW A GOOD DEAL ABOUT THE DETAILS OF ROMAN PUNITIVE
procedures from the Gospels and from other ancient texts, but
the case of Jesus of Nazareth was not a routine one. He was condemned for letting people hail him as their King; and so the Roman executioners decided to have a little extra fun at his expense after they flogged him
to within an inch of his life and led him forth for his execution. These cruel-
ties are recorded in the Gospels, too, of course, but their full meaning is clear
only in the context of secular history and archæology.

Pagan Romans had scant respect for Jewish kings, even though they
themselves had placed them in office. For instance, when King Herod
Agrippa was visiting Alexandria, Philo says, the Alexandrians took up an
idiotic beggar, wrapped him in a mat, handed him a reed as a scepter, and
paraded him through the streets just as the King of the Jews was arriving:
and they crowned their parody king with the bottom of an old basket.

Mat, reed, and basket seem to be items that would be ready to hand in
Alexandria, the capital of the land in which everything possible was made
out of papyrus, and a city that stood on the Nile delta beside the marshy
Lake Mariotis. But all of this basketry also calls to mind the Gospel
accounts, especially details like the reed that the Romans handed to Christ
to use as a scepter (Mt 27:29). And it also recalls the relic of the Crown of
Thorns that's been kept in Paris since Louis the Saint brought it back from
the Crusades and built the Sainte-Chapelle to keep it in.

The Crown of Thorns, now at Notre-Dame-de-Paris, is nothing more
than a few ancient reeds woven together as if they were part of a basket.
This doesn't meet our expectations, but Louis the Saint evidently knew
what to look for; and he must have found the description in the writings of
the Fathers of the Church. In the fifth century, St. Vincent de Lérins for
example, wrote in a sermon on the Passion that the Romans placed on
Christ's head "a crown of thorns, which was in the shape of a *pileus*, so that
it touched and covered his head at every part."

A *pileus* is a freedman's cap, sometimes called a *phyrigium*, after the
province of Phrygia where it was said to have originated. A *pileus* is
a kind of oval or rather half-oval cap that covers the top, sides, and
back of the head—a sort of beehive-shaped cloth hat worn with the

empty top part flopped forward. Personifications of Liberty in American art, like the one on the Morgan silver dollar, often wear the *pileus* as a sign of their status.

Of course, it wouldn't be difficult to find a basket shaped like a *pileus*, but more to the point the *pileus* itself was shaped like the *tiara*, the customary crown of levantine monarchs. It would also recall the headgear worn by the priests of the Temple, as described by Josephus (*Antiquities* 3:7:4 *ff.*). In fact, the freedman's cap is the prototype of priestly headgear: it's the direct ancestor of the papal *tiara*, the *biretta* worn by priests, the white *pileolus* of the Pope and the red *zucchetto* of cardinals, and even of the college mortarboard, from the days when universities were Church institutions. Pagan kings, and Roman priests, wore a *pileus* distinguished by the addition of an *apex*, a spike, of olive wood stuck through the crown of it. Apparently, this feature of the priestly and royal headgear gave the Roman soldiers the perverse idea for the thorns.

Early representations of Christ during his Passion don't show the Crown of Thorns at all; early Christian paintings in the catacombs, Byzantine icons, and any number of other images simply leave it out. Even early Renaissance paintings like those of Giotto show no Crown. After Louis the Saint brought the relic back, though, virtually every representation of the Passion includes the Crown of Thorns. But despite the form of the relic, virtually every image after that date shows the Crown in precisely the same inaccurate way, as a simple wreath of interwoven thorns, not as a cap-shaped parody of the tiara worn by the divine kings of the Levant.

There is a perennial debate about exactly what kind of plant produced the thorns that the Romans used. It seems a trivial question, but meditating on the wounds that the Crown of Thorns caused is made easier and more vivid if you know something about what the thorns were probably like. Most authorities agree that the thorns must have been those of the jujube shrub, *Zizyphus spina Christi*, or of a very similar plant related to the jujube, the *Paliurus spina Christi*, which is why both of those plants are given the botanical name "thorn of Christ".

The *Zizyphus* was evidently unknown in the Holy Land until the end of the imperium of Cæsar Augustus, when Sextus Popinius carried it out of its native Syria so that its small, sweet fruits—still used to make candies—could be cultivated in the region. Like many another imported garden plant, it quickly escaped, went wild, and became a noxious pest that bore not fruit but only thorns. By Holy Thursday it was growing in every land around the Mediterranean.

THE CROWNING WITH THORNS

It's entirely possible, even likely, that both of these species were heaped up in the courtyard of the Prætorium; the hewers of wood were not likely to care much about which kind of waste wood they piled up for fuel (*cf.* Ec 7:6). Other kinds of brush was undoubtedly there, too. But the surviving relics of thorns from the Crown agree with these two species as the source of the original; even those thorns that are kept as third-class relics, having been touched to the authentic Thorns, have virtually always been taken either from *Zizyphus* or *Paliurus*. The thorns from either kind of plant are identical: long, hard, very sharp, growing both curved like claws and straight as needles on the same plant.

The soldiers themselves would hardly go to the trouble of weaving thorns into a wreath-shaped crown, and in fact it's hard to see how that could be done. Those thorns are tough, long, and very sharp, and the twigs that carry them are hard and woody. So they evidently broke thorny branches off and stuck them into an old reed basket. That would hold the thorn branches steady while the soldiers drove them into Christ's scalp with their sticks. They probably also stuck some thorny twigs into the outside of the basket, like the spiky rays that evidently ornamented levantine crowns and priestly headdresses.

This configuration wouldn't carry an appropriate symbolism to a mediæval European viewer, though. For one thing, the popes since Innocent II had been wearing a tiara like those of the old monarchs of the Levant, a *pileus*-shaped crown with a spiky ring of gold (later two and then three of them) around it. An accurate representation of the Crown of Thorns, then, would provoke comparison with the crown of the Pope, which would make the wrong point entirely. Still, there was a much more appropriate image of the crown, and one just as rich in associations. The artists of Europe, one and all, gave the Crown of Thorns form of a horrible parody of the floral chaplet of rejoicing.

Whatever form it took, the Crown of Thorns inflicted both physical and emotional pain on Jesus of Nazareth. Like that poor nameless idiot of Alexandria, he was held up in ridicule as a mock King of the Jews; and those thorns lacerated the thin skin of his scalp, tearing through it and covering his face and body with blood. The scalp is what you call highly vascularized tissue; that is, it is particularly rich in blood vessels, which is why scalp wounds bleed so abundantly. It's also particularly rich in nerves, which is why it's so sensitive. Having a basket full of hard thorns pressed or beaten onto the scalp is itself more than enough to seriously weaken a person, or, if left unattended, to kill.

But beyond this physical pain came the shame of ridicule. Having crowned Jesus with thorns, the soldiers put a cloak on him, a *paludamentum* that was the short mantle of a centurion. Centurions, so called because they were officers in charge of one hundred soldiers, were always around when criminals were to be executed; they were the ones who herded condemned criminals through the streets to crucifixion. The Apostles must have been appalled that Christ went to see the centurion who asked him for help (Lk 7:3-10)—not just a Roman, but a Roman soldier, and a Roman executioner of Israelites besides. The centurion's primary insignia were the vine-stem walking stick that he always carried, and his cloak: a short, dark-red cloak, a cloak of the imperial purple, the color common to emperors, kings, and gods; a centurion was evidently the lowest-ranking Roman permitted to wear it.

All things considered, they evidently enjoyed their work, those Roman soldiers on that cold Friday, to flay this man alive, to tear his scalp to shreds, and to mock him, to laugh at what they had done; to push him through the city in disgrace, and then to kill him in the cruelest way the human mind could devise.

THE CARRYING OF THE CROSS

NORMALLY, JEWS WHO WERE CONVICTED OF BLASPHEMY WERE STONED to death, as St. Stephen was (Ac 7:54-60). When the Jews of Antioch and Iconium stoned St. Paul at Lystra for blasphemy (Ac 14:18-19), the Roman government evidently ignored the whole proceeding. Blasphemy against the Hebrew God was a matter for Hebrew law.

But after St. Paul recovered miraculously and returned to Jerusalem, the Jews seized him again in the same way (Ac 21:30-32). But this time the tumult constituted civil disorder, so the Roman tribune arrested St. Paul—not for blasphemy against a God that Roman law didn't recognize, but for inciting a riot, which was an offense under Roman law.

The tribune apparently didn't think that he needed to try Paul; he could summarily declare a Jew guilty, have him flogged, and condemn him to crucifixion. Citizens of subjugated nations had no more rights under Roman law than slaves did. But Paul mentioned that he had the privilege of being a Roman citizen, and that changed everything. A Roman citizen had rights under Roman law: he could not be flogged, not in any particularly horrible way, in any case; he had the right to a trial before a Roman magistrate. He could appeal the decision to Cæsar, and if found guilty he could not be crucified.

That's why St. Paul was eventually beheaded in Rome. But Jesus of Nazareth was not a Roman citizen; he had no such rights. And when the Jews clamored for his death the most they could hope for was permission to stone him (Lk 4:28-30). They wanted him crucified; so they manoeuvered their charges purposefully to put him under Roman law, where he would be subject to that punishment (*cf.* Lk 13:1). They had a problem thinking of a reason for handing him over to the Romans (Jn 18:29-40), but eventually they charged him with a capital offense under Roman law: treason (Jn 19:12). For letting his followers hail him as King of the Jews (Mt 2:2, 21:6-10), Jesus of Nazareth was condemned to the cross.

Roman crosses consisted of two pieces. The *stipes* (STEE-pez) was the upright piece, set up at some desolate place outside the city—a Field of Blood or, in the case of Jerusalem, the Place of the Skull. Usually, in peaceful times when government was just and tranquil, judges would order the *stipes* set up as need arose. But governments in restless areas seem to have left whole groves of *stipites* standing in the ground, serving one execution after another. Tyrannies did the same thing, of course; the permanent plantation of death-trees set up in the Field of Mars was one of the reproaches that Cicero leveled at Labienus (*For Rabirius; Verrine Orations*). There was already another, larger killing field outside the Esquiline Gate, and the Romans set up the same permanent facility outside of Jerusalem, during the Jewish Wars, according to Josephus. But in any case the *stipes* was there waiting for the condemned man when he got there. He had to carry the other part of the cross on which he would die.

The horizontal piece was called the *patibulum*; that means the beam that people put over brackets to bar a door, or that slides into sockets in the door-jamb for the same purpose. So the cross-piece was a good heavy beam, more than would be strictly necessary to hold the weight of a man nailed to it. Ancient texts suggest that the average *patibulum* must have weighed about a hundred pounds, and the upright stipes was heavy enough to support it.

But they were two separate pieces. The phrase that sentenced a person to crucifixion, then, was *Pone crucem servo*—"Put the cross on the slave", not the other way around. The *patibulum* would be tied to the outstretched arms of the condemned man—the *patibulatus*, they called him—who would of course have been stripped naked and flogged, usually to within an inch of his life anyway. This is what Christ predicted to St. Peter when he said that the Apostle's arms would be stretched out, and that others would lead him where he'd rather not go (Jn 21:18); and St. Peter, like anybody else in the Empire, must have known exactly what that meant.

Everybody in the city turned out to watch the condemned man being marched stumbling through the streets in his shame, the target of any abuse that anybody cared to hurl, physical, verbal, or otherwise. It was probably a good idea to take the opportunity to show your support of the administration that could do precisely the same thing to you, if it wanted to, so this abuse of the *patibulatus* became a custom throughout the Empire. This part of crucifixion became a metaphor for just making cruel fun of somebody, as we would say that we'd "roast" somebody with humorous insults—*Patibulum ferat per urbem*, Plautus wrote, *deinde affigatur cruci*: "Let him carry his crossbeam through the city, and then let him be nailed to his cross", and he wrote that in a comedy (*Casina*).

When they crucified Jews, the Romans accommodated Jewish sensibilities, though, to an extent. Jesus was not subjected to the usual indignity of carrying his cross naked (Mt 27:31), for instance, although he may have been nailed to the cross that way (Mt 27:35; Jn 19:23). But carrying the cross was an ordeal, and one that was all too familiar to the Jews of the time. In this light, it's significant that Christ stressed the delights of Heaven less than he talked about the need for his followers to take up their crosses and follow him; and in the Roman empire they knew precisely what that promise meant. As Jews, they may also have understood the promise of prophecy. "Isaac is another symbol of the Lord, too," St. Clement of Alexandria explained (*Christ the Educator*; cf. Gn 22). "He was a son just as is the Son; he was a victim, just as the Lord was a victim… [A]nd he carried the wood to his own sacrifice, just as the Lord bore the wood of the Cross."

When Jesus of Nazareth had carried his sacrificial wood to the Place of the Skull, the Roman soldiers stripped off his garment, pulling open again all of the wounds of the Flagellation that covered his back, sides, and legs entirely. Then they prepared to nail him to his *patibulum* and hoist him up onto the *stipes* that stood there waiting for him.

THE CRUCIFIXION

T HINKING ABOUT WHAT HAPPENED AFTER JESUS GOT TO GOLGOTHA MIGHT be difficult, not only because the idea of being nailed to a cross is so horrible but also because we just don't remember what crucifixion really is. About fifty years before Christ was born, Marcus Tullius Cicero (*Verrine Orations* 2:5:170) remarked that it was a crime to put a Roman citizen in chains, an enormity to flog one, and outright murder to slay one; but "what shall I say of crucifixion?" he asked. "There is no way to find words for such an abomination." It's undoubtedly the worst and most agonizing way to kill a person ever devised.

Herodotus (*Historia* 9:20) suggests that crucifixion was invented by the Persians in about the sixth century before Christ, and although the classical Greeks knew about it they only told of its horrors; they never inflicted it on anybody. After Alexander the Great united the old Persian Empire to his own collection of Greek-speaking states, he and his successors used it, but only seldom. It was the Romans who made crucifixion universal, and, as they practiced it, crucifixion includes enough wounds and enough torture to kill a person five times over.

The Romans practiced it often, too. Roman law specified crucifixion as the penalty for theft, murder, and a wide variety of other crimes, particularly treason; and as they imposed their rule on unwilling people from Palestine to Spain and Britain, they encountered almost infinite numbers of people who resisted them—traitors by definition. Six thousand of the followers of the rebel slave Spartacus were crucified as traitors in 73-71 BC, their crosses lining the road all the way from Capua, the hotbed of their rebellion, to Rome itself.

Even these thousands were comparatively few. Rather than pay for the support of a veteran slave or bother with a recalcitrant one, Romans evidently just crucified them on some pretext. Slaves were born into "the Companionship of the Cross," as the slave Palæstrio remarks in a comedy by Plautus (*Miles Gloriosus*)—my father, grandfather, great-grandfather, and great-great-grandfather all died on the cross, his fellow slave Sceledrus adds. There is some truth in these dark jokes; Cicero, Livy, and Tacitus suggest that crucifixion was the usual way that slaves died under Roman rule.

But it was in Judea that the Romans got the most practice in the art of crucifixion. Just after Herod the Great died (4 BC), the Roman legate to Syria, Quintilius Varus, crucified more than two thousand Israelites, not for treason, exactly, but for sedition—for simply planning treasonable activities. Josephus says (*Jewish Wars* 5:11) that the legions of Titus crucified five hundred

Israelites a day during the siege of Jerusalem. So many thousands were crucified that the Roman executioners varied the positions in which they nailed them "by way of jest", just to keep from being bored with their butchery.

Josephus's estimate might be conservative, because he was Roman governor of Galilee and naturally sympathetic to his Latin overlords. Even so, the Israelites around the time of Christ knew exactly what crucifixion meant and exactly what happened to a crucified man. As a physician (Cl 4:14), St. Luke was particularly well equipped to convey the pathology of crucifixion; he uses the same vocabulary as Hippocrates, Dioscurides, Galen, Aretæus, and other ancient physicians, and he uses it with professional skill. St. John records details that affirm that he really did see Jesus's crucifixion, although his account sounds as if he hadn't seen many others—which makes sense, given that he was the youngest and gentlest of the Apostles.

But the significance of these details has faded over the centuries. You can't really take artistic representations of the Crucifixion as conveying accurate information. Because crucifixion was the most shameful execution known, the early Christians were reluctant to depict it—representations like that would focus on the death of their leader, not his resurrection, and his death was not the point that the early Church wanted to make. So, for the first three or four hundred years of the Church's life, the Crucifixion was virtually never depicted. The Lamb or the Fish stood as the Church's primary symbol, not the Cross.

In life as in symbolism, the Church abhorred crucifixion; Christianity could not tolerate so cruel a penalty for anybody. So, in the first piece of social legislation that the Church was able to achieve, Constantine the Great abolished it in the fourth century. But this meant that people soon forgot how to represent one of the crucial events—literally, *the* crucial event—of Christian history. It took about two hundred years after Constantine's abolition before the shame and horror of the penalty faded enough for the event to be frankly represented in Christian art, and by then people had forgotten the details entirely.

Nobody who has ever designed a crucifix has seen a person crucified (which is itself a testimony to the efficacy of the religion). So, although some crucifixes depict wounds and suffering in vivid detail that can only be called excruciating, virtually none depicts those sufferings with complete accuracy. The truth is much worse than artistic imagination has ever been able to invent.

After the *patibulatus* carried the crosspiece of his cross out to the field of execution, he'd be attached to it with ropes or with nails—hence the term *crucifixio*, from *crux*, cross, and *figo*, to affix. Then he'd be hauled up so that the *patibulum* could be fastened to the *stipes*. We tend to think of the two pieces being mortised into each other to form a familiar Latin-cross shape (†). More probably the Roman army carpenters, with hundreds and thousands of crosses to make, didn't bother with that kind of fancy joinery. They probably just fixed a peg in the top of the *stipes* and bored a hole in the *patibulum*; that would make it easier to assemble the cross in a single motion, and it would make the weight of the crossbeam and the crucified man hold the cross together; it would result in a shape like the Greek letter *tau* (T).

Either way, the sufferings of the crucified are almost beyond imagination. Some modern surgeons and pathologists have researched the matter, delving into archæological records, patristic writings, the classics, and the Gospels themselves, and some have even done studies with cadavers. But most of the details of crucifixion emerge clearly if you just spend some time thinking about what must have happened. And thinking about these episodes in Christ's life is precisely what the Rosary is all about.

Remember first of all that even before crucifixion itself, the condemned man was always scourged, and always with the *flagellum*. The loss of blood and trauma of flagellation drastically weakened him, and his sure and detailed knowledge of what would happen to him at the field of crosses certainly caused stress that not even informed meditation on the Agony in the Garden can quite grasp. There was also the exertion of carrying the *patibulum* across the city to the killing field. If the Roman soldiers had not known, by horrible practice, exactly when to withhold the whip, and exactly when to relieve the condemned man of his load (Mt 27:32), no one would have survived these preliminary tortures. Yet they were only preliminaries.

It may not be immediately apparent to us nowadays, but simply having the wrists tied to the *patibulum* with ropes is enough to kill a person. Obviously, when the hands are held above the head, the heart has to work far harder than usual to keep blood supplied to them. That's an additional stress, particularly for a person lacerated by the whip. This cardiac stress isn't enough to kill a person, but having the entire weight of the body suspended from the hands makes breathing impossible.

Normally, of course, inward breathing happens when the muscles of the diaphragm contract, pulling air into the lungs; when those muscles relax, the air is pushed out without any real effort, mainly by the elasticity of the muscles of the thorax and the lungs themselves. But this kind of suspension causes cramps, spasmodic contractions of the muscles of the thorax; and because the body is stretched out that way, the muscles in spasm can't relax. So a person simply suspended with his arms above his head can't exhale. Crucified people suffocate. And they suffocate very slowly.

When this form of punishment was reinvented in the First World War, miscreants were left with their arms tied above their heads so that their toes barely touched the ground, but not for more than about ten minutes. Almost immediately, the cramping set in; the victims would begin to writhe, to try to pull themselves upward so that their thorax muscles could relax and let them gasp for air, but, already short of oxygen, they could not. They turned first red and then purple, and finally blue, as they progressively asphyxiated. At that point, they were cut down, during the First World War, their panic and distress being regarded as sufficient punishment.

But in Hitler's camps a decade later people were suspended with their toes above the ground until they died. The executioners of Dachau, for instance, tied weights to the feet so that the victims couldn't pull themselves up to get a breath of air. After three or four minutes, they'd lift the weights, allowing the victim to take in a quick gasp. This way, the Nazis prolonged the torture for only a few hours; but if, like the victims of Roman-style crucifixion with ropes, those crucified at Dachau had been able to shift their weight around by pushing against ropes on their legs, they might gasp for enough breath to keep themselves alive for as long as three days.

The Romans evidently didn't accelerate death on the cross with weights on the feet, but they invented the breaking of the legs, the *crurifragium* (Latin *crur-*, leg, and *frangere*, to break), which made it impossible for the rope-crucified victim to lift himself even briefly to relieve the stretching of his arms so that he could gasp for air. His lower body was then just dead weight, having the same effect as weights strung from sound limbs. But whether the rope-crucified person hangs immobile for a few hours or writhing for a few days, the general lack of oxygen in the blood inevitably makes waste products build up in the muscles all over the body, and the cramping paralysis gets worse and worse anyway, until the victim can't shift his weight any more.

At Dachau, after only about an hour of unrelieved hanging by the hands, the jerky pulls upward became involuntary as the muscles went into final spasm; the legs hung blue and useless, because the victims couldn't move them any more. The chest was expanded far more than usual, and the pit of the stomach was sucked in deeply. Finally the skin all over the body—which could be seen because the Nazis were no less likely to shame their victims by nakedness than the Romans were—turned a deep violet color, and sweat poured copiously from every pore, puddling on the concrete below. None of the weighted victims of this crucifixion without nails lived more than three hours in this position.

The spasms and paralysis that suffocate people suspended in this position indicate that the manacles still hanging high in some mediæval dungeons are a mode of execution, not of imprisonment. During the

Reformation, a good many martyrs, such as Bl. John Rochester and Bl. James Walworth, were just suspended this way in chains and left to suffocate, suffering just as crucified people suffer even if they're only tied to the cross.

In Roman times, though, some of the condemned men were roped and others nailed, and it made a terrible difference. Josephus records that he saw three of his friends being led to crucifixion during the siege of Jerusalem in 70 AD, when the Temple was destroyed. He ran out to the Roman camp and, being a co-operator with the Romans, used his influence to get them pardoned. He rushed to the Place of the Skull to have them taken down from their crosses. One of them who had been roped to his cross was revived on the spot, but it was already too late for the others. They had been nailed to theirs.

Presumably, the two thieves crucified that same Good Friday were roped; otherwise, they would not have been able to talk long enough to mock him (Mt 27:44; Lk 23:39-43). But Christ was nailed. Nailing a person to a cross was something of a specialty for the Roman legionaries, one in which they had considerable practice. They knew precisely where to set the nails, and exactly what kind of nail to use. Most crucifixes show the nail going through the palm of the hand, but obviously that wouldn't work; the weight of the body would simply tear the hand through, splitting it up to the fingers, and the man would fall forward.

The Romans put the nail instead through the wrist, just at the hollow where the two bones of the forearm, the ulna and the radius, come together in a kind of gothic arch, piercing straight through the process known as Destot's space. That puts the whole support of the body on that mass of bone and tendon that shapes the wrist and the heel of the hand. It locks the nail into the skeleton, although it breaks no bones (Ex 12:46; Nm 9:12; Ps 33:21). And it severs all, or most, of those veins that pass through the wrist, but it doesn't cut any important arteries; bleeding would be serious, of course, but not quickly fatal.

So a person hung on a cross by nails in the wrists is doomed for several reasons. Mere suspension in that position would cause cramps leading to fatal asphyxia; his heart, already stressed by the loss of blood and trauma of the scourging, would be unable to maintain circulation to his elevated limbs, and even as it tried to do so it would only be pumping his lifeblood out through his pierced wrists.

Beyond even that, the nails in the wrists cut the median nerves, which are not just motor nerves, the kind that induce motion in muscles. They're also sensory nerves, trunks of feeling that branch out to the hands and fingers, some of the most sensitive tactile tissues of the body. Crucifixion does not feel simply like stepping on a nail; those nails, punctured through the body with the blows of heavy hammers, break the nerves themselves, opening the sensations to an entirely different order of pain, pain removed from the mere mechanical discomfort of the flesh to an amplified, pure, and oceanic searing that might only be compared to electrocution by tens of thousands of volts; and electrocution moreover that lasts hours or days at that same lightning pitch.

Every time the victim tried to move, to shift his weight from his wounded wrists to his wounded feet and gasp for air, the nails—forged square because that takes less effort—would grind into his bones, pressing upon, and tearing, the severed ends of those nerve trunks, blood vessels, and tendons all the more. The nails in the feet themselves made it nearly impossible for the victim to shift his weight anyway. There really is no arch in the foot that's parallel to the arch of bone in the wrist; the only place to put a nail is straight through the top of the foot.

So the Roman executioners seem to have simply bent the knees to force the feet flat against the *stipes* and then hammered them down—the little foot-ledge usually shown on crucifixes is a mediæval invention, put there because people after Constantine's day had forgotten how crucifixion worked. The more the victim tried to bear his weight on his feet the more he would tear his feet. And the more they would bleed—largely blood from the veins that would pool in the lower legs, which, being paralyzed by cramps brought on by lack of oxygen, could no longer return it to the heart.

Crucifixion by nails was an unspeakably agonizing death, but it was not nearly so slow as crucifixion by rope. Certainly, no man could endure that kind of crucifixion for more than about three or four hours, and all existing records testify that no one ever did. The *crurifragium*, in fact, was never necessary for a man crucified by nails. Writhing to shift the weight and gasp for air only made death come faster. Naked, beaten nearly to death, crowned with thorns, and mocked by the same crowd that had hailed him as King of the Jews only days before, Jesus of Nazareth hung nailed to his cross, twisting in torment and gasping for air for three long hours before he died.

Even when they knew that the victim was dead, the Romans never failed to perform another procedure: the law of executions required that the crucified be given a final wound to the heart, a *coup de grâce* that ensured death. The heart is on the left, of course, but the soldier stood on the victim's right; and he pierced a lance straight through the side of the victim until he was sure that he had stabbed through the heart. He could do this almost horizontally, and without much inconvenience, because crosses weren't normally all that tall, probably only six and a half to seven feet.

The extra stab of this *percussus*, this blow, was the Roman equivalent of the extra gunshot in the ear administered to persons shot by firing squads;

it's given not because of need but for the sake of certainty, whether there's any doubt of death or not. In the case of Jesus, the soldier saw that he was already dead, but he did his duty anyway (Jn 19:33-34). And the issue of water with the blood is consistent with piercing the pericardium, the membranous sac filled with lymphatic fluid, that surrounds the heart. Blood alone would have indicated that the *percussus* had not penetrated enough to pierce the heart; but blood and water meant that the heart had unquestionably been pierced, and that the man was dead.

All of this Mary watched, standing at the foot of the Cross while her only son died; "he offered a single sacrifice in union with her," St. Louis-Marie Grignion de Montfort wrote, "and was immolated to the Eternal Father with her consent, as Isaac was once immolated to the divine will with the consent of Abraham" (*True Devotion*; *cf.* Jn 19:25; Gn 22:1-10).

More than that, more than the unspeakable horror of seeing her son sacrificed, Mary had to watch him insulted at every step of the way. The soldiers who beat him mocked him as well, in addition to executing the sentence; the people who had welcomed him as King in triumph insulted him, spat upon him, and jeered at him even in his death throes. They added insult to those injuries of the Cross by offering him, under pretext of assuaging his thirst, a drink of wine mixed with myrrh or gall (Mt 27:34; Mr 15:23).

> Myrrh, even with wine, wouldn't do anything to relieve the pain of a crucified man, and the Jews of Christ's day knew it. It's a bitter resin that comes from a small tree that grows in the Levant, *Balsamodendron myrrha*. In ancient times, it was prescribed for disorders of the reproductive organs, and it has always been used to relieve the griping and gas pains caused by some purgatives like aloes. But its very name is synonymous with bitterness—it comes from the Hebrew root מר (mr), which means exactly that.
>
> Gall is the yellow bile secreted by the liver and stored in the gall bladder. It's extracted from beeves, sheep, or other animals. Like myrrh, and like the wormwood (*Artemisia absinthum*) that's often mentioned with it (Dt 29:17; Lm 3:19), gall is extremely bitter. The Jews applied it topically for some medicinal uses (Tb 6:5), and until the early years of this century it was listed in medical books under its Latin name, *fel bovis*, as a tonic and laxative.

This combination of the two most bitter things the Jews knew was intended as an insult (Mt 27:39, 48-49; Lk 23:36-37). Its administration to Jesus fulfills prophecies like Ps 68:22 where, as everywhere else in the Old

Testament, gall symbolizes the bitterness of punishment for sins (*cf.* Dt 29:18; Jr 8:14). And it points to his own prophecy, in Mt 26:39.

Even after her son died before her eyes, Mary's sorrows were not quite over. The Roman practice was to leave the bodies hanging on the crosses on the blood-field outside the city, a final disgrace that was considered part of the punishment. They even made the crosses comparatively short so that dogs, wolves, and other beasts could tear the bodies to pieces in contention with the carrion birds that flocked around these hideous forests of crosses.

But the Old Law was hedged in with countless regulations about the disposal of the dead because bodies were ritually unclean and had to be handled accordingly (Nm 5:1-2, 19:11-22); and for any dead person, even an executed criminal, to remain unburied and exposed overnight was considered a great disgrace (4Kn 9:10; Ps 78:3; Jr 14:16; Dt 21:22-23).

In fact, the very first crucifixion mentioned in the Bible, the execution of the king of Hai related in the Book of Josue, shows that even in that case Josue would not permit the body to remain exposed overnight, but had let it hang on a cross only until evening (Js 8:29), at which time he ordered the body taken down, thrown on the ground, and covered with a heap of stones—a disgraceful burial, but a burial nonetheless.

Leaving a body exposed overnight was a great reproach to those who let such a thing happen and, on the other hand, burying those who had no other family to bury them was a great work of mercy, a sacred duty (Tb 1:20-21, 2:3-9), and so was providing for those whose families could not attend to them (Gn 23:4-11; Mt 27:57-61). So the Israelites hastened to get the bodies off of the crosses and buried before the end of the day, sunset.

To avoid the final disgrace prescribed by Roman practice, the Israelites took advantage of an easement in Roman law. "The bodies of the executed," the ancient law compiled in the *Digest* of Ulpian specifies, "shall not be buried unless permission has been asked and has been granted", so the Israelites simply took advantage of this policy and asked for the bodies of the crucified. For their part, the Romans usually accommodated Jewish law by releasing the condemned dead for burial before sunset of the day they died—*percussos sepeliri carnifex non vetat*, "the executioner doesn't prohibit the burial of those who have been struck with the *percussus*", Quintilian wrote in the first century.

In fact, that final mercy is why the Israelites asked Pilate to have the legs of the thieves broken (Jn 19:31-32). And although that same law quoted by Ulpian notes that permission was sometimes refused, "particularly for the bodies of persons condemned for the crime of treason," Pilate hadn't found any fault in Jesus (Jn 18:39, 19:6), and, judging from the Gospel accounts, he must certainly have regretted the whole chain of events. So when Joseph of Aramathea, in accordance with custom and with the Law, plucked up his courage and asked for Christ's body (Mt 27:57-58; Mr 15:43; *cf.* Philo Judæus, *On Governor Flaccus*), Pilate confirmed that the *percussus* had been delivered (Mr 15:44-45) and released the body.

Although the practice of crucifixion was abolished by the early fourth century, Sacred Tradition preserved a surprising amount of information about Christ's death through the centuries. Just as St. Vincent de Lérins knew about the *pileus*-shaped Crown of Thorns, St. Augustine and the other Fathers of the Church knew that the wound to the heart was inflicted from the right, although most people would assume that it was from the left, and it's represented on the right in most crucifixes and crucifixion scenes, and in images of the resurrected Christ. The Church's great mystics have often been favored with visions and infused knowledge about the Passion that are confirmed by pathologists' experiments centuries later—Julian of Norwich, for example, saw the face of Christ turning different colors as he slowly suffocated, although until the sad days of our own century nobody knew that this was a symptom of the torment that crucified people endure.

But no record of the details of Christ's suffering and death is more detailed or more accurate than the image and the bloodstains on the length of linen cloth known as the Holy Shroud of Turin. It, too, shows the wound to the heart on the right, but it carries accurate information far beyond that. Nobody knew until experiments with cadavers in the middle of this century, for instance, that nails in the wrists lock the thumbs across the palms in a way impossible in a healthy hand, but the Shroud shows that this happened to the man whose imprint it bears. In fact, the information on the Shroud has been confirmed to a microscopic level, in terms of the pattern of the wounds, the pathology of the torture, and even the chemical nature of the bloodstains that the Passion left behind.

It's also interesting, from the standpoint of prophecy, that the first crucified person mentioned in the Bible is a king. And it's no wonder that so many of the great saints, meditating on the death inflicted upon Christ, have collapsed in the most abject tears.

There are still one or two details recounted in the Gospels that cause a certain amount of confusion. One is Christ's perceived despair on the Cross, when he cried out, "My God, my God, why hast thou forsaken me?" (Mt 27:34-36). Some of the bystanders didn't understand the reference then, and, in the centuries since, many a pious tract has been spun out to explain how this indicates that not even Christ himself could maintain his certainty of God's goodness while on the Cross.

But that's a flatly incorrect, even ridiculous, topic for a discussion of Christian principles. A better familiarity with Scripture, or indeed the cross-references in a good Bible, would reveal that this cry is the first verse of the great Psalm of prophecy, which today is numbered 21. The Evangelists, the Fathers of the Church, and the Church as a whole have always understood what Christ meant by quoting that particular verse, out of all of the things that he could possibly have said at that moment.

Because schools taught children how to read—Hebrew, Greek, or Latin—by having them memorize the Book of Psalms, quoting the first verse, or really any verse, of any psalm is a universal and age-old way to remind educated people of the whole psalm. That's why so many psalmodic verses turned into proverbs in their own right, and why public and private devotions so often include only one or two verses of Psalms interspersed between the principle divisions of the texts.

It's the same with other quotations—the brief readings at Mass, for instance, are supposed to put you in mind of the whole contexts in which they occur, and to prompt to you study those longer passages, to think about them, and to study how they relate to other parts of Scripture. Certainly a single verse of Psalms is really all that's needed to convey the whole psalm to people, so whenever you find one cited—even in this book—it's a good idea to study the whole psalm in which it appears.

The psalm of which Christ reminded us in his distress is the most detailed psalmodic prediction of the Passion. It made more sense to the Evangelists after the Crucifixion, and it makes more sense to us now, than it could have to David when he wrote it and to those who heard him sing it. Because it compresses so many facts about the Crucifixion, the Son of David quoted it, as best he could under that torture, but sufficiently for it to echo from age to age. It was another way for Christ to remind those who hear him that this day this Scripture is fulfilled before them (Lk 4:16-21).

His intention in crying out this way should be forever clear, too, because while hanging on the Cross he also quoted—loudly—a verse from Psalm 30, which is not only a prayer for aid in distress but a song of absolute confidence in God's justice and thanksgiving for escape: Into your hands I commend my spirit (Ps 30:6; Mt 27:50; Mr 15:37; Lk 23:46).

THE GLORIOUS MYSTERIES

G LORIOUS MYSTERIES ARE THE KEY EVENTS in Christ's triumph over sin and death, as well as his fulfillment of his promises with regard to Mary, who passed early through the sequence of events that Christ promised for the happy souls after death. The first Glorious Mystery is the Resurrection, celebrated liturgically at Easter, the greatest holy day of the year; its solemnity takes place on the first Sunday after the first full Moon after the vernal equinox. The Easter season continues, liturgically, through the feasts of the next two Mysteries, the Ascension (celebrated forty days after Easter) and Pentecost (fifty days after Easter). The fourth and fifth Glorious Mysteries are the Assumption (August 15) and the Coronation of Mary as Queen of Heaven, which is commemorated on the memorial of the Queenship of Mary, August 22.

A ❀ Ω

THE RESURRECTION

C HRIST'S RESURRECTION FROM THE DEAD IS THE SUPREME EVENT IN Christianity; it's the capstone of everything that Christ taught. Without it, Christianity would make no sense (1Cr 15:14). Because the Resurrection is so central to the Gospels and the Epistles, and because each book of the New Testament takes its facts from various witnesses to make various points, it may be difficult to see an overall structure for the sequence of events. Yet all of the details come together into a coherent narrative.

One outline that would bring all of the accounts together would begin probably just after midnight—a point of Tradition that seems to signify that Jesus stayed among the dead only as long as necessary to touch that third day, and arose quickly to be with his loved ones again (*cf.* Ps 118:62; Jg 16:3; Mt 28:9). The minute the prophecies were fulfilled, Christ arose. He left his shroud (a long linen cloth about fourteen feet long, laid under the body, folded over the head, and laid over the top of the body) lying empty, flat on the ground, which indicates that his body had left it without touching it (Jn 20:6-9). Then he folded the cloth that had been tied around his head to keep the jaw from falling open, put it to one side, and came out of the tomb.

Mary Magdalen, Mary of Cleophas (the mother of James), and Salome— not the one who danced before Herod (Mt 14:6)—started out from Jerusalem before dawn, with the spices and other supplies that they need- ed to complete the burial ritual, which had been abbreviated because of the approaching Sabbath (Mr 15:42; Lk 23:54-24:2). They didn't know about the guards, and they weren't sure who would roll back the stone for them (Mt 28:1; Mr 16:1-3; Lk 24:1; Jn 20:1).

Either before Christ left the tomb, just after, or just before the women arrived, an angel dazzled the guards by his brightness, put them to flight, and opened the tomb; then he sat himself above the stone—not on it (ἐπ᾿ αὐτοῦ), but above it (ἐπάνω αὐτοῦ; Mt 28:2-4).

The women arrived just after dawn and saw the stone rolled back (Mr 16:4; Lk 24:2; Jn 20:1). Mary Magdalen ran back to the Apostles to tell them. The other women entered the tomb and heard the angel tell them what had happened; he told them also to go back and tell Peter and the others that they would see Jesus in Galilee (Mt 28:5-7; Mr 16:5-7). At this point, appar- ently, a second group of women, including Joanna and her companions, arrived at the sepulchre; two angels told them that Jesus had risen, as he had said he would (Lk 24:10).

Soon after that, Peter and John arrived, having been told by Mary

Magdalen but not having believed her. They found the cloths, and when John saw them he understood what it all meant (Jn 20:3-10). Mary Magdalen arrived again at the tomb just after that; she saw the two angels and then Christ himself (Mr 16:9; Jn 20:11-17). The other women saw Christ, too, and he told them to inform the others that they would see him in Galilee (Mt 28:8-10; Mr 16:8-11). But when the women did this, the Apostles didn't believe them (Mr 16:10-11; Lk 24:9-11).

Jesus then appeared to two disciples, one of whom is Cleophas, and to Peter himself, but the others still didn't believe (Mr 16:12-13; Lk 24:13-35). But after Peter, John, Cleophas, and all of the others except Thomas had gathered together, Jesus came to them and demonstrated his bodily resurrection to them (Mr 16:14; Lk 24:36-43; Jn 20:19-25). After that, he was seen and heard preaching by at least five hundred people (1Cr 15:1-6). Then he was seen by James and then by all of the apostles, however many they were at the time (1Cr 15:7; Lk 10:1-17; *cf.* Mt 4:23-25, 13:1-2, 14:13-21, etc.).

As an historical fact, Christ's resurrection can't be ignored; all philosophies, all avenues of thought about life in general, have to confront it, at some point, which is really not the case with any other fact of his life on Earth. The facts of his birth, his teachings, and even his death can be rejected, and their significance can be evaded, because everybody is born, many teach, and all die; but his resurrection is not so easily put aside. Every detail in the Gospels affirms the facts of his bodily death and his bodily resurrection.

He had been in the tomb three days; we don't count time as the Hebrews did but, as St. Ignatius of Antioch explained it on his way to the lions of the Coliseum, "The day of the preparation comprises the Passion; the Sabbath embraces the burial; the Lord's Day contains the Resurrection" (*Epistle to the Trallians*). A man crowned with thorns, flogged without the protective benefits of Roman citizenship, and then crucified could have no spark of life in him, but even if he did he would still bleed to death, suffocate, or simply die of shock locked in a tomb that long. Christ was not in a coma; the nails and the lance to the heart make a coma impossible, but even a man in a coma with those wounds would not survive.

Nor were the witnesses ignorant; they were soldiers, executioners, and people who had seen hundreds, perhaps thousands, of crucifixions that were designed, from long experience, to ensure death many times over. If there were no Gospels at all, if there were only those few passing remarks in the works of Roman historians that state that Jesus of Nazareth was crucified and the accounts that tell what crucifixion was, it would be enough. He was dead.

But on that third day he arose from the dead; he was alive again. Just as the details of his execution preclude any end short of death, so the details of his emergence preclude anything like a merely natural recovery. A man simply recovering from intense trauma could hardly crawl out of his tomb, much less open it; and if he were found still alive he would still need intense care—like the friends of Josephus who hadn't even been nailed— and many months of recovery. Jesus needed none. He immediately walked, spoke, and taught coherently, and he even ran (Mt 28:9; the Vulgate has *occurrit*, "he ran toward them"). His was not a recovery from wounds, but a recovery from death.

There were other prodigies, too, such as an earthquake (Mt 28:2), that might be relegated by skeptics to the purely natural order. But Jesus of Nazareth didn't arise from the dead alone. As he had revived Lazarus after four days, he brought back any number of other people, too, some of whom had been dead for years (Mt 27:52)—among them, early Christian writings say, Simeon and his sons. When Christ himself rose, the fact of it was seen by too many people to be dismissed; the truth of his teachings couldn't be denied.

L ooking at it with a cold eye, the New Testament might be dismissed as the assertions of interested parties *ex post facto*. But Christians had no control over what the prophets had written and taught in the millennia before them. Virtually every historical account in the Old Testament prefigures the rising of the Messiah from the dead as it foreshadows the resurrection of his Faithful; and virtually every prophecy proclaims the Resurrection that was to come. Nor can it be asserted that you can go back after the fact and make prophecy say anything that you like: the prophecies of the Old Testament don't talk about anything else. The Resurrection is closely integrated with the rest of revelation not only in prophecy but in historic prefigurations and in the miracles that Christ himself performed as well.

The Resurrection is the final accomplishment of every promise of salvation, the ones made to Adam and Eve (Gn 3), Abraham (Gn 12, 15; Ac 3:25-26; Hb), David (Ac 2:30-31), and all of the patriarchs. As a promise of the general bodily resurrection of the Faithful, it's presumed by Job (19:25-27), by the Machabees (2Mc 7:11, 12:43), and by Daniel (12:2) and Ezekiel, in his vision of the dry bones (37:1-14). In fact, most of the prophets speak of it in advance, from the moment that death becomes Man's lot, as the wage of sin. Isaia is incomprehensible unless the Messiah, and his Faithful, are to die and then rise from the dead (Is 42-53, 26:19); so are Psalms (26:13), even those that speak of the Messiah's death. They, too, make no sense unless followed by the Messiah's triumph over that death, and over death in general (1Cr 15:12-28).

The Resurrection of Christ also makes sense of the historical prefigurations in the Old Testament—all of the resurrections recounted in the Old Testament point to the physical reality of the teaching. Joseph is cast into a well and delivered, and later locked in prison only to be elevated to the right hand of Pharaoh (Gn 37:1-36, 39:21-23, 40:1-41:46); Jeremia is brought forth from the dungeon and from the cistern wrapped in linen (Jr 37:1-38:13). Daniel is sealed into the lions' den (for simply adhering to the Faith), and then escapes the jaws of death, brought out to counsel the King (Dn 6:2-29). David escaped the soldiers of Saul by leaving a dummy behind in his bed (1Kn 19:11-16), returning later as King himself. Jona lay three days in the whale and then came forth to preach judgement (Jo 2:1-3:10), which example Christ applied to himself (Mt 12:40).

Early events in Christ's own life prefigure the Resurrection, too; his birth in the stable-cave where he lay, wrapped in linen (Lk 2:7), his recovery from the Temple on the third day (Lk 2:46)—even the Circumcision prefigures survival of a blood sacrifice. The actual bodily resurrections that he performed, like raising the widow's son (Lk 7:11-17) and the daughter of Jairus (Mr 5:40), elevated the prophetic episodes to a higher level, fulfilling those performed by the prophets (3Kn 17:17-24; 4Kn 4:8-37). Unlike the prophetic revivifications, but like the evangelical accounts of the Resurrection itself, Christ's resurrections of the dead are presented in sufficient detail to preclude coma or other insensibility absolutely, and Christ performed them in such a way that they would prefigure his own Resurrection with some precision. In fact, his resurrection of Lazarus demonstrated almost exactly what was to happen at his own resurrection, with some significant differences.

Lazarus was in the tomb four days, Christ three. Either length of time is enough to make survival impossible, but the body of Lazarus had already begun to decay (Jn 11:39), and Christ's body didn't (Ac 2:23-27, 13:35-37; Ps 15:10). Like all of the other people whose resurrection from the dead is recorded in Scripture, Lazarus died again; but Christ rose glorified, as the Just will arise on the Last Day (Cl 1:18; 1Cr 15:20), to everlasting life. It took some effort to open the tomb of Lazarus (Jn 11:41), but, of course, the stone sealing Christ's tomb was rolled back without human intervention.

Lazarus emerged bound hand and foot with bandages, and with a cloth tied around his face (Jn 11:44). Jews of the time were buried that way, with their wrists and their ankles tied together with strips of cloth to keep the limbs from moving during and after *rigor mortis*, and with a kind of kerchief around the chin to keep the jaw shut; they were laid then on half of a strip of linen about twelve feet long and three feet wide, which was then doubled, coming over the head and down to the feet. All of these cloths, of course, are accounted for in the Gospels as left behind in the tomb when

THE RESURRECTION

Christ arose (Jn 20:6-7; Lk 24:12), a detail that was prefigured by the priest-ly garments of the Old Covenant (Ex 28:39, 29:21, 34:29-35; Lv 16:4, 23) and by St. Mark's own experience at Jesus's arrest (Mr 14:50-52), and that itself prefigures Christ's own return (Rv 19:11-14).

The Resurrection is the principal—the only—object of the message of sal-vation in the Bible, prophetically and historically, and it's really the point of everything in Scripture, the keystone of the plan of salvation outlined in every book since Genesis. The need to testify to this single fact is the motive of the Book of Acts; it's the central point of the Epistles, and with-out it the Gospels themselves would be an empty promise.

That's why the most astonishing thing about the Resurrection is that the Apostles themselves didn't understand it; they thought that the women were talking nonsense (Lk 24:11), and they didn't believe the two witness-es from Emmaus (Mr 16:9-13). Despite Jesus's own explanations in advance, they were appalled and, certainly, their faith was sorely tried when he was taken and killed, as any common traitor could be killed.

After all, people generally expected the Messiah to establish his tri-umphant kingdom on Earth at once, when he came; and there had been others in the Apostles' lifetime who had seemed to be the Messiah but were killed, their movements snuffed out with them. None had ever been reported to rise from the dead and resume his teaching. It was not some-thing that people expected (Jn 20:9).

But after the Resurrection, after Christ's own fuller explanation of prophecy (Lk 24:13-27), the Old Testament fell into perspective. That's why time and again the Church adds the phrase "in fulfillment of the Scriptures" when she mentions the Resurrection (1Cr 15:4); look to Scriptures, she says, if you want to understand, just as Christ himself said (Mt 21:42; Jn 5:39).

And it's why the resurrection of Christ is a kind of watershed in the New Testament as a whole. Before it, the Apostles speak of the Kingdom of God to come, but after it they speak of that Kingdom achieved. They speak of the risen Christ.

I f the Resurrection is acknowledged as true, then its obvious implica-tion—that Christianity and Christianity alone is true—has to be con-fronted, and other systems of thought about the meaning of life are hard pressed to stand up against it. The historical reality of the Resurrection, once fully realized, compels a person to give up trying to integrate religion into his life, and to start the struggle to integrate his life into religion. That's not easy; and the difficulty of living in accordance with the Resurrection and all that it implies is undoubtedly why some people acknowledge that Jesus walked, talked, and taught after the Crucifixion and yet try to account for these facts in different ways that would accommodate the reality of the Resurrection and yet keep it from challenging any of their own beliefs and preferences.

Even the Apostles and the others who saw him in Jerusalem (Lk 24:36-43) tried to fit Christ's reappearance among them into some smaller frame of reference that wouldn't challenge the perspective to which they'd grown accustomed—they thought at first that they had seen a spirit. Ever since, there have been those who acknowledge that people saw and heard Christ after the Crucifixion but profess that the risen Christ was only an apparition, a ghost, or an angel whom God allowed to take the appearance of Christ.

Those schemes fall in self-contradiction, though. If Christ can come back as a ghost by his own power or show himself as an apparition when he wants to, then there seems to be no reason that he couldn't rise from the dead. If God can order an angel to manifest himself in the appearance of Christ, then, too, what theological system limits his power so that he can't revive the body of Christ, which is really the simplest explanation.

Besides, these positions are contradicted by the very texts that they take as evidence. If God formed Man from earth and breathed a soul into him, then he can certainly reunite a body and a soul that already exist (Gn 2:7; Acts 26:8). And Jesus demonstrated to them that his body was real, and that his soul was reunited to it. The witnesses didn't just see and hear him; they touched his body as he stood before them, beginning with Mary Magdalen. When she saw him and recognized him in the garden (Jn 20:11-17; cf. Mt 28:9), she evidently embraced him: "cease clinging to me," he said (in Greek, μή μου ἅπτου), which she could not have done to a phantom or an apparition.

The Gospels also recount the events surrounding the Resurrection with great attention to detail, telling exactly what the witnesses did and what they said, drawing their facts from testimony from people who saw Christ alive and teaching after the Resurrection (1Cr 15:6). Most compelling of all, they don't add anything. The easiest and least disputable way to assert anything is to claim that you saw it yourself; but none of the Gospels claims that anybody saw Christ at the moment of his resurrection. The very fact that none of the Evangelists ever claims that anybody saw him at the instant of his revivification argues for the truth of their accounts. But the fact that none of the writers claims to be an eyewitness of the event does not mean that all of the evidence is circumstantial.

Circumstantial evidence consists of facts that are consistent with the proposed chain of events but don't directly prove it. The material facts related in the Gospels—leaving aside the angels and other events of the supernatural order—present the Resurrection as an inferential fact, which means that if these accounts are factual then the bodily resurrection of Jesus of Nazareth must also be factual. In the broadest and simplest terms, he was dead when he was buried, and three days later he was alive again, in the flesh. Obviously, between the two events, there was resurrection.

I n Apostolic days as now, acceptance of the fact of the bodily resurrection of Jesus of Nazareth split the world into two opposing camps. Many of the people who believed it were Pharisees, and Christ's expectations of them was apparently why he went to such lengths to correct them (Mt 23:1-31); he never spoke so specifically or so much to any other group. They were in a position to understand the meaning of his return from the dead; they were the strictest sect (Ac 26:5), the majority party who maintained the whole of revelation to the Jews.

They respected Tradition, the "Oral Torah", as inseparable from the written Torah (Mt 23:2); they credited prophecy and the promise of individual salvation for those faithful to the Covenant; and they understood bodily resurrection of the dead as an integral part of the plan of salvation. Lazarus and his family, like most of those who followed Christ when he walked among us, were Pharisees (Jn 11:23-27), and it was this understanding of the Messiah's purpose that brought so many of the Jews into the Church just after the Resurrection.

Of course, the Pharisees weren't easy to convince, but those among them who opposed Christ (Mt 9:11, 12:2, 14, etc.) didn't dispute that the Messiah was to make possible bodily resurrection of the Faithful. They just questioned whether Jesus of Nazareth was that Messiah, which is why they pestered him with questions and why, ultimately, some of them resisted the Christian movement as vigorously as they could (Jn 12:42-43).

The other party, the Sadducees, refused to believe either the resurrection of Jesus or the whole principle of resurrection in the Covenant (Mt 22:23; Lk 20:27). They were the minority party, the party of the powerful and the rich; they controlled the administration of the Temple and of the state, and they were the ones who eventually put Jesus to death (Mt 26:57-68). Taking a more liberal view of religion, they dropped many of the teachings of the prophets one by one, and many of the requirements of those teachings. By the time of Christ they denied Tradition entirely, holding only to the written Torah, and they considered the mandated sacrifices and observances of the Temple as merely symbolic and more or less optional.

So, when Jesus's resurrection became known, the Sadducees in power did everything that they could to preserve their positions and authority, but the Pharisees converted in their thousands. That left basically the Sadducees as the remnant of Judaism. They determined the character of modern Judaism, which is profoundly different from Judaism before Christ. Resurrection to everlasting life for the Faithful of the Covenant is either ignored or relegated to minor importance for most Jews today, and, not surprisingly, Jewish texts that mention the Resurrection of Christ frankly label it a myth, as do any number of latter-day academic studies. Resurrection myths do occur in a lot of religions around the world, but this isn't one of them.

Myths are different in substance from the accounts in the Gospels, the Epistles (which in fact are older than the Gospels), and Acts. Myths use highly symbolic language to explain recurring natural events. The resurrection of Osiris and Adonis, or the return of Persephone from the underworld, are figurative accounts of the yearly seasons of generation in the Spring. They start with an observed natural phenomenon and then construct a story to account for it.

A myth never really leaves its connection to some recurring process in nature; they're not talking about the man but about the phenomenon, illustrated as a fictitious man. "Whenever Spring drives Winter out, each year when Ram succeeds to Fish," Ovid wrote to explain where hyacinths come from, "he comes to life again and sprouts to blossom on the sward of green, this Hyacinthus", and then he relates the myth of how the friend of Apollo was accidentally killed and how his blood was transformed into the springtime flower (*Metamorphoses* 10:163-219). His poem is not directed at explaining why Hyacinthus rose from the dead, and it doesn't claim that he did. It isn't about Hyacinthus at all; it's about flowers.

Christians sometimes use this phenomenon of annual regeneration as a metaphor for the resurrection of the dead (Mt 13:36-43; Jn 12:23-26), but this use of symbolic language works exactly in the opposite way from the way that the language of myth works. Christian symbolic rhetoric doesn't start with the progression of the seasons or anything else observed in nature and then develop a symbolic account of it; it starts with a promise of something that is not observed in nature—something moreover that's contrary to the observed natural order—and then strives to convey that idea by reminding people of something that they see around them. Christian tracts comparing bodily resurrection to seeds lying dormant in the ground and then bursting forth with new life aren't intended to explain why seeds sprout, but to illustrate a truth about the supernatural order. They're parables, never stated as anything other than a metaphor. But the New Testament proclaims the Resurrection without metaphor, without figurative language, and without hesitancy, in detail as a material event that occurred at a specific time and place. They testify to it as to a fact. And, unlike the mythic accounts of annual revivification, they testify to Christ's resurrection as a fact that happened only once.

So, intellectually as well as historically, it's more valid to reject the Gospels completely as fabrications than to classify them as myths, because structurally and rhetorically they are not myths. It's the same with Christianity itself, the religion established on the Resurrection as a fact; it's not like the pagan cults founded on the myths about Osiris or Adonis or Persephone. Those cults have to do with the generative power that shows itself in Spring, and usually the generative power of human sexuality; so they were structurally and substantively different from Christianity, a religion of salvation that looks beyond the natural order of this life and beyond Time itself to everlasting life in a resurrected body.

For that matter, pre-Christian salvational cults like those of Hercules or of Isis didn't promise bodily resurrection of the dead; they either destroyed the body through cremation to release the spirit for disembodied life among the stars, or they preserved it so that the spirit could remain tied to it. Any way you look at it, the accounts of the Resurrection and the history of the religion that burst forth after it can't be relegated to the same shelf as myth and cult. They are of an entirely different order, and of an entirely different nature; and they're based on a certain historical fact.

The immediate results of the Resurrection are just as compelling as what was predicted and what happened immediately before it. There were those hundreds of people whose dead relatives rose, too (Mt 27:52), who could hardly deny the reality of the situation. But even in the natural order of things there is overwhelming testimony to the fact of the Resurrection.

For example, look at what happened to the Apostles themselves. Only three days before Christ rose, they had seen the whole nation of Israel turn into a mob that compelled the Roman governor to crucify Christ. Simply being known as his associate made them targets for execution, too (Mt 26:69-75; Jn 20:19). The false Messiahs had not gone to their crosses alone, and it was nothing exceptional for the Romans to crucify hundreds or even thousands of rebels. Not even the five hundred who saw and heard Jesus of Nazareth after that first Easter (1Cr 15:6) could stand against the whole state. Attesting to the Resurrection was certain suicide; nobody would stand forward to testify to it, in those circumstances—unless it was true.

The Apostles did attest to it, and so did the five hundred. They were transformed when the news of the Resurrection came to them, and when its implications sank in. Beyond that, they were able to transform the world itself, regenerating all nations with a dynamic religion that even today has that same power to change Man's heart and give meaning to his existence. The Resurrection of Jesus is the pivotal event in human history; even secular history shows that the world before that first Easter was an utterly different place from the world after it. No myth, no error, no deceit has ever been able to work that kind of change.

The reality of the Resurrection was so indisputable at the time that some of the Sadducees converted, too. But those who loved their positions struggled to suppress news of Christ's return from the dead even if they themselves believed it—after all, these were the same people who had plotted to kill Lazarus precisely because they knew that Jesus had raised him from the dead (Jn 12:9-11). Yet, in the end, the reaction to the Resurrection was a popular movement that left behind the sacrifices and ceremonies of the Temple, along with the whole hierarchy of the Levitical priesthood.

And even the opposition of the chief priests at the time gave unwitting confirmation of the fact of the Resurrection. Unable to ignore the evidence, unable to account for it otherwise, they simply bribed the guards—the only witnesses under their control—to change their stories (Mt 27:62-66, 28:11-15). It didn't work, of course, and, according to the Gospel of Nicodemus, when the guards later told the truth anyway, the Sadducees harangued the people not to believe them, "because we have given them money not to say such things."

The Gospel of Nicodemus also relates more details of what the guards said to the chief priests when they reported what had happened (*cf.* Mt 28:11-15). It was at midnight, the guards said, when the stone was rolled back by an angel, and when the women came. Why did you not lay hold of these women, and this young man—the one you called an angel, the priests asked. "We were like men dead from fear," the guards answered, "and not expecting to see the light of day; and how could we lay hold of them?" As the Lord lives, the priests said, we do not believe you.

The guards cited all of Jesus's miracles, but still the priests refused to admit what they must have already believed. So, the guards said, we know that you have locked up the man who begged the body of Jesus of Pilate, and put your seal upon the door, lest he come out and steal the body; and now you have opened that door, and found him gone. Do you then give us this man whom you were guarding, and we will give you Jesus whom we were guarding.

"Joseph has gone to Arimathea, to his own city," the priests grumbled.

"And Jesus has risen from the dead," the guards replied.

THE ASCENSION

SOME OF THE EVENTS OF CHRIST'S WORK ON EARTH HAVE TO DO WITH things that are beyond Earth. So do many of the prophecies that came before him, and many of the doctrinal statements that have clarified his teachings after him. These things of Heaven can't be captured in human language, because our language is confined to our three-dimensional world measured in the boxlike space of height, width, and breadth—or, really, in our four-dimensional world, which is trapped also in Time.

That's why the prophets so often spoke in highly symbolic language, and it's why Christ himself spoke in parables, *parabolæ*. Like the geometric figure that shares its name, a parable gets from one point to another, but it doesn't get there by a straight line.

The ineffability of the mysteries of the Faith is also why Christians have always expressed them visually. The silent communication of art gets to the point immediately, bypassing the limits of words altogether. And yet Christian art, like representational art always and everywhere, still operates according to an elevated form of those same mechanisms of grammar and rhetoric that shape human language. Mysteries that pierce the skies, those that open a view of Heaven to those of us on Earth, are really most clearly grasped in this wordless language of visual symbols; and, because everybody can understand the mechanisms by which they are formed, the visual arts are among the most effective aids to meditation. No Mystery of the Rosary illustrates this better than the Ascension.

On the fortieth day after his Resurrection, Christ went with his Disciples to a place outside of Jerusalem—Tradition says that it was the Mount of Olives, and naturally the Bible account is consistent with that (Ac 1:12). Then he returned to Heaven (Mr 16:19-20; Lk 24:51; Ac 1:1-12). He himself said that he would ascend to the Father after his Passion (Jn 6:63, 20:17), and the Epistles (Eph 4:8-10, 1Tm 3:16), as well as Sacred Tradition, affirm it as an historical fact. Still, it's an historical fact performed in a highly symbolic way, and it's recorded for us in highly symbolic language.

When Christ came back to the Apostles after his Resurrection, he didn't stay with them between visits; he left, somehow, but Scripture is silent on exactly when he left and exactly how. So when he wanted to convey to them the idea that he was departing until the end of Time, he had to arrange the event in a way that they—and people always and everywhere—would understand. This makes sense Scripturally, because God has always communicated to Man by shaping phenomena of the material world in ways that humans at that place and time can easily understand (Ex 19:16-19; Jb 36:29-33, 38:1-7; Mt 3:16). In fact, the language of the accounts in the Gospels indicate that his physical ascent is most interesting from a symbolic point of view.

All of the words that the Evangelists chose indicate that Jesus of Nazareth, risen from the dead, ascended bodily upward; the accounts say that the witnesses, astonished even after all of the astonishing things that Christ had done, stood staring after him into the sky (Ac 1:9-11). But the words used to describe the event itself also have rich figurative associations that bring out the full significance of this levitation.

St. Luke uses the word ἀναφέρειν, which is more usually used in the Septuagint—the Greek Old Testament used in Jesus's day—to mean offering up a sacrifice, just as we say "offering *up*". In Acts (1:9), he uses the word ἐπήρθη, which literally means elevated or lifted up; but figuratively ἐπήρθη means exalted. In his Gospel he says that it came to pass, in the blessing of them, he withdrew from them (διέστη ἀπ᾽ αὐτῶν) and was transported into Heaven—τὸν οὐρανόν, which can mean either the sky above us or Heaven itself (*cf.* Lk 9:34-35; 4Kn 2:10-12; Ps 103:3).

So, although it's correct to take all of these words of ascension literally, they don't mean that Heaven is the same as the sky—although the two are intimately related in human thought and language around the world.

In every language of the Indo-European family, words having to do with the divine—"divine" itself, *divus, deus, diós, dieu,* and some specific names of gods like Ζεύς—all stem from the primordial root-word usually represented as *deiw-*. This root-word refers to the sky, and it's also the root from which we get words about light, like *div, dies, día,* and "day". In fact, the sky is associated with the divine precisely because the sky is where light comes from. Here below, things are dark; but in the sky, all is light—the Sun, the Moon, the stars, even the lightning that probably brought fire to early Man, are all in the sky. So the association between *up* and *light*, and between *down* and *dark*, is elemental.

Our experience also teaches us that darkness is dangerous, cold, frightening, full of injury, decay, and death; but light is clear, warm, constant, and safe (Is 2:21, 9:1; Ps 103:20-23; Ml 3:19-21). And darkness can envelop anything except light itself; light is power over darkness and all of its attendant evils (Gn 1:1-4; Jn 1:5). Since light comes from the sky, it's perfectly reasonable for people to suppose that, if there are any beings who are greater, stronger, brighter, and better than we are, they must be above the sky, somehow. So the connections that human thought makes among the divine, the sky, light, safety from harm, and happiness are elemental, too.

THE ASCENSION

These inter-relations are part of how we understand our world, so they're universal in human language and art. And it seems that they've always been so, too, although since the First World War we've lost track of them. To see clearly how all of this opens the Mystery of the Ascension, it's helpful to get to the kernel of these universal thoughts and images, and to remember the way that the ancients saw the structure of the universe—the way most of us do today, really, in the course of our daily lives.

People tend to think of the sky as a kind of dome, or a kind of hollow sphere, with the Earth in the middle and the Sun, Moon, and stars either set like jewels in that shell itself or moving around us in the space left inside. This is what things look like from our point of view, and even today teachers of astronomy assume that viewpoint so that they can map the positions of the heavenly bodies. Our ancestors, very reasonably, thought of things as being this way in actual fact. The Chinese understood the sky as a kind of celestial bell standing like a vault over the Earth; and the Greeks, Romans, and Indians considered the sky as a shell in which the Earth hangs like the yolk of an egg. The Hebrews described the sky as *rakia* (רָקִיעַ), the "firmament" on which God walks, spreading the clouds as the carpets in his tent (Gn 1:6; Jb 36:29; Is 19:1; Ez 1:26; Rv 6:14-16; *cf.* Lk 21:27). People in ancient and mediæval Europe developed detailed theories about how many crystalline spheres there were up there, nestled inside one another, how they moved, and what moved them.

Within this sky-shell, the heavenly bodies go around, moving from place to place, from there to there; and as they move, they mark off days, months, and years, the limits of mortal human life and the life of everything else—animals, plants, every living thing on Earth, which invariably ends in death (*cf.* Gn 1:6, 14-15, 2:17, 3:17-19).

The most important idea that people everywhere derive from all of this is that this sky-shell, because it contains the Sun, the Moon, the Earth, and all the planets, also contains Time. Here on Earth, things are born at a certain point, they live a while, and they die; existence here is linear, you might say, beginning at a certain point, lasting only a while, and then ending at a certain point, which is bodily death. Everything here dies, and it all decays; it falls into darkness, so to speak. So Time itself is understood to have had beginning—which is why Genesis starts out at that point (Gn 1:1)—and it's understood to have an end, after which Time will be no more. But most cultures on Earth have seen that the light above the sky never really goes out; it seems to come through the sky-shell itself constantly, in one way or another.

The Sun is perpetually reborn every morning, and the Moon goes endlessly through a cycle of growth, diminishment, and growth again; and, most particularly, there are the stars that shine constantly generation after generation, although they give way to the Sun. That's why people everywhere develop the idea that Time exists inside the sky-shell but not outside of it.

Jews and Christians understood that outside of the sky-shell, outside of Time, there's *Eternity*. In Hebrew, it's called נצח (ne-tsach); our word "Eternity" is based in the Latin *æternitas*, which really refers to changeless duration. It's not just an endlessly long time; it's a wholly different state of being, in a dimension outside of Time itself. Eternity is understood as being the dimension of God alone (Is 57:15); only God has no beginning and no end, only God always was and always will be. Eternity is bornless, endless, and changeless, the dimension of absolute perfection. St. Augustine described this dimension of Eternity as "a 'now' ever standing", and Dante saw Eternity as standing outside the succession of events that mark linear Time; he called it "the point at which all times are present" (*Paradiso* 18:18).

We humans are trapped here in Time. We can't see Eternity, and we can't reach into it, any more than we can touch the sky; we can't get out of the sky-shell that contains Time. So the sky is generally understood as the barrier between the two dimensions of Time and Eternity. The idea of God's Eternity existing somehow outside of the sky is why the prophets visualized him as being enthroned atop a clear blue firmament (Ex 24:9-10; Ez 1:22-28). It's also why his presence in the Temple was set apart from this world by means of a sky-colored curtain; here, too, the sky is used as the symbol of the barrier between Time and Eternity (Ex 26:31-33; Mt 27:51; Rv 11:19).

But even in those cultures that didn't know the Eternal Father, people understood that beyond Time, yet not quite in Eternity, there's another dimension. The ancient Romans called it *ævum*, but Christian thought calls it *Sempiternity*, from the Latin *semper*, always, and *æternitas*, bearing the sense of duration. "Sempiternity differs from Time, and from Eternity, as a middle term existing between them," St. Thomas Aquinas explained. "Eternity has no beginning and no end; Sempiternity has a beginning, but no end; Time has a beginning and an end" (*Summa* 1:10:5).

This is a critically important distinction, because "eternal" is so often misused to refer to the sempiternal, even in translations of the Bible. The King James Version has it wrong from its beginning to its end, although King James certainly knew better; he got the distinction clear in everything that he wrote himself, and he wrote rather a lot about these matters. It's a common fault; the Greeks tended to use the same word, αἰών, to refer to both dimensions, and they left it to the reader to decide which was meant. Cicero knew the difference, too, but he still said *æternitas* sometimes when he should have said *ævum* or *sempiternitas*, because the more absolute word has more poetic force—even the Church's own translations of Scripture and liturgy sometimes slip across that boundary and ask *vitam æternam* for the souls of the Faithful Departed. In any case, in any denomination, Christians don't aspire to eternal life, because only God has that; Christians aspire to everlasting life, or endless life. But all human life has a beginning, so it can't be called eternal. It's sempiternal.

In the Christian view of things, Sempiternity is the dimension of the angels, good or fallen, and of human souls whether they're in Heaven or Hell, in Purgatory or here on Earth conjoined to our bodies—angels and souls are creatures called into being by the Eternal Father, so their existence had a beginning, but they won't die, so their existence will have no end. Beyond that, Sempiternity is recognized by all organized cultures, usually as the abode of the immortal gods, demons, and other deathless beings. Unlike plants, animals, and our own human bodies, creatures that exist in Sempiternity know no death, no decline, no past, and no future, nor any other feature of Time-bound existence.

But, like us, they had a beginning. Sempiternals are universally understood as being able to move and think and act, although we can't really conceive of how that can be, because our experience is trapped in material bodies that exist and move only in the three dimensions of height, width, and breadth, and all material bodies are trapped in that fourth dimension of Time.

St. John saw into Sempiternity while he was on the island of Patmos, and language failed him in describing it, which is why the Book of Revelations relies entirely on symbolism of word, number, and color. That dimension simply can't be grasped in terms of this one, as St. Cyril of Jerusalem reported in a letter to St. Augustine about what he'd been told about all of this by a man who had been raised miraculously from the dead.

"You know that you have a soul," the man said, "but you can't know what it is; you know that angels exist, but you're ignorant of their nature. You also know that there's a God, but you can't comprehend how he can be. So it is with everything that has no body; our understanding can't grasp these things." Even so, St. Thomas Aquinas was able to deduce a tremendous amount of information about what these incorporeal beings are like, and what they can do; but, still, he could not explain how they can be that way, nor how they can do those things.

It is difficult to conceive of existence outside of Time and space, but this dimension of Sempiternity is the crucial concept for understanding the relationship between Heaven and Earth, and Earth and Hell. Above all, it's absolutely essential for understanding the Ascension. In fact, it's absolutely essential for understanding anything that you see in Christian art or hear in Christian Scripture. For that matter, the idea of Sempiternity—as the abode of the gods—pervades and structures the literature, mythology, and art of those cultures that came before Christianity or stand outside of it, from the most sophisticated to the most primitive, the world around, in every age. Without this simple concept, very little in the world's visual and literary art really makes clear sense; but if you approach art or literature, or even law, with a knowledge of Sempiternity, it all explains itself, as it is always intended to do.

At first, people understand Sempiternity to exist, like Eternity, somehow above the sky, in the region of everlasting light (Dn 12:3). But sooner or later people's science leads them past the primitive idea of a physical sky-shell in favor of a wider view of space as extending beyond the atmosphere, beyond the solar system, and beyond even the galaxy. Even so, by the time they've started to discover the scope of Creation they've also come to understand that Eternity and Sempiternity exist as dimensions distinct from the Time-bound dimension that we perceive in physical objects and bodies, and that the sky-shell, conceived as a physical object itself, has nothing to do with it.

And by then they also understand that, whatever the laws of physics might be here on Earth, they don't apply in those dimensions outside of Time and space. That's why even today the reality of these dimensions is universally recognized, and why both Eternity and Sempiternity are understood to have a certain definite set of characteristics: they're immaterial, invisible, and inaccessible to us while the mortal clay holds us down, and whatever is thought to live in them is invariably understood to have perpetuity of existence.

Far from being primitive or childlike, this sense of parallel dimensions is really quite sophisticated, when you think about it, and it stands at the foundation of civilized life. No society, no code of civil law, can be structured unless it is raised to immortality above Time; the state must not be considered bound by Time, or it would fall to pieces when its ruler dies. That's why states and rulers are virtually always considered in law as if they could not die; it's why our corporate entities are constituted in law to have perpetuity of existence, and it's why titles and offices are considered to survive the death of any particular incumbent or the expiration of his term—the immortal creature of law, the King, the President, or the Chieftain, conjoins itself then with the human body of the successor, and thus the office lives on.

No matter where you look on Earth, and in whatever century, the same understanding of Sempiternity that stands as the cornerstone of religion is also the basis of the constitutions of states and of the laws that govern them. In fact, while St. Augustine and St. Thomas Aquinas wrote about Sempiternity at some length, the western writers who explained the most about that dimension aren't theologians at all but jurists like Franciscus Accursius, Henry of Bracton, the Norman Anonymous, and Lothario dei Conti di Segni, better known to history as Innocent III.

The importance of the idea of Sempiternity in organized civic life, no less than its importance in religion, is one major reason that people continue to use the old idea of the sky-shell as a symbol even after their awareness of material creation has outgrown the idea that there really is a celestial dome over the Earth. Their civic and religious laws have been long established on the basis of everlasting life, and their language itself has fossilized the connections among "up" and "light" and "Heaven" and "sky", and among all of these concepts and the concept of divinity. Our word "Heaven", for instance, comes from the Anglo-Saxon word for the sky, *heofon*, and we still use that single word to refer to the dimension of everlasting life and, without the capital letter, to refer to the sky we see above us. It's the same in most other languages, too.

The Latin *cœlum* (the root of our word "ceiling") and the Greek οὐρανός also mean both the sky that we see domed above us and the Heaven that we can't see, the dimension of perpetual life that's figuratively and morally above us. The Hebrew שׁמים (shamayim) comes from שׁמה (shamah), which means "to be high"; שׁמים refers to the upper regions, whether literally the level of the sky-hanging clouds or figuratively the abode of the eternal God and the ever-living angels and saints. The language of the Bible is incomprehensible if you don't understand that words indicating the idea of *up* have a symbolic, not a literal, meaning. And when God communicated through visions or images, or even with acts, he uses the same kinds of metaphors without words.

That's why St. Stephen, at the moment of his martyrdom, "being full of the Holy Spirit, looked up to Heaven and saw the Glory of God; and he said, Behold, I see the heavens opened, and the Son of Man standing at the right hand of God" (Ac 7:55-56). It's why *The Martyrdom of St. Polycarp* written in about the year 156 noted that the martyrs "despised worldly tortures ... with the eyes of their heart they looked up, to the good things reserved for those who persevere, things that neither has ear heard nor eye seen ... but to them ... a glimpse of these things above was granted by the Lord... [And thus they] gained an imperishable crown".

But whether we're particularly religious or not, we can't escape the metaphor that lasting good is up, and transient decay and corruption are down. These ideas are why we speak of high-mindedness when we mean thoughts in accordance with the ever-living divine, or why we talk of doing the right thing as taking the high road. So language maintains the metaphor of deathless perfection as being *up*, and art and literature maintain the metaphor of the sky-shell as the boundary between mortal Time and immortal Sempiternity and endless Eternity.

Because the imagery of the old sky-shell is a universal feature of human thought and language, representations of relationships between Heaven and Earth, between this world and the next world, use the symbolism of the sky-shell even today. That symbolism occurs in the visual arts, in ceremonies, and in liturgy whenever and wherever people want to convey the distinction between the short span of life of bodies here on Earth and the endless life of the spirit. And just as the words for all of this are remarkably similar in all human languages, and the symbols are surprisingly few, no matter when or where you find them.

The Romans called images of the sky-shell by the word *mundus*. That's the root of words like the French *monde*, the Spanish *mundo*, and the Italian *mondo*, all of which mean world, and our word "mundane", meaning of this world. To understand all of the symbolic representations of these concepts in art and language, it's important to distinguish clearly between our words "Earth" and "world": Earth (γῆ in Greek, *terra* in Latin) is this planet on which we walk; the world is that planet and everything above it up to the boundary of the sky-shell, which is the *mundus*.

The most familiar *mundus* in the Roman world was the golden ball that was carried by the Emperor or put into the hand of images of Jupiter, the god of light and sky. "The *mundus* gets its name from the sky above our heads," Cato wrote; "indeed, its shape resembles the sky." We'd call this symbolic model of the sky-shell an *orb*, using a word that's related, obviously, to words like "orbit"; it comes from the Latin *orbis* used for the circuit of the heavens or for the ring of constellations that encircles the sky, through which the Sun moves to complete the cycle of the year—the Zodiac (from the Greek ὁ ζῳδίων κύκλος, ring of life).

The idea of the sky-shell as the boundary between Time and Eternity is why God the Father and Christ are so often shown holding an orb, and its symbolism of the barrier between Time and Sempiternity is why so many western monarchs carry one; it shows them to be outside of Time and not subject to the decay and death that go on inside that sphere. "The Emperor," Gervaise of Tilbury explained fourteen centuries after Cato, "carries in his left hand an orb of gold filled with dust and ashes, that by way of the gleam of the gold the everlasting glory of the Emperor may be represented, and that by means of the insignificant ashes may be designated the transitory glory of this Time-bound Earth" (*Otia Imperialia*).

Sometimes western monarchs put a little orb atop their crowns—it's still called a "mundus", when they do that—and they almost always put a cross on top of the orb, no matter where or how they displayed it. That's intended as a symbol that the True Faith exists in Sempiternity, outside the sky. The English coronation ritual, for example, reminds the monarch, as he takes the Orb in his hand, "When you see this Orb thus set under the Cross remember that the whole world is subject to the Power and Empire of Christ our Redeemer." In fact, the orb is what we refer to when we say that the Lord has the whole world in his hands.

Two symbols based on the idea of the sky-shell as the boundary of Time and space are particularly important for Christian art and language. One is the idea that we mortals pass through that barrier into endless life when we die, and the other is that ever-living beings can occasionally move through the barrier represented by the sky-shell to make themselves visible here below.

The ancient Greeks referred to the passage of a mortal to the other side of the sky as *apotheosis* (ἀπο-, completely, and θεοῦν, to make divine), and we do, too. The passage of a sempiternal through the figurative sky-barrier to be seen among us mortals here in Time is an *epiphany* (ἐπιφαίνειν, to make [oneself] manifest), which is where we get the name of the holiday commemorating the Adoration of the Magi—Christ showed himself as Messiah to the Gentiles that day. But any appearance of any sempiternal or eternal being to us mortals is an epiphany.

The appearance of angels to the prophets and patriarchs (Gn 16:7, 22:15), of saints seen by Apostles (Mt 17:3), of God the Father made visible as the Burning Bush (Ex 3:2-14), the Holy Spirit as a dove or tongues of fire (Mt 3:16; Ac 2:3-4), are all epiphanies. The Blessed Sacrament is always an epiphany, the immortal Jesus showing himself to mortal Men in the appearance of bread and wine. In fact, it's a special kind of epiphany, a *theophany*, a showing forth of God.

Because Eternity and Sempiternity are conventionally spoken of as existing above the sky or outside of it, art and architecture in virtually all cultures around the world have always conveyed the idea of epiphany or the idea of apotheosis by showing the immortal entity as coming through the sky, as just having come through it, or just as being somehow up above us.

For that to happen, the sky-barrier, the veil or the shell that keeps us from seeing Sempiternity, has to be broken or at least opened (Mt 27:51; Ac 7:56; Rv 4:1, 6:14, 19:11). When the barrier of Time pulls back to show us Sempiternity, the edge of that barrier is universally represented as making an unstable border, an undulating, shimmering, or pulsating zone of light around the doorway between the two dimensions.

Wavy lines (often punctuated with groups of three dots to represent the perfection of Sempiternity and its inhabitants), interlaces of rainbow stripes or lightning patterns in stridently contrasting colors (Ez 1:28; Rv 4:3), fluttering mosaic ribbons of colored glass and gold, or S-curves one after another have always been very popular decorative motifs for representing the shimmering boundary around portals to endlessness. That's why you see them on ancient sarcophagi, around the doorways of gothic churches, in the frames around the illuminations of epiphanies in mediæval manuscripts, and in the borders around stained-glass windows.

The spiral columns around the high altar of St. Peter's respond to that same idea as they frame the epiphany of Christ in the Eucharist, and so did those similar columns that stood before the door of the Temple in Christ's day, as Josephus says (*Antiquities* 15:11)—they marked the spot at which God made himself visible above the Ark, and in the Tablets of the Law. And the roiling clouds around images like that of Our Lady of Guadalupe mark just such a portal to Sempiternity, as do the radiant spikes of light around her (Mr 13:26; Rv 14:14).

> The halo on images of angels and saints conveys exactly the same idea. It got its start as a little hole in the sky-shell through which sempiternal beings look down on us, and through which the everlasting light of Heaven shines around their heads as they do. The idea of everlasting light in Eternity and Sempiternity is the reason that churches are so often decorated with mosaics or stained glass; you're supposed to understand that those images are windows that give you a view out of Time into a dimension of endless glory.

In addition to these representations of an ever-living being coming through the sky-shell, people often convey the idea of epiphany or apotheosis—depending on whether the immortal is moving out of Sempiternity into Time or out of Time into Sempiternity—by showing the sempiternal entity in some other significant relationship to an image or a model of the sky-shell.

These models come in many forms: domes, round rooms, niches, arches of triumph, bowers, and canopies are all models of the sky as the barrier between dimensions, and so are palls, and curtains and veils when they're used ceremonially. The Church uses all of these images to point to the epiphany of Jesus in the Eucharist, to the epiphanies of saints, to events like the Assumption and the Ascension that parallel the ancient idea of apotheosis, and to the fact of salvation—"One who has died in Christ … merits surviving beyond death… He is among the stars and cannot die," a typical early-Christian epitaph in Milan says, and the same image shows up in language and in art wherever Christians bury their dead.

Christianity is so dominant in the culture of the West, in fact, that people sometimes mistake these images, furnishings, and features of our buildings as indicating holiness, but they don't: they indicate immortality.   To Christians immortality in the light is attained only by the holy, but if you look around you'll notice that all of these same images are used in civic art and public ceremonies exactly as they are used in liturgy: to indicate that the entity presented to your view belongs to that dimension of endless life on the other side of the sky and has come through that symbolic sky-shell to make itself visible to you.

That's why, from Lhasa to Constantinople, from Persepolis to Tahiti, from the Vatican to Washington, rulers—by necessity considered in law to have perpetuity of existence—are so often presented to us sitting on elevated thrones, showing themselves to us standing before curtains or remaining hidden behind them, meeting us under arches or bowers or domes, wearing crowns (which are nothing more than haloes of immortality), or even depicted standing on clouds, precisely as angels and saints are shown to us. It's why we call princes "Your Highness"; it's why we put people, and statues of apotheosized people, on pedestals. But a king does not have to be holy to appropriate a throne, and a president does not have to be a saint to sit in an oval office. Wings on devils mean precisely what wings mean on angels: simply that the creature is immortal and that it has the superhuman power to travel through that barrier between Time and Sempiternity to be seen here in this Time-bound world.

All images and accounts of the End of Time naturally arrange these images to convey the idea of the barrier between the dimensions dissolving or at least opening up in a final dissolution of the world as we know it. That's why the fullest catalogue of all of these images of Time Without End in Christian literature is the Book of Revelation. But images of the Ascension also convey the meaning of that Mystery through one or more of these conventional symbols. Most often Christ is shown simply rising up to the Father; often the bright cloud (Lk 21:27; *cf.* Mt 17:5) is shown under his feet or behind him, which is to say around him. Sometimes his head alone remains visible; sometimes his feet, recognizable by the wounds of the nail, are the only part of him represented as the rest of his body disappears above the upper edge of the picture. The two kinds of image represent both sides of the same coin, really: "the head means the divine nature of Christ," St. Cyril of Jerusalem explained, "the feet, his manhood" (*Catecheses* 12:1).

Sometimes he's shown rising effortlessly, and sometimes he strides purposefully across the sky, as in Ps 18:5-6: "He has pitched a tent [a model of the sky] for the Sun [a symbol of Christ], which comes forth ... and, like a giant, joyfully runs its course" (*cf.* Lk 1:78; Ws 5:6; Zc 3:8, 6:12; Ml 3:20). This kind of image underscores the fact that Christ ascended by his own power, rather than being taken up like Elias or assumed like Mary. An eleventh-century Ascension scene in the Bamberg Gospels, for instance, shows Christ striding forcefully across the sky-shell, and it ensures that this connection won't be missed; it bears the legend *Maximus ecce gigans scandit super astra triumphans*—Behold, the greatest giant strides over the stars in his triumph.

After about the year 300, a good many Ascension scenes in the West build on St. Mark's account of the Mystery (Mr 16:19) to display the fuller meaning of the event through a combination of images: they show Christ moving upward under his own power, and they show him holding an orb in his right hand, or extending his right hand upward to take the right hand of the Father, which reaches back to him through the clouds.

Some representations of the Ascension show the Hand of God reaching through a circle of rainbow colors that ripple out on the dimensional barrier like wavelets across still water; sometimes the Hand comes through its own halo, or through a burst of light. However it appears, it's not intended to mean that Christ needed help in moving back to the Father; he and the Father are one (Jn 10:30), and that's exactly the idea that their extended right hands are intended to convey. Joining right hands is the age-old sign of concord, of harmony, and most of all of union between two people, which is why it's still done on signing a contract, on meeting someone to whom you bear good will, or when getting married. We still combine those symbols, just as they're combined in the old Ascension scenes, when we raise our right hands upward, toward the immortals on the other side of the sky, to take an oath—a gesture that was already old when Abraham did it (Gn 14:22).

Of course, the hand has always been a powerful symbol in its own right—in fact, it's a symbol of power, as when we say that something is in someone's hands (Ps 30:6), meaning that he'll manage it. Even "manage" comes from the Latin *manus*—hand. The Hebrew word יד (yad), which also happens to sound like the name of the first letter of the Tetragrammaton, means both "hand" and "power". Moses and Aaron worked their wonders by stretching forth their hands, or rather the Lord used their hands as his own (Ex 6:1, 7:5, 19; 8:1; *cf.* Ac 3:1-7). The right hand is a particular symbol of power and authority, the right hand of God being the most powerful of all. Figuratively, any act of God performed on Earth is ascribed to his hand (Ex 15:6,

31:18; Jn 8:6; Rt 1:13; Jb 2:10-11). In fact, images of his right hand are the oldest of all pictorial representations of God the Father.

Specifically, in representations of the Ascension, the Annunciation, the Baptism of Christ, the Transfiguration, and a few other applications like images of Christ in Glory or Christ the King, the extended right hand of God shows that Christ is truly God, truly the Messiah who was promised (Mr 16:19; Ac 7:55-56; *cf.* Ps 15:8; Mt 25:31-46; Ac 2:25-28, 33-34). His legitimacy, his authority, his right to rule, and in fact his godhead are all summed up in that simple phrase, "he sits at the right hand of God". At his trials, that was the only confession of his nature that he needed to make (Mt 26:64; Mr 14:62-64; *cf.* Ps 15:8, 11; Mt 22:44; Rm 8:34; Cl 3:1; etc.).

The right hand also means that Christ has the power to save. The power of the right hand is justice, and that means salvation from evil and injury; that's why blessings are given with the right hand extended (Gn 48:14-18; Ps 16:7, 19:7, 20:9, 47:11; 76:11, 97:1; etc.). And it's why we make the Sign of the Cross with the right hand.

Naturally, each particular symbol used to refer to the Ascension has its own long and complicated history, but they all focus on that same simple idea of Sempiternity, of immortality, by making reference to a dimension that's somehow beyond the sky. And of course you have to use common sense when you interpret these images; the same form can mean somewhat different things in different contexts, just as the same word can mean different things in different contexts. The curtain before the Ark of the Covenant means something, and so does the curtain behind the Speaker of the House; the curtains in your living-room don't.

But it is certainly true that by the time of Christ, Greek and Roman literature, art, and law already had an ancient heritage of sophisticated expressions of the imagery of Time, Sempiternity, and Eternity; the Hebrews themselves had a tradition even older and, in some ways, even more sophisticated. In Christianity, too, these indications of movement through the sky-barrier mean that someone is moving from a dimension of endless life to this mortal world, or from this mortal world to endless life. And because that barrier is represented by the old sky-shell, movement up invariably means movement to the dimension of endless beatitude: Heaven.

So when Christ wanted to indicate that he was returning to Heaven, he had to go up; he certainly couldn't go down. If he had gone off to one side or another, that would have indicated that he had gone to some other place on Earth. He had to go up. And he had to go up bodily, until he could no longer be seen. If he had simply disappeared it might have been thought that his resurrected body was just an immaterial phantom, which it is not.

C hrist's risen body was different, in many ways. He ate and drank (Lk 24:43; Acts 1:4), but then again he could pass through doors—the stone had been rolled back to show that the tomb was empty, but some commentators have posited that he came forth before that, moving out of the tomb as he was born without breaking his mother's seal of virginity. After he arose he could vanish, and he could traverse long distances quickly or instantaneously (Lk 24:13-15, 31), and somehow he could withhold his appearance so that even his friends wouldn't recognize him until he willed it (Lk 24:15-16).

These are characteristics of what's called the *glorified* body. The Resurrection is a proof of the doctrine of general resurrection of the Faithful; it was intended, evidently, as a glimpse of what life is like in Heaven, and how different it is from bodily life on Earth since the Fall (Jn 17:22; 1Cr 15:12-28; Phl 3:21). So Christ's risen body has the same identity that it had before (Lk 24:39; Jn 20:24-29; Jb 19:25-27), and it was reunited to the same soul. Resurrection in the Christian understanding is not a matter of the same imperishable soul being united to a new and different body, one created from nothing, made from other elements, or generated from procreation of other bodies—it's resurrection, not reincarnation (Hb 9:27). Christ obviously values the human body, or he would not have healed it so often, and he would not have rejoined his soul to his own body if he despised it.

That's why the Church, like the Pharisees before her, has always insisted on treating the body as sacred during life, not allowing it to sin (1Cr 6:13-20), keeping it healthy (1Tm 5:23; Jm 5:14), and burying it respectfully to await the resurrection—in those times and places where heretical or pagan sects adopted cremation specifically as a denial of the resurrection, the Church has discouraged it, but it's not unlawful if abuses are avoided.

Slowly if buried, quickly if cremated, the body dissolves into the elements after death (Gn 3:19), but as God formed it out of earth to start with, he gathers that same matter together again when it is to arise (Ez 37:1-14). "For the resuscitation of our bodies, far be it from us to fear that the omnipotence of the Creator cannot call back all of the portions that have been consumed by beasts or by fire, or have disintegrated into dust or ashes, or have dissolved in water, or evaporated in the air," St. Augustine said (*City of God* 22:20). "From all of this ... we gather this conclusion: that in the resurrection of the flesh the body shall be of the size that it had attained or should have attained in the flower of its youth".

Like many other theologians before him and since—St. Paul (Eph 4:13) and St. Thomas Aquinas among them—St. Augustine estimated that the risen will all seem to be about thirty, the age at which Christ died and rose.

Each person's risen body will be recognizable as that of the specific human person, but it won't have any of the defects that the person endured in life.

St. Thomas Aquinas pointed out (*Summa*, Suppl. 69-85) that whatever the body had in earthly life that pertains truly to human nature will rise again; otherwise the risen body would not be perfect. But defects, injuries, the ravages of Time, and the like are things that happen to bodies, not truly part of their nature; so those erosions are not part of the glorified bodies of the blessed. God established human nature without defect, and the point of salvation is to attain that same state that Adam and Eve had before the Fall (Rm 5:14; 1Cr 15:22), so the Faithful in Heaven don't have any defects, either. Youth is a defect because the body has not yet attained its full growth, any more than the soul has, and old age is a defect because, although the soul has had time to gain wisdom, the body has already begun to lose its vigor.

The scars of martyrdom, St. Thomas Aquinas adds, aren't defects but signs of the most steadfast virtue, so they only increase the joy of those who bear them (Jn 20:27). "A certain beauty will shine from them," St. Augustine explained, "a beauty that, though in the body, is not of the body, but of virtue" (*City of God* 22:19).

In addition to freedom from defects, the glorified body is understood to have gifts above and beyond the perfection of human nature—supernatural gifts, literally, like Adam and Eve had. One of these is *impassability*, which means that glorified bodies don't age, weaken, get sick, or, of course, die (1Cr 15:42-58; Phl 3:21). The bodies of the condemned will be *imperishable*, too, after the Last Day (Rv 9:6), but they'll feel the unspeakable torment of being forever separated from God. The happy souls in Heaven won't feel any pain, because that's part of what Heaven's about (Ps 83; Is 35:10; Rv 21:4), but they won't be insensible, because the senses are properly part of human nature—and grace perfects nature; it doesn't destroy it. If they could not see (Rv 1:7), hear (Rv 5:11, 15:3), taste (Lk 24:41-43; Rv 10:10), touch (Mt 28:9), or smell (Rv 8:3-4), then resurrected life would be no different from the silence of death; it would be the virtual extinction of the self.

Glorified bodies are also understood to be *subtle*, in the sense that they aren't restricted by physical obstructions like material objects or barriers (Mt 14:22-27; Lk 24:36, 50-51; Jn 20:19, 26; Ac 1:9). They're also understood to be *agile*; like the angels, they can traverse great distances quickly or even immediately (Tb 8:3; Is 40:31; Ws 3:7). Those who pass Judgement are also understood to have *clarity* (Mt 13:43; Phl 3:21), a splendor like that of the angels (Mt 17:1-3). All in all, an astonishing beauty (Dn 10:4-7; Mt 17:2).

T he Ascension asserts that Christ's body, glorified and living, is now in Heaven, with the living glorified bodies of Mary and all the saints, in fact, of all the Faithful Departed. This is confusing. We

Time-bound humans see that people die, that their bodies are buried, and that they are not resurrected, not as far as we can see (Ws 2:1-5). But Christ's own career, his teachings, and the prophecies that came before them, promise that the soul will be reunited with the body so that the whole person can stand and face judgement, and then be sent to everlasting reward—the immediate presence of God—or everlasting punishment, the perpetual denial of the presence of God, which is Hell. In a word, Christ teaches the resurrection of the dead, and we usually picture that as happening on the Last Day, at the End of Time.

This event causes no end of worry, all of which is really pointless; Christ himself said that, although there would be signs, we'd never know when it would happen (Mr 13:32-33). A certain segment of the population—of every population—still panics whenever a year that happens to have an otherwise significant number comes up, even though those numbers don't accurately reflect any chronological landmark in Christ's career. We know that Herod the Great died some four years before the Incarnation, but St. Luke says that the Annunciation happened in his reign (Lk 1:5), and that event is the era of our calendar. So our dates are off by at least four years from that alone, not to mention the many vagaries that the calendar has gone through since.

That's one reason that the Church doesn't get involved in millennial movements. She concentrates, as Christ himself concentrated, on the fact that for each of us individually the moment of death is our last day, the end of our Time. All of the talk about being ready for the End of Time is intended to encourage us to keep our own souls in order; but since death takes the soul out of Time and into Sempiternity, what happens from the soul's point of view at the instant of death is very different from what those of us who are left behind on Earth might think. And although it may be a little hard to grasp, it really carries an immense consolation.

When the body and soul separate at the instant of death, the soul is in Sempiternity, the dimension of the angels, in which existence has a beginning but has no end. It's outside of Time as it's outside of space.

It's always been difficult for medical science to determine the moment of death precisely. That spark of divine fire in us is surprisingly tenacious, and the soul can evidently stay tied to the body by the merest thread for a surprisingly long time, even without audible heartbeat or other signs of bodily life. People can be revived from conditions that even sophisticated diagnostic machines interpret as death, and they are every day. However, death is by definition final; there is no human agency that can grasp a soul and rejoin it with its body. Experiences that seem to be near death are not death. Dreams and illusions that happen during extreme stress can be induced arti-ficially, and their similarity from case to case isn't really surprising, either. They all seem to refer to those universal symbols of endless life that are embedded in human thought and language and expressed in human art that everybody knows implicitly, if not sub-consciously.

At the instant of death, though, when the soul stands instantly in Sempi-ternity, the body is left behind in Time, the dimension that governs all of our perceptions. So we still see the body; like it, we're trapped in Time, too. We may go on visiting the burial site for years and decades after the soul departs. But years and decades are parts of Time. From the soul's point of view, things must be entirely different.

The soul in Sempiternity probably notices no delay between the instant of death and the instant of its renewed conjunction with that body, risen and immortal—after all, delay is a function of Time (Lk 23:43; *cf.* Lk 16:22). The body, separated from the soul, can remain here on Earth (as far as we can tell) and be conjoined with the soul in Heaven or in Hell (as far as the soul can tell), but that's not being in two places at one time, because Heaven and Hell are not physical places, and they stand outside of Time. Exactly how glori-fied bodies can exist in Sempiternity, we can't tell; but the Ascension and the Assumption show that they do, as do the events after the Resurrection.

So each person faces an individual judgement at his last instant, the instant of death that takes him out of Time and space. But Time itself will come to an end; all material bodies are perishable, and those perishable bodies are what mark the succession of Time for us (Gn 1:14); without mat-ter, there is no Time. This is the event that St. John described as the rolling back of the sky, as a scroll (Rv 6:14) and Isaia compared to seeing the sky vanish like smoke (Is 51:5-6): the Second Coming of Christ to judge those living on Earth and all of the dead (Rv 19:11-13; Mt 24:29-31, 25:31-46; 1Cr 15:12-55, 1Th 4:16-18, etc.).

Divine judgement is the act of retribution, a word that shouldn't sound entirely negative—it's from the Latin *re-*, again or back, and *tribure*, to pay, so it means both reward for merit and punishment for sins and crimes. By your acts, you either adhere to or deviate from God's laws, so you put yourself either in the light of God's approval or in the shadow of his condemnation. Because Christianity is a covenant, the choice is yours, with each act you perform (Sr 15:11-20; Jn 3:20). That's why Christ said that he hadn't come to judge, as some in Israel had expected the Messiah to do, but to save (Jn 3:17, 8:15, 12:47). He will come again in glory to judge (Mt 16:27).

But that General Judgement, like the individual judgement that each person faces, happens outside of Time, too, because at that event Time has come to an end. That's not to say that the General Judgement has already happened, because you can't properly use words like "already" for matters of Sempiternity or Eternity, and because as far as we can tell—trapped in Time as we are—it hasn't happened. We have to await individual judgement at the instant of our death, and the General Judgement at the instant when Time itself comes to an end; but it's meaningless to say that one happens "before" the other.

By ascending at the end of his earthly career, Christ showed us what the culmination of our earthly careers will be like, and he did it precisely to evoke all of the universal images that have to do with passing from Time into Sempiternity. So it doesn't matter whether the Apostles thought that the blue sky was a shell-like firmament or not. The symbolism of Christ's departure upward, wrapped in a cloud of glory, told them precisely what he meant it to convey: that he was returning to Heaven, and more than that he meant them to know that where he went, the Faithful would be able to follow (Mt 25:34). That's what the Church has always understood as the promise of his Ascension (Eph 4:7-14; *cf.* Ps 67:19), and it's why hymns like the old *Salutis humanæ* sung on the Feast of the Ascension, praise Christ by calling him *tu dux ad astra*: thou guide to the stars.

This view of Heaven and Earth, the contrast between the everlasting splendor of Heaven and the fragile uncertainties of Earth, and the fact that none of us can know for certain which hour will be his last, urge the Church to exhort the Faithful to pray always.

"Don't say, 'I'll start on such and such a day,'" Francisco de Osuna advised. "Remember that everything can be retrieved, except time… Time rushes on, carrying with it your life; and yet you let it go… I don't think that it's such a grievous loss when things of the flesh are lost over the years, because they are of Time, and they aren't meant to endure. But it's a great misfortune if your spiritual advantage slips away… When the new Heaven and the new Earth appear and our bodies are made new … they will be renewed and purified … but … what you lose spiritually, at whatever age, is gone forever and cannot be recovered… I beg you to consider the counsel of the sage: 'Anything that you can turn your hand to, do with what power you have; for there will be no work, nor any reasoning, nor knowledge, nor wisdom in the nether world where you are going' (Ec 9:10)… Here, and in countless other passages … Holy Scripture warns us to pray always, and to persevere in praying to the Lord".

PENTECOST

PENTECOST HAS A LONG, LONG HISTORY IN THE CHRONICLES OF REVELATION. It's been celebrated since early Hebrew days. But throughout its long history it's been celebrated in many different ways, and for many different reasons. That's how revelation works: certain things happen, although the reason for them might not be clear, and then gradually everything crystallizes into something ordered and transparent that catches the light and lets us see it in all its splendor.

It started as a harvest feast of the Hebrews (Ex 23:16), the celebration of the presentation of the "first fruits" to God. This Feast of the First Fruits is unique on several levels of meaning. For one thing, other Hebrew festivals commemorated things that had happened to Israel, or they were directly commanded by God; but this one seems to have begun as a Cananite festival that the Hebrews took up when they reached the Promised Land. And even among harvest festivals it was unique. All agrarian cultures have harvest festivals, but those of the Mediterranean, like the Akitu festival of the Babylonians and even the Cerealia of the Romans, correspond more directly to the Feast of Unleavened Bread, the festival that celebrated the beginning of the grain harvest, than they do to First Fruits, which came seven weeks later (Dt 16:9).

In fact the Hebrews had a third festival of harvest, Asif (אָסִיף), later called the Feast of Booths or of Tabernacles, *Succoth* (חג הסכות, hag hasukot), which marked the completion of the harvest of all kinds of crops (Ez 45:21 *ff.*). Of these three, First Fruits seems to have been the least important observance. Psalms (4:8) and Isaia (9:2) indicate that it was celebrated, but they also suggest that it didn't rank as equal to the Feast of Unleavened Bread or to Succoth. Still, it bore the most potential as prophecy.

The public liturgies of First Fruits centered on the presentation of the first fruits of the harvest to God in his sanctuary (Lv 23:10-21; Nm 28:26 *ff.*). A priest waved a sheaf of grain before Yahweh, and fine flour was offered, as were new-baked loaves of leavened wheat bread and wine; and a spotless male lamb was sacrificed. All of these symbols were later used by the prophets and by Christ himself as both image and substance of his New Covenant (Mt 6:11, 26:26; Jn 1:29, 6:22-60), obviously; but it was not so obvious to the Jews that the focus of their Harvest Feast shifted slowly as the centuries rolled on.

At some point in the history of Judaism, the Feast of Unleavened Bread was combined with Passover (Mt 26:17), and the Feast of First Fruits, the feast of leavened bread (Lv 23:17), was fixed as seven weeks after the time of that combined feast. That's why First Fruits became known as the "Feast of Weeks" or just "Weeks", *Shevuot* (שָׁבוּעוֹת, חַג שָׁבוּעוֹת). But that name didn't last long, because of the way that the Israelites counted days, which is different from our own. If we were to set a date fifty days after a certain event, or three days after it, we'd count the day after the event as the first day. But the Israelites counted days between events starting with the day of the first event itself; that's why Christ was three days in the tomb, Friday, Saturday, and Sunday. It's also why the Jews considered that seven weeks add up to fifty days, not forty-nine.

So, because they reckoned fifty days between the offering of the first fruits of the barley harvest and the Feast of Weeks on the day after the seventh sabbath (Lv 23:11, 15-16), because this holiday didn't have a descriptive name rooted in Hebrew history like the others, and because by the time of Christ so many Jews spoke Greek, the holiday came to be called simply the Fiftieth Day—Pentecost, πεντηκοστή, from the Greek πεντηκοστός meaning "fiftieth day" (2Mc 12:31-32; Tb 2:1).

Pentecost was always a time of rejoicing, like most harvest festivals. Besides the presentation of the gifts and sacrifices to the Creator, there were hymns of thanksgiving and praise; which evidently made the Israelites think about thanking God for his spiritual gifts, like the Law. There was also the fact that, after the date of Pentecost was shifted around, it coincided with the dates of several other commemorations.

In Ex 19:1, the Hebrews are said to have arrived at Sinai on the first day of the third month after leaving Egypt. Passover, now combined with the Feast of Unleavened Bread, was fixed in the middle of the first month, so the seven weeks that followed until Pentecost approximated the time between the Exodus and the arrival at Sinai. The first clear evidence that Pentecost had become a celebration of the Covenant comes from the Book of Jubilees, which isn't exactly Scripture; but then the festival of Asa (2Pr 15:10-12) may stand as evidence that Pentecost had already taken on this new significance. So the original Feast of First Fruits, the Cananite harvest festival that the Israelites had some trouble integrating into their own religion and history, developed into Pentecost, the Feast of the Fiftieth Day, and its focus turned gradually away from the bounty of God's crops to center on the providence of his Law.

Christ also used the metaphor of crop and harvest again and again to signify the establishment of his kingdom (Mt 13:3-43; Lk 10:2; Jn 4:35), but his Apostles don't seem to have expected anything in particular to happen on Pentecost—in fact, the account in Acts doesn't really point to any subtle comparisons between the first fruits of the harvest and the first fruits of the

Spirit, nor between the thunderous descent of the Old Law on Sinai and the fiery descent of the New at Jerusalem. Of course, the fact that the Descent of the Holy Spirit happened on the old feast of Pentecost makes the connection well enough, and it ties together all of the different strands of the history of that Jewish holiday.

There is still some debate about what, exactly, happened at the first Christian Pentecost, but the general outline in Acts (2:1-41) is clear. The Apostles were gathered together in one place, with those loyal Christians who had stayed faithful despite the Crucifixion and the persecutions that followed it. Mary was there—it's always been understood that the people mentioned in Ac 1:14 are included in the hundred and twenty of Ac 1:15, and that "they were *all* gathered together" means exactly that.

Then there was a theophany, an epiphany of the Holy Spirit. There was a strong wind in the house, apparently as a kind of warning. Then the Spirit appeared as a large flame that separated into individual flames that settled above the heads of those present, "and they were filled with the Holy Spirit". In Christian art and language, flames always represent love, specifically the ardent love of God for humans, which is why virtually every image of God in Scripture and since, from the Burning Bush to the Sacred Heart, is shown in flames like those of a furnace. Both great deliveries of the Law to Man, the great theophany at Sinai and the descent of the Holy Spirit, happened in the imagery of fire from Heaven; both speak eloquently and elementally about charity, about the love of God for his creatures, and the establishment of his Law in love.

Jesus himself had said that this particular event would happen at the end of the Old Covenant and the establishment of the New (Ac 1:5; Mr 13:11; Lk 12:11-12, 24:46-49; Jn 14:16-17; Ac 1:8, 2:17; *cf.* Ex 4:12; Is 44:3; Jl 2:28, or in some editions 3:1-2). The Spirit would dwell in the Faithful, and the Faithful in the Spirit, as he is in the Father and the Father is in him. That is, the advent of the Holy Spirit upon the Faithful would mark the taking up of the first fruits of Christ's teachings—the birthday of the Church.

The Christians gathered together received both kinds of grace, sanctifying and actual, and they received them in accordance with their vocations (*cf.* 1Cr 12:4-31). The grace most often celebrated in the liturgy of Pentecost is the sanctifying grace that vivified the Church at that moment and that has sustained her ever since. Here, as the Spirit breathed upon her in that mighty wind, the Church received her soul, as it were. The Apostles knew what they had to do—get people to repent and be baptized.

To accomplish this, they received two distinct actual graces. First, the Apostles were confirmed in priestly office or, more specifically here, in episcopal office; they were to lead, to shepherd, the Church. As part of this grace, they knew how to do this, which is itself unprecedented. Other religions of the time were more or less available to initiates, but they didn't necessarily recruit. In fact, there had never been an organization like the Church on Earth before, an organized body of men and women who moved out purposefully to bring everybody's attention to a new religion and a new way of life.

With the light of this actual grace, the Apostles saw the whole world united in a single creed, a vision that no religion on Earth had ever shared. They understood what the sacraments were and how to administer them; they understood how to direct missionaries to the far ends of the Earth. They had a lot to work out, of course, but after Pentecost they knew how to work it out. Even when they disagreed with each other about discipline (Ac 15:1-35), they knew how to work it out. We may take the innovations of the earliest days of the Church for granted, business as usual, but that's only because what the Apostles did in the days after Pentecost has remained the norm for two thousand years since. We forget how utterly different the world, the Faith, and religion were before that first Pentecost.

Secondly, the Apostles, Mary, and the others that were with them—about a hundred and twenty persons in all, men and women alike—received whatever actual graces they needed to perform their particular tasks, to live up to their individual vocations. Evidently some among the hundred and twenty had received some official recognition in the Church before this (Lk 10:1), but none had the authority of the Twelve. There were no priests, yet, and no deacons (Ac 6:1-6), and the only one of the followers who assumed the office of Bishop with the remaining Apostles was Matthias (Ac 1:15-26). So the majority of the Christians visited by the Spirit that day must have been laymen—which includes women.

But Mary had not received any priestly office from Christ as the Apostles had; she had not received any special charge of primacy as St. Peter had. She had received no priestly or pastoral office whatsoever. Still, John Paul II said, "the fact that the Blessed Virgin Mary, Mother of God and Mother of the Church, received neither the mission proper to the Apostles nor a ministerial priesthood ... cannot mean that women are of lesser dignity, nor can it be construed as discrimination against them" (*Ordinatio sacerdotalis*, 1994). Acts doesn't say that some of the tongues of fire were larger than others; all are represented as equal. But each of those flames of love was intimately suited to the person on whom it rested; each had a precise configuration of particular gifts, in particular degree, to bestow on each individual person, almost as if that person were the only one involved with the Spirit.

PENTECOST

Two extraordinary linguistic graces in particular were bestowed, two miracles of language. One was that the devout people in the crowds understood the Apostles simultaneously, no matter what their native languages were. That is, the Apostles spoke ecstatically about the wonderful works of God—as Mary had done in her *Magnificat* after the Holy Spirit had come upon her—but the devout Jews from Rome heard them in Latin, those from Parthia heard them in Pehlevi; people from the Greek-speaking cities of Asia Minor must have heard them in their own local dialects. Acts specifies that this phenomenon didn't affect everybody in the crowd, only the devout (Ac 2:5, 12-13, 41), which would indicate those who already sought to do the will of God; Christianity is a covenant (Lk 2:14, 11:9), and a covenant requires the free consent of both parties.

The second miracle of language was that the Apostles were able to speak intelligibly in languages that they had not learned naturally. This was obviously necessary for the immediate spread of the Church. None of the Apostles, evidently, was an educated man (Ac 4:13, for instance). None would have been prepared to speak intelligibly to the Gentiles. And yet St. Peter went to Rome; St. Jude went to Edessa, where people spoke Syriac. St. Philip, the example to them all, was taken instantaneously to Azotus— that is, to Ashdod (1Kn 5; 1Mc 5:68, 10:77-78, 16:10)—where he preached to the Philistines, whose language was only slightly, but significantly, different from his own. St. Bartholomew taught successfully in India, the mother of languages where even today hundreds of tongues are spoken, none of them known in the rest of the world until modern times. No matter where they went, they were able to address the people in the native language of the country, and convey to them the Good News of the Gospel.

The purpose of both of these miracles, the miracle of hearing and the miracle of speaking, was specifically to spread the Gospel to all peoples (Mt 28:19; Ac 1:8), so the language was intelligible. It's interesting, in this light, to reflect that when God appeared as fire to propagate the Old Law among the people there was smoke around the flame (Ex 19:18; *cf.* Is 6:4), because the Old Testament is veiled in prophecy and obscure; but the Spirit appeared at Pentecost as clear flames like the flames of lamps, that illumined the minds of those who received him; there was no smoke at Pentecost. The message of Pentecost was to be understood directly and clearly.

This Gift of Tongues is called *glossolalia*, from the Greek γλῶσσα, meaning tongue, and λαλέειν, to speak. It has happened in the Church since the days of the Apostles, but only very, very rarely. St. Irenæus, for instance, notes (*Against Heretics* 5:7) that many people in his congregation were heard speaking in many tongues. It's not clear whether this was a matter of

their suddenly knowing foreign languages that they hadn't learned naturally or of their listeners' understanding them in their own native tongues, but
either way the discourse was intelligible and instructive.

In later ages, St. Vincent Ferrer, who preached only in Limousin, the
language of his native Valencia, was understood by each person in the huge
congregations who flocked to hear him speak; but the Church has never
stated officially that he had the Pentecostal gift. It's sometimes reported,
vaguely, that once when St. Anthony of Padua addressed the Pope and
Curia, each heard him in his own native language, but this was a singular-
ly educated audience, and one Romance language is much like any other,
and they're all like Latin. It's sometimes said, too, that St. Francis Xavier
was supernaturally empowered to speak oriental languages, but those
reports came from people who hadn't noticed that he studied while they
slept. Other than these rare cases in which a population must be instructed in the Faith by someone who does not speak their language, any cred-
itable phenomenon resembling glossolalia is unknown.

When the Corinthians started mistaking other linguistic behavior for the
Gift of Tongues, St. Paul wrote to them very clearly about it, requiring that
the distinction be made between those who spoke actual understandable
languages by infused knowledge and those who babbled (1Cr 14:10-11); he
uses the word "barbarian", from the Greek βάρβαρος, someone who
speaks in an uncouth or crude way, or someone who stammers meaninglessly (as, in the Greek view of things, anybody who wasn't Greek spoke).

To keep the distinction clear, St. Paul specified that there had to be an
interpreter to confirm that the person was, in fact, speaking a known
human language and speaking it properly. Even when a person could
miraculously speak a genuine language that he hadn't studied, being
understood and understandable, St. Paul ranked the gift low on the scale of
spiritual favors, and he specified that it was intended for unbelievers, not
for believers. He interrupts his discourse on the proper reception of the gift
(1Cr 12-14) with a digression on charity, the love of God that the stammer-
ing babble violates; and he commanded the Corinthians to use only articulate and plain speech (14:9); they were to refrain from even that in church
unless even the unlettered could grasp what was being said (14:16).

There is no mention in Scripture of people's speaking "angel languages" or
ancient and extinct tongues, because none of the bystanders would be able
to learn about Christ from unintelligible utterances, and nobody could distinguish those utterances from the babble that susceptible people perform in
all cultures. Modern experts can make those distinctions, though. Linguists
can describe and transcribe utterances even in languages that they themselves don't know, so that they can analyze the patterns of sounds. They can

even determine, with surprising accuracy, the basic grammatical structures in languages that they've never heard before.

Naturally, linguists are intensely interested in how humans use language and how they acquire it, so if it is indeed possible for people to suddenly begin speaking a language that they've never heard before, linguists want to know about it, and they have no particular doctrinal axe to grind.

The modern phenomenon has been studied in great detail for many years, now, since it began to show up again in Pentecostal sects. In all cases, analysis of tongue-speaking in this century shows that the behavior is no known ancient or foreign language; that it is far too simple to be a regular language of any kind; that it is learned, often in subtle ways, from charismatic leaders who expect it from followers; and that it is possible to chart the chain of teaching from teacher to disciple and then to more followers by following the patterns of the sounds that they make.

It isn't glossolalia; it's more properly called *idioglossia*, from ἰδιο-, meaning personal or peculiar to one person, and λαλέειν, to speak. It means going off on one's own, linguistically, speaking in a way that one makes up inside himself that nobody else can understand. This is a behavior that anybody can learn, given sufficient motivation to be a follower or a leader of followers; it's very easily faked, and in fact it has to be started by someone before it spreads in a group. Those who claim to interpret, too, fall short on analysis; foreign students who recite, for instance, the Our Father in their native language may be interpreted as prophesying Armageddon or a particular person's marriage, depending on which interpreter interprets.

Bystanders may not be able to distinguish the linguist's genuine Aramaic or Greek from the tongue-speaker's utterances, but in Pentecostal groups no tongue-speaker has ever been found who can converse in genuine languages that he has not learned by natural means. That's another critical distinction between what happened on Pentecost and what happens today: genuine extraordinary spiritual gifts always serve some good purpose, but the modern behavior does no good; it conveys no information about Christ or anything else. It puffs up the idioglossic (1Cr 13:4), making him feel special and superior.

There are any number of reasons that a person might start talking incomprehensibly, but they are psychological, not spiritual; largely, it's a kind of regressive behavior—a return to infantile or childlike behavior (1Cr 13:11)—that begins spontaneously in response to certain kinds of stress or is learned by persons wanting to escape such stress. In fact, this particular behavior occurs worldwide, which is another distinction between it and the Apostles' gift, which was unique to the Church; and it occurs in predictable circumstances to persons of predictable susceptibility. Some claim to be possessed by demons or by the souls of the dead; some claim to be reincarnated from unknown ages past. But most usually tongue-speakers here and abroad claim that they are "gifted" in this way for something other than religious reasons, such as being from another planet or conversing with beings who are.

There is an immense clinical literature on the subject, both in linguistics and in clinical psychology, that should be reviewed carefully by anybody whose friends or relatives are attracted to idioglossic groups, and by those who have to handle the problem pastorally. Not surprisingly none of the facts seem make much difference to those who want to believe, any more than Acts or the Epistles do. The usual refutations are that the investigator is not spiritually gifted enough to understand the tongues of angels, that it's blasphemy to reason about divine revelation, or that God will not be tested. So the idioglossic person can seldom be talked out of the behavior; the underlying causes of it have to be approached and healed instead.

The Church herself speaks of the distinction between idioglossia and glossolalia when she has to, but by and large she has found, since the Corinthians, that people attracted to this kind of behavior attach more importance to its emotional consolation—chiefly its feelings of relief and cleanliness—than to the spiritual treasures of their religion. If asked to stop, they will leave the Church to join sects that focus centrally, or even exclusively, on this behavior, as the Messalians and the Jansenists did. So, by and large, the Church concentrates on assisting them in managing the stresses that have provoked the behavior in the first place. As the person makes progress in coming to terms with those problems in life, the behavior disappears.

B ecause Pentecost reunited peoples of all tongues into the single body of the Church, the scene is often shown in parallel with the miracle of the Tower of Babel (Gn 11), which it reversed as Mary's obedient approval of Christ's coming reversed the disobedience of Eve. And because Mary, as prophetess, speaks for the whole body of the Faithful in the Gospels—as at the Annunciation, in the *Magnificat*, and at the foot of the Cross—she is usually shown as the central figure in images of Pentecost, representing the Church.

The burst of flame is sometimes shown around the Hand of God, but more usually around a dove, which is a kind of hieroglyph of the Holy Spirit. Pentecost is the Baptism of the Spirit that Christ spoke of (Ac 1:5), and the central Dove connects this theophany to the one at his Baptism by water (Mt 3:16). Sometimes, as in the thirteenth-century Pentecost mosaic in the cupola of St. Mark's in Venice, the Dove comes through a glittering rainbow portal from Eternity into Time to distribute the tongues of fire; he's also shown there sitting on a book on an otherwise empty throne.

PENTECOST

The Dove on the throne, surrounded by countless tongues of fire, is not too common in recent pictures of Pentecost, but the image used to appear in countless Pentecost scenes, and it makes an important point. An empty throne, usually radiant in glory, is called an *etoimasia*, from the Greek ἑτοιμασία, which bears the sense of ready to come or certain to come—it refers to that which is imminent. The whole phrase that describes this kind of symbol is ἑτοιμασία τοῦ θρόνου, the "preparation of the throne" or the "readiness of the throne", and it comes from Roman imperial legal practice.

Roman law courts were run in a building called a *basilica*, from the Greek word βασιλική, derived from βασιλεία, meaning majesty. The word "basilica" applied to a building indicates that, metaphorically, it's a building in which an otherwise invisible ever-living being descends to make itself visible in Time and space; a basilica is the setting for an epiphany. That's why the form of the ancient Roman law-court was adopted by the Church as the preferred shape for churches, which are designed to accommodate the epiphany of the Eucharist in a suitable and significant way.

The epiphanies that happened in imperial law-courts before the advent of Christianity, though, were not religious. The same everlasting majesty appeared there as appears today in our own law-courts: the majesty of the law (Jn 18:28, 33; *cf.* Pr 20:8; Ps 100:8, 103:22). The judge, then as now, was understood to embody that law, and so did the book that put it all in writing. So, when the judge rose to leave the court, he left a book on his empty seat. It was either the volume of the imperial law code or the *liber mandatorum*, the book of his written orders that described the powers that the Emperor had granted to that judge. Either way, the book embodied the law, and it had a picture of the Emperor in majesty on its cover.

The book on the empty throne was a sign that the judge would come back, and that until he did the law itself was still in force, still embodying the majesty of the state. The enthroned book of the law was treated exactly as the person of the judge himself—or the Empire's supreme judge, the Emperor—was treated. It was flanked by ever-burning lamps or candles, and the throne-chair on which it was placed had a cushion or a cloth of estate on it, the ancestor of the rich cloth draped over pulpits today. Right up to the French Revolution, images of empty thrones, sacred, secular, or divine, might bear the legend *Hinc Suprema Lex*: from here comes the Supreme Law. Naturally, Christianity adopted this symbol, too, but the Church replaced the books of the old imperial system with the books that embody the supreme Law of the New Covenant: the Gospels.

St. Cyril of Alexandria explained that it was customary at synods and councils to put up a throne and put the books of the Gospels on it, to show that Christ was presiding, as for example at Ephesus in 431 (*Explanation to the Emperor).* It's the same reason that Gospel books so often have a picture of Christ on the cover, and it's why they're carried into Mass today exactly as the old Roman law-books came into court: preceded by the imperial standard of the Cross, flanked by acolytes carrying lights, and followed by the officer who will preside at the epiphany in the basilica, the priest. That symbolism, as much as simple convenience, is why the priest leaves his Missal on his seat when he rises to deliver the Word. And it's why the tabernacle—the סֻכָּה (sukah), as in the Feast of Tabernacles—in which the Body of Christ rests is always flanked by at least one perpetual light; it's the throne of his embodiment, the Eucharist.

Of course, the same imagery pertains to the Judgement-Seat, too (Ps 9a:8, 121:5; Pr 20:8; Mt 27:19; Jn 19:13). When the judge comes again to take that seat, it's a sign that he is there in his official capacity, the embodiment of the law. In the Old Testament, the "Judgement Seat" is the same as the "Mercy Seat" (Ex 25:17, etc.), the lid of the Ark on which the visible majesty of God sat, flanked by ministering angels (Ex 25:18-19; Is 6:2; Ez 10) and surrounded by ever-burning lights (Ex 25:37; Lv 24:2; Rv 4:5), which is obviously the same set of images arranged for the same purpose.

In Christian imagery, Mary, the Ark of the New Covenant, is the Throne of Wisdom, too, the *sedes sapientiæ,* which is what the images of the Madonna and Child mean, basically: Christ, Divine Wisdom embodied, sits enthroned upon Mary. At Pentecost, the majesty of the Holy Spirit descended to touch the Apostles on Earth, and to dwell in a special way in Mary—who is, again, the symbol, prototype, and embodiment of the whole Church. Pentecost, then, is the empowerment of the institutional Church (Lk 24:49; Ac 1:8).

For their part, the Apostles in Pentecost scenes usually assume various postures of teaching, with the right hand extended significantly—one finger pointing up, or two, or with the palm open and forward to the listeners, or in any other pose that people use when they explain something. That's a visual means of conveying what happened to them when the Spirit came upon them as tongues of fire. It was only later, after the Renaissance, that artists began representing them stunned by the impact of the infused knowledge and the other Gifts of the Spirit. Either way, they're presented to us at Pentecost as embodying the First Fruits of the Spirit; they are the fulfillment of the prophecy inherent in the use of leavened bread at Pentecost. From this moment, they would expand the unleavened bread of the Passover to feed the whole world (Ex 12:39; Mt 13:33; Jn 6:22-60; 1Cr 5:6-8).

That's why, at this moment, more than any other in Scripture, the fact that there are twelve of them carries immense meaning. Twelve is a number of completeness, or, more specifically, a complete cycle, a sort of circular completeness that includes both beginning and end, in perpetuity. That's why pictures of Pentecost fit so well on domes: the Twelve stand around the perimeter, and the light comes through a central oculus. The dome, a model of the sky, makes the Twelve around it correspond to the twelve "stars", the months of the Zodiac, which is the "ring of life" that surrounds the sky.

Even the numbers of people with the Twelve multiply and reinforce their significance of universality. Acts 1:15 says that there were a hundred and twenty people there that day. That means that each Apostle in conventional Pentecost scenes stands for ten others as well; and ten is another number that represents totality, in the sense of completeness—ten Commandments embody all of the Old Law, and Ws 7:2 counts ten lunar months as the time it takes between conception and birth. So Pentecost, the birthday of the Church, is the fulfillment of Christ's command to teach all nations, the whole world, and of the prophecies of the Messiah's universal reign (Dn 6:2; Ps 2; Gn 17:20, 49:28; 3Kn 4:7; and, most insistently, 1Pr 25:8-31). And the first stage of their universal teaching is already indicated in the sixteen nations that heard them that first day, and understood (Ac 2:7-11): ten plus six, a number twice as perfect as three.

Liturgically, Pentecost doesn't seem to have been celebrated as a separate feast in the first centuries of the Church's life. It was a Jewish festival, after all; and usually the Church waited patiently and developed her liturgies gradually, and as the other religions gradually died out, Christian feasts eventually replaced the Jewish or pagan observances held on those dates. St. Paul's remark about the holiday, for instance (1Cr 16:8), seems to refer to the Jewish observance, not to a Christian feast; and while the oldest surviving Syrian missal includes readings for that day taken from Ex 19—the great theophany of Sinai. This, too, was most likely carried over from Jewish observances.

Origen and Tertullian wrote about Pentecost as a Christian celebration, but the earliest clear reference to Pentecost as a Christian holiday comes from the second-century *Letter of the Apostles*. It evidently reflects only the practice of the eastern Church, and not even all of that. The significant event recorded in Acts, the descent of the Holy Spirit, seems to have been celebrated more usually with the Ascension, as the culmination of the Easter Mystery—Easter marked the inception of grace, St. Augustine explained, and Pentecost its crown (Jn 7:39). By his day, though, Pentecost had come into its own, clearly focussed on the Holy Spirit and, eventually, moved to a separate feast day.

But the connection between Pentecost and Easter has never been forgotten: the two holidays are seen together as beginning and end of the same process. In fact, they were often called "White Easter" and "Red Easter", distinguished by the color of the vestments worn. That's why Pentecost is still called *Pascha rosatum* sometimes in Latin, *Pascha rossa* in Italian, and *Pâque rose* in French; and that, in turn, is evidently why people in the Middle Ages began the custom of scattering red rose petals on the congregation during the singing of the *Veni, Sancte Spiritus*.

Like the red rose petals, the red vestments of Pentecost recall the flames of the Holy Spirit, and they foreshadow the blood that the Apostles would shed in establishing the Church, the blood of martyrs that Tertullian called the seed of the Church. That color might be confusing to speakers of English, because the old English name for Pentecost is White Sunday, Whitsunday; but that comes from the white baptismal robes worn by catechumens who were customarily baptized—with water, not with fire—on Pentecost. In fact, the eve of Pentecost used to be the preferred time for blessing baptismal fonts.

Two other sacraments are intimately associated with Pentecost. Confirmation is the sacrament through which the Gifts of the Holy Spirit can be obtained, of course. But there's also a close connection between Pentecost and Holy Orders. Nobody knows when the custom of ordaining during Pentecost season started; it seems so obviously appropriate that ordinations may have been the first commemorations of the event, in the lifetimes of the Apostles themselves. By 494 Pope Gelasius I put ordinations definitively on Ember Saturdays, days of fast and abstinence that fall four times a year.

These are called "ember" days, a term that, despite folklore, has nothing to do with letting the fire go out. "Ember" in this case may derive from the Old English *ymbryne*, meaning recurrence; *ymber-daeg* meant a day—an observance—that recurred during the cycle of the year. Because this three-day observance comes around four times a year, the term "ember days" may have been influenced by a corrupted pronunciation of the Latin phrase *quatuor tempora*, the "four times" or the "four seasons". There's a somewhat similar development in German, in which ember days are called *Quatember Tage*. Wherever the name came from, ember days are days of fast and abstinence mandated in the earliest days of the Church for the four major divisions of the year. Oddly enough, their observations had a festive character to them, because the readings at Mass on those days focussed on hope, expectation, and thanksgiving; people celebrated with everything but fancy food.

Ember days were more or less optional in some dioceses, and they still aren't customary in the eastern Rites. Even in the West they weren't universally fixed in the calendar until 1078, when Pope St. Gregory VII fixed ember days on the Wednesday, Friday, and

Saturday after the Feast of St. Lucy on December 13; after Ash Wednesday; after Pentecost; and after the Exaltation of the Cross on September 14. They were omitted from the requirements for penitential practices in 1966 when Pope Paul VI Montini issued his apostolic constitution *Pœnitemini*, reorganizing the disciplinary regulations of fasting and abstinence.

The Ember Saturday that falls after Pentecost has always been the preferred time for ordinations, because the whole liturgical cycle of the week builds up an appropriate context for the sacrament: the seven days of the week celebrate the Seven Gifts of the Holy Spirit (Is 11:2-3). Wisdom, the gift by which one can judge all things as God sees them—Divine Wisdom, which is Christ himself—is celebrated in the liturgy of Pentecost Sunday. Understanding, the Gift that helps one understand what God has revealed, dominates the liturgy of that Monday. Counsel, the Gift of knowing what to do in a difficult situation, is celebrated on Tuesday.

On Wednesday, the first ember day of Pentecost week, the liturgy focusses on Fortitude, the courage to do what is right—which is appropriate for the customary public scrutiny of the candidates for the priesthood, a kind of ritual final examination. Thursday's liturgy speaks of Knowledge, through which one sees this world as it really is. Piety, the proper regard for God and things related to God, is celebrated on Friday; that's when the candidates would meet again for public approbation, which was sort of like a graduation ceremony. Then on Ember Saturday, the celebration of Fear of the Lord, the candidates came together again for a vigil that lasted until their ordination there on Sunday morning, at dawn.

All of these liturgies gathered together passages from both Testaments and arranged them meaningfully to constitute a vast, week-long prayer for Wisdom and enlightenment; as preserved in the old Roman Missal, they are a rich store of meditation and reflection. The arts assisted in the celebrations, too, of course; a good many major monuments, churches that customarily held these ember-day ordinations, still echo visually this week-long plea for the Gifts. For example, the whole oratory of the University of Rome, S. Ivo alla Sapienza, is a temple to the Divine Wisdom (the University's nickname, *Sapienza*, means Wisdom in Italian). And it's configured to represent Pentecost from the ground up, or rather from the dome down. It's dedicated to S. Ivo, St. Yves Hélory of Kermartin in Brittany, by the way, not just because his feast day falls on May 19, on or around Pentecost, but because he once called down actual fire from Heaven, to give force to his arguments in favor of orthodoxy—which won him the epithet "Tongue of Fire".

THE ASSUMPTION

THE ASSUMPTION OF MARY ISN'T RECORDED IN THE BIBLE, BUT IT IS PERfectly consistent with everything that is. In fact, it's a necessary consequence of Christ's teachings, the example and the promise of what those teachings are intended to accomplish. But it was accomplished after Christ's own work was done, and the authors of the New Testament evidently saw no need to write it down. Christ's own resurrection and ascension are proof enough that what he said is true, and Mary's progress through that sequence of events doesn't add anything to what Christ taught. It simply confirms what he taught; it demonstrates that same truth, and it shows us what is supposed to happen to each of us.

Christ's promise of life after death included the human body, too, as well as the soul, "for God formed Man to be imperishable; the image of his own nature he made him. But by the envy of the Devil death entered into the world, and they who are in his possession experience it" (Ws 2:23-24; 1Cr 15:14-22). So the immortality of human beings, and the resurrection of the dead, have always been integral parts of Christian doctrine. The teaching is that after we die we're judged, and that our state of everlasting life accords with the record that we've established during our temporary life on Earth.

Those whose sins are grave, who have stubbornly and proudly turned away from the way of life that Christ requires as part of his Covenant, are farthest from God, in everlasting torment because they are permanently unable to experience the divine love that they've willfully rejected. There are others who have embraced that love and have tried to live in accordance with it, but they have failed slightly to achieve its standard and have not had those sins forgiven or have not had the effects of those sins removed—which is normally done through the ministry of the Church. These people have to be purified before being admitted forever to the sight of God, so they are delayed a while on their way. They suffer, of course, from that same torment of distance from God, but they know that they are on their way, and that their suffering won't last forever.

But those who are entirely without sin would move directly to the presence of God. Like Christ, they stand in their resurrected bodies, which are now "glorified"—that is, free from the imperfections and debilities that afflict all humans in this life, and more like the bodies of Adam and Eve must have been before the advent of sin. In fact, it's original sin that exposes our bodies to corruption, in the first place. And because Christ was free from the effects of original sin, and free from any other sin because it's impossible for

God to do anything contrary to God's will, he rose from the dead quickly; and he, being God, ascended into Heaven by his own power. Anybody else who would be born free from original sin, and who lived absolutely free from actual sin, would likewise pass into Heaven without delay. But such a person could not ascend into Heaven by his own power. Such a person would have to be taken up—assumed—by God's power.

Mary's immediate assumption into Heaven is prefigured in Scripture by the passing of the prophet Elias, who was taken up to Heaven body and soul (4Kn 2:1-11), and before that by the carrying of the Ark of the Covenant into Jerusalem (2Kn 5:6-6:15). The transport of the Ark, particularly, is often depicted in Christian art as prophecies of Mary's being carried into the heavenly Jerusalem and crowned as Queen of Heaven, as the Ark was received into the Holy of Holies and crowned with the Presence of God.

The perfect conformity of Mary's will to the will of God kept her from actual sin, but her freedom from original sin required a special dispensation. That dispensation is part of the doctrine of the Immaculate Conception, which is a necessary precondition of the Assumption.

The phrase "Immaculate Conception" is sometimes misunderstood as referring to the Incarnation of Christ, but the two events are entirely different. The Incarnation (Latin *in-*, into, and *carnem*, flesh) is the moment of the conception of Jesus through the agency of the Holy Spirit in the womb of Mary; it took place at the Annunciation, which is usually celebrated on March 25, nine months before Christmas. The Immaculate Conception is the conception of Mary herself by her parents Joachim and Anna.

We know something about Mary's parents solely from the Church's collective memory. None of the official records survive because, according to the old *Ecclesiastical History* and the *Chronicle* written down by St. Bede, Herod burned all of the genealogical books that were stored in the Temple of Jerusalem—that way, nobody would notice that he was not of noble birth, not even of Jewish birth, really; and nobody would be able to trace the ancestry of anybody else who came along and claimed to be the Messiah. Without the records, he thought, he could even claim to be not just King of the Jews but the Messiah himself, as his grandson Herod Agrippa tried to do later (Ac 12:21-23; Josephus, *Antiquities* 19:8).

Of course, the whole chain of "begats" in the Bible ends directly in Jesus and nobody else (Mt 1:1-17); the Bible is the history of that one family from which the Messiah was to come. And while the records in the Temple were the official lists they weren't the only ones; the Jews knew their own families, and the Apostles were perfectly able to recite who was descended from whom. Mary's ancestry was repeated generation to generation, and occasionally written down—St. Jerome, for one, said that he learned the whole history of Mary's ancestry and birth from a little book on the subject in his youth, and he wrote it down himself in his *Prologue* to the Vulgate. Later Fathers, such as St. John Damascene repeated her genealogy, too, so it has never departed from the Church's memory. Of course, like the genealogies in the Bible, this chain of procreation skips a few generations and mentions only the most prominent of her forefathers, but Nathan, son of David, begat Levi, who begat Panthar, who begat Barpanthar, who begat Joachim, and Joachim begat the Virgin Mary.

All of these old writings give at least a general outline of the history of Mary's parents. Joachim, from Nazareth in Galilee, married Anna, who was from Bethlehem in Judea, David's city. Anna had a sister named Ismeria, who was the mother of Elizabeth, wife of Zachary and mother of St. John the Baptizer. But Anna herself had no children, and although she and Joachim hoped and prayed for a child, she passed the years of child-bearing without issue.

The *Protevangelion of James* and the *Gospel of Pseudo-Matthew* both relate the story of Anna's seeing a sparrow's nest, full of cheeping chicks, in a laurel tree, and groaning aloud to the Lord, "You have given offspring to every living thing, and they rejoice over their young; but you have shut me out alone from the gift of your goodness. Yet you know, O Lord, that from the beginning of my marriage I have vowed that, if you would give me son or daughter, I would dedicate the child to thee in thy holy Temple."

Still, her heartfelt prayer went unanswered. Then, in their old age, they went up to Jerusalem to celebrate the Feast of the Dedication (2Pr 7:9; Jn 10:22). Joachim approached the altar to offer his sacrifice, but a priest drove him away angrily, saying for all to hear that nobody who had not given increase to the people of God should dare to approach the altar. So Joachim left, but he was ashamed to go home to face his kinsmen, who had all heard the priest's words. Instead, he went out into the fields to spend some time among his shepherds, and to think and pray.

While he was there, an angel appeared before him, and said, "I am sent to thee to announce that thy petitions are granted, because thine almsdeeds have ascended to the sight of the Lord. I have seen thy shame, and I have heard the reproach of barrenness that has been wrongly cast upon thee. Yet God does not punish nature, but sin: and when he closes a womb, it is only so that he might open it wondrously later, so that everyone may know that the child born of it is not the fruit of lust, but the reward of divine generosity."

The angel reminded Joachim of Sara, and of Rachel, who bore pivotally important children in their barrenness, and of the great judges Samson and

THE ASSUMPTION

Solomon, who were also born of mothers called barren.

"Therefore," the angel said, "take credit at my words, and believe these examples; and remember that those conceived of barren mothers after long delay are likely to be more admirable than those born in the usual way. And Anna thy wife shall conceive and bear thee a daughter; and thou shalt call her Name Mary. In fulfillment of thy vow, she shall be consecrated to the Lord from her infancy, and filled with the Holy Spirit from her mother's womb. And she shall not live in the world among ordinary people, but in the Temple itself, so that no evil can be thought of her."

According to some ancient texts, the angel confided to Joachim that his daughter would be the mother of the Messiah, but all agree that he gave the man a sign to look for. "When thou shalt come to the Golden Gate of Jerusalem, Anna thy wife shall meet thee there—she who now mourns at your absence shall rejoice at thy coming." For her part, Anna had not seen her husband since that embarrassing day when he went up to the altar. But the angel came to her, too, and told her the same things, so she hurried out to the Golden Gate to be there when Joachim came, rejoicing in their news and thankful for the great blessing that God had given them.

Of course, Joachim and Anna probably didn't know that this child of the miracle was conceived free from the stain of original sin. And although St. Anna and St. Joachim do have their own feast days in the universal calendar—his used to be the day after the Feast of the Assumption itself—none of these old accounts is taught as an article of faith. But the Church does teach that Mary was preserved, by a unique grace, from ever contracting original sin; her human nature was unstained, free from the corruption of sin that afflicted Adam and Eve and all of their other children.

This is extraordinary, of course, but it isn't unprecedented: Mary was endowed with supernatural gifts like those given to Adam and Eve themselves, but lost by them through sin. That's why she is called the New Eve; and what happened to Mary is what was supposed to happen to Eve, and to Adam, and to all of their descendants, if the first parents of Mankind had kept from sin. She was accorded this privilege, of course, so that she would be a suitable mother for the Son of God. She was conceived without contracting the taint of original sin; hence the term Immaculate Conception.

The Immaculate Conception of Mary is included in the Deposit of Faith, the body of doctrine originally given to the Apostles and passed on by the Church. This does not necessarily mean that Christ told the Apostles about it explicitly while he walked among them, though. It means principally that the doctrine is implicit in everything that Christ did teach explicitly, including all that he revealed about his own nature and all of those parts of his teachings that eventually were written down and compiled into the Bible. Like many other doctrines that must also be true if anything that Christ said explicitly is true, the doctrine of the Immaculate Conception has crystallized over the centuries, becoming sharper and clearer through years of meditation and study.

But the fact of it has always been taught and celebrated by the Church. And the definitive doctrinal statement issued by Pius IX Ferretti in 1854 accords perfectly well with the decree of the Lateran Council of 649, which called Mary Immaculate, with the affirmation of the doctrine promulgated in 1661 by Alexander VII Chigi, and with the tracts, histories, sermons, and liturgies dating from patristic and indeed from apostolic times. Since Genesis, in fact.

It's often been said that Gn 3:15, the promise of a woman who will crush the head of Satan, refers to Mary's sinlessness. The Messiah is, obviously, the offspring of the woman who will crush the serpent's head (in Hebrew, Greek, and Syriac texts, the pronoun referring to the person who will crush the serpent is masculine; it's feminine in the Vulgate, but the idea is the same: the woman is the source of Satan's utter defeat).

The passage can't refer to Eve, the only woman in existence at the time, because she could only convey to her posterity a fallen condition, a life wounded by sin. And in any case she had agreed with the serpent, so there was no enmity between them—or at least, having given in to him, she did not have the power to defeat him permanently. Only a person preserved from the effects of Eve's sin could defeat Satan utterly; so Mary, immaculately conceived, is contained in that passage of Genesis as a lily is contained in the bulb. Mary and Eve were both innocent at first, St. Ephrem the Syrian explained, "but Eve became the cause of death, and Mary the cause of life".

Gabriel's salutation to Mary, *Ave gratia plena*, "Hail, full of grace", has also been interpreted, customarily, to mean that Mary was endowed with as much grace as a human being could receive, which would also put her on that same prelapsarian plane as Adam and Eve in the beginning, exempt from original sin and its effects. Evidently this, too, was understood from earliest times; the oldest formal treatment of it is by St. Ephrem the Syrian, who died in 373.

Just before the Council of Ephesus was convened to correct the heresy taught by Nestorius, any number of eastern Fathers spoke eloquently on the matter, among them St. Proclus, who said that Mary "was formed from stainless clay". Later, the same doctrine was articulated by other great saints and Fathers like St. Sophronius of Jerusalem and St. Andrew of Crete. St. John Damascene wrote that the angelic salutation shows that the holy daughter of Joachim and Anna "who has escaped the fiery darts of the Evil One" (*Sermon 1 On the Nativity* 7), is a new Paradise to which the serpent has no access (*Sermon 2 On the Dormition*).

These interpretations harmonize with the doctrine, but it's more to the point to take a broader view of Scriptural passages on the matter. The story of Mary as related by St. Luke and St. Matthew definitely shows her to be a particularly holy person, endowed with special graces by her Creator; and it's clear that only a perfect holiness would be appropriate to the perfect holiness of the office for which she was created.

Certainly God fashions his saints according to his own ends (Rm 8, 9), and he requires holiness of all who draw near him (1Pt 1:16). St. Thomas Aquinas (*Summa* 3:27:1-5) notes that St. John the Baptizer, like Jeremia, was sanctified in the womb, so it's reasonable to believe that Mary was sanctified before birth, too. And, he adds, because grace must increase as one draws nearer to the source of all grace, and because Mary as close as anybody possibly could be to the Messiah who is the "principle of grace", it is reasonable to understand that her sanctification was complete (*cf.* Jr 1:5; Lk 1:41).

T he implications of all of this became clear slowly in the West, more quickly in the East, in the areas more directly under the influence of councils like those of Ephesus and Constantinople, where ecumenical councils had discussed the basic theology involved in the matter. By the eighth or ninth century, though, the doctrine of the Immaculate Conception was already universal. (The Greek Orthodox Church taught the doctrine for several centuries after the schism that started in the eleventh century, but they've gradually replaced it with the idea that Mary was like everybody else until she was made sinless at the time of the Annunciation. This is now the principal doctrinal point on which the Greek Orthodox Church differs from the Church as a whole, but because it originated, historically, in a well-documented drifting away from the authentic teachings of the Apostles, it doesn't seem to be much of a bar to reunion.)

In any event, Christians everywhere had always understood the Immaculate Conception of Mary to be a fact, and they celebrated it in literature and song, in art and in liturgy, across the known world. The Immaculate Conception had a special feast day as early as the year 700, and by the year 1050 it was celebrated from Syria to Scotland.

But when the Normans invaded Britain in 1066 they undertook the reorganization of the institutional Church there, trying to bring the English Church into conformity with Norman French practices. As it happened, the Normans were practically the only people in Christendom who didn't celebrate the Immaculate Conception, and oddly enough those among them who were made bishops in England had never noticed that everybody else had been doing so since time immemorial. The Feast was new to them; so they suppressed it at Winchester and Canterbury, and most of the other major churches in the kingdom followed suit.

Even so, local celebrations of the Immaculate Conception went on all over England anyway, no matter what the government had to say about it; the

English have always been particularly good friends of Mary's. By about 1125 these observances had virtually displaced the official ban, and more churches in England were celebrating the feast than not. But because the Feast of the Immaculate Conception wasn't officially on the calendar of the English Church, the practice had to be investigated. This led to about six hundred years of intensive study of the doctrine that, until then, had been neither seriously challenged nor definitively stated.

By the twelfth century, most authorities understood the doctrine more or less as it was to be stated by Pius IX, and therefore they had no objection to the liturgical celebration of the event—even in Normandy, by that time, the Immaculate Conception was celebrated as a feast equal in rank to that of the Annunciation. On the other hand, two English bishops, Roger of Salisbury and Bernard of St. David's, raised the issue of discipline. They had no objection to the doctrine of the Immaculate Conception, but they said that since the celebration of the Feast had been prohibited by the King's council under William the Conqueror, it was not to be celebrated in England, period. But the provincial Council of London of 1129 decided that, since nobody in England doubted the doctrine, the celebration was perfectly permissible.

There were still opponents of the doctrine, though. Even St. Bernard of Clairvaux wrote a stern letter to the canons of Lyons cathedral asserting that the Holy Spirit could not possibly be involved in anything as inherently evil as the conception of a child. But he was wrong; even great saints can be wrong. It's surprising that he was that wrong on something that integral to the Faith, but he was. The conception of a child is not perceived as inherently evil, but inherently good, an unqualified good in the fulfillment of God's commandment (Gn 1:26-31; Is 9:5; Sr 40:18; etc.). And anyway the Holy Spirit was involved in the conception of the child Jesus of Nazareth, wasn't he, and he's involved in the conception of every other human child—which is why the Nicene Creed repeats at every Mass that he is the Lord and Giver of Life.

So after about the twelfth century those who objected to the doctrine most strenuously found themselves in the position of Devil's Advocate; their questions served only to clarify the concept and strengthen the terms in which it was presented. Nobody brought forward any objection to the doctrine serious enough to condemn the doctrine or even to bring it into question. You can still review the learned documents of these teachings in collections like those of the industrious Pedro de Alva y Astorga, O.F.M., whose *Monumenta Antiqua Immaculatæ Conceptionis Sacratissimæ Virginis Mariæ* and *Monumenta Italo-Gallica ... pro Immaculata Virginis Mariæ Conceptione* (both Louvain, 1664), are still basic reference works on the subject.

The classic answer to the last basic objection, though, came from Bl. John

Duns Scotus, the Franciscan from Oxford. Some theologians still wondered whether the idea of Mary's preservation from original sin ran contrary to the whole idea of Christ's redemptive work. No, it doesn't, said Scotus: "More than anyone else, Mary needed Christ as her Redeemer, because she would have contracted original sin ... if the Mediator's grace had not prevented it. So, as others need Christ so that sin already contracted may be remitted for them through his merit, Mary needed a preventive, an anticipatory, Mediator even more, lest there be sin to be contracted, and lest she contract it". Christ redeemed Mary, in other words, just as he redeems anybody else; he just did it in a slightly different way, because he had a very special vocation—a unique vocation—for her.

After the debates settled down in the late seventeenth century, virtually no more objections were raised, and the doctrine had been clarified and stated precisely. It could be seen now more fully in light of its deep relationships with the rest of revelation, yet still it was essentially exactly as the body of the Faithful had always accepted it. The Feast of the Immaculate Conception, after all, is ancient, dating at least to the seventh century. Sixtus IV della Rovere approved a new proper for the Feast in 1476, and he dedicated his new private oratory in the Vatican (the Sistine Chapel) to Mary in that title when he built it in 1477.

By 1846 the Sixth Provincial Council of Baltimore adopted Our Lady of the Immaculate Conception as the patroness of the United States. Finally, in 1854, Pius IX Ferretti proclaimed (*Ineffabilis Deus*), from the Throne of Peter, that "the doctrine that the Most Blessed Virgin Mary, from the first instant of her conception, was, by the singular grace and privilege of God, in view of the merits of Christ Jesus, the Savior of the human race, preserved free from every stain of original sin, has been revealed by God and is therefore to be firmly and constantly believed by all the Faithful."

Mary's sinlessness means that her body would not have to undergo that delay that comes for the bodies of the rest of us between departing this life and beginning everlasting life, with the soul reunited to a glorified body and standing forever in the presence of God. It was sin that brought corruption into the world, and, because Mary is free from sin, she could not undergo corruption. "Today the Immaculate Virgin ... returns not to dust but to the mansions of Heaven," St. John Damascene explained to his eighth-century congregation on the Feast of the Assumption (*Sermon 2 On the Dormition*; cf. Gn 3:19). That is, having completed the course of her earthly life, she was assumed body and soul into heavenly glory, passively drawn there by God's power.

The collective memory of the Church on the Assumption is assisted by sermons written by any number of Fathers, including St. Andrew of Crete,

St. John Damascene, St. Juvenal of Jerusalem, St. Modestus of Jerusalem, St. Jerome, St. Augustine, and many others of the patristic age, as well as by a book written by, or attributed to, St. Melito of Sardis (*On the Passing of the Virgin*, before 190) and another ascribed to St. John the Evangelist (*On the Passing of Our Blessed Lady*).

The most popular source for many of these elaborations is the *Book of the Names of God* written by Dionysius, the disciple of St. Paul. It's structured on the framework of the main points of the occurrence, but, as St. Jerome wrote to St. Paula and St. Eustochium, "many other things are set down in it as symbols rather than as facts ... that, manifestly, are to be set aside rather than believed." For instance, there's the story that St. Thomas, the Doubter, wasn't at the tomb at that moment and refused to believe the other Apostles, so the Virgin's girdle—her belt—dropped into his hands, still tied, as a proof to him that she had passed into Paradise body and soul, like Elias (4Kn 2:11-14). Many of the other written records also add little scenes like this, and lots of them have been depicted in devotional art over the centuries. Yet the framework of narrative that organizes all of these embroidered texts is remarkably stable.

St. John, Mary's son by adoption at the foot of the Cross (Jn 19:25-27), lived with her until her days on Earth were over, although there's no reliable record as to just how long that was. St. Epiphanius, for example, records that Mary lived for twenty-four years after the Ascension, but he says that he doesn't really know anything definite about the details (*On Heresies* 79:11); other sources say, probably for symbolic reasons, that she lived on for anywhere from three to thirty-three years, achieving the age of sixty or seventy-two, or some other symbolically significant number.

However long it was, Mary's life was not intended to last forever, any more than anybody else's is. What happened when the number of those days was fulfilled is clear enough from Sacred Tradition and from ancient texts, although the written sources are a little sketchy on details—again, because their authors liked to fill out their accounts with features that would carry moral symbolism to their readers and hearers.

Evidently, Mary lived on Earth until she was overcome with memories of Christ's death and resurrection; that is, until she could no longer bear the separation from her Son—St. Alphonsus of Liguori, in his eighteenth-century *Glories of Mary*, muses that she may well have recalled the psalm of David, "had I but wings like a dove, I would fly away and be at my rest" (Ps 54:7). Some old sources recount that an angel told her that the Apostles would gather around her that day and give her a noble burial—the eleventh-century Symeon Metaphrastes, Symeon "the Compiler" mentions the angel, and three hundred years later the historian Nicephorus Gregoras still reported the visit in his *History of Rome* as a fact.

Whether by angelic prompting, supernatural agility, or more pedestrian means, the Apostles gathered around Mary, coming back to her from their missions across the known world. She told them what the angel had said, and St. John told his brethren to see to it that no one should weep for her passing, so that nobody could say, "See! These men preach the resurrection of the dead, but they themselves fear death, and mourn the loss of their friend and mother!"

Of course, Mary probably didn't need an angel to announce her passing; her will is in perfect accord with God's. And St. John probably didn't need to warn the other Apostles; Christians have a tendency to rejoice at funerals, which mark the transition to everlasting happiness—we're supposed to agree with St. Laurence Justinian, who told the weeping companions around his deathbed, "Get out of here with your tears. This is a time to rejoice, not to mourn." Whatever the details, when the Apostles saw that Mary's time had come, they laid her on a bier and took her outside the city to a tomb.

They were concerned because some of the Jews had threatened to violate her burial and destroy her body because she had borne the one who converted so many thousands from the Old Covenant to the New. So the Apostles kept watch, and on the third day they found that the otherwise empty tomb was filled with flowers, the old sources relate—roses of an ineffable heavenly fragrance. "The Immaculate Mother of God," as Pius XII Pacelli wrote, "having completed the course of her earthly life, was assumed body and soul into heavenly glory" (*Munificentissimus Deus*).

Nobody knows precisely where this tomb was; almost all of the old legends say that it was in the Valley of Josaphat outside Jerusalem, but this detail is not intended as an historical fact, it seems. That valley lies about eleven miles from Jerusalem, far from Ephesus (which is evidently where Mary and St. John lived), and it's not likely that the Apostles took Mary to a tomb there.

Josaphat isn't a valley, in any case, but a man, the fourth king of Juda, the son of Asa, who reigned from about 914 to 889 BC. The only valley in Scripture that carries this name is the one mentioned by the prophet Joel: "Yes, in those days, and at that time, when I would restore the fortunes of Juda and Jerusalem, I will assemble all the nations and bring them down to the Valley of Josaphat, and I will enter into judgement with them" (Jl 4:1-2). He didn't mean that there was a specific valley anywhere near Jerusalem that was called that, because there wasn't. Joel probably meant this simply as a reference to the place of the Last Judgement on Earth, wherever that will be, because in Hebrew Josaphat, יהושפט (yahošafat), means "God has judged".

But then in 333 a literal-minded pilgrim from Bordeaux visited the Holy Land, coming from France through northern Italy and the Danube Valley to Constantinople, and then down through Asia Minor and Syria. He must have been fairly wealthy, because we still have the itinerary that he wrote along the way, and it records the stops that he and his party made to change horses; an ordinary person would have had to walk. The Pilgrim of Bordeaux was certainly no scholar, and he, or his guides, made a lot of mistakes about what he was looking at—he thought that the Transfiguration took place on the Mount of Olives, for instance (Mt 17:1-8).

Somebody evidently told him that the Valley of Kidron east of Jerusalem was the Valley of Josaphat that Joel talked about, and, with the tomb of that king there before him, he took it literally. Then the Pilgrim of Bordeaux went home and published his travel notebook as the *Itinerarium Burdigalense* or *Itinerarium Hierosolymitanum*; it was popular for centuries, and although people saw his obvious mistakes in it, the Kidron was known forever after as the Valley of Josaphat. Even St. Jerome adopted that name for it, and his opinion bears a lot of weight.

But the name probably would have endured anyway because there are so many associations that support it. For one thing, that valley runs from the Tombs of the Kings to the Tombs of the Judges, so it's always been an important burial site, which is suitable to the idea of the Last Judgement—right up to the twentieth century pious Jews have asked to be buried there, so that they will be in the first rows at the end of Time. This valley is where Helcias, Ezechias, and Josais threw all of the things that had polluted the Temple (4Kn 23:4; 2Pr 29:16, 30:14), and it's where Asa himself destroyed the idol of Priapus that his mother had brought to Jerusalem (3Kn 15:13); so Josaphat's Valley of Kidron suggests purification and restoration of the worship of the True God, as Joel said.

But this valley is more important prophetically for what happens to people who cross it. David escaped with his life by crossing the Kidron when Absalom pursued him to kill him (2Kn 15:23), but Solomon set it as a limit for the prophet Semei and gave him a prophetic warning: stay in Jerusalem, he said, "for on what day soever thou shalt go out and shalt pass over the brook Kidron, know that thou shalt be put to death" (3Kn 2:37). In fact, Jesus crossed it on his way to Gethsemani (Jn 18:1). The Valley of Kidron, the Valley of Josaphat, is the Valley of the Shadow of Death, in a way, the depths that mark the transition from one life to the next; Christ's crossing over it shows that it has to be passed on the way to the heavenly or the earthly Jerusalem, and to judgement.

All of these associations persisted through early Christian times: the tomb of St. James is there in the Valley of Josaphat, too. After the *Itinerarium Burdigalense* was known across Europe, pilgrims flocked to the site, looking thoughtfully on the valley as they meditated on the Last Things. And by about 450, when the time had come to build a pilgrimage church there, the only logical dedication for it was to Mary of the Assumption, in memory of the first, and so far the only, Christian lifted up body and soul to everlasting life in Heaven.

Commemorations of the Assumption came to be centered on this church to the east of Jerusalem, not at Ephesus; but nobody ever said that Mary's tomb was in Jerusalem until more than a hundred years after this church was built. From then until the Moslems of the area changed the building into a little mosque dedicated to Abraham, Christian pilgrims always had a tendency to call it the Tomb of the Blessed Virgin.

Like the doctrine of the Immaculate Conception, the doctrine of the Assumption wasn't defined in precise and official terms until comparatively late, and in fact times didn't require a definitive formulation of the teaching before Pius XII published his encyclical in 1950. But, also like the teachings about the beginnings of Mary's life on Earth, the teachings about the end of it are implicit in the Deposit of Faith. The Fathers of the Church and virtually every great saint who came after them uniformly testify to Christian belief in the event, which was celebrated liturgically since about the fourth or fifth century, at least.

Some of the surest evidence for the continuity of any teaching, apart from the Bible itself, consists of the liturgies that celebrate that point of doctrine. These have to be composed very carefully, because they structure the Mass on that day; and what has been said on what occasions over the centuries testifies unanswerably to the substance of the Church's understanding of the point.

In fact, the Feast of the Assumption of Mary is the oldest Marian feast on record. Evidently, it was first celebrated in Jerusalem; an Armenian lectionary from 434 gives the text of a commemoration kept there on August 15, the date that St. Jerome recorded as that of the actual event. The observance got a boost from the Council of Ephesus in 431, although the exact date of the Feast varied according to the province. In Egypt, Arabia, and France it was observed in January; the Greek-speaking parts of the Church celebrated it in August, as the Church in Palestine had since before the year 500, according to the oldest surviving biography of St. Theodosius.

Eastern Christians, displaced by the Moslems, carried the texts and customs of their Marian feast days westward, and by turn of the eighth century, in the pontificate of St. Sergius I—who was himself a Syrian—the Assumption had become one of the major feasts of the city of Rome. It was celebrated there on August 15, too, but other western dioceses kept the Feast on August 23, August 29, or September 13, and some preceded their observance with a vigil or followed it with another observance on the octave or on the fortieth day afterwards. Whenever and wherever it was observed, it was always a major feast. Until the early years of this century, for example, the city of Gerace in southern Italy celebrated for three days, commemorating Mary's passing on the fifteenth of August, her Assumption on the sixteenth, and her coronation as Queen of Heaven on the seventeenth.

By the eighteenth century the Feast of the Assumption was virtually universal. As theologians studied the Assumption itself, of course, questions about the details arose, and speculations about the precise nature and extent of its theological implications; these musings evidently gave some people the wrong impression, because Benedict XIV Lambertini reminded the Faithful in an encyclical (*De Festis Beatæ Virginis Mariæ*) that denying the fact of the Assumption was impious and blasphemous. In the nineteenth century, scholars sought to establish clearer statements of this truth and explore its more profound connections to the rest of revelation, and its implications for the whole cycle of redemption. In the twentieth, with the world's eyes turned so tragically downward to the Earth and all of its empty promise, Pius XII decided that the time was right to remind us all of the promise of the resurrection and the life.

There's still another body of evidence that supports the historical fact of the Assumption unanswerably—or, rather, the lack of a body of evidence does. Think about this: although Mary is indisputably the most loved, most revered, and most honored saint of all, there is not one record in the history of Christianity of any relic of her body. Christians have flocked to venerate the head of St. John the Baptizer, the grave of St. Peter, and physical remains of thousands of other saints for centuries, but there have never been any physical relics of Mary.

Relics still draw crowds of pilgrims, and even a spurious relic of the Mother of God would make any shrine an unsurpassed attraction, if people would think that it was real: but none has ever been claimed to exist. The complete absence of Marian relics makes sense only if Christians have always known that her body was not available on Earth for the taking of relics. That's the only condition that would have made such a claim nonsense; and, integral as the Assumption is to the Christian faith, it's the only fact that would make even frauds aware that nobody would take seriously the claim of having some relic of Mary's body.

The exceptions prove the rule. Just about the only major blunder on record in the matter came from the fifth-century Emperor Marcian, who began life as a simple unlettered soldier. Evidently he was sufficiently unaware of Christian doctrine to ask the bishop of Jerusalem, St. Juvenal, to send him the body of the Mother of God as a relic for the Holy Palace in Constantinople, which is where most major relics were kept. St. Juvenal, then attending the Council of Chalcedon, responded patiently that Mary had passed from this life in the presence of all of the Apostles, who had buried her and sealed her in a tomb; which, when they opened it on the request of St. Thomas, was found to be empty. The Apostles, St. Juvenal concluded, knew this to mean that Mary had been assumed, body and soul, into Heaven, in perfect fulfillment of her Son's teachings. So, he said, no relics of her body have been left behind for the veneration of the Faithful.

In fact, the lack of relics of the Blessed Mother is one reason that liturgical feasts in honor of Mary—although they started very early on—started somewhat later than those of other saints. Feast days commemorating saints took shape around the celebrations of martyrs (Rv 6:9), and almost always took their start at the churches built over their relics tombs; but Mary was not a martyr, and no church claimed to be built over her final resting place—the church in the Valley of Josaphat wasn't put up until much later, and it was built to commemorate the fact of her assumption, not the spot on which it happened. So, although there's plenty of documentary and archæological evidence that her intercession was implored by public prayers since at least the third century, the lack of relics of the Blessed Mother apparently kept those prayers distinct from liturgy, until at least the fifth century.

And there's one other consideration that ought to be remembered in thinking about the Assumption. The bodies of many of Mary's friends—St. Catherine Labouré, St. Bernadette Soubirous, Ven. Jacinta Marto—didn't decompose when they died (Ps 15:10; Acts 2:27). They remained fresh, supple, and perfectly intact long after the spirits of these favored ladies departed from them; in fact, they remain fresh and rosy to this day. For that matter, the incorrupt bodies of hundreds of other saints are rosy in another way, too, emanating—like the flowers that the Apostles found in Mary's tomb—the penetrating fragrance of roses sweet above the flowers of nature.

E VA ❀ AV E

THE CORONATION OF MARY

L IKE THE ASCENSION AND THE ASSUMPTION, THE CORONATION OF MARY as Queen of Heaven is understood as a symbol; but unlike any other Mystery of the Rosary, it's understood as a symbolic way of expressing a reality, not as an actual event performed in a significant way. No doctrine teaches that Mary, once assumed into Heaven, was given an actual crown to wear on her head. This Mystery expresses the truth that Mary, once received into Heaven, stands higher than anybody else there, except Christ himself. "She alone excels, both in Heaven and on Earth; who is holier than she?" St. John Chrysostom asked. "Prophets are not, nor martyrs, nor patriarchs; no, not even Angels, Thrones, Dominations, Seraphim, nor Cherubim. No creature can be found, visible or invisible, to excel her; she is both handmaiden and mother of God" (*Metaphrases; cf.* Lk 1:38, 43).

Her sinlessness is essential to the unparalleled rank that she holds, so the idea of her queenly status in Heaven is implicit in the doctrine of the Assumption; but primarily she holds that title as she holds every other title and honor: because she is the mother of Jesus. "Call her Queen of Heaven, Sovereign Mistress of the Angels, or any other title you please; but you can never honor her more than by simply calling her the Mother of God," St. Peter de la Celle concluded (*On the Bread, to John of Salisbury*).

Pius XII recalled that "like her son before her, she conquered death and was raised body and soul to the glory of Heaven." And just as Jesus, the Christ, the King of Heaven, sits at the right hand of the Father, he said, Mary, the Queen "sits in splendor at the right hand of her son, the immortal King of the Ages" (*Munificentissimus Deus; cf.* 3Kn 2:19-20; Ps 46). In his encyclical *To The Queen of Heaven*, he instituted the Feast of the Queenship of Mary explicitly "so that everyone may more clearly recognize and more zealously venerate the kind and maternal rule of the Mother of God."

The title "Queen of Heaven" itself comes straight out of the Gospels, in Elizabeth's greeting to Mary at the Visitation: "and how have I deserved that the Mother of my Lord should come to me?" (Lk 1:43). It's the same phrase that you find in 4Kn 10:13, when the brethren of the King of Juda explained that they had come to salute the sons of the queen mother. But notice that Elizabeth doesn't ask, "How have I deserved that my Queen should come to me?" That's not how queenship worked in antiquity. Mary is of the royal house of David, but that wasn't enough to make her a queen in earthly terms, and her earthy ancestry has no real relation to her title Queen of Heaven.

In fact, our word "queen" comes from the same ancient root as the Greek γυνή, which simply means woman. A queen, to the Greeks and Romans, was exactly that: a person who took her rank not in her own right but by virtue of the son she produced; a queen was simply a woman who produced the child of a king, or a child who became a king. The pattern of thinking reflected in these ancient words is interesting, almost ironic, because it describes exactly the basis of Mary's queenship, and yet Mary is the one who utterly reversed it.

Pagan antiquity didn't really have sovereign queens. Cleopatra of Egypt, Dido of Carthage, and Zenobia of Palmyra were seen as aberrations, women who acted like men and—to the surprise of the Greeks and Romans—actually accomplished things. Like the mythic Amazons, these women were pointed out as bizarre departures from the order of nature. Greco-Roman historians praised them for their "masculine" minds and always concluded that some feminine frailty brought these presumptuous ladies the correction that was coming to them: defeat and annihilation at the hands of a state more normally constituted.

It was an attitude that grew naturally out of the ancients' view of womanhood; and a culture's view of women always pivots on its definition of marriage. To the pagans, marriage was a contract that largely consisted of proprietary considerations. Daughters were transferred from father to husband along with property, and in fact as property themselves. The husband virtually owned his wife as he might own a house or a horse; women were generally not permitted to appear in public nor to own property in their own right, because they were understood to have no rights. Even those formidable Roman matrons who moved and shook did so through their husbands or sons; Zenobia and Cleopatra seized power in the names of their infant sons. None held office.

This view of women as property is what makes marriages easily dissoluble by divorce—any civil proprietary contract can be abrogated with the consent of both parties who make it, which would be the husband and his father-in-law, not the wife, not the property herself. In most cultures that practice this kind of marriage, any children of the union also belong to the father as property, just as the children of his slaves would. Under Roman law, the *pater familias* could order his children aborted, or he could have them abandoned to die, or he could kill them by his own hand without committing a crime. And he could throw his wife out or send her back to her father, whenever he liked.

To Christians, Matrimony is a sacrament, instituted by Christ (Mt 5:31-32,

19:3-9). This makes the world a very different place. Nobody can be forced to receive a sacrament; it requires the consent of free will, because the recipient has to be properly disposed to receive it. Matrimony involves two persons, usually two baptized persons, so both have to consent, and their individual consent weighs equally in the balance. Because the bride has to consent as freely as her groom has to consent, she must be as fully a person as he is. Both men and women must have the same nature and the same rights, in this view, so a woman can own property: but she can't be property. She has every right that anybody else has, and she can determine her own course of life.

> The little ritual of "giving this woman to this man" has never been part of the sacrament of Matrimony. It used to be part of the old English betrothal ceremony, and the Church of England transferred it to the marriage ceremony to fill the void left when the sacrament of Matrimony was displaced in the Reformation. But in the Church's view no human being can own another, so none can "give" another to anybody. That's why bride and groom in Catholic ceremonies walk down the aisle together. That custom reflects their status as equal, free human beings who together consent to the sacrament.

All of this equality of women was unheard of in the Hellenistic states and in the Roman Empire itself, and it's very different from Jewish practice (Dt 24:1, etc.). When Christ came, all of the civil laws in the known world reduced women to the status of property; all of the institutions that structured society supported this view, even to prescribing the death penalty for women who tried to move toward recognition of equal rights.

Christians simply could not live in denial of the equality of all the baptized. They certainly couldn't accommodate their way of life to a society that denied the humanity of some class of humans; they couldn't refuse self-determination, freedom of conscience, and even property rights to women, any more than they could consider children as anything less than human. Christ's teachings on these essential matters can't be changed, so society itself had to be restructured. In the end, the Christian view prevailed; it was the sacrament of Matrimony, more than any other factor, that brought down the Roman Empire. And Matrimony was instituted because Mary decided to make her son's work possible.

M ary's unique position in Christian theology is the focus of all of the honor paid to the dignity of women in Christian cultures, and it's really the foundation stone of the recognition of women's rights in civil law. Her revolutionary achievement is what has often led philologists to think that her name itself comes from the Hebrew word for rebellion, ‏במרים‏, but it most probably has nothing to do with that word. Still, "the modern woman will note with pleasant surprise that Mary of Nazareth, while completely devoted to the will of God, was far from being a timidly submissive woman or one whose piety was repellent to others," Paul VI wrote in his *Apostolic Exhortation on Devotion to the Blessed Virgin Mary*. "On the contrary, she was a woman who did not hesitate to proclaim that God vindicates the humble and the oppressed, and removes the powerful people of the world from their privileged positions."

She took the first of her revolutionary steps when she agreed to co-operate fully when the Word was made flesh (Jn 1:14); this was accomplished through Mary, and by her will (Lk 1:38). She was the first Christian, the first to know who Jesus of Nazareth is (Lk 1:30-33), and she nurtured him (Lk 2:7); with the aid of St. Joseph, she protected him (Mt 2:13-15) and guided him until he began his public ministry (Lk 2:51), and she stood by him through all of it, the sorrowful parts as well as the glorious (Lk 2:34-35; Jn 2:12, 19:25). Clearly, a woman who played such an active part in the work that re-structured the world is not to be treated as mere property; in fact, her power requires that she be treated with the respect properly rendered to one who commands.

Christ treated her exactly that way, and she was mindful of the honor he paid her. She herself sang of the great things that God had done for her (Lk 1:49), although "she did not explain them, because they are inexplicable," St. Thomas of Villanova explained (*The Shadow of the Virgin*). But the Church has found ways to symbolize the unparalleled dignity to which God raised Mary of Nazareth, largely from the prophetic texts of the Old Testament. Not surprisingly, homilists, theologians, and artists have looked back to the mothers of the kings to deepen their understanding of this relationship between King and Queen Mother, and—because the Father is God just as Christ is God—between King and Spouse.

Esther, queen and intercessor, is one precedent whose history prefigures Mary's career, but the most obvious precedent is Bathsheba, although that comparison can't be pressed too far. Her son Solomon is one of the great prototypes of Christ, a figure presented to us in the Old Testament to help us understand the nature and the function of the Messiah who was to come (3Kn 3:12; Mt 12:42). Like Jesus of Nazareth, he was of the House of David; in his wisdom he foreshadowed the Wisdom of God. And Solomon was the one who built the Temple that Christ tore down and replaced with his Church (Mr 14:58; Jn 2:19-22).

In a wider perspective, David, Bathsheba, and Solomon are prophetic prototypes of God the Father, Mary, and Christ himself. In fact, just as Mary stands always in Scripture as the representative of the whole Church,

Bathsheba's history (2Kn 11-12) was taken by mediæval theologians as a kind of allegory of the relationship between that Church and Christ. Bathsheba was the daughter of a man named Eliam, but her name (שֶׁ־בַּע־בַּת, literally the daughter of Seba) might indicate some connection with the Kingdom of Sheba, a Semitic state in what's now Yemen—the Queen of Sheba visited Solomon, later (3Kn 10:1-13).

In any case, Bathsheba was the wife of Uriah the Hittite. Looking down into her garden from his rooftop, David happened to see her at her bath, and he was ravished by the sight of her. For St. Bruno, among others, this pre-figured the intense love that Christ feels for his Church, cleansed in Baptism—a love so strong that he takes her from her husband, Uriah, or from the world, or from the Devil, to bring her to himself (2Kn 11:15; *cf.* Dn 13:1-63). Eventually David married Bathsheba, and their son Solomon reigned after him; but he only attained the throne through his mother's initiative.

That throne of spotless ivory and incorruptible gold that Solomon made for himself (3Kn 10:18-20), like his carriage (Cn 3:9-11), is yet another symbol of Mary, the Throne of Divine Wisdom. And when Solomon ascended to that throne Bathsheba was given the same title that Elizabeth used in reference to Mary—even before David died she was referred to as Mother of Solomon (3Kn 1:11, 2:13). Bathsheba used her queenly status to intercede with her son on behalf of those who had offended him (3Kn 2:18), just as Mary was to do.

But, unlike Bathsheba, Mary carries petitions to God whether she is asked to or not; she actively looks to the needs of good people, as she asked her son to help the host of the wedding at Cana without being directly asked to. Her queenship is based on her maternal relationship to the Messiah, but it takes its power from the fact that she is the first, and most effective, inter-cessor. After all, Christ was subject to her while he walked among us (Lk 2:51; Jn 2:1-12), and the examples of her effectiveness as intercessor record-ed in the Gospel do something more specific than show us the power of prayer for others; they show the power of Mary's special closeness to Christ. Nobody else in the Gospel has so much influence over him as his mother.

This makes perfect sense, if it's sin that keeps a person's prayers from being heard (Ps 49; Sr 35:16); the prayers of the sinless Virgin must be heard without any delay or barrier whatsoever. God by his nature concurs with anything that is good, so he can hardly refuse the petitions of one whose will is in perfect accordance with his own (Sr 35:17-18). So she rules in Heaven as an earthly queen might manage works of mercy in a kingdom here below: not by taking a seat in the council, but by ruling over the heart of her lord.

Bathsheba's son Solomon left the greatest and most exultant Biblical reference to the Queenship of Mary, the Song of Songs, the Book of Canticles. It's a representation of the sacred conversation between

Mary and Christ, and through her between Christ and his Church; it's the source of her allegorical titles such as "Tower of David" (Cn 4:4) or "enclosed garden" and "fountain sealed" (Cn 4:12), which refer to her virginal fertility.

Everything in the book—the plants, the flowers, animals and birds, the colors and materials, the gardens, the fountains, and all—is a specific symbol that ties the Song of Songs to every other part of Scripture and to virtually every aspect of western and levantine art, architecture, and literature. Verse by verse, its elaborate allegories and metaphors can be taken as the starting-points for endless meditation; Canticles is one of the books most frequently quoted in the Church's devotional literature, and it's one of the most fertile fields for symbols that communicate through the visual arts.

The symbols through which Canticles speaks of Mary come in bewildering array, so rich, so diverse, and so concentrated, that in pictures of Mary from early Christian days to the present, virtually every flower has its roots, every animal its pedigree, in the Song of Songs. Each is a symbol of some facet of Mary's relationship with God.

But the largest, most comprehensive symbol of that relationship in all of art and literature is that of coronation; and that image comes primarily from the vision that St. John had of the Heavenly Jerusalem. Like Canticles, the Apocalypse of St. John is a confusing book if you take it out of context. Apart from Sacred Tradition, it doesn't make much sense, and if subjected to private interpretation (2Pt 1:20) it gives rise to all kinds of unnecessary worries, and even to bizarre views of the whole economy of salvation. The way to extract the fullest and most accurate meaning from St. John's description of his vision is to look to the Fathers of the Church, to the great saints who have commented on this book, and to the popes who have steadily clarified the Church's understanding, starting while St. John himself was still among us.

None of these interpretations cites one, definitive significance for any of the symbols in the Book of Revelations, because that's not how these kinds of symbol work. In the same passage, the same verse, a dragon can represent Satan or the Antichrist—but then it can represent Satan and the Antichrist, too. The Woman Clothed with the Sun can stand for Mary, or for the Church, or for Mary and the Church, at the same time. While each entity has a distinct role to play in the economy of salvation, similarities among the parts played by many different entities can be captured in a single image. Searching for a single, exclusive interpretation of St. John's symbolism is simply the wrong way to go about it, rhetorically as well as doctrinally.

When the skies opened to show Heaven to St. John, he saw in the center of the city the new Temple, brilliant with the light of God; and in the center of it was the glorified Ark of the Covenant (Rv 11:19). This vision opened up to stand as a woman clothed with the Sun, with the Moon under her feet, and crowned with twelve stars. Taken in reference to Mary, this is the Queen of Heaven; the "stars" are the twelve signs of the Wheel of Life that surrounds the orb of the heavens: the Zodiac.

The Zodiac was simply the way that people mapped the sky in ancient times, and in fact it's still used that way. From any vantage point in the northern hemisphere, the Sun apparently rises farthest in the south on the winter solstice, against the backdrop of the constellation Capricorn. Then it moves the site of its rising north toward the summer solstice and then south again to the next winter solstice; then it starts to move north again. During one of these cycles, the Moon goes through its phases almost exactly twelve times. That's why there are always twelve months in a year; the annual solar cycle is divided according to the waxings and wanings of the Moon.

> Obviously, the signs of the Zodiac themselves are arbitrary, imposed on whatever pattern of stars happens to show within that particular thirty-degree arc of the sky that's marked by the sunrises during one month, one Moon. In most cases the pattern of stars themselves bears no imaginable resemblance to the animal or figure that they're said to represent; those images were chosen for symbolic reasons when people first started trying to find correspondences between the life above and the life below. The whole business of casting horoscopes (from the Greek ὥρα, hour, and σκοπός, watcher) from the relative positions of these celestial features is different from the early kind of science that sought to marshall countless observations into an intelligible and predictable system.
>
> The business of horoscopes was reserved to pagan priests, and it's properly called *astromancy*, from the Greek ἀστρο-, star, and μαντεία, divination. *Astrology* ("star-study") was run by mathematicians, not priests, and they didn't interpret their data to make personal predictions. That's why astrology survived the demise of paganism, and why it's still worthwhile—classical astrology is the root of *astronomy* ("star-laws"), and three or four thousand years of art and literature are incomprehensible without it. Even the Bible depends heavily on astrological symbolism. There's really nothing holy about astrology or unholy, as long as it doesn't substitute for religion (*cf.* Gn 1:14; 4Kg 23:5). The worst that could be said about it now—in the absence of any logically valid theory that unifies it with the rest of science and explains how it works—is that it's fatuous.

The occurrence of twelve lunar months in a solar year is the reason that twelve is always a number of completeness. In particular that number symbolizes the whole world, everything contained within the band of the Zodiac. A woman touching all three of these celestial symbols—clothed with the Sun, making the Moon her footstool, and having twelve stars her crown—is obviously Queen of Heaven.

Mary's title as Queen of Heaven, propelled by its precedents in the Old Testaments and glorified by the symbolism of the New, was accorded to her without dissent by Christians from the beginning. Naturally, Christian artists and writers have always expressed that title through its clearest and most economical symbol, showing her receiving her celestial crown from the hands of her son, from the Father (as when the Hand of God is shown piercing the sky to place the crown on her head), or from the Trinity together.

During the Middle Ages, the chivalric culture that exalted womanhood and idealized devotion of brave knights to their ladies made it seem just as natural to surround that scene with all of the symbols and trappings of earthly royalty. The French were particularly fond of hailing Mary as Queen in art and poetry, which is why you can still see sculptural groups of the Coronation over the portals of most gothic cathedrals—like Notre-Dame-de-Paris—and why the great rose-windows over their western doors are often wheels of the Zodiac recalling the Woman of the Apocalypse and the Queen of Heaven at the same time. Between about the tenth century and the eighteenth, when the Age of Chivalry at last came to an end, there is hardly a great master of painting or sculpture who didn't depict the Coronation of Mary as Queen of Heaven.

The chivalric impulse to do honor to Mary as *Notre Dame*, Our Lady, is also the reason that love songs were written to Mary—chaste and high-minded love songs, but love songs, none the less for that. The thirteenth-century hymn *Regina Cœli*—Queen of Heaven, rejoice, alleluia!—is one product of this courtly culture, but by no means the earliest. Mary had been hailed as Queen of the World, *Regina Mundi,* as early as the tenth century. In fact, the greatest compendium of her royal titles is the Litany of Loreto, named for the city where the Holy House in which Mary heard the Annunciation stood, miraculously transported from Nazareth, and where it still stands today, encased in a sculpted marble shell.

The Holy House of Loreto is a stone cottage thirty-one by thirteen feet, supposedly carried by angels from Nazareth to Tersato in Illyria in 1291. Three years later it disappeared from there to reappear near Recanati in Italy, where it reportedly moved three times in a year; then it was translated again to Loreto, where a basilica has been built around it. On the one hand, nobody mentioned such a house at

Nazareth before the sixteenth century, when people there heard about the Holy House of Loreto and wanted it back, and in fact no surviving Italian document before 1472 mentions the movement of the relic to Loreto. On the other hand, the Santa Casa itself is made of stone and brick notably different from those available at Loreto but chemically similar to materials commonly found around Nazareth; and (perhaps significantly no matter which way you take it) it stands intact on the ground with no foundation whatsoever.

The House of the Virgin made Loreto a major pilgrimage center, and the city has been the site of any number of miraculous cures over the centuries, but the Litany evidently came from the East into Italy about a hundred years before the Holy House itself; it's called "of Loreto" because St. Peter Canisius heard it there and published it under that title in 1558. It's an exceptionally beautiful litany, and it follows a very old pattern that shows up first in Exodus, in the song of Miriam (Ex 15:21). So this system of prayer was ancient when Daniel recorded the litany of the Children of Israel (Dn 3:57-87), and it was already old when the Psalmist used it.

Like Psalm 135 with its lists of divine accomplishments and responsorial "for his mercy endures forever," the Litany of Loreto consists of the various approved titles of Mary, each followed by the petition, "Pray for us", and like the ancient Litany of the Saints and all other approved litanies, it begins with the *Kyrie*. Like the old psalmodic devotions themselves, the litanies tended to get very long and very complicated; so the popes since St. Gregory the Great have standardized and controlled the titles and petitions that approved litanies contain, adding items only very seldom through the centuries.

Today, the Litany of Loreto calls Mary by twelve royal titles. Each is the summit of a whole mountain of theology explored by the Fathers of the Church and saints from St. Ephrem the Syrian in the fourth century to St. Alphonsus of Liguori in the eighteenth, and in every generation since. Each is a worthy object of meditation summing up whole regions of her relationship with God and with Man, but the reasons for each can be stated briefly.

Mary is called *Queen of Angels* because she outranks all of the angels; none of them was created to give birth to the Second Person of the Trinity, none has a body to give birth with, and none shares so intimately the nature of the Messiah. *Queen of Patriarchs* denotes that her virtues surpass even the virtues of Adam; she kept her free will in perfect accord with God's, and unlike Adam she didn't sin. No patriarch—not Abel, Noe, Abraham, Isaac, Jacob, or Joseph—was ever more intimately close to God; and when she was called upon to sacrifice her son as Abraham was called to sacrifice Isaac, she was not excused from that horror. They were the tree, and she is the flower; they were the promise of the glory of that family, and she is its fulfillment.

THE CORONATION OF MARY

Queen of Prophets means that she had the gift of prophecy to a level of perfection that nobody else equalled and only Christ himself surpassed. Mary understood the word that was given to her; she knew fully who her son was to be. And although the great prophets of the Old Testament all begged God to remove this gift from them, either in knowledge of their own unworthiness (Ex 3:11, 4:10; Is 6:5; Jn 1:27) or because they knew the consequences of it (3Kn 18:4; Jo 1:3; Jr 20:1-2; Mt 10:16-31), Mary accepted the gift and its consequences immediately, without hesitation, and in full knowledge, when she said simply, "Let it be done unto me according to thy word."

Queen of Apostles indicates that Mary played a role more central to Christ's mission than any of the Apostles could. She received the Holy Spirit at Pentecost when they did (Ac 1:14-15, 2:1-4), of course, but her position in the cycle of redemption is obviously different from theirs. On the one hand, she received no priestly ministry from Christ as they did, but then on the other hand none of the Apostles was called upon to give birth to the Messiah. Long before they heard their vocations, she was appointed to nurture him in his infancy. After the Ascension—after the Crucifixion—Christ left Mary to his Apostles to guide and counsel them with maternal care (Jn 19:25-27), and she was certainly an unparalleled source of information to them. St. Ambrose, for instance, remarked that St. John writes most fully about the Mystery of the Incarnation because he lived at the source of heavenly secrets (*On the Education of the Virgin* 9). That's why the image of Mary standing crowned with twelve stars is often interpreted also as a symbolic reference to her standing in the midst of the Apostles, all of whom point to her glory (*cf.* 3Kn 10:20).

Queen of Martyrs is a reminder of her sufferings, the "white martyrdom" of a life utterly devoted to the service of God. The sufferings of martyrs is proportionate to their charity, their love of God (1Cr 10:13; 2Pt 2:9), and no one has ever loved God more perfectly than Mary. And—just as her gifts and graces were unparalleled—her suffering was greater than that of any other saint (Lk 2:35). That's why she's also called *Queen of Confessors*: a confessor is someone who stands forth to martyrdom by admitting that Jesus is the Lord and Messiah but is not called upon to end his life in blood shed by hatred of that Faith.

Queen of Virgins is a title of praise accorded to Mary because her virginity surpasses that of all other earthly virgins; she kept it not only intact but spotless. In fact, it surpasses even the perfect virginity of the angels, because they have no bodies with which they might compromise it. *Queen of All Saints* is a title that explains why groups of saints are so often shown around her in pictures of the Coronation; like Queen of Apostles and Queen of Patriarchs, it refers to Mary's superior rank among the blessed in

Heaven, which she enjoys because of her unparalleled intimacy with God as Mother of the Redeemer. Of course, this unique favor is also why she's hailed as *Queen Conceived Without Original Sin*.

The last three royal titles accorded to Mary in the Litany of Loreto are somewhat more specific. The title *Queen Assumed into Heaven* was added to the Litany after the doctrine was officially clarified, and *Queen of the Most Holy Rosary* was inserted after the Battle of Lepanto awakened Christendom to the full power and effectiveness of that method of prayer.

Finally, Benedict XV della Chiesa added the title *Queen of Peace* to the Litany during the First World War, when the whole world cried out for peace. Still, this is an old title for Mary; the picture kept at St. Mary Major in Rome, which was supposed to have been painted by St. Luke himself, carries the legend "Hail, Most Sublime Queen of Peace, Most Holy Mother of God". In fact, it's implied in Scripture—Isaia called the Messiah Prince of Peace (*cf.* Hb 7:1-2), and the mother of the prince, as Elizabeth pointed out at the Visitation, is the queen. Even passages like Lk 2:14 speak of Mary as Queen of Peace: Peace on Earth among Men of good will, it says, and human will is good insofar as it accords with God's will; Mary's human will coincides exactly with God's, so Mary is unequalled among all who have the peace of God.

But when the War of 1914 broke out it seemed that there was no peace on Earth, whatsoever. We don't quite realize what a watershed in western civilization—in the world's civilization—that War was. But it's not easy to find a more significant era in the history of the world since the birth of Christ.

The governments in power when the War broke out in Europe had started to form in the fifth and sixth centuries when the first missionary monks and nuns went up into Europe. In fact, they had started their evolution when the Roman legions came, and those legions themselves were the agents of a culture that had grown up in Italy since prehistoric times. The first Frankish kings took their authority from their recognition by the Cæsars in the sixth century, and for the next twelve hundred years their successors ruled in France. The German Kaisers, the Holy Roman Emperors, had a pedigree not much newer than that, and of course the Pope had ruled in Rome, formally, since Constantine's day. Even in China the Son of Heaven ruled as he had ruled, through upheavals and changes in dynasty, since palæolithic days.

There had been disruptive wars, of course, and one or another government had fallen, one or another title had shifted. But generally the course of things was upward, one generation building on the accomplishments of their parents, and generally the framework of western society was stable. No war had definitively ended the development of civilization, not even the French Revolution.

THE CORONATION OF MARY

The War to End All Wars ended that development. Wise men knew this; by 1900 many saw the great sunset coming, and they saw that there would be no winners. That's why so many Europeans emigrated to the United States at that time; it's why scholars hurried to save all they could of the accumulated learning of the West, and why so many definitive editions, so many great compilations, and so many excellent textbooks date from the first decade of the twentieth century. And, in the end, that War is the reason that nothing has quite worked very well in the world since.

One of the farsighted men who saw all of this through the gathering gloom was the archbishop of Bologna, Giacomo della Chiesa. He was a scholar and a realist, a civil attorney and a canon lawyer, and an experienced papal diplomat; his view of things was sufficiently broad to make him deeply anxious about the tottering structure of Europe and the world. He worked tirelessly to call the people and the powers of the world to peace: surely, he wrote, there are other means than war by which violated rights may be rectified. Let them be tried honestly and with good will, and meanwhile let arms be laid aside.

Nobody listened to him, any more than they had listened to the other prominent men and women, the prudent statesmen, the professors and the teachers, all of whom cried out for peace. The strain finally broke on June 28, 1914, when an assassin shot the Austrian Archduke Franz Ferdinand in Sarajevo. Within days, within hours, the card-castle of alliances among European powers collapsed in a flurry of declarations of war, and on August 2 the guns began to thunder. On August 20, Pope Pius X Sarto died, and on September 3 Giacomo della Chiesa was elected Pope, taking the name Benedict XV.

His inaugural encyclical letter, *Ad Beatissimi Apostolorum* (November 1, 1914) outlined the situation eloquently. "What could prevent the soul's ... being most profoundly distressed by the spectacle presented by Europe—indeed, by the whole world, perhaps the saddest and most mournful spectacle of which there is any record."

> On every side the dread phantom of war holds sway; there is hardly room for another thought in the minds of men... [W]ell provided with the most terrible weapons that modern military science has devised, they strive to destroy one another with refinements of horror. There is no limit to the measure of destruction and slaughter. Every day the Earth is soaked with new-shed blood and covered with the bodies of the wounded, the corpses of the slain.
>
> With numberless troops the battle is engaged, and in fury; sorrow and distress, those sad cohorts of war, swoop down upon every city, every home; every day sees increase in the mighty number of wid-

ows and orphans. And with the interruption of communications trade stands still; agriculture is abandoned; the arts reduced to inactivity. The wealthy themselves are in difficulty, and the poor are sunk in abject misery.

But, he said, however horrible it is, this war was not really the point; it came from deeper causes. "In the very heart of human society rages another entity, a source of dread to all who really think, [that] may rightly be called the root cause of this present awful war".

He saw that this war had been brought about by "a general disregard and forgetfulness of the supernatural, a gradual falling away from the strict standard of Christian virtue"; he saw Mankind "slipping back more and more into the shameful practices of paganism" (*Humani generis redemptionem*, June 15, 1917).

> For ever since the precepts and practices of Christian wisdom have ceased to be observed in the ruling of states, it has followed—because those precepts and practices comprise the peace and security of states—that the very foundations of the states have trembled. And moreover such has been the change in the ideas and morals of men that unless God come soon to our aid, the end of civilization appears at hand (*Ad Beatissimi Apostolorum*).

In fact, he was right. By the Armistice in 1919 not one of the European governments still stood. Indeed, few houses stood. Looking across the face of the Earth after the War, Benedict saw "immense regions utterly abandoned, multitudes in want of food, of clothing, of shelter; widows and orphans beyond number and bereft of everything; an incredible number of human beings, especially children and the young, carrying on their very bodies the ravages of this atrocious war" (*Pacem Dei munus pulcherrimum*, May 23, 1920).

He worked heroically, as he had worked during the War itself, to relieve the suffering and to prevent further damage. He arranged massive exchanges of prisoners and the repatriation of refugees; he established international programs of civilian relief and funded the hospitalization of thousands of the wounded. He exhausted himself and the Church's resources—when he died in 1922 the Vatican had to borrow money to give him a simple funeral.

His efforts so impressed the world that the Turks erected a bronze statue of him in Constantinople itself even before he died. But his exhausting efforts could not possibly have been enough to repair the devastation. Life in 1919 was worse even than life had been in 919, worse even than it had been in the year 19; in those days people were still struggling upward, but after the War the survivors knew what they had lost. There were no utilities, no crops, no transportation, no effective money—without a government there can be none, and all of the governments were gone. There were no police and no one to command any police; no schools, no universities, no libraries functioning. People scurried to survive among the ruins, and they hastened to pick up the fragments; but the scholarship, the learning, won at such great cost over so many ages was devastated. The western world was set back to its beginnings—except for those fragments, and except for the living presence of the Church.

Separated sects, and governments that turn away from the principles of religion, have not been able to establish a lasting order of life since the Great War. War has followed war ever since, and, naturally, countries in communion with the Church have been embroiled in them, too. But we still have the Church herself, the sole and only institution that survived the First World War, the only stronghold of our continuity. The Church is the only institution in which sacraments—rituals that work changes in the soul—substantively unite this world to the next and open dependable channels for the constant flow of grace. She is the enduring repository of our collective memory, the only framework in which music, poetry, painting, sculpture, architecture, and the arts of learning still really live, not just as pastimes to dabble in but as vital forces shaping a lasting, reliable, and ennobling way of life, raising Man's eyes to God and to the divine in himself. She's the only institution that can still teach those arts of civilization, and the art of peace.

Benedict XV was just as generous with the Church's treasuries of mind and spirit as he had been with her human and material resources, but while everybody scrambled for the Church's material aid, they had to be persuaded to accept her intangible treasures, to take up again the path of individual conversion that alone could prevent future conflagrations.

He considered the observation made so long ago by St. James (4:1): "Whence come wars and quarrels among you? Is it not from this, from your passions, that wage war in your members?" Obviously, he wrote in 1920, "there can be no stable peace, no lasting treaties ... without a return to mutual charity".

> Never was there a time when we must stretch the bounds of charity farther than in these days of universal suffering and sorrow. Never so much as today, perhaps, has humanity so needed that universal beneficence that springs from the love of others, and that is full of sacrifice and zeal... It would be difficult to overstate the effects of manifold acts of Christian beneficence in softening the heart and facilitating the return of tranquillity to the nations... For the Gospel does not have one law of charity for individual persons and another for states and

nations, which are indeed nothing more than collections of individual persons (*Pacem Dei munus pulcherrimum*).

He knew that the internal war from which all external wars spring forth cannot be won without prayer; he knew that nothing but prayer can cultivate charity in the hearts and minds of humankind. And looking back on the floods of graces that civilization had received through devotion to Mary—the healing of the Albigensian heresies, the reform of England through St. Æthelwold and St. Dunstan, the Italian peace led by St. Peter Damiano, and so many more—Benedict XV saw the cure as clearly as he had seen the crisis.

He encouraged people to pray, and particularly he encouraged them to invoke Mary's aid. Throughout his pontificate, at every opportunity, he asked people to beg the prayers of the Mother of Jesus. And in an *allocutio*—an address to the Consistory of Cardinals—on Christmas Eve, 1915, he hailed Mary as "Mother of the Prince of Peace, Mediatrix between rebellious Man and merciful God," and reminded the assembly that

> She is the dawn of peace shining in the darkness of a world out of joint; she never ceases to implore her Son for peace, although his hour is not yet come. She always intervenes on behalf of sorrowing humanity in the hour of danger. Today she, who is the mother of so many orphans and our advocate in this tremendous catastrophe, will most readily hear our prayers.

And then he continued, giving specific purpose to those prayers for which he so desperately asked. "In view of these considerations," he said, "and the better to direct Christian thought and trust in the most powerful intercession of the Mother of God, We, in response to the requests of many children far and near, consent that they address the Blessed Virgin in the Litany of Loreto with the invocation 'Queen of Peace'. And will Mary, she who is Queen of a Kingdom of Peace and not of wars and disasters, reject the desires and prayers of her trusting children?"

EVA ✸ AVE

THE PATTERN OF THE PRAYERS

AFTER ITS CENTURIES OF DEVELOPMENT, THE Rosary has crystallized into a standard pattern of vocal prayer that, with practice, becomes automatic. After all, the beads serve to regulate the time that you spend in meditative prayer without your having to think about it consciously. But the vocal prayers themselves are the pathway between everyday thoughts and the elevated thoughts of meditative prayer, so they have to be said carefully, and with a view to that goal. "To recite the Our Father or the Hail Mary," St. Teresa of Avila said (*Way of Perfection* 25), "is vocal prayer. But behold what poor music you produce when you do this without mental prayer".

The short string of beads between the crucifix and the circlet are to mark the customary prayers before the Rosary itself, so that you can recollect yourself; many people like to begin the prayers of recollection before even that, praying perhaps the Soul of Christ.

Holding the crucifix, or at least looking at it, make the Sign of the Cross, and then pray the Apostles' Creed.

On the first bead, pray the Our Father.

On each of the group of three small beads, pray the Hail Mary.

On the following single bead, pray the *Gloria Patri*.

On the last bead before the circlet begins, bring the first Mystery to your mind. Some people pray the Joyful Mysteries on Mondays and Thursdays, the Sorrowful on Tuesdays and Fridays, and the Glorious on Wednesdays, Saturdays, and Sundays; but some pray all fifteen every day, and others may be able only to set aside enough time each day to meditate well on one Mystery.

Whatever pattern you choose, call that Mystery to mind, read the Bible passages, patristic commentaries, or devotional tracts about it if you wish, and begin the vocal prayers on this bead with the Our Father.

On each of the ten small beads of the decade, pray the Hail Mary while meditating on that Mystery.

At the space on the chain following those ten beads, you can pray the *Gloria Patri.* There is no bead for this prayer because by the time St. Louis-Marie Grignion de Montfort suggested the practice the conventional arrangement of beads had long since been established. If you intend to offer your Rosary in reparation for sin, say the Fátima Prayer at this space on the chain, too.

On the next bead, bring the first Mystery to your mind and heart, and pray the Our Father. Then continue until you have passed through all of the beads. If you wish, and according to your intention, pray the Hail, Holy Queen or the Prayer to St. Joseph when you've finished.

THE ROSARY IN THE CHRISTIAN COMMUNITY

B ECAUSE THE ROSARY DEVELOPED ALONG WITH THE CHURCH'S OTHER devotions, it's intertwined with them today. In places where the bells of the Angelus can still be heard, many people pause for those few seconds to remember Christ and his Mother, and they take the few minutes longer to pray the Rosary when they can. Many people combine the private prayer of the Rosary with the public prayers of the Little Hours or the Little Office, and many gather together regularly to meditate on the Mysteries in groups formed for the purpose of praying the Rosary. All of the older forms of praying the Rosary are still available, if you can find the books from ages past that preserve them, and even today you can find devotional books that suggest various forms of the "Scriptural Rosary" or "spiritual Rosary", listing verses of Gospel or prophecy before each Hail Mary.

The Rosary has also served as a framework for spiritual exercises that have developed since it reached its definitive form, as with the ones written by St. Ignatius of Loyola, which you can always find conducted somewhere near you by an experienced director. These, and other kinds of spiritual exercise, formalize the process of meditations, petitions, and resolutions and extend it to other areas of prayer.

Integrating the Rosary into your individual prayer life is one of the most powerful methods of working toward the deepest possible spiritual improvement, but the Rosary has always had something of the character of communal prayer.

N ow, as the Rosary itself developed in Christendom, it was always understood to be the highest and most effective form of family prayer. As a private devotion, it found its center not in the church but in the home, and the collective family Rosary was usually the way that children learned the Church's basic vocal prayers and the key mysteries of Christ's life on Earth.

"And that old custom of our forefathers ought to be preserved, or else restored," Leo XIII urged (*Fidentem piumque animum*), "according to which Christian families, whether in town or country, at the close of the day when their labors were at an end, were religiously wont to assemble before a figure of Our Lady and alternately recite the Rosary. She, delighted at this faithful and unanimous homage, was ever near them like a loving mother surrounded by her children, distributing to them the blessings of domestic peace, the foretaste of the peace of Heaven."

Praying the Rosary together in this way becomes a special time of closeness each day, or one or two days a week, during which the family can join in praise, petition, thanks, and love. Infants held in the arms feel the quiet and respectful atmosphere, and children as young as two can join in repeating the vocal prayers and listening to the Gospel readings that encapsulate the Mysteries.

Often the father of the family reads the Bible verses that tell of the Mystery before each decade; sometimes the mother does, or the family reads them in rotation. Customarily, a family prays as many decades as the littlest ones can manage; or the youngsters are excused at the end of the fifth decade, or the first, to go and play quietly while the rest of the family finishes their devotions.

The place at which the family gathers should be special, somehow— before a crucifix or a picture of Mary and Jesus, perhaps at a little tabletop shrine brightened by flowers and haloed with candlelight. The time should be special, too. Some choose a certain night during the week to pray the Rosary after dinner, or between dinner and dessert on that special night. Dinner, after all, has been called the liturgy of civilization, an image in daily life of the great liturgy of the Mass, which is itself a continuation of the Last Supper. Family dinner makes a suitable prelude to the family Rosary, and that evening becomes a time sacred to God and to the family alike.

Naturally, there will be times when a son or daughter will have an important engagement that can't be broken, when a spouse is called away to work, or when the whole family's schedule is interrupted by illness or emergency. These cases may shift the devotion to another time or to the side of the sickbed; but however the Rosary is scheduled, it has to remain voluntary. Nobody can be forced to pray, after all, and family devotions ought to be entirely disconnected from punishment in every way.

The Rosary hour is a special time, set apart to keep company with Jesus and Mary, from which nobody can be excluded because of earlier misbehavior, and to which nobody can be sentenced. Even when the rotation of the chaplet turns to the Sorrowful Mysteries, the Rosary is a crown of flowers, not of thorns; it's to be offered in gladness, sympathy, and relief from the concerns of this sin-worn world. And anyway if we were kept from prayer because of transgressions, who could pray at all.

But if the family takes the word "devotion" literally the little ones will see that joining in the prayers is a privilege and a pleasure—and the Rosary makes better people of those devoted to it. In fact, many families who observe this ancient custom testify that the benefits of the Rosary are so profound, and so obvious even to the youngest of those devoted to it, that after even a short time the whole family takes care to schedule passing pleasures around that holy time, and bustles through dinner to ensure enough time, and time quiet enough, to devote to the Rosary. It is morally impossible, the saints have said again and again, for children to go wrong when they have the chain of the Rosary linking their families together.

C hrist asserted that his own family extends to all who hear his word and keep it, when he told his followers to call God "Our Father"; and in saying it he underlined his desire that this family should extend to all Mankind (Mt 28:19). That's why your parish almost certainly has a chapter of one of the great confraternities of the Rosary, a kind of organization with a history as old as that of organized prayer itself. When St. Peter was cast into prison in chains, Leo XIII recalled (*Octobri mense*, 1895), the Church in Rome gathered together and prayed without ceasing for his release from Herod and his deliverance from all the hopes of the people of the Jews (Ac 12:5-11). His liberation from the cell and from the chains—which have been piously kept ever since as a physical reminder of the miracle—stands as a constant reminder of the power of united prayer, and the gathering of that early Christian community to beg God for the release of their bishop is the Church's great prototype of collective prayer in emergencies. In much the same way, the historical record of the England of St. Dunstan, the Italy of St. Peter Damiano, or the France of St. Dominic and St. Louis-Marie Grignion de Montfort show that the emergency may be simply a matter of grave disorder in daily life. And that the cure consists of gathering as many people as possible together in devotion to the Rosary.

Bl. Alan de Rupe, working to restore the Church's ancient devotional practice of communal prayer, established the Confraternity of the Most Holy Rosary in France, Germany, and the Netherlands, but in his lifetime it did not receive papal approval. But on September 8, 1475, the very day that Bl. Alan died in Zwolle, another Dominican, the abbot Jacob Sprenger, established the Rosary Confraternity in the city of Köln. The Kaiser Frederick III, who happened to be in that Dominican church that day, signed his name in the membership book and asked the papal nuncio to ask the Pope for official approval of the organization. The matter was investigated again, and in 1478 Sixtus IV della Rovere approved the organization.

Thousands of local chapters of the Confraternity blossomed around the world in the following centuries. In the United States, the organization is often known as the Rosary Society or, sometimes, as the Rosary Altar Society, because one altar in the chapter's home church must be designated as the altar of the Society. Anyone—man, woman, or child—can join the Confraternity worldwide, but in the United States the Rosary Altar Society restricts its membership to women.

Today, the collective prayers of these fellowships link together in a perpetual Rosary around the whole globe, from the rising to the setting of the Sun, and then around again, every day and every night. "Indeed," Leo XIII remarked,

> Catholics are so closely drawn together and united by the bonds of charity that they are truly brethren... [O]rganizations for excellent purposes [have always been] legally approved, distinguished by special emblems, enriched with privileges, [and] associated with divine worship in the churches... We do not hesitate to assign a pre-eminent place among such societies to the one known as the Confraternity of the Most Holy Rosary... Prayers acquire their greatest efficacy when offered publicly, by large numbers, constantly, and unanimously, so as to form a single chorus of supplication, as it were, as those words in the Acts of the Apostles declare clearly, in which the disciples of Christ ... are said to have been "persevering with one mind in prayer" (Ac 1:14) ...
>
> The Rosary unites everyone who joins the Confraternity in a common bond of paternal and military comradeship, so that a mighty host is formed, marshalled and arrayed, to repel the assaults of the Adversary, both interiorly and exteriorly... The history of the Church bears witness to the power and efficacy of this method of prayer, recording as it does the rout of the Turkish forces at the naval battle at Lepanto ... [and] Pius V declared that by virtue of this kind of prayer "Christians suddenly began to be transformed ... the darkness of heresy dispelled, and the light of the catholic Faith to shine forth." ... We cherish the strongest hope that these prayers and praises, rising incessantly from the lips and hearts of such a great multitude, will be most efficacious (*Augustissimæ Virginis Mariæ*).

Saturday has always dedicated to Our Lady. By at least the fourth century, Saturday was referred to as the "Brother of Sunday" in the East and marked as a special day of fasting and reparation in the West. Missals and sacramentaries from the earliest days of the Church give the propers for regular votive Masses to ask Our Lady's intercession, and the devotion of the Little Office has centered on Saturday since at least the eighth century. But after the reported apparitions of Mary at Fátima in Portugal in 1917, the day took on a renewed significance as a day of reparation for sin.

On May 13, 1917, the Lady of Light first appeared to Lucia dos Santos, Jacinta Marto, and Francisco Marto. She said, just before rising into the eastern sky, "Pray the Rosary each day, to obtain peace for the world and an end to the War." The next month, on the thirteenth, the Lady returned and repeated her request:

> I want you to pray the Rosary every day... [I]f people do not stop
> offending God another and worse [war] will begin during the reign
> of Pius XI... God ... is going to punish the world for its crimes by
> [permitting] war, famine, and persecution of the Church and the
> Holy Father. To prevent this I will come to ask for the consecration
> of Russia to my Immaculate Heart, and for communions of repara-
> tion on the First Saturdays.

This last request was left incomplete, but on the thirteenth of July the Lady
repeated her request about the Rosary: "Continue to say *o terço* (the third)
every day in honor of Our Lady of the Rosary to obtain peace for the world
and an end to the War; for she alone can aid you." On August 13 the children had been kidnapped by the local Socialist administrator, who wanted
to put a stop to the happenings at Fátima, but they prayed the Rosary in
prison anyway, and enlisted the hoodlums in the common cell to pray it,
too. Then on September 13, 1917—the anniversary of the Battle of Muret
seven hundred and four years earlier—the apparition said comparatively
little, but she repeated her request that people "continue to pray the Rosary
to bring about the end of the War."

October 13, 1917, is the date of the Great Miracle of Fátima, the day that
the Sun danced in the sky. On that day the Lady repeated her request yet
again: *Que continuem sempre a rezar o terço todos os dias.* She identified
herself as the Lady of the Rosary, and then she summed up everything that
she had said before—in fact, most of what Mary has said in apparitions
since the second century: People must not offend Our Lord any more, for
he is already greatly offended.

At these words, the apparition opened her hands to the overcast sky and
dispelled the heavy clouds. Rays of light from her palms reflected off the
Sun, which was seen by the hundred thousand pilgrims that day to spin as
a disk of brilliant silver. For the three little seers, though, the Sun itself was
eclipsed by a vision of the Lady of the Rosary in the sky to its right, with St.
Joseph and the Child to its left.

The Sun continued to dance in the sky, flashing brilliant colors, and
apparently fall nearly to the Earth, for some time, witnessed not only by the
crowd but by people throughout the region. At last the skies over Portugal
were normal again, but that was not the end of the matter.

The apparition came again, not to Fátima but to the Spanish town of
Puy, where Lucia dos Santos lived as a nun. "Look at my heart," she said
to Sor Lucia, "encircled by these thorns with which mankind pierces it
every moment by blasphemies and ingratitude." Do you, at least, try to

console me, she said, and announce this:

> I promise to assist at the hour of death with the grace necessary for
> salvation all those who, with the intention of making reparation to
> me, will on the first Saturday of five consecutive months go to con-
> fession, receive Holy Communion, say five decades of the beads, and
> keep me company for fifteen minutes while meditating on the fifteen
> Mysteries of the Rosary.

After this, the devotion of the First Saturdays spread across the world,
working not only to encourage individual conversions but to balance their
collective weight against the rising tide of disorder in the world. Today,
through the efforts of many different kinds of Rosary organization, the connection between prayer and peace, indeed between prayer and simple civil
order, is expressed forcefully and as effectively from Jerusalem (1Mc 3:45-
55) to Plainfield, New Jersey.

Plainfield was where Monsignor Harold V. Colgan, pastor of St.
Mary's Parish, founded The Blue Army of Our Lady of Fátima in
1947. The year before, he had suffered a severe heart attack from
which his doctors thought that he would never recover, but during his hospitalization he implored Mary to intercede for him and obtain a postpone-
ment of his death. If this favor were granted, he said, he would spend his
extra years promoting devotion to her.

After he recovered, Msgr. Colgan reflected on the spread of
Communism across the face of Europe and the world, and he remembered
the words reported of Mary at Fátima in 1917: "If my requests are not heed-
ed, Russia will spread her errors throughout the world, provoking wars
and persecutions of the Church... Pray the Rosary every day to obtain
peace for the world and an end to the war." For three weeks he preached
this message in his parish, and then he announced that "we in this parish
will be the Blue Army of Our Lady, against the Red Army of Communism."
He outlined a life of daily Rosaries, acts of penance, frequent Reconciliation, devotion to the Immaculate Heart of Mary, and the First Saturdays;
and he asked each member of his Army to wear something blue as a way
to engage others in conversation about Fátima.

John Haffert, one of the speakers that Msgr. Colgan invited to address
his organization, consulted with Sr. Lucia dos Santos to develop a pledge
for members that would fulfill the basic requirements of the Fátima message. By 1950 more than a million members had taken it. With the support
of pastors who, like Msgr. Colgan himself, had made the Marian consecration suggested by St. Louis-Marie Grignion de Montfort, the Blue Army

soon had chapters or "cells" across the United States and in Europe, at Fátima itself. Msgr. Colgan himself asked the stigmatic Padre Pio to accept members of the Army as his spiritual children. I will if they are faithful, Padre Pio responded, and I believe that Russia will be converted when there is a member of the Blue Army for every Communist.

Today, the Blue Army sponsors the annual National Rosary Congress and a National Rosary Crusade for America; arranges and supervises apostolate programs, including some centered on the devotion of the First Saturdays, all-night vigils, and "prayer cells", the basic unit of the Army; and it operates programs of teaching youth groups, visiting prisons, and establishing the Rosary as a regular devotion in families. The Army offers for sale rosaries and books on the skills and techniques of all kinds of prayer, and it publishes *Soul*, a bimonthly magazine at a nominal subscription fee. The Blue Army can be reached at Post Office Box 976, Washington, New Jersey 07882-0976, the city at which it maintains the Shrine of the Immaculate Heart of Mary, a major pilgrimage center.

The circle of vocal prayers of the Rosary can be counted on the fingers, of course, or with pebbles or even knots in a length of string; but it's best to have a proper set of beads, and to have them properly blessed. Some people, like the princes of the Middle Ages, still prefer fancy or expensive beads, but nobody has to go without a rosary for lack of funds. Any number of devoted souls work constantly to supply beads to anyone who can't afford them.

For example, Brother Sylvan, C.F.X., was a teacher at St. Xavier High School in Louisville, Kentucky, who used to turn bits of wire and pieces of broken rosaries into usable, durable chaplets for those who might not be able to afford new ones. He did it at first occasionally, but then he started hearing from his fellow Brothers of St. Francis Xavier at their missions in Kenya and Uganda. They had few materials to teach with, and no rosaries at all.

So Brother Sylvan set about teaching other people in Louisville to make rosaries for the missions, and eventually he organized them into the "Our Lady of Fatima Rosary Making Club". By the time of his death in 1951 the club was well established, and by 1954 it included more than twenty-five hundred members across the United States. Today the organization, renamed Our Lady's Rosary Makers, supplies the necessary materials at nominal cost to more than twenty thousand members worldwide—housewives and political prisoners, assembly-line workers, invalids, retired people, and school children. Together, they make more than seven million rosaries a year in their spare time, sending them to missionaries who need them most. More than a hundred and fifty thousand chaplets went to Russia in one year alone, twenty thousand to the Levant; and a shipment of three hundred supplied the needs of the parish in the South Pacific that had until then shared a single public set of beads kept hanging from the hands of a statue of Mary when not in use.

Yet the four thousand rosaries that the association produces every day supply only about ten percent of the demand; the need is particularly acute in developing countries. The association can be contacted at Post Office Box 37080, 4611 Poplar Level Road, Louisville, Kentucky 40233-7080.

אמת

FURTHER READING

CITING A SINGLE VERSE OF SCRIPTURE IN A BOOK OR AT MASS IS INTENDED to call your attention to the whole passage in which it occurs and its relation to the rest of the Bible. In the same way, books are cited here because they're worth reading in full; they include some of the most basic books on prayer. Their authors brought together immense amounts of Christian writing spanning the centuries since before the Bible to their own times, and they in turn had immense influence on the theology and literature of the ages that followed them.

In fact, they defined not only our religion but our culture; so, starting with the books mentioned here, your further reading can branch out to include whole libraries of worthwhile texts—it's easier to understand Ophelia's burial scene in *Hamlet*, for instance, if you know that Shakespeare assembled it from passages in Ven. Luis de Granada's *Book of Prayer and Meditation*.

Unfortunately, it's not easy to get good translations of the works of the Fathers of the Church. Jacques-Paul Migne's *Patrologiæ cursus completus, Series græca* (usually abbreviated *PG*), 161 vol., Paris, 1857-1866, and his *Patrologiæ cursus completus, Series latina* (*PL*), 221 vol., Paris, 1844-1855, are the basis for all subsequent editions, but the texts are in the original languages, and most have been superseded by more accurate recensions after more than a century of further scholarship; and in any case few libraries have a full set of Migne. William A. Jurgens's *The Faith of the Early Fathers*, Collegeville, Minnesota, 1970, gives a good selection of passages from the best recent editions of each Father's works, so it's a useful guide to those editions; it's also easily accessible, and it has both general and doctrinal indices. The series of new translations begun at Catholic University of America in Washington, D.C., under the general editorship of Roy Joseph Deferrari is in English, but it's not yet complete; some of the volumes suffer grievously from misprints, and none has a useful index.

The series edited by Alexander Roberts and James Donaldson, *Ante-Nicene Fathers* (1885), usually sold today in a uniform set including Philip Shaff's *Nicene and Post-Nicene Fathers* (1886), is more fully indexed, but the index is hotly partisan, listing, for example, the heresies of Tertullian and Origen as if they were correct and denying correct teachings whenever possible. Worse, in these series the texts themselves are corrupted— Roberts, Donaldson, and Shaff took the liberty of "conforming" the Father's quotations of the Bible "to the Revised Version of 1881", which is to say that whenever the Fathers contradict a Protestant teaching the editors changed the text to say what they wanted it to say, as indeed the Revised Version of 1881 did to the Bible itself. The Church herself urgently needs to produce an accurate, standard English-language edition of the Fathers, fully indexed and well; but until that happens perhaps the best strategy is to use the index in Roberts, Donaldson, and Shaff to find the locations of what you want, and then look it up in Deferrari or Migne.

All of the works by saints or other theologians cited in this book went through scores of editions during the lifetimes of their authors, and after the fifteenth century they were printed again and again in every language from Swedish to Japanese. Most never fell into disuse until about the time of the First World War. Some of them are available in English translations, although they may not be so easily found. Religious-book stores sell some of the more important ones, of course. Catholic university libraries may have copies of others, and you may be able to arrange to borrow them.

Encyclicals are a primary source of authoritative information about the Church's teachings on just about everything. Like the Epistles, encyclicals are written to clarify the doctrine that applies to questions that have come up at a certain time; so papal encyclicals are binding on the Faithful, and it's important to know what they contain. They're usually titled by the first few words of their text, in Latin or whichever language they're written in, so that you can find them easily. Many are available in collections of translations like *The Papal Encyclicals 1878-1903* compiled by Claudia Carlen Ihm, Raleigh, North Carolina, 1981.

Unfortunately, these collections are not always complete, and it's not often easy to figure out the editorial parameters that governed the selection; important encyclicals are often missing, while others specific to a single occasion or addressed to a single group are often included. In any event, no single compilation could hold all of the papal encyclicals, and even a collection that aimed at completeness would naturally lag behind somewhat while new volumes are being compiled.

Apart from papal and conciliar documents, there are also letters from the various Congregations, like the letter *On Some Aspects of Christian Meditation* (1990) by the Congregation for the Doctrine of the Faith, that are direct, authoritative, and brief. You can usually get copies of recent encyclicals for a few cents at religious-goods stores.

אמת

INDEX

Saints, popes, and monarchs are referenced here by first name. The Blessed and Venerable, like ordinary people, are listed by family name. Apostles, Evangelists, and prophets are listed by name for their personal acts, but the books of the Bible that bear their names are listed under "Bible".

Books of the Bible are abbreviated by any numeral that the title includes followed by the initial letter of its title and the next distinguishing consonant in the title; if no consonants distinguish two books, the first distinguishing vowel is used. See the table of abbreviations on the next page.

Paragraphs under the entry "Bible: citations" group the abbreviated titles of biblical books that begin with the same number or letter, and each Gospel is set off in its own paragraph. Subdivisions of other entries are referenced in **bold type**, as seems convenient, and particularly long entries are divided into paragraphs at those points.

Other written works are referenced by title, usually by both the original title and its most usual English equivalent, and also by author; writings are grouped at the end of the author's entry. Encyclicals are listed by the most usual title, which is normally the first word or words of the Latin text.

Spellings of proper names and the titles of the books of the Bible follow those in the *New American Catholic Edition of the Holy Bible*, Confraternity version, Benziger Brothers, New York, 1961.

INDEX

A ❁ Ω

INDEX

tius) 139

Catherine Labouré, St. (1806-1876) 351

Catherine of Bologna, St. (1413-1463): *Treatise on the Seven Spiritual Weapons* 197

Catholic: defined 147

Cato (M. Porcius Cato, 234-140 BC) 314

Cattle: gall of 292

Cecilia, St. (*d. c.* 178) 87

Cedron *see* Kidron

Celestine I, Pope St. (*r.* 422-432) 166

Cerealia 325

Cerinthus (*fl. c.* 88) 212

Cervantes Saavedra, Miguel de (1547-1616) 34, 65; *Don Quixote* 65

Chaplet *see* wreath

Charlemagne (742-814) 11, 19, 22, 34

Charles Martel (*c.* 688-741) 59

Charles V, Holy Roman Emperor, King of Spain (Carlos I, 1500-1558) 225

Cherubim 352

Chiasmus 231

Chivalry 34; 359

Christ the Educator (St. Clement of Alexandria) 285

Christmas 205, 238; Annunciation and 219, 339; banquets 239; carols 41, 238; feast of 238, 244, 256; Irenaeus and 238; Julius I and 244; midnight Mass of 239; Origen and 238; presents 239; Purification and 257; secular observances of 238; significance of 241; St. Augustine and

238; St. Clement of Alexandria and 238; St. Cyprian of Carthage and 238; St. Cyril of Jerusalem and 244; St. Gregory Nanzianus and 238; St. John Chrysostom and 244, 245; St. Justin Martyr and 244; Tertullian and 238, 244; trees 238; yule logs 239; *see also* Nativity

Chronicle (St. Bede) 339

Church: **America** 68 (*see also* American Heresy); **Arabia** 349; as urban phenomenon 11; authority of 68, 102, 103, 104, 111; Bible and 135, 136, 214, 215; civilization and 34, 365; abolishes crucifixion 287; communion of saints and 46; devotional practices of 19, 20, 24, 159, 228; Doctors of *see* Doctors of the Church; **Egypt** 349; End of Time and 322; **England** 26, 30, 66, 343; Fathers of *see* Fathers of the Church; foundation of 70, 111, 129, 136, 157, 270, 327, 335, 355; **France** 66, 349; **Germany** 66; growth of 303, 306, 329; heretics and 51, 52, 68, 69, 73, 74, 75, 165, 180, 275; in Creed 142; **Italy** 28; Mary and 44, 46, 63, 71; Militant 57; missions 85, 111; name of 147; **Palestine** 349; prayer and *see* prayer; review of texts 73, 215; **Rites of** 142: Gallican 177, Latin 177, Mozarabic 11, 177; **Rome** 371; stability of practice 365; stability of teachings 68, 107, 143, 147,

166, 214, 274, 295, 324, 341 (*see also* Tradition, Sacred); symbols of 210, 226, 357; uniqueness of 328, 331; universality of 45, 46, 67, 68, 86, 94, 335; *see also* Tradition, Sacred

Church of England 354

Cicero, Marcus Tullius (106-43 BC) 286, 310; *In Verrem* 284, 286; *Pro Rabinio* 284

Circumcision 247, 248; Feast of 244; Presentation and 247, 250; in art 247; prophecies 300

City of God (St. Augustine) 107, 320, 321

Clare of Assisi, St. (1194-1253) 86

Claudius (Tiberius Claudius Drusus Nero Germanicus Cæsar, Emperor of Rome, 10 BC-54 AD) 234

Clavis Salomonis (*Key of Solomon*, Abraham Colorno) 130

Clement of Alexandria, St. (Titus Flavius Clemens, *d. c.* 215) 83; Christmas and 238; doxology and 173; *Christ the Educator* 285

Clement VIII Aldobrandini, Pope (1536-1605): *Dominici gregis* 213

Clement XI Albani, Pope (1649-1721) 76; Feast of Our Lady of the Most Holy Rosary and 77; St. Louis-Marie Grignion de Montfort and 77

Cleopatra, Queen of Egypt (68-30 BC) 353

Colgan, Harold V. (*d.* 1972) 374

INDEX

H

Haffert, John 374

Hail Holy Queen (*Salve Regina*) 124, 175, 176, 368

Hail King of Eternal Mercy (*Salve Rex æternæ misericordiæ*, Martin Luther) 179

Hail Mary 160; 31; analysis of 161, 163

Hallowe'en 151

Halo 316

Harmony of the Gospels (St. Augustine) 263

Haurietis aquas (Pius XII Pacelli) 48

Heaven: derivation of word 313; dimensionality of 150, 307, 313, 323; St. Augustine on 150, 310, 312; St. Thomas Aquinas on 311 (*see also* Sempiternity); perfection of 107, 153, 321; Queen of *see under* Mary, titles of; rank in 106; St. Cyril of Jerusalem on 154

Helena, St. (*c.* 250-*c.* 330) 243

Hell 145; 322; Apostles' Creed and 145; Christ's descent into 140, 142, 145; dimensionality of 311, 323; harrowing of *see* Christ's descent into, *hereunder*; predestination and 110; Purgatory and 103; Rosary and 88

Henry III, King of England (1207-1272) 58

Henry of Bracton (*c.* 1210-1268) 313

Henry of Kalkar (1328-1408) 198, 199; *Monastic*

Exercises (*Exercitatorium monachale*) 198

Henry VIII, King of England (1491-1547) 15, 149, 189

Hercules 244, 305

Heresy and heretics 66, 67; **Adoptionism** 274; **agnoetæ** 274; **Albigensianism** 50, Mary and 55; **Apollinarists** 274; **Arians** 165, 274; **Catharism** 50; conversion and 67; **Corinthians** 74, 123, 330, 332; **Ebonites** 212; **Jansenism** 73, 74, 75, 76, 332; **Manichænism** 50, Mary and 112; **Messalianism** 74, 75, 332; modern 67; **Nestorianism** 166, 274, 342; **Novatianism** 165; **Pelagianism** 165; prayer and 70; **Quartodecimanism** 165; **Quietism** 73, 75; **Socinians** 213; St. Louis-Marie Grignion de Montfort and 71; union with Church 69; **Waldensianism** 50

Herman the Cripple, Bl. (Hermannus Contractus, 1013-1054) 176, 178

Herod and Herodians 232, 268, 279, 286, 297, 322, 339, 371

Herodotus (*c.* 484-425 BC): *Historia* 286

Hilary of Poitiers, St. (*c.* 315-*c.* 367) 97

Hilton, Walter (*d.* 1396): *Ladder of Perfection* 117, 123

Hinduism 7

Hippocrates (b. 460 BC) 287

Hippolytus, St. (*d. c.* 236): *Apostolic Tradition* 143

Historia (Herodotus) 286

History of Rome (Nicephorus Gregoras) 347

History of the Church (Eusebius) 255

Hitler, Adolf (1889-1945) 289

Holy Name Society (1274) 133

Holy Shroud of Turin 189, 294

Holy Spirit: Gifts of 246 (*see also* Mary, Adam, Eve); Hours of 24; in art 217, 315, 332

Homily on the Annunciation (St. Bede) 219

Hours: canonical 20 (*see also* names of individual hours); Little 23; of the Cross 24; of the Holy Spirit 24; of the Virgin *see* Office, Little; *see also* Office

Human beings: God and 83; nature of 73, 81, 84

Humani generis redemptionem (Benedict XV della Chiesa) 364

Hyacinthus 304

Hyperdulia 44

I

Idioglossia *see under* Tongues, Gift of

Ignatius of Antioch, St. (*d. c.* 110) 85, 147; on devotion to Mary 97; on Incarnation 248; on Resurrection 298

Ignatius of Loyola, St. (1491-1556) 85, 369; on prayer 95, 123; recollection of 8; *Spiritual Exercises* 123, 175, 191, 198

Ildelphonsus, St. (*d.* 667):

INDEX

130

Livy (Titus Livius, 59 BC-17) 286

Loreto: Holy House 359, 360; *see also* litany

Lothario dei Conti di Segni *see* Innocent III

Lotto, Lorenzo (*c.* 1480-1556) 190

Louis IX the Saint, King of France (1214-1270) 33; Crown of Thorns and 279; devotional practices of 33, 117

Louis VIII, King of France (1187-1226) 33

Louis XIII, King of France (1601-1643) 66

Louis XIV, the Great, King of France (1638-1715) 179

Louis-Marie Grignion de Montfort, St. (1673-1716) 71; 374; Gloria and 71, 171, 367; Jansenism and 75; miracles of 76; on intercession of saints 45; on the Our Father 57, 148; Rosary and 71, 76, 124, 171, 367; sacramentals and 121; schooling of 72; Simon de Montfort and 72; St. Dominic and 72; *Secret of the Most Holy Rosary* 42, 171, 203, *True Devotion to the Blessed Virgin* 122, 292

Lucernarium *see* Vespers

Lucy, St. 87

Ludolph of Saxony (*c.* 1295-1377) 170; *Life of Christ* 185

Luis de Granada, Ven. (1505-1588): *Book of Prayer and Meditation* 377; *Memorial of the Christian Life* 197

Luke, St.: as painter 362

Lull, Ramon, Bl. (*c.* 1235-1315) 36

Lully, Jean-Baptiste (1632-1687) 179

Lumen gentium (*A Light unto the Nations*) 43, 108

Luther, Martin (1483-1546) 52, 136; on Christ's knowledge 274; *Salve Rex æternæ misericordiæ* (Hail King of Eternal Mercy) 179

M

Magi 268; *see also* Adoration of the Magi

Magnificat 25, 226; analysis of 229; composers and 227; precedents 228; rhetoric of 227; salvation and 228

Man: symbolism of 220

Manasse 129

Manichænism *see under* heresy and heretics 50

Manuscripts 13; *see also* printing

Marcella (friend of St. Jerome) 13

Marcian, Emperor of the East (*c.* 390-457) 350

Marialis cultus (Paul VI Montini) 1, 71, 87, 160

Mark Anthony (Marcus Antonius, *c.* 83-30 BC) 232

Mark, St.: churches dedicated to, Venice 332

Martin of Tours, St. (*c.* 316-400) 87

Marto, Ven. Francisco (1908-1919) 372

Marto, Ven. Jacinta (1910-1920) 351, 372

Martyrdom of St. Poly-

carp 313

Mary 43; ancestry of 232, 254, 339, 340, 352

apparitions of: to Bl. Alan de Rupe 79, to St. Dominic 79, to St. Eulalia 182 (*see also* Fátima); as author 227 (*see also Magnificat*); Assumption of *see* Assumption; beauty of 122; chivalry and 34, 359

churches dedicated to: 36, 65, 257, Chapel of Our Lady of the Rosary, Muret 60, Holy House, Loreto 360, Lady Chapel, Versailles 221, Mary of the Assumption, Josaphat 349, Notre Dame, Paris 221, 359, Panaya Kapulu, Ephesus 167, Sistine Chapel, Vatican 342

conduct of 223

devotion to: 36, and predestination 112, benefits of 93, 97, 366, Immaculate Heart 253 (*see also* Hyperdulia, Laudesi) emblems of 41; Eve and 178, 332, 341, 342; gifts of 208, 269, 328, 341, 343; glorified body of 321; heretics and 55, 97, 273, 343; house of 359; humility of 229; Immaculate Conception of 339, 341

in art: 65, 217, 221, 223, 225, 248, 332, 334, 343, 359, prohibited images 218 (*see also* names of Mysteries)

intercession of: 31, 44, 46, 48, 63, 66, 87, 108, 167, 260, 356, for Alan de Lanvallay 72, for Maréchal Foch 66

INDEX

Q

R

INDEX

Saints 112, 343; abode of 313; commemorations of 25, 351; communion of *see* communion of saints; devotion to *see* dulia; epiphanies 316; errancy of 344; glorified bodies of 321; in art 316, 317; intercession of 45, 46, 109, 116, 158, 167, differs from Mary's 48, 109; lives of 22; Mary and 112; merits of 100, 104; patronage of *see* patronage of saints; personalities of 85; prayers of 95, 109, 294; recollection of 8, 115, 118; *see also* communion of saints

Salome 297

Salutation, Angelic 168

Salutatis humanæ 324

Salvation 321; Annunciation and 12; Apostles' Creed and 147; available to all 251; Christ and 101, 229, 269; Christianity and 46, 80, 82, 83, 305; Christmas and 245; Church and 57; death and 46; difficulty of 268; distinct from redemption 82; faith and 110, 156, 201; final end of Mankind 101, 178; free will and 85; graces and 80, 84, 85, 101; heretics and 51, 52, 179, 187, 273, 357; *Magnificat* and 228, 235; Mary's role in 34, 43, 44, 47, 48, 97, 167, 225, 236, 250; merit and 100, 101, 108, 109, 110, 146 (*see also* Treasury of the Church); morals and 156; not assured 106, 155; not free 82, 101, 156 (*see also* redemption);

Our Father and 149, 156; preaching about 55, 203; predestination and 110, 111; reason and 201; redemption and 12, 206; Resurrection and 299, 301, 303, 316; right hand and 146, 319; Rosary and 79; sacramentals and 125; saints and 109; Sign of the Cross and 138; symbols of 357; vocal prayer and 183; works and 110, 156

Salve Regina see Hail, Holy Queen

Salve Rex æternæ misericordiæ (*Hail King of Eternal Mercy,* Martin Luther) 179

Salvifici doloris (John Paul II) 92

Samson 255, 340

Samuel 255

Sappho (*fl. c.* 610-c. 580 BC) 41

Sara 97, 128, 340; Name of 129

Saul 263, 300; *see also* Paul of Tarsus, St.

Savonarola, Girolamo (1452-1498) 168

Scotland 27, 343

Scupoli, Dom Lorenzo, C.R. (*c.* 1530-1610): *Spiritual Combat* 120

Second Book on Luke (St. Ambrose) 202

Second Sermon on the Dormition (St. John Damascene) 236

Secret of the Most Holy Rosary (St. Louis-Marie Grignion de Montfort) 42, 171, 203

Seed-Christ 243

Self-examination 191, 193,

195

Selim II Mest, Sultan of Turkey (1524-1574) 62

Semei 348

Sempiternity 310; dimensionality of 311, 312, 324; incomprehensibility of 311, 312; law and 312, 313, 317, 333; Revelation and 317; St. Thomas Aquinas on 310; *see also* Eternity, Time

Seraphim 352

Sergius I, Pope St. (*r.* 687-701) 349

Sermon 1 on St. Andrew (St. Bernard of Clairvaux) 193

Sermon 1 on the Circumcision (St. Bernard of Clairvaux) 247

Sermon 1 on the Nativity (St. John Damascene) 342

Sermon 18 On the Saints (St. Augustine) 226

Sermon 2 on the Dormition (St. John Damascene) 342, 345

Sermon 310 On the Nativity of St. John the Baptizer (St. Augustine) 210

Sermon 32 (St. Bernard of Clairvaux) 190

Sermon 35 (Pope St. Leo the Great) 224

Sermon 38 (St. Ambrose) 143

Sermon 47 On Mark (St. Augustine) 275

Sermon 56 (St. Augustine) 16

Sermon 6 on the Annunciation (Origen) 208

Sermon 64 on John (St. Augustine) 166

INDEX

Stipes see under cross

Strife 267

Subjunctive mode of speech 151, 152

Succoth 325, 334

Suffering: significance of 92

Summa Theologica (St. Thomas Aquinas) 107, 114, 213, 216, 265, 310, 321, 343

Sun: symbolism of 243

Superstition 126

Supremi Apostolatus Officio (Leo XIII Pecci) 66, 78

Swift, Jonathan (1667-1745): *Argument to Prove that the Abolishing of Christianity in England May, as Things Now Show, Be Attended with Some Inconveniencies* (1708) 67

Sylvan, Bro., C.F.X. 375

Symbols 357; ass 243; Burning Bush 315; cross *see under* cross, Cross, Holy; dove 217, 223; dragon 243; eagle 221; fire 315; fish 287; lamb 287; lion 239, 243; man 220; ox 221, 243; panther 243; sky 316; Star of David 130; Sun 243; weasel 218; wolf 243

Symeon Metaphrastes (*c.* 950-*c.* 1000) 346

Syria 329, 343

T

Tacitus, Cornelius (*c.* 55-120) 286

Talent 84, 196

Talmud 122

Teaching of the Twelve

Apostles (*Didache*) 172, 173

Terce 21

Tercer Abecedario (*Third Alphabet Book*, Francisco de Osuna) 111, 118, 119, 121, 190, 195, 196, 324

Teresa of Avila, St. (1515-1582) 85, 186, 196; on devotional feelings 192; on emotions 192; on meditative prayer 184, 367; on perseverance in prayer 96, 185; on recollection 121; on Rosary 2; on vocal prayer 8, 367; spiritual exercises and 191; *Book of Her Life* 96, 191, 192; *Interior Castle* 192; *Way of Perfection* 8, 184, 185, 367

Tertiary *see* third, *under* Order

Tertio millennio adveniente (John Paul II) 217

Tertullian (Quintus Septimus Florens Tertullianus (*c.* 155-*c.* 222): Christmas and 238, 244; heresy of 377; on martyrdom 336; on Pentecost 335; on sport 265; on the Our Father 57, 148, 154

Testem Benevolentiæ (Leo XIII Pecci) 68, 94

Tetragrammaton 131, 132, 319

Thee and thou 152

Themistius (*fl. c.* 540) 274

Theodas (Matthias) 260

Theodosius II, Emperor of Rome (401-450) 165

Theodosius, St. (*c.* 423-529) 349

Theology: ascetic 80; doc-

trinal 80; moral 80; mystic 80; pastoral 80; spiritual 80; structure of 80

Theophany *see under* epiphany

Theophronius of Cappadocia (*c.* 370) 274

Thérèse of Lisieux, St. (1873-1897) 45, 85

Third Alphabet Book (*Tercer Abecedario*, Francisco de Osuna) 111, 118, 119, 121, 190, 195, 196, 324

Third Tract on First John (St. Augustine) 85

Thomas à Kempis (*c.* 1380-1471) 49, 148, 198

Thomas Aquinas, St. (*c.* 1225-1274) 145, 243; education of 54; on Christ's descent into Hell 145; on dimensionality of Heaven 311; on divine judgement 107; on friendship 115; on glorified bodies 320, 321; on grace 81; on Mary's virginity 213, 214; on self-love 114; on sport 265; on St. John the Baptizer 343; on the Annunciation 216; on the dimensionality of Heaven 312; on the Our Father 150; on Time 310; patron of schools and universities 87; *Summa Theologica* 107, 114, 145, 213, 216, 265, 310, 321, 343

Thomas of Chantimpré: *Book of the Bees* (*Liber de apibus*) 38, 42; *De Natura rerum* (*On the Nature of Things*) 38

Thomas of Villanova, St. (1488-1555) 217; *Shadow of the Virgin* 355

407

U

V

LAUS ❦ DEO